The **Rough Guide** to

Chicago

written and researched by

Rich McHugh

this edition researched and updated by

J.P. Anderson and Caroline Lascom

NEW YORK • LONDON • DELHI

www.roughguides.com

Contents

◄◄ Chicago skyline ◄ Sculpture in Grant Park

Introduction to

Chicago

Soaring skyward from the pancake-flat prairies of the Midwestern heartland, Chicago has the feel of the last great American city. Having come into its own during the late nineteenth century, the city remains an economic hub and still evinces its traditional blue-collar roots. Chicago delivers all the excitement of a pulsating metropolis with a small-town spirit and refreshing lack of pretension, giving coastal rivals cosmopolitan New York and glittery LA more than a run for their money. Millions of visitors flock annually to Chicago, seduced by its pioneering architecture, world-class museums and galleries, vibrant nightlife, shopping along glitzy Michigan Avenue, and the raw energy of the downtown Loop.

Founded in 1833, Chicago was a raw frontier outpost on the sharp edge of civilization and wilderness. Owing to its strategic position as a mid-continental hub, Chicago soon became the engine of the growing nation's westward expansion, reaching its zenith during the industrial age. The grain, lumber, meatpacking, steel, and railroad trades all took turns dominating the economic landscape, bringing hitherto unbridled opportunity for thousands of immigrants and fostering a can-do spirit; every man was for himself, and the dollar was king.

In 1871, the city emerged from the ashes of one of the worst fires in US history to redefine American urban architecture. Chicago became a crucible of innovation, where visionary designers, ambitious industrialists, and ingenious inventors could find their greatest expression. Prototypical skyscrapers soon rose gloriously along the shores of Lake Michigan; meanwhile, Chicago's cultural importance bloomed following the creation of the University of Chicago in 1892 and the city's prestigious hosting of the World's Columbian Exhibition in 1893.

▲ Aerial view of downtown Chicago

While the lurid legacy of Al Capone and his empire of organized crime is still one of the city's overarching associations, most traces of the mob-run opium dens, brothels, and speakeasies that studded the city during the 1920s Prohibition era have disappeared. Cleansing the deep stains of "machine" politics has proved a more difficult undertaking, however, with allegations of corruption and fraud over city contracts tainting the accomplishments of City Hall to this day. Contrary to popular belief, the name "Windy City" does not refer to the gusts that whip up over the lake but the city's history of bellicose "windy" politicos, notorious for spinning a line.

Along with a compelling history and a panoply of attractions, Chicago is also one of America's great lifestyle cities. Cycling along the lakefront, sauntering through parks, wandering down hushed tree-lined streets punctuated by turreted brownstone mansions and chichi restaurants, or delving into distinctive neighborhoods where traditions of first-generation immigrants are interwoven with the classic Americana of hot dogs, pizza, and baseball – each experience contributes to the dynamism and diversity of this formidable city.

Chicago is America's geographical and cultural crossroads. It's no exaggeration to say that **modern blues** was invented here during the first half of the twentieth century, tens of thousands of African Americans migrating from

Fact file

- Chicago covers approximately **228 square miles**, of which 5 percent (7300 acres) is devoted to parkland.
- The city's **population** has been on the decline since 2000. The estimated figure for 2004 was 2,870,122 – down just under 1 percent from the 2000 census. 36 percent is black, 31 percent white, 26 percent Hispanic, and 4 percent Asian. The population of the greater metropolitan area is 8,840,080 (2004 estimate).
- The big and busy city boasts the world's largest public library (Harold Washington Library), biggest illuminated fountain (Buckingham Fountain), largest free public zoo (Lincoln Park Zoo), largest food festival (Taste of Chicago), and largest aquarium (Shedd Aquarium) – as well as the world's busiest roadway (Dan Ryan Expressway), busiest futures exchange (Board of Trade), and busiest airport (O'Hare International Airport).
- Chicago is known as the birthplace of roller skates, the blood bank, the electric iron and cooking range, the cafeteria, *McDonald's*, spray paint, the grain reaper, the window envelope, the winding watch, the zipper, the bifocal contact lens, the railroad sleeping car, the malted milkshake, the pinball machine, the bowling tournament, and the steel-frame skyscraper.

the South bringing with them the music of their birthplace. With the relocation of legendary blues clubs from the South Side to the more polished North, performances have become a more diluted tourist spectacle. However, **live music** is something Chicago does with aplomb, spanning every conceivable genre. Alternative rock came of age here in the 1990s with the Smashing Pumpkins and today the scene is one of the healthiest in the country. There is a phenomenal array of venues ranging from smoky jazz bars to Art Deco theaters and edgy, hole-in-the-wall clubs.

With its rough and tough spirit and competitive zeal, Chicago is passionate about sport. **Baseball**, **basketball**, **football**, and **hockey** dominate the sporting agenda and Chicagoans are fiercely loyal to their teams; the ever-inconsistent Chicago Cubs' games remain well attended thanks largely to the atmosphere at the ivy-covered Wrigley Field, bastion of baseball traditionalism. Occasionally, as with the Michael Jordan–led Bulls of the Nineties and the 2005 World Series champions, the White Sox, local fervor is rewarded with championships.

▲ Murals near Wicker Park

Immigrant Chicago

From the mid-nineteenth century, over 2.5 million **immigrants** including Swedes, Italians, Poles, Russians, Ukrainians, Germans, Greeks, Puerto Ricans, Japanese, Mexicans, and Chinese flocked to this pulsating industrial metropolis, enticed by Chicago's frontier spirit and endless opportunities in transportation, construction, and manufacturing.

Fleeing the devastating famine of 1845, **Irish** immigrants came here, rising from their humble beginnings digging canals to dominate the urban linchpins of politics, police, and religion – most Chicago mayors since 1933 have been of Irish origin. The mid-nineteenth century also saw the arrival of **Poles and Ukrainians**, who settled in Bucktown and Wicker Park, and **Swedes**, who made Andersonville their home. Following the 1893 World's Columbian Exposition, Chicago became a truly international city, inspiring a new wave of immigration. In the 1890s, impoverished **Italian and Greek** immigrants, settled in the West Side, which encompasses the neighborhood of Pilsen, currently home to the largest concentration of **Mexicans** living outside of Mexico. While much of this area has suffered from Disneyfication, immigrant cultures are still preserved and nurtured through the much-vaunted Greek school system as well as the Mexican Fine Arts Center.

What to see

The compact heart of Chicago is the Loop; from here the city spreads to the north, south, and west, bounded to the east by Lake Michigan, which provides Chicago with some of its most attractive open space, and serves as a clear point of reference for getting your bearings – the lake is always east of the urban grid. The Chicago River, which cuts through the heart of downtown Chicago to Lake Michigan, separates the business district from the shopping and entertainment areas of the North Side, which merit, at the very least, several days' worth of exploring. Usually bypassed, Chicago's dichotomous South Side and increasingly gentrified immigrant enclaves to the west provide a rewarding and well-rounded insight into Chicago's history.

The best place to start exploring Chicago is **the Loop**, the city's downtown and birthplace, and home to perhaps the finest display of modern architecture in the world, from the prototype skyscrapers of the 1890s and the "Chicago School" period to Mies van der Rohe's Modernist masterpieces and the

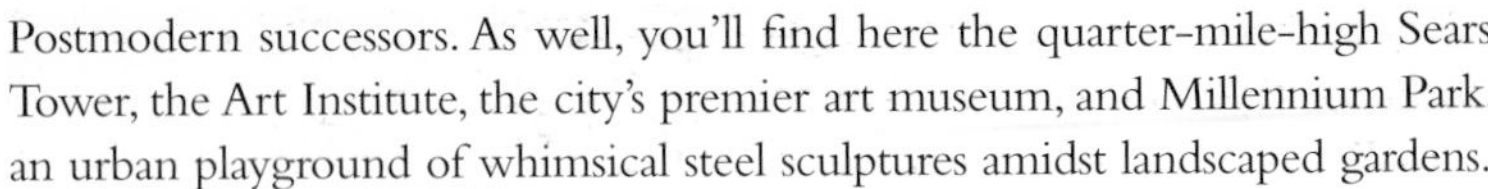

Postmodern successors. As well, you'll find here the quarter-mile-high Sears Tower, the Art Institute, the city's premier art museum, and Millennium Park, an urban playground of whimsical steel sculptures amidst landscaped gardens.

Chicago's most commercial area – **Near North** – is where you're likely to spend much of your time. Just north of the river and divided into the River North, N Michigan Avenue, and Streeterville areas, Near North is where most of the city's hotels and restaurants are concentrated, as are its fashionable shops, designer boutiques, and department stores, on the famed Magnificent Mile. East of Michigan Avenue, on Streeterville's lakefront, is Chicago's most popular tourist destination, Navy Pier, a promenade of chain restaurants, shops, and concert venues marked by the hard-to-miss giant Ferris wheel. On the other side of Michigan Avenue, **River North** is to Chicago what Soho is to New York, a thriving gallery district where former run-down warehouses now house a diverse array of art works and antiques, not to mention a number of the city's finest restaurants.

The name "Windy City" does not refer to the gusts that whip up over the lake but the city's history of bellicose "windy" politicos, notorious for spinning a line

Further north brings you to the **Gold Coast**, where a few streets of upscale boutiques and gorgeous brownstones make a pleasant stroll, while **Old Town** to the west is artsier and more unbuttoned, home to the venerable Second City improvisational comedy club and a host of colorful Victorian homes.

Old Town blends into **Lincoln Park**, a leafy residential area that borders the park of the same name and is home to an enclave of young professionals. The streets, lined with restored apartments and condos, also hold some of the city's best restaurants and bars, giving the neighborhood a lively social scene.

One of the most rapidly developing neighborhoods, **Lakeview**, further north, draws a younger crowd than Lincoln Park with its myriad cafés, bars, restaurants, and boutiques. Baseball fans will want to pay homage at the shrine of Wrigley Field stadium, home to the much-loved Chicago Cubs. A quintessential sporting preamble requires a hop around the bevy of raucous sports bars in the surrounding **Wrigleyville** neighborhood.

▲ The El train

Beyond here, the distinct city neighborhoods thin out, save for **Andersonville**, where a worthwhile selection of restaurants, delicatessens, and bakeries still serve the remnants of a Swedish enclave, and **Rogers Park**, further north, which is home to one of the largest South Asian and Indian populations in the United States.

Heading south from the Loop, the **Near South** encompasses the lakefront Grant Park, with its world-class museums, the historic **Printers Row district**, and **Chinatown**'s kaleidoscopic restaurants and street life. Further south, the **South Side** proper takes over, much of it a no-go zone for visitors, except for **Hyde Park and Kenwood**, an island of middle-class prosperity around the Gothic campus of the **University of Chicago**.

Chicago's **West Side** holds the twin culinary attractions of **Greektown** and **Little Italy**, the latter mainly a tourist hangout, and the former considerably less so. The city's large Mexican community makes its base southwest of here in **Pilsen**, known as well for its home-style eateries, Fine Arts Center, and colorful murals.

Northwest of here, Chicago's blue-collar side takes over; among the warehouses and old churches are a few areas worth your attention. The **Ukrainian Village**, with its wonderfully ornate churches and Eastern European roots, is worth a stop on your way to the city's most bohemian neighborhood, **Wicker Park**, full of carefully restored Victorian homes, a flourishing alternative music scene, edgy bars, and eclectic thrift stores.

Chicago's lakefront

The third largest of the Great Lakes and the sixth largest freshwater lake in the world, **Lake Michigan** is to Chicagoans what Central Park is to New Yorkers – an oasis in which to escape the grinding congestion and frenetic pace of downtown, a place to relax, play, exercise, and socialize.

Defining the iconic cityscape where glass-and-steel architectural marvels rise above undulating waters, the lake is gloriously fronted by manicured parks, a marina, and beaches. During the summer, young and old play volleyball, bask in the sun or rollerblade, run, or cycle along mile after mile of serpentine pathways, which skirt the water's edge.

Some of the best places to luxuriate along the waterfront are **Grant Park** west of the Loop with the new, sculpture-filled **Millennium Park; Oak Street Beach** a popular place to sun and be seen; **Navy Pier**, a playground of shops, amusement rides, museums, and shows; and **Lincoln Park**, which boasts a zoo, a conservatory, and a gorgeous stretch of lakefront path that's perfect for running, rollerblading, or biking.

Suggested itineraries

Chicago can be experienced in an endless number of ways – architecture tours, baseball or football games, blues clubs, and so on. The following are suggested itineraries for trips up to a week, while giving you an idea of what's possible to see in one day. They're mainly designed around the key sights and include suggestions for where to have lunch. Of course if any of the days seem too sight-oriented, don't be afraid to simply wander around.

Two days

• Sears Tower observatory, Historic Skyscrapers Tour, shopping along Michigan Ave, *Atwood Café* (lunch), Steppenwolf Theatre, *Morton's of Chicago* (dinner)

• Art Institute of Chicago, Millennium Park, *Billy Goat Tavern* (lunch), shopping or amusement rides at Navy Pier, blues show at *Buddy Guy's Legends*

Four days

As above plus…

• River North galleries, Oak Street Beach, Italian beef sandwiches at *Mr. Beef*, drinks at the *Drake Hotel*, *Second City* comedy show, *Frontera Grill* (dinner)

• *House of Blues* Gospel Brunch, Museum Campus, Wicker Park Historical District, jazz or blues show at *Green Mill Tavern*

Seven days

As above plus…

• Cycling, rollerblading, or walking along Chicago's lakefront, the Maxwell Street Market (lunch), Mexican Fine Arts Museum, walking around Greektown (dinner)

• Tour of the University of Chicago, *Ribs 'N' Bibs* (lunch/dinner), the Museum of Science and Industry, and the Robie House.

• The Lincoln Park Zoo, walk around Lincoln Park neighborhood (brunch), Frank Lloyd Wright's Home & Studio and Unity Temple in Oak Park.

Bucktown, just north, is a more gentrified version of Wicker Park, with plenty of restaurants, bars, and nightclubs to choose from, along with correspondingly high rents and an increasingly homogenous make-up.

Nine miles west of the city, the affluent and attractive suburb of **Oak Park** holds the childhood home of Ernest Hemingway and more than a dozen well-preserved examples of the influential architecture of Frank Lloyd Wright; the most interesting and groundbreaking of these are maintained as monuments and open for viewing.

North of Andersonville, the thriving neighborhood of **Rogers Park**, centered around Devon Avenue, is home to a variety of ethnic groups from Vietnamese to Peruvian as well as one of the largest South Asian populations in North America. The suburban **North Shore** is home to the scholarly Northwestern University and has a wealth of scenic beaches and parks, as well as a burgeoning art scene.

▲ Nightlife on Rush Street

When to go

Chicago's **climate** ranges from the unbearably hot and humid in midsummer to well below freezing from December through February, with spring and fall amounting to little more than a month or two in between. The **best times to visit** are in the early summer (May–July) and early fall (Sept & Oct), when the weather is at its most pleasant; there's usually snow from December to March, while the heat of late summer is best avoided. Whatever time of year you come, be sure to dress in layers: buildings tend to be overheated during winter and air-conditioned to the extreme in summer. Also bring comfortable, sturdy shoes – you're going to be doing a lot of walking.

Chicago climate

	Jan	Feb	Mar	Apr	May	Jun	Jul	Aug	Sep	Oct	Nov	Dec
Average daily temperature												
Av. high (ºC)	-2	1	7	14	21	27	29	28	24	17	9	2
Av. high (ºF)	29	34	45	58	70	80	84	82	75	63	48	35
Av. low (ºC)	-11	-8	-2	4	9	14	17	17	18	6	-1	-7
Av. low (ºF)	13	18	28	39	48	57	63	62	64	42	31	20
Average rainfall												
in mm	43	35	68	91	81	96	9	104	89	66	74	56
in inches	1.7	1.4	2.7	3.6	3.2	3.8	3.6	4.1	3.5	2.6	2.9	2.2

22 things not to miss

It's not possible to see everything that Chicago has to offer in one trip – and we don't suggest you try. What follows is a selective and subjective taste of the city's highlights: stunning architecture and engaging museums, wide-ranging cultural events, and memorable restaurants and bars. They're arranged in five color-coded categories to help you find the very best things to see, do, and experience. All entries have a page reference to take you straight into the Guide, where you can find out more.

01 Boat tours Page **49** • The Chicago River, which snakes through the city center, is best experienced on a boat tour, with the Chicago Architectural Foundation's cruises being the best. A great way to see the city skyline, if the crowds at the Sears Tower and John Hancock Building are too much to handle.

02 Maxwell Street Market Page **134** • A long-standing West Side tradition, this open-air bazaar is a great place to meander through on a Sunday afternoon, featuring a variety of ethnic food stands, live music, antique-peddlers, and sketch artists.

04 Frank Lloyd Wright Home & Studio Page **151** • The great and innovative American architect left a hefty number of structures in his native Chicago, including his own home and studio in Oak Park.

05 Gospel Brunch at the House of Blues Page **220** • Indulge in a heavenly and fattening brunch buffet with everything from biscuits and gravy to jambalaya, while taking in soulful gospel music by top musicians.

03 Steppenwolf Theatre Page **228** • Founded in a basement, the Steppenwolf has grown into a world-renowned theater company, counting such members as John Malkovich and Laurie Metcalf.

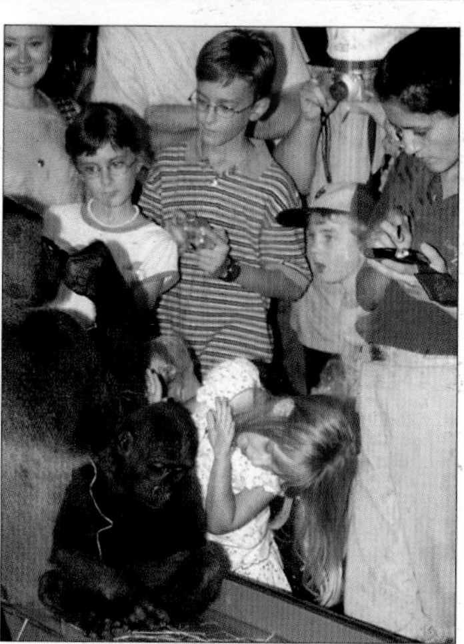

06 Lincoln Park Zoo Page **119** • The nation's oldest and one of its last free zoos, this Lincoln Park menagerie is home to a wide variety of primates, and particularly famous for its collection of apes.

07 Museum of Science and Industry Page **141** • Behind the stately exterior of this popular museum, you'll encounter everything from a submarine to a live-chick hatchery to a replica of a coalmine, among hundreds of other exhibits.

08 Green Mill Tavern Pages **221** • Take in some stellar jazz during the wee hours of the morning at this former speakeasy and pretend you're living during the Roaring Twenties, when Al Capone might easily have been sitting next to you.

09 Oak Street Beach Page **88** • A glamorous summertime playground, right off Michigan Avenue, in a somewhat unexpected location.

10 Second City comedy club Page **92** • *Second City* rarely disappoints with its raucous brand of improv – chances are good you'll wake in the morning with sore stomach muscles.

11 Glessner House Page **104** • Considered a plain-faced addition to Prairie Avenue District when it was built in the late 1800s, the house and its decorative interior are among the well-preserved survivors of Chicago's gilded age.

12 Chicago's lakefront Page 09 • Jog, walk, or even better, rent a bike and explore the spectacular shores of Lake Michigan.

13 Millennium Park Page 98 • The embodiment of Chicago's visionary zeal and innovation, Millennium Park is an urban playground of whimsical steel sculptures and fountains, landscaped gardens, theater and music venues, and an ice-skating rink in winter.

14 Navy Pier Page 81 • After soaring through the sky on the giant Ferris wheel or spinning on the merry-go-round, make for the promenade for a relaxing beer and a bite to eat.

15 Printers Row Page 95 • Though most of the presses that packed this small stretch in the South Loop in the late nineteenth century have since moved on, the buildings are immaculately preserved.

16 Seeing a game at Wrigley Field Page 124 • The ivy-covered walls, the boisterous crowd, and free-flowing hot dogs and beer all add up to the quintessential baseball experience, no matter who wins the game.

17 The Oriental Institute Page 145 • This University of Chicago research institute uncovers their newly excavated ancient Near and Far Eastern finds for public viewing.

18 Chicago Symphony Orchestra concerts Page **230** • When the world-renowned symphony plays at its stunning venue, you're assured of one of the most rewarding high-culture experiences around.

19 Tiffany Dome, Chicago Cultural Center Page **50** • Your eyes will be glued to the sparkling roof of Preston Bradley Hall, particularly if you can take in a concert at the Center.

21 Art Institute of Chicago Page **66** • With one of the largest art holdings in North America, the Art Institute of Chicago is sure to keep you occupied for hours. Be sure to visit the Impressionist wing.

20 Ravinia Festival Page **256** • This complex of music venues is the place to go for summertime outdoor concerts, a treat whether you're in view of the stage under the Pavilion or sprawled on the adjacent lawn.

22 Ba'haí Temple Page **162** • Gazing at this gleaming, peculiar temple in Wilmette on the North Shore might make you wonder if you're no longer in Illinois, or America for that matter.

Basics

Basics

Getting there

A major hub for domestic and international travel, Chicago is well served by air, rail, and road networks. Flying into O'Hare International Airport – the country's busiest – is your quickest and easiest approach, given the sheer volume of domestic and international flights that route through here. One of the country's largest carriers, United Airlines, is based here, and nearly every major airline offers service to Chicago, either through direct flights or in conjunction with other airlines. Midway Airport, on the city's southwest side, sees a much smaller flow of mostly domestic commuter flights, but is nonetheless an option for those already in the US or who have included Chicago on a multi-city itinerary.

Trains can offer a scenic alternative to flying, if you have time and don't mind paying the equivalent of airfare. The national train network, Amtrak, runs frequent service between Chicago and most major US cities, all of them arriving at Union Station, just west of the Loop.

Far cheaper and more frequent than trains, **buses** can be uncomfortable and time-consuming. The sole long-distance carrier servicing Chicago is Greyhound, whose buses arrive at the Greyhound station southwest of the Loop.

Shopping for air tickets

Within the US, prices for domestic flights to Chicago depend more on passenger volume than anything else, so it pays to search for flights leaving from an airport with plenty of traffic to the city. Airfares always depend on the season, with the highest being around May to September, when the weather is best; fares drop during the low season, December to March (excluding around Christmas and New Year's Day when prices are hiked up and seats are at a premium). Note also that flying on weekends ordinarily adds substantially to the cost of a round-trip fare; the price ranges quoted on p.20 assume mid-week travel.

If you want to travel during major American holiday periods (around the Fourth of July, Thanksgiving, and Christmas and New Year's Day), be sure to book well ahead. While prices fluctuate wildly around these times, it's possible to find cheaper fares with some digging, though they'll require at least the standard three-week (or 28-day) advance purchase.

You can often cut costs by using a **specialist flight agent** – either a consolidator, who buys up blocks of tickets from the airlines and sells them at a discount, or a discount agent, who in addition to dealing with discounted flights may also offer special student and youth fares and a range of other travel-related services such as travel insurance, rail passes, car rentals, tours, and the like. Some agents specialize in **charter flights**, which may be cheaper than anything available on a scheduled flight, but again departure dates are fixed and withdrawal penalties are high.

If you're traveling from Europe or Australasia and the US is only one stop on a longer journey, you might want to consider buying a **Round-the-World (RTW) ticket**. Some travel agents can sell you an "off-the-shelf" RTW ticket that will have you touching down in about half a dozen cities; others will have to assemble one for you, which can be tailored to your needs but is apt to be more expensive. Chicago does figure on some standard itineraries, but cities on the US East and West coasts are more typical stopovers.

Bookling flights online

Many airlines and discount travel **websites** offer you the opportunity to book your tickets online – often at a small discount – which may also cut out the costs of agents and middlemen. Good deals can often be found through discount or auction sites, as well as through the airlines' own websites. As Chicago isn't a popular package-tour destination, you're likely to find better deals on your own, especially through one of the online booking sites (see below), who can set you up with air tickets, lodging, and car rental. It usually works out much more cost effective to book a flight and accommodation package offered by companies, such as Orbitz and Expedia, although your accommodation choices will be quite limited.

Online booking agents

Ⓦ **www.airline-network.co.uk** UK flight bookings, car rental, lodging, and last-minute special offers.
Ⓦ **www.a2btravel.com** Flight comparisons from major airline carriers and very good value hotel/flight packages.
Ⓦ **www.cheapflights.com** Bookings from the UK and Ireland only. Flight deals, travel agents, plus links to other travel sites.
Ⓦ **www.cheaptickets.com** Discount flight specialists.
Ⓦ **www.etn.nl/discount** A hub of consolidator and discount agent Web links, maintained by the nonprofit European Travel Network.
Ⓦ **www.expedia.com** Discount airfares, all-airline search engine, and daily deals.
Ⓦ **www.flyaow.com** Online air travel info and reservations site. Accommodation, including condo rentals, and up to 70 percent discount on hotel bookings.
Ⓦ **www.gaytravel.com** Gay online travel agent, concentrating mostly on accommodation. Good destination guide.
Ⓦ **www.geocities.com/thavery2000** Has an extensive list of airline toll-free numbers and websites.
Ⓦ **www.hotwire.com** Bookings from the US only. Last-minute savings of up to 40 percent on regular published fares. Travelers must be at least 18 and there are no refunds, transfers, or changes allowed. Log-in required.
Ⓦ **www.lastminute.com** Offers good last-minute holiday-package and flight-only deals.
Ⓦ **www.orbitz.com** Partnership of the top airlines in the US, offering the cheapest fares published, as well as hotel and car booking; best used from within the US.
Ⓦ **www.priceline.com** Name-your-own-price website that has deals at around 40 percent off standard fares. You cannot specify flight times (although you do specify dates) and the tickets are non-refundable, non-transferable, and non-changeable.
Ⓦ **www.skyauction.com** Bookings from the US only. Auctions tickets and travel packages using a "second bid" scheme. The best strategy is to bid the maximum you're willing to pay, since if you win you'll pay just enough to beat the runner-up regardless of your maximum bid.
Ⓦ **www.smilinjack.com/airlines** Lists an up-to-date compilation of airline website addresses.
Ⓦ **www.travelocity.com** Destination guides, hot Web fares, and best deals for car rental, accommodation, and lodging, as well as fares. Provides access to the travel-agent system SABRE, the most comprehensive central-reservations system in the US.
Ⓦ **www.travelshop.com.au** Australian website offering discounted flights, packages, insurance, and online bookings.
Ⓦ **travel.yahoo.com** Incorporates a lot of Rough Guides material in its coverage of destination countries and cities across the world, with information about places to eat, sleep, and so on.

Flights and other approaches from North America

From most places in North America, flying is the fastest and easiest way to reach Chicago. The city is connected with all of the major US cities – New York, Boston, Washington DC, Atlanta, and Miami on the East Coast, and Seattle, San Francisco, and Los Angeles on the West – with at least several flights a day from each.

Sample round-trip fares and flight times to Chicago

From	Flight time	Fare
Boston	2hr 30min	$230
Dallas	2hr 15min	$230
Denver	2hr 30min	$180
Los Angeles	4hr	$240
Minneapolis	1hr 30min	$210
Montréal	2hr	Can$300
New Orleans	2hr	$300
New York	2hr	$220
Orlando	2hr 30min	$290
San Francisco	4hr 30min	$275
Toronto	1hr 30min	Can$270
Vancouver	3hr	Can$410
Washington DC	1hr 30min	$190

As Chicago isn't a popular package-tour destination, you're likely to find better deals on your own, especially through one of the online booking sites (see above), which can set you up with air tickets, lodging, and car rental.

Airlines

Unless specified, all the following fly into O'Hare.

Aero Mexico ⓣ1-800/237-6639, ⓦwww.aeromexico.com/ingles/home

Air Canada ⓣ1-888/247-2262, ⓦwww.aircanada.ca

Alaska Airlines ⓣ1-800/252-7522, ⓦwww.alaskaair.com

America West Airlines ⓣ1-800/235-9292, ⓦwww.americawest.com

American Airlines ⓣ1-800/433-7300, ⓦwww.aa.com

American Trans Air (to Midway Airport) ⓣ1-800/225-2995, ⓦwww.ata.com

Continental Airlines ⓣ1-800/525-0280, ⓦwww.continental.com

Delta Air Lines ⓣ1-800/221-1212, ⓦwww.delta.com

Frontier Airlines (to Midway Airport) ⓣ1-800/432-1359, ⓦwww.flyfrontier.com

Mexicana ⓣ1-800/531-7921, ⓦwww.mexicana.com

Northwest ⓣ1-800/225-2525, ⓦwww.nwa.com

Southwest Airlines (to Midway Airport) ⓣ1-800/435-9792, ⓦwww.southwest.com

Spirit ⓣ1-800/772-7117, ⓦwww.spiritair.com

United Airlines ⓣ1-800/241-6522, ⓦwww.united.com

US Airways ⓣ1-800/428-4322, ⓦwww.usairways.com

Discount travel agents

Air Brokers International ⓣ1-800/883-3273, ⓦwww.airbrokers.com. Consolidator and specialist in Round-the-World and Circle Pacific tickets.

Airtech ⓣ212/219-7000, ⓦwww.airtech.com. Standby seat broker specializing in flights to/from Europe, USA, Hawaii, and the Caribbean; also deals in consolidator fares and courier flights.

Airtreks.com ⓣ1-877/AIRTREKS or 415/977-7100 (calling from outside North America), ⓦwww.airtreks.com. Round-the-World and Circle Pacific tickets. The website features an interactive database that lets you build and price your own itinerary.

Educational Travel Center ⓣ1-800/747-5551 or 608/256-5551, ⓦwww.edtrav.com. Student/youth agent offering discounted airfares, accommodation, and rail passes. Standard fares also available.

STA Travel ⓣ1-800/781-4040, ⓦwww.sta-travel.com. Worldwide specialists in independent travel; also student IDs, travel insurance, car rental, rail passes, and more.

Student Flights ⓣ1-800/255-8000 or 480/951-1177, ⓦwww.isecard.com. Student/youth fares, student IDs.

TFI Tours ⓣ1-800/745-8000 or 212/736-1140, ⓦwww.tfitours.com. Low cost consolidator with some of the best deals you will find anywhere.

Travac ⓣ1-800/TRAV-800, ⓦwww.thetravelsite.com. Consolidator and charter broker with offices in New York City and Orlando.

Travel Cuts Canada ⓣ1-800/667-2887, US ⓣ1-866/246-9762, ⓦwww.travelcuts.com. Canadian student-travel organization.

Travelers Advantage ⓣ1-877/259-2691, ⓦwww.travelersadvantage.com. Discount travel club; annual membership fee required (currently $9.99 per month; often runs a special offer $1 for 2 months' trial).

Worldtek Travel ⓣ1-800/243-1723, ⓦwww.worldtek.com. Discount travel agency for worldwide travel.

Tour operators

AmeriCan Adventures ⓣ1-800/TREK-USA, ⓦwww.americanadventures.com. Camping and youth hostel trips that feature Chicago on various cross-country itineraries. Note that trips do not originate in Chicago.

Contiki Holidays ⓣ1-866/CONTIKI, ⓦwww.contiki.com. Planned vacation packages geared to 18–35-year-olds; the 10-day "North by North East" tour (from $1269, land only) begins in New York and ends in Chicago and includes a day of sightseeing, plus one night's accommodation.

Suntrek Tours ⓣ1-800/SUNTREK or 707/523-1800, ⓦwww.suntrek.com. Small group tours that mix sightseeing in cities with the outdoors; a few tours stop in Chicago for a night. The two-week "Eastern Pioneer Tour" beginning in New York and taking in Chicago costs from $1229, including basic accommodation and land transportation.

United Vacations ⓣ1-800/377-1816, ⓦwww.unitedvacations.com. Vacation packages that can combine airfare with hotel accommodation, car rental, and other services.

By rail

Travel **by train** can be a picturesque and leisurely option, though not likely to be much cheaper than air travel. Amtrak

(Ⓣ1-800/USA-RAIL, Ⓦwww.amtrak.com) services Chicago and runs trains from most major US cities. It also jointly operates trains between Toronto and Chicago with Canada's national rail company, VIA Rail (in Toronto Ⓣ416/366-8411, rest of Canada Ⓣ1-888/842-7245, in US Ⓣ1-800/USA-RAIL, Ⓦwww.viarail.ca); several trains make the twelve-hour trip daily.

Peak **fares** are usually in effect from June to September. Round-trip fares from New York (19hr) $170–220, from Boston (17hr) $190–275, San Francisco or Los Angeles (40hr) $700, Seattle (45–50hr) $250–500, Detroit (5hr) $50, Milwaukee (1.5hr) $40, San Antonio (31hr) $200, New Orleans (19hr) $235–335, and Toronto (14hr) around Can$215.

You'll also find seasonal special offers (30 percent discount on select routes during the fall and spring etc), as well as discounts of 15 percent for seniors and students, for most Amtrak rail journeys; check the company's website or call them for details. If Chicago is part of a longer itinerary, you might consider buying one of Amtrak's **rail passes**. For US and Canadian residents, the North America Rail Pass allows thirty days' unlimited travel throughout Amtrak and VIA Rail's networks ($766 in high season, $543 in low season).

Overseas visitors can buy USA Rail passes, which cover six different regions and are valid for fifteen or thirty days with unlimited stopovers. Of these, the most suitable for visits to Chicago are the West Rail Pass, allowing travel between Chicago and New Orleans, and westward to the Pacific during a fifteen-day period ($210 in low season, $325 in high season) and thirty-day periods ($270 in low season, $405 in high season); and the National USA Rail Pass, good for fifteen days of unlimited travel anywhere in the network for $440 (high season) or $295 (low), or thirty days for $550 (high season) or $385 (low). Passes must be bought before you travel to North America, and you'll need to present it, along with a passport, at an Amtrak office to be issued tickets before you board your train. Note that reservations are usually required, and are best made before you arrive in North America.

Sample round-trip fares and bus times to Chicago

From	Trip time	Fare
Boston (9 daily)	23hr	$200
Cleveland (6 daily)	6hr	$83
Indianapolis (9 daily)	3hr 20min	$59
Los Angeles (6 daily)	50hr	$239
Milwaukee (14 daily)	1hr 45min	$23
Minneapolis (8 daily)	8hr	$115
New York City (6 daily)	16hr	$168
Washington DC (5 daily)	17hr	$159

By bus

The national bus line, **Greyhound** (Ⓣ 1800-231-2222, Ⓦwww.greyhound.com), runs frequent buses from major Midwestern cities (Cleveland, Indianapolis, Milwaukee, or Minneapolis), usually around ten per day from each city. Beyond the Midwest, Greyhound does run a few buses daily from New York, Washington DC, and Denver, plus a few that make the two-day journey from the West Coast. Two smaller companies stop at Greyhound's station: Lakefront Lines (Ⓣ1-800/638-6338, Ⓦwww.lakefrontlines.com) operates service between Charleston (West Virginia) and Chicago, passing through Ohio, Indiana, and Kentucky, while the Michigan-based Indian Trails (Ⓣ1-800/292-3831) runs buses between Chicago and points in Michigan.

Fares depend on the season, though on all routes you'll pay slightly more if you travel between Friday and Sunday (see below for standard midweek round-trip fares). The price drops if you buy your ticket seven days in advance or take advantage of student and senior discounts or special offers (eg "two-for-one" companion fares). If Chicago is just one stop on a longer itinerary, check out the various **Discovery passes**, which includes the International Ameripass, open to overseas travelers. It offers unlimited travel in the entire Greyhound network for as little as four days ($1179) up to sixty days ($639).

By car

Though **driving** to Chicago will give you some flexibility, once you reach the city you're not likely to need a car unless you're short on time or want to explore outlying areas like Oak Park. You'll pay a lot for parking, so having a car over a long period of time can add up. (For more about driving in Chicago, see "Arrival," p.30.)

Arranging a car in advance, either online or over the phone, will also save you money. Most rental agreements will include unlimited mileage, though you should confirm this when arranging a car and again when you pick it up. If you want to pick up the car at one location and leave it at another, rates can go up by as much as $200. If you are under 25, expect to pay high surcharges on top of the initial rental charge. A mid-sized car rental for one week will cost around $180-250, plus tax. Be sure to read the agreement carefully before signing out an automobile, especially for details on Collision Damage Waiver (sometimes called Liability Damage Waiver), a form of insurance that often isn't included in the cost of the initial rental charge but is well worth having. At $10–15 per day the waiver can add up, but without it you could end up paying hefty fees for any scratches, dents, and other damage to the car – even those that aren't your fault. Credit-card holders should inquire with their credit-card companies beforehand as some include this type of coverage if you use your card to pay.

Car rental agencies

Alamo US ⓣ1-800/522-9696, ⓦwww.alamo.com
Avis Australia ⓣ13 63 33, ⓦwww.avis.com; Canada ⓣ1-800/272-5871; New Zealand ⓣ09/526 2847; Republic of Ireland ⓣ353/214 281 111; UK ⓣ0870/606 0100; US ⓣ1-800/230-4898; ⓦwww.avis.com
Budget Australia ⓣ1300/362 848; New Zealand ⓣ0800/283 438; UK ⓣ8701/565 656 181; US ⓣ1-800/527-0700; ⓦwww.budgetrentacar.com
Dollar US ⓣ1-800/800-4000, ⓦwww.dollar.com
Enterprise Rent-a-Car US ⓣ1-800/325-8007, ⓦwww.enterprise.com
Hertz Australia ⓣ13 30 39; Canada ⓣ1-800/263-0600; New Zealand ⓣ0800/654 321; Republic of Ireland ⓣ01/660 2255; UK ⓣ0870/844 8844; US ⓣ1-800/654-3001; ⓦwww.hertz.com
National Australia ⓣ13 10 45; New Zealand ⓣ0800/800 115 or 03/366 5574; UK ⓣ0870/5365 365; US ⓣ1-800/227-7368; ⓦwww.nationalcar.com
Suncars UK ⓣ0870/500 5566, ⓦwww.suncars.com
Thrifty Australia ⓣ1300/367 227; New Zealand ⓣ09/309 0111; US ⓣ1-800/367-2277; UK ⓣ01494/751 600; ⓦwww.thrifty.co.uk

Driving to Chicago

From	Driving time	Distance
Miami	23hr	1380 miles
Montréal	14hr	840 miles
New York	15hr	780 miles
San Francisco	35hr	2135 miles
Toronto	9hr	513 miles
Washington DC	12hr	699 miles

Flights from the UK and Ireland

There are several direct flights leaving daily **from London**'s Heathrow Airport to Chicago's O'Hare. British Airways offers two flights, one in the morning, the other in the afternoon, while United has three – usually in mid-morning, around noon, and in the late afternoon. United Airlines partners with British Midland to service major UK cities, offering direct flights from Manchester to Chicago (one daily, leaving mid-morning). All other British Midland flights first route through London Heathrow before heading to Chicago, which will add extra to the transatlantic fare.

Round-trip fares to Chicago can cost as little as £260 and as much as £600 (June–Aug and at Christmas). If a direct flight to Chicago is not a priority, your flight options increase substantially: several carriers – KLM, Alitalia, and Northwest Airlines among them – fly between the London area airports and route either through a European city (Amsterdam, Milan, Paris) or a US city (New York, Washington DC, Detroit, Atlanta) before continuing on to Chicago.

American Airlines and Aer Lingus fly direct to Chicago **from Ireland** with fares starting from around €475. Although other major carriers (such as British Airways, Continental, Delta, and Northwest) do route through Ireland, they don't link directly with Chicago, so you'll be forced to deal with layovers and transfers. Your best bet is to stick with Aer Lingus or American Airlines and make sure to reserve in advance.

Airlines

Aer Lingus UK ⓣ0845/084 4444, Republic of Ireland ⓣ0818/365 000, ⓦwww.aerlingus.ie
Air France UK ⓣ0870/850 1839, ⓦwww.airfrance.co.uk; Republic of Ireland ⓣ08/1821 0013, ⓦwww.airfrance.com/ie
Alitalia UK ⓣ0870/544 8259, Republic of Ireland ⓣ01/677 5171, ⓦwww.alitalia.co.uk
American Airlines UK ⓣ0845/7789 789 or 020/7365 07777, Republic of Ireland ⓣ01/602 0550, ⓦwww.aa.com
British Airways UK ⓣ0870/850 9850, Republic of Ireland ⓣ1890/626 747, ⓦwww.ba.com
British Midland UK ⓣ0870/607 0222, Republic of Ireland ⓣ01/407 3036, ⓦwww.flybmi.com
Continental UK ⓣ0845/607 6760, Republic of Ireland ⓣ1890/925 252, ⓦwww.continental.com
Delta UK ⓣ0800/414 767, Republic of Ireland ⓣ1800/768 080, ⓦwww.delta.com
Iberia Airlines UK ⓣ0845/601 2854, Republic of Ireland ⓣ0810/462 000, ⓦwww.iberiaairlines.co.uk
KLM UK ⓣ0870/507 4074, Republic of Ireland ⓣ1850/747 400, ⓦwww.klmuk.com
Lufthansa UK ⓣ0845/7737 747, ⓦwww.lufthansa.co.uk
Scandinavian Airlines (SAS) UK ⓣ0870/6072 7727, Republic of Ireland ⓣ01/844 5440, ⓦwww.scandinavian.net
Swiss UK ⓣ0845/601 0956, Republic of Ireland ⓣ1890/200 515, ⓦwww.swiss.com
United Airlines UK ⓣ0845/844 4777, ⓦwww.unitedairlines.co.uk
Virgin Atlantic Airways UK ⓣ0870/380 2007, ⓦwww.virgin-atlantic.com

Flight and travel agents

Expedia UK ⓣ0870/050 0808, ⓦwww.expedia.co.uk. Easy-to-navigate online agent offering a diverse range of holiday packages and good deals on flights.
Flightbookers UK ⓣ0870/814 0000, ⓦwww.ebookers.com. Low fares on an extensive selection of scheduled flights, plus Chicago accommodation packages. Recommended.
Flynow UK ⓣ0870/660 004, ⓦwww.flynow.com. Wide range of discounted tickets.
Joe Walsh Tours Ireland ⓣ01/241 0800, ⓦwww.joewalshtours.ie. Family run, general budget fares agent.
North South Travel UK ⓣ01245/608 291, ⓦwww.northsouthtravel.co.uk. Discounted fares worldwide – profits are used to support projects in the developing world, especially the promotion of sustainable tourism.
Quest Travel UK ⓣ0870/442 3542, ⓦwww.questtravel.com. Specialists in Round-the-World and Australasian discount fares.
STA Travel UK ⓣ0870/1600 599, ⓦwww.statravel.co.uk. Worldwide specialists in low-cost flights and tours for students and under-26s, though other customers welcome.
Trailfinders UK ⓣ0845/058 5858, ⓦwww.trailfinders.com. One of the best-informed and most efficient agents for independent travelers; Amtrak passes available.
Travel Bag UK ⓣ0800/082 5000, ⓦwww.travelbag.co.uk.com. Specializing in Round-the-World tickets, with good deals aimed at the backpacker market.
United Vacations UK ⓣ0870/606 2222, ⓦwww.unitedvacations.co.uk. Tailor-made package holidays, fly-drive deals, rail tours, cruises, organized sightseeing tours, and more.
ⓦwww.travel4less.co.uk UK ⓣ0871/222 3423. Good discount airfares and package deals, including three-night city breaks to Chicago, from £439 in low season (flight and accommodation included).

Tour operators

American Adventures UK ⓣ01295/256 777, ⓦwww.americanadventures.com. Small-group camping trips and adventure tours, including hiking and mountain biking throughout the US and Canada.
American Holidays UK ⓣ028/9023 8762, Dublin ⓣ01/673 3840, ⓦwww.american-holidays.com. Specialists in travel to the US offering tailor-made city breaks and escorted tours.
British Airways Holidays UK ⓣ0845/606 0747, ⓦwww.britishairways.com/travel/holidaysindex. An exhaustive range of package and tailor-made holidays around the world, with Chicago city breaks.
Kuoni Travel UK ⓣ01306/747 734, ⓦwww.kuoni.co.uk. Build your own holiday package to Chicago; good family offers.
Thomas Cook UK ⓣ0870/750 5711, ⓦwww.thomascook.com. Long-established one-stop 24-hour travel agency for package holidays or scheduled flights, with bureaux de change issuing Thomas Cook travelers' checks, travel insurance, and car rental. Three-night city breaks in Chicago start from £357 per person, staying in a three-star hotel.

Twohigs Ireland ⓣ01/648 0800, ⓦwww.twohigs.com. Specialists in US travel, among other regions.
World Travel Centre Ireland ⓣ01/416 7007, ⓦwww.worldtravel.ie. Discount flights and other travel services.

Flights from Australia and New Zealand

There are no direct scheduled flights to Chicago from either Australia or New Zealand.

Most Chicago-bound flights **from Australia** leave from Sydney or Melbourne and usually route through Tokyo, Los Angeles, or Las Vegas. The major carriers – Qantas (in partnership with American Airlines) and United Airlines – offer several flights a day to the US West Coast, from which onward travel to Chicago is easily arranged. Flights take about thirteen hours to the West Coast, and five hours onward to Chicago.

Fares vary depending on the season (between June and September being the most expensive) and flight availability, with fares as low as A$1200 and as high as A$3600, though A$2300–2640 is the more usual range.

Chicago-bound flights **from New Zealand** leave Auckland, Christchurch, or Wellington and route through Los Angeles, before making the onward flight to Chicago. The two major carriers, Air New Zealand and Qantas, and their US partners, United Airlines and American Airlines, generally fly from Auckland (add about 15 percent to the fare for Christchurch and Wellington departures). In general, expect to pay NZ$2830–4100.

Airlines

Air Canada Australia ⓣ1300/655 767 or 02/8248 5757, New Zealand ⓣ0508/747 767, ⓦwww.aircanada.ca
America West Airlines Australia ⓣ02/9810 7400, ⓦwww.americawest.com
American Airlines Australia ⓣ1300/650 747, New Zealand ⓣ0800/887 997, ⓦwww.aa.com
British Airways Australia ⓣ1300/767 177, New Zealand ⓣ09/966 9777, ⓦwww.britishairways.com
Continental Airlines Australia ⓣ02/9244 2242, New Zealand ⓣ09/308 3350, ⓦwww.continental.com
Delta Air Lines Australia ⓣ1300/302 849, New Zealand ⓣ09/977 2235, ⓦwww.delta-air.com
Japan Airlines Australia ⓣ02/9272 1111, ⓦwww.au.jal.com, New Zealand ⓣ09/379 9906, ⓦwww.nz.jal.com
KLM/Northwest Airlines Australia ⓣ1300/303 747, ⓦwww.klm.com/au_en, New Zealand ⓣ09/309 1782, ⓦwww.klm.com/nz_en
Korean Air Australia ⓣ02/9262 6000, New Zealand ⓣ09/914 2000, ⓦwww.koreanair.com.au
Qantas Australia ⓣ13 13 13, ⓦwww.qantas.com.au, New Zealand ⓣ0800/808 767, ⓦwww.qantas.co.nz
Singapore Airlines Australia ⓣ13 10 11, New Zealand ⓣ0800/808 909, ⓦwww.singaporeair.com
United Airlines Australia ⓣ13 17 77, ⓦwww.unitedairlines.com.au, New Zealand 0800/747 400, ⓦwww.unitedairlines.co.nz
Virgin Atlantic Airways Australia ⓣ1300/727 340, ⓦwww.virgin-atlantic.com

Travel and flight agents

Budget Travel New Zealand ⓣ0800/808 480, ⓦwww.budgettravel.co.nz. Round-the-World tickets and tours.
Destinations Unlimited New Zealand ⓣ09/414 1680, ⓦwww.travel-nz.com. Round-the-World tickets, flights, packages, car rental, insurance, and more.
Flight Centre Australia ⓣ13 31 33 or 02/9235 3522, ⓦwww.flightcentre.com.au, New Zealand ⓣ0800/243 544, ⓦwww.flightcentre.co.nz. Specialist agent for budget flights, especially Round-the-World tickets.
STA Travel Australia ⓣ1300/733 035, ⓦwww.statravel.com.au, New Zealand ⓣ0508/782 872, ⓦwww.statravel.co.nz. Discount flights, travel passes, and other services for youth/student travelers.
Trailfinders Australia ⓣ1300/780 212, ⓦwww.trailfinders.com.au. One of the best-informed and most efficient agents for independent travelers; Amtrak passes also available.

Specialist agents

Adventure World Australia ⓣ02/8913 0755, ⓦwww.adventureworld.com.au, New Zealand ⓣ09/524 5118, ⓦwww.adventureworld.co.nz. Chicago hotel bookings, car rental, and organized tours.
Canada & America Travel Specialists Australia ⓣ02/9922 4600, ⓦwww.canada-americatravel.com.au. Flights and accommodation in North America, plus Amtrak passes and Greyhound Ameripasses.
Sydney International Travel Centre ⓣ02/9250 9320, ⓦwww.sydneytravel.com.au. US flights, accommodation, city stays, and car rental.
travel.com.au Australia ⓣ1300/130 482 or 02/9249 5444, ⓕ02/9262 3525. Comprehensive online travel company.

United Vacations Australia ⓣ1300/887 870, ⓦwww.unitedvacations.com.au. Features hotel deals for Chicago.
Viator Australia ⓣ02/8219 5400, ⓦwww.viator.com. Small selection of Chicago tours and discounts; also sells City Pass – admission to six top Chicago attractions for 50 percent off regular admission (from US$50 per person).

Red tape and visas

Citizens of the UK, Ireland, Australia, New Zealand, and most Western European countries (check with your nearest embassy or consulate), who plan to visit the US for less than ninety days, need only a round-trip ticket, passport, and a visa waiver form. The latter (an I-94W) is available from your travel agency, at the airline check-in desk, or on board the plane, and must be presented to immigration once you arrive.

All **passports** must be machine readable, and governments of countries that participate in the visa waiver program must issue passports with biometric identification. Note that all travelers after October 2006 will be required to present a biometric passport with microchip biographical data to immigration; consult your embassy for further information well in advance of travel.

For a brief excursion, **Canadian citizens** will need only proof of citizenship (passport or birth certificate in conjunction with a photo ID) to enter the US.

Residents of countries not mentioned above will need a valid passport, as well as a non-immigrant visitor's visa, which is valid for a maximum of ninety days. Visa procedures vary by country and by your status on application, so contact the nearest US embassy or consulate for details. Most travelers won't need to be inoculated to enter the US, unless they're en route from areas where cholera and typhoid are endemic; check with your doctor before you leave.

The date stamped in your passport by immigration upon arrival is the latest you're legally allowed to stay. Leaving a few days later may not matter, especially if you're heading home, but more than a week or so can result in a protracted, rather unpleasant interrogation from officials, which may cause you to miss your flight. You may also be denied entry the next time you try to visit the US.

Should you need a **visa extension**, you'll have to apply through the nearest US Immigration and Naturalization Service (INS) office before your time is up. In Chicago, the office is at 10 W Jackson Blvd (Mon, Tues, Thurs, Fri 7.30am–2pm, Wed 7.30am–noon; ⓣ312/385-1500 or 1-800/870-3676, ⓦwww.ins.usdoj.gov). Be prepared to discuss why you're hoping to stay on – they're likely to assume you are working in the US illegally, so any evidence of your pre-existing (and abundant) funds might strengthen your case. If you can, bring an upstanding American citizen to vouch for you. You'll also have to explain why you didn't plan for the extra time initially.

US embassies

For details of foreign embassies and consulates in Chicago, see p.270.

Australia Moonah Place, Yarralumla, Canberra, ACT 2600 ⓣ02/6214 5600, ⓦusembassy-australia.state.gov/embassy
Canada 490 Sussex Drive, Ottawa, ON K1P 5T1 ⓣ613/238-5335, ⓦwww.usembassycanada.gov
Ireland 42 Elgin Rd, Ballsbridge, Dublin 4 ⓣ01/668 8777, ⓦwww.Dublin.usembassy.gov.ie
New Zealand 29 Fitzherbert Terrace, Thorndon, Wellington ⓣ04/462 6000, ⓦwww.usembassy.org.nz
UK 24 Grosvenor Square, London W1A 1AE ⓣ020/7499 9000, ⓦwww.usembassy.org.uk

Insurance

Even though EU health-care privileges apply in the US, residents of the UK would do well to take out an insurance policy before traveling to cover against theft, loss, illness, or injury. Before paying for a new policy, it's worth checking if you are already covered – some all-risks home-insurance policies may cover your possessions when overseas, and many private medical schemes include cover when abroad. In Canada, provincial health plans usually provide partial cover for medical mishaps overseas, while holders of official student/teacher/youth cards in Canada and the US are entitled to meagre accident coverage and hospital in-patient benefits. Students will often find that their student health coverage extends during the vacations and for one term beyond the date of last enrolment.

After exhausting these possibilities, you might want to contact a specialist travel insurance company, or consider the travel insurance deal Rough Guides offers (see box, below). A typical travel-insurance policy usually provides cover for the loss of baggage, tickets, and – up to a certain limit – cash or checks, as well as cancellation or curtailment of your journey. Most of them exclude so-called dangerous sports unless an extra premium is paid: this can mean whitewater rafting and trekking, though probably not kayaking. Many policies can be chopped and changed to exclude coverage you don't need – for example, sickness and accident benefits can often be excluded or included at will. If you do take medical coverage, ascertain whether benefits will be paid as treatment proceeds or only after return home, and if there is a 24-hour medical emergency number. When securing baggage cover, make sure that the per-article limit – typically under £500 – will cover your most valuable possession. If you need to make a claim, you should keep receipts for medicines and medical treatment, and in the event you have anything stolen, you must obtain an official theft report from the police.

Rough Guide travel insurance

Rough Guides has teamed up with Columbus Direct to offer you travel insurance that can be tailored to suit your needs.

Readers can choose from many different travel insurance products, including a low-cost backpacker option for long stays; a short-break option for city getaways; a typical holiday-package option; and many others. There are also annual multi-trip policies for those who travel regularly, with variable levels of cover available. Different sports and activities (such as trekking and skiing) can be covered if required on most policies.

Rough Guides travel insurance is available to the residents of 36 different countries with different language options to choose from via our website – Ⓦwww.roughguidesinsurance.com – where you can also purchase the insurance. Alternatively, UK residents should call Ⓣ800/083 9507; US citizens should call Ⓣ1 800/749-4922; Australians should call Ⓣ1 300 669 999. All other nationalities should call Ⓣ44870 890 2843.

Information, websites, and maps

The main source of city information for tourists is the Chicago Office of Tourism (see below for details). You can contact them before your trip for glossy brochures, maps, visitor guides, and event calendars. It also runs the Chicago Greeter service (ⓣ312/742-1284, ⓦwww.chicagogreeter.com): a great way to learn more about the city from a local's perspective, these city tours lasting between two and four hours are led by passionate volunteers. Tours depart from the Cultural Center (see p.50) Mon–Fri 9am–5pm. Seven days' advance booking is required. Once in Chicago, you can visit its walk-in branches. There are also several excellent Chicago-related websites with current information on tours, museums, and the newest restaurants and clubs.

Information

Before setting off for Chicago, you may want to contact one of the tourist organizations listed below for help in planning your itinerary.

Once in the city, you'll want to head for the Chicago Office of Tourism, which has three locations, the best and most accessible of which is on the first floor of the Chicago Cultural Center, 77 E Randolph St (Mon–Fri 10am–6pm, Sat 10am–5pm, Sun 11am–5pm; ⓣ1-877/CHI-CAGO, ⓦwww.ci.chi.il.us/Tourism/CulturalCenter/index), which can help you with maps, tours, and citywide information. The Office of Tourism has a second location inside the Chicago Water Works building, 163 E Pearson St at Michigan Avenue (daily 7.30am–7pm), and an Explore Chicago kiosk at 2 N State St at Madison Street (Mon–Sat 10am–6pm).

Tourist offices

Chicago Convention and Tourism Bureau Mailing address 2301 S Lake Shore Drive, Chicago, IL 60616 ⓣ1-877/244-2246; outside the US, Mexico, and Canada ⓣ312/201-8847, ⓕ567-8533, ⓦwww.chicago.il.org

Illinois Bureau of Tourism 100 W Randolph St, Suite 3-4000, Chicago, IL 60601 ⓣ312/814-732 or 1-800/226-6632, ⓦwww.enjoyillinois.com

Websites

The following is a selective list of Chicago-related websites to help get you started.

Chicago Public Library ⓦwww.chipublib.org. A handy resource whose encyclopedic "Learn Chicago" section covers just about everything you want to know, from vital city statistics and symbols to major and minor disasters.

Chicago Reader ⓦwww.chicagoreader.com. The city's free and voluminous entertainment weekly newspaper has an excellent website with day-by-day details of what's on when and where: music, galleries, restaurants, bars, clubs, theater, and readings, as well as reviews and features.

Chicago Tribune ⓦwww.chicagotribune.com. Homepage of the city's morning newspaper, covering local news, sports, and weather updates, plus arts, entertainment, restaurant, and bar listings in its extensive Metromix search engine (ⓦwww.metromix.com).

City of Chicago ⓦwww.egov.cityofchicago.org/city. The city's official homepage, with links to major attractions, accommodation, tours, an events calendar, and more in its "About Town" section. There is also an excellent guide to the city's Historical Landmarks.

Illinois Hotel and Lodging Association ⓦwww.stayillinois.com. The Association's comprehensive website has detailed summaries of and links to most hotels in Chicago and throughout Illinois.

League of Chicago Theaters ⓦwww.chicagoplays.com. Provides details on venues, showtimes, and ticket prices for plays being performed in Chicago. Includes a link to a list of half-price theater shows (under "Hot Tix").

Mayor's Office of Special Events ⓦwww.ci.chi.il.us/SpecialEvents. The best source for information on festivals, parades, holidays, and sporting events, as well as what films are currently being shot in Chicago. Updated regularly.

National Weather Service Ⓦweather.noaa.gov/weather/IL_cc_us. The organization's Illinois page provides up-to-the-minute weather conditions at O'Hare, Midway, and regional airports.
Sports Illinois Ⓦwww.sportsillinois.com. Part of the Illinois Bureau of Tourism's extensive site, covering every conceivable sport, and where to participate, throughout the state.

Maps

Our maps should be sufficient for most purposes; commercial maps and the free city plans available from tourist offices can help fill in the gaps. For a pocket-sized map, try the laminated *Streetwise Chicago* ($5.95; Ⓦwww.streetwisemaps.com), which is available from most book, travel, and map stores.

The American Automobile Association (Ⓣ1-800/222-4357, Ⓦwww.aaa.com) provides free maps and assistance to its members, and to British members of the AA and RAC.

Map outlets

In the US and Canada

AdventurousTraveler.com US Ⓣ1-800/282-3963, Ⓦatb.away.com.
Book Passage 51 Tamal Vista Blvd, Corte Madera, CA 94925 Ⓣ1-800/999-7909, also in San Francisco Ⓣ415/835-1020, Ⓦwww.bookpassage.com
Elliot Bay Book Company 101 S Main St, Seattle, WA 98104 Ⓣ1-800/962-5311, Ⓦwww.elliotbaybook.com
Globe Corner Bookstore 28 Church St, Cambridge, MA 02138 Ⓣ1-800/358-6013, Ⓦwww.globecorner.com
Rand McNally nationwide Ⓣ1-800/275-RAND, Ⓦwww.randmcnally.com. Around thirty stores across the US; dial ext 2111 or check the website for the nearest location. In Chicago: 150 S Wacker Drive, IL 60606 Ⓣ312/332-2009; 444 N Michigan Ave, IL 60611 Ⓣ312/321-1751.
The Travel Bug Bookstore 2667 W Broadway, Vancouver, BC V6K 2G2 Ⓣ604/737-1122, Ⓦwww.swifty.com/tbug
World of Maps 1235 Wellington St, Ottawa, ON K1Y 3A3 Ⓣ1-800/214-8524, Ⓦwww.worldofmaps.com

In the UK and Ireland

Blackwell's Map and Travel Shop 50 Broad St, Oxford OX1 3BQ Ⓣ01865/793 550, Ⓦmaps.blackwell.co.uk
Eason 80 Middle Abbey St, Dublin 1 Ⓣ01/858 3881, Ⓦwww.buy4now.ie/eason
Heffers Map and Travel 20 Trinity St, Cambridge CB2 1TJ Ⓣ01223/333 536, Ⓦwww.heffers.co.uk
Hodges Figgis Bookshop 56–58 Dawson St, Dublin 2 Ⓣ01/677 4754, Ⓦwww.hodgesfiggis.com
National Map Centre 22–24 Caxton St, London SW1H 0QU Ⓣ020/7222 2466, Ⓦwww.mapsnmc.co.uk
Newcastle Map Centre 55 Grey St, Newcastle-upon-Tyne NE1 6EF Ⓣ0191/261 5622
Ordnance Survey Ireland 34 Aungier St, Dublin 2 Ⓣ01/476 0471, Ⓦwww.osi.ie
Ordnance Survey of Northern Ireland Colby House, Stranmillis Court, Belfast BT9 5BJ Ⓣ028/9025 5755, Ⓦwww.osni.gov.uk
Stanfords 12–14 Long Acre, London WC2E 9LP Ⓣ020/7836 1321, Ⓦwww.stanfords.co.uk
The Travel Bookshop 13–15 Blenheim Crescent, London W11 2EE Ⓣ020/7229 5260, Ⓦwww.thetravelbookshop.co.uk

In Australia and New Zealand

The Map Shop 6–10 Peel St, Adelaide, South Australia 5000 Ⓣ08/8231 2033, Ⓦwww.mapshop.net.au
Mapland 372 Little Bourke St, Melbourne, Victoria 3000 Ⓣ03/9670 4383, Ⓦwww.mapland.com.au
MapWorld 173 Gloucester St, Christchurch Ⓣ0800/627 967 or 03/374 5399, Ⓦwww.mapworld.co.nz

Arrival

Those traveling to Chicago by bus or train arrive just west of the Loop, within a stone's throw of public transportation and dozens of hotels. While flights touch down at O'Hare and Midway airports in Chicago's outlying areas, at least a dozen miles from the city center, efficient El trains will take you downtown within a half hour to 45 minutes. Taking a taxi from the airport won't save you much time and can be expensive, especially if you're going it alone. Alternatively, airport shuttles will cost less but tend to make multiple stops on the journey downtown.

By plane

If arriving by air, you'll most likely be coming into **O'Hare International Airport** on the city's northwest side, about seventeen miles outside the city center. There are several ways of getting into Chicago proper from here, the quickest and most reliable option being the forty-minute ride on the Chicago Transit Authority (CTA) Blue Line El train, which runs 24 hours and costs $1.75 one-way. You'll reach downtown from O'Hare in about 45 minutes, and just under half that time from Midway. The station is underneath the main parking garage, a short walk from most of the airport's terminals. From Terminal 5, though, you'll need to take the free Airport Transit System shuttle to Terminal 3 and follow the signs marked "City Transport."

Another option is taking one of the airport shuttles, which drop you off at your requested hotel for around $24, plus tip – half the equivalent taxi fare. Shuttles pull up in front of the main entrances of each terminal every ten to fifteen minutes. Most of the shuttle companies have information desks inside by the baggage claim area. Shuttles generally run between 6am and 11.30pm. If you want to try and reserve ahead, call Continental Airport Express (☎1-888/284-3826), one of the better shuttle services.

Taxis are your most expensive option, and you're at the whim of Chicago traffic – a single fare could run you anywhere from $38 and up, plus tip. Even in off-peak times, however, cabs are plentiful and can be found curbside at any terminal, outside of baggage claim. Usually the ride takes twenty minutes, but with traffic you could be looking at up to an hour. If you can find someone to split the fare, then a cab could be decent value.

From **Midway Airport**, on the southwest side of the city, the quickest and cheapest way to reach downtown is to take the CTA Orange Line El train, which departs every five minutes (off-peak, every 15min) and makes the ten-mile trip in just under half an hour. To find the El stop, follow the signs to the parking garage – the station is directly behind the garage. If you arrive at Midway late at night or very early in the morning, bear in mind that the Orange Line stops running between 1am and 4am Monday to Saturday, and between 1am and 7am on Sundays and holidays.

You can pick up a taxi just outside the baggage claim area. Fares are metered, and a ride into downtown will set you back about $24 (plus tip), taking anywhere from fifteen minutes to an hour, depending on traffic. If you're with other travelers, you might try the shared-ride service, whereby passengers can share a cab for a flat rate of $19 per person; however, be sure to let the driver know beforehand that you want to do this.

Another option is taking the Continental Airport Express shuttle (6am–11.30pm; ☎1-888/284-3826), which leaves from just outside the main terminal. Shuttles run every fifteen minutes between Midway and downtown Chicago (for around $15), and also the northern suburbs.

For driving directions from both airports, see p.31.

By train and bus

Chicago is the hub of the nationwide Amtrak rail system, and almost every cross-country route passes through Union Station (Ⓣ312/558-1075), at Canal and Adams streets, just one block west of the Loop. The closest El stop is about four blocks away at Quincy and Wells streets, while cabs are available outside the station on the upper and lower levels.

Greyhound and a couple of regional bus companies pull into the large modern terminal at 630 W Harrison St (Ⓣ312/408-5980 in Chicago, Ⓦwww.greyhound.com), between Des Plaines and Jefferson streets, a ten-minute walk from the Loop. The nearest El stop (Blue Line) is on Clinton Street, two blocks northeast of the terminal.

By car

When driving to Chicago you'll need to be aware of at least four major **expressways** feeding into downtown Chicago: I-90/94 from the northwest and north; I-290 from the west; I-55 from the southwest; and I-90/94 from the south.

From O'Hare International Airport (on the northwest side), take I-90 East to Ohio Street, which will take you to Michigan Avenue, just north of the Loop. From the northern suburbs, take I-94 to the same Ohio Street exit. Alternatively, take the scenic route along Lake Shore Drive (Highway 41).

From the west, take I-290 East directly into downtown – it becomes Congress Parkway and runs along the Loop's southern edge.

Approaching the city from the south (from Indiana, near Lake Michigan), use I-90, following it over the Chicago Skyway's long bridge to merge onto I-94 North. Stay on this past the juncture with I-290, then exit at any of the next three streets and drive east to reach the heart of downtown. Alternatively, from Indiana via I-80/94, take the expressway to the Calumet Expressway, then to I-94 North and follow the directions from I-290, as given directly above.

From Midway Airport (and the southwest), take Cicero Avenue north to I-55. Take I-55 east to either I-94 North, past I-290 and exit east at any one of the streets thereafter, or simply stay on I-55 to Lake Shore Drive north and exit at Wacker Drive.

Major expressways

I-55	Stevenson Expressway
I-90 East	Kennedy Expressway
I-94 North	Dan Ryan Expressway
I-290 East	Eisenhower Expressway

Leaving Chicago: reserving a shuttle seat

If you plan on taking a **shuttle** to either O'Hare or Midway, it's worth booking a seat in advance as vans can book up fast, especially around the holidays. Be sure to give yourself plenty of time to get to the airport.

Costs, money, and banks

Chicago is relatively inexpensive compared to the major US cities: public transport is efficient and reliable enough in most instances, many of the museums are affordable (under $10) and offer free days; unless you're intent on dining in high style, the food can be relatively cheap too.

Average costs

Accommodation is likely to be your biggest single expense. The least expensive, reasonable double hotel rooms go from $95 a night, though you'll probably find some good deals on weekends and during Chicago's winter; see Chapter 13, "Accommodation," for more details. After accommodation, you could get by on $50–65 per day, which will buy you a basic diner breakfast, a fast-food lunch (pizza, burger, sandwich), and a budget sit-down dinner with beer, plus El fare. Beyond this, a little more luxury – such as fancier meals, taking taxis, going to a concert or play – will mean more like $100 a day. Bear in mind that sales tax is added to just about everything you buy in stores, except for certain groceries.

Bear in mind that **tipping** is customary and expected at restaurants (usually not less than 15 percent) and bars ($1 for a round of drinks), though you needn't feel pressure to leave a large tip if service is especially poor.

Banks and ATMs

With an ATM card, you'll be able to withdraw cash just about anywhere in Chicago, though you'll be charged a fee for using a different bank's network. If you have a foreign **cash-dispensing card** linked to an international network such as Cirrus or Plus – be sure to check with your home bank before you set off – you can make withdrawals from ATMs in the US. The flat transaction fee is usually quite small – your bank will able to advise on this. Make sure you have a personal identification number (PIN) that's designed to work overseas. You may also be able to use your debit card for purchases, as you would at home.

Most banks in Chicago are open Monday to Friday, 9am–3pm, though a limited number have Saturday hours, usually open no later than 1pm. For a list of downtown banks, see p.270.

Travelers' checks

Travelers' checks in US dollars are widely accepted as cash in restaurants, stores, and museums. The usual fee for travelers' check sales is one or two percent, though this may be waived if you buy the check through a bank where you have an account. It pays to get a selection of denominations so you'll have some flexibility. Make sure to keep the purchase agreement and a record of check serial numbers safe and separate from the checks themselves. In the event that checks are lost or stolen, the issuing company will expect you to report the loss immediately to their office; most companies claim to replace lost or stolen checks within 24 hours.

For a list of currency exchange offices, see p.270.

Credit and debit cards

Credit cards are a very handy backup source of funds, and can be used either in ATMs or over the counter. MasterCard, Visa, and American Express are accepted just about everywhere, but other cards may not be recognized in the US. Always carry with you a **photo ID** or your card may be refused. Remember that all cash advances are treated as loans, with interest accruing daily from the date of withdrawal; there may be a transaction fee on top of this.

A compromise between travelers' checks and plastic is Visa TravelMoney, a disposable pre-paid **debit card** with a PIN that works in all ATMs that take Visa cards. When your funds are depleted, you simply throw the card away. Since you can buy up to nine cards to access the same funds – useful for couples or families traveling together – it's a good idea to buy at least one extra as a backup in case of loss or theft. To order or activate a card, call ⓣ1-877/394-2247 in the US; visit also the Visa TravelMoney website at ⓦinternational.visa.com. The card is available in most countries from branches of Thomas Cook and Citicorp.

Wiring money

Having money wired from home using one of the companies listed on p.33 is never convenient or cheap, and should be considered a last resort. It's also possible to have money wired directly from a bank in your home country to a bank in the US, although this is somewhat less reliable because it involves two separate institutions. If you go this route, your home bank will need the address of the branch bank where you want to pick up the money and the address and telex number of the bank's head office, which will act as the clearing house; money wired this way normally takes two working days to arrive, and costs around $40 per transaction.

The quickest way to have money wired to you is to have someone take the cash to the

A note for foreign visitors

US currency comes in $1 bills and coins, bills of $5, $10, $20, $50, and $100, plus various larger (and rarer) denominations. All are the same size and same green color, making it necessary to check each bill carefully. The dollar is made up of 100 cents (¢) in coins of 1 cent (usually called a penny), 5 cents (a nickel), 10 cents (a dime), and 25 cents (a quarter). Fifty-cent and $1 coins are less frequently seen.

Change – especially quarters – is needed for buses, vending machines, and telephones, so always carry plenty, though automatic machines are increasingly fitted with slots for dollar bills.

nearest money-wiring company and have it wired to the office nearest you – a process that should take no longer than ten to fifteen minutes. The fee depends on the amount being sent, where it's being sent from and to, and how fast you need it. This service is offered by Travelers' Express Moneygram (also available at participating Thomas Cook branches) and Western Union. Travelers' Express only accepts cash, while the Western Union office sending the money will accept credit cards. The latter has slightly higher rates, and if a credit card is involved, they'll probably charge an extra fee.

If you have a few days' leeway, it's cheaper to send a postal money order through the mail; postal orders are exchangeable at any post office. The equivalent for foreign travelers is the international money order, but it may take up to seven days to arrive by mail. An ordinary check sent from overseas usually takes two to three weeks to clear.

Money-wiring companies

Thomas Cook Canada ⓣ1-888/823-4732, Republic of Ireland ⓣ01/677 1721, UK ⓣ01733/318 922, US ⓣ1-800/287-7362, ⓦwww.us.thomascook.com
Travelers' Express Moneygram Canada ⓣ1-800/933-3278, US ⓣ1-800/926-3947, ⓦwww.moneygram.com
Western Union Australia ⓣ1800/501 500, New Zealand ⓣ09/270 0050, Republic of Ireland ⓣ1800/395 395, UK ⓣ0800/833 833, US and Canada ⓣ1-800/325-6000, ⓦwww.westernunion.com

Phones, mail, and email

As one of the country's major business hubs, it should go without saying that Chicago has a speedy and efficient communications infrastructure, so staying in touch shouldn't be a problem.

Telephones

All telephone numbers within Chicago use either the **ⓣ312 or 773 area code**, which you need to dial if you are calling from within the city. Outside Chicago, dial 1 before the area code and the seven-digit phone number. For detailed information about calls, area codes, and rates in the Chicago area, consult the front of the telephone directory in the *White Pages*.

In general, calling from your hotel room will cost considerably more than if you use a pay phone, where you can make local calls for 35¢ for the first three or four minutes, 10¢ more for each additional two minutes. Hotels often charge a connection fee of at least

$1 for all calls, even if they're local or toll-free, and international calls will cost a small fortune.

Long-distance and international calls

For overseas visitors, one of the most convenient ways of phoning home from abroad is with a **telephone charge card**, available from your phone company back home. Using access codes for the country you are in and a PIN number, you can make calls from most hotel, public, and private phones that will bill to your own account. The benefit of calling cards is mainly one of convenience, as the rates aren't necessarily cheaper than calling from a public phone abroad and can't compete with discounted off-peak times many local companies offer. Since most major charge cards are free to obtain, however, it's certainly worth getting one at least for emergencies; contact your phone company for more details.

In the **US and Canada**, AT&T, MCI, Sprint, Canada Direct, and other North American long-distance companies all enable their customers to make credit-card calls while overseas, billed to your home number. Call your company's customer-service line to find out if they provide service from the US, and if so, what the toll-free access code is.

In the **UK and Ireland**, British Telecom (Ⓣ800/345 144, Ⓦwww.payphones.bt.com) will issue free to all BT customers the BT Charge Card, which can be used in 116 countries – calling a UK landline from the US using the Charge Card will cost £0.78 per minute; AT&T (dial Ⓣ1-800/833-3232 for further information) has the Global Calling Card.

To call **Australia and New Zealand** from overseas, telephone charge cards such as Telstra Telecard or Optus Calling Card in Australia and Telecom NZ's Calling Card can be used to make calls abroad, which are charged back to a domestic account or credit card. Apply to Telstra (Ⓣ1800/616 606), Optus (Ⓣ1300/300 990) or Telecom NZ (Ⓣ04/801 9000).

An alternative to telephone charge cards is cheap pre-paid phone cards offering cut-rate calls to virtually anywhere in the world. Various stores in Chicago sell them; look for signs posted in shop windows advertising rates.

A less well-known option is to call home through an Internet-phone service, usually available from one of the better cyber cafés. The audio quality isn't nearly as good as with a regular phone and there's usually a slight delay, but calling via the Internet ($5/30min) can work out to be cheaper than calling on a regular phone. Calls are patched through like any other phone call. (See p.271 for addresses.)

Mobile phones

If you want to use your **cell phone**, you'll need to check with your phone provider whether it will work in Chicago, and what the call charges are. Many phones only work within the region designated by the area code in the phone number.

Useful telephone numbers

For international calls to Chicago, dial your country's international access code + 1 for the US + 312 or 773 for Chicago.

Emergencies Ⓣ911 for fire, police, or ambulance
Directory assistance Ⓣ411 (for numbers in Chicago); Ⓣ1 + (area code) + 555-1212 (for numbers in other area codes)
Operator Ⓣ0

International calls from Chicago

Australia Ⓣ011 + 61 + phone number
Canada Ⓣ011 + 1 + phone number
New Zealand Ⓣ011 + 64 + phone number
Republic of Ireland Ⓣ011 + 353 + phone number
UK Ⓣ011 + 44 + phone number

If you are visiting the US, your cell phone probably won't work unless you have a **tri-band phone**, for example. For details of which phones work in the US, contact your service provider. Should you have a phone that works in the US, you'll probably have to inform your service provider before going abroad to get international access switched on. You may get charged extra for this depending on your existing package and where you are traveling to. Tri-band phones will automatically switch to the US frequency, but these can be pricey, so you may want to rent a phone if you're traveling to the US. If you want to retrieve messages while you're away, you'll have to ask your provider for a new access code, as your home one is unlikely to work abroad. You are also likely to be charged extra for incoming calls when abroad, as the people calling you will be paying the usual rate. For further information about using your phone abroad, check out Ⓦwww.telecomsadvice.org.uk/features/using_your_mobile_abroad.

For time differences between the US and the rest of the world, see p.271.

Mail

Ordinary **mail** sent within the US costs 37¢ (at press time) for letters weighing up to an ounce, while standard postcards cost 23¢. For anywhere outside the US, airmail letters cost 80¢ up to an ounce and 70¢ for postcards and aerograms. Airmail between the US and Europe may take a week and 12–14 days to Australasia.

You can have mail sent to you c/o General Delivery (known elsewhere as **post restante**), Chicago, IL 60601. Letters will end up at the post office at 200 E Randolph St (Mon–Fri 7.30am–5.30pm; Ⓣ312/861-0473), which will only hold mail for thirty days before returning it to sender – so make sure the envelope has a return address. Alternatively, most hotels will accept and hold mail for guests.

Email

One of the best ways to keep in touch while traveling is to sign up for a free Internet **email** address that can be accessed from anywhere, for example YahooMail or Hotmail – accessible through Ⓦwww.yahoo.com and Ⓦwww.hotmail.com. Once you've set up an account, you can use these sites to pick up and send mail from any Internet café, or hotel with Internet access.

A useful website – Ⓦwww.kropla.com – has information on how to plug your laptop in when abroad, on phone country codes around the world, and about electrical systems in different countries.

Finding an Internet outlet is fairly easy in Chicago – the city has numerous **Internet cafés** (see p.271) that charge, on average, $5 for half an hour's use. You're likely to spend twice as much ($5–10/hr) at the many business centers inside hotels. The hostels also have a few terminals (*Hostelling International – Chicago* has eight), though they charge the same as Internet cafés. Another option is to head to the Harold Washington Library in the Loop, where you can log on for free.

City transportation

For a city as spread out as Chicago, the public transportation system is extensive, and service is remarkably efficient. Most sights can be reached on the city's El train system, while buses, though slower, fill in the gaps. Other options include taking a taxi, or renting a car or bike.

The CTA

The Chicago Transit Authority's **subway and elevated train system** – also known as the "El" – runs on seven lines that cover most downtown areas and neighborhoods, with the exception of parts of Lincoln Park toward Lake Michigan, the area east of Michigan Avenue toward Navy Pier, and Hyde Park. Each color-coded line (Blue, Brown, Green, Orange, Purple, Red, and Yellow) radiates from the Loop. Trains are clean and run frequently during the day – roughly every fifteen minutes or so – though at night service on most lines is sporadic between 2am and 5am; the Red Line and Blue Line (between Forest Park and O'Hare), however, run 24 hours.

Fares are $1.50 a ride; you'll need to buy a **transit card** from a vending machine at El stations before you pass through the turnstiles. Cards will hold as little as $1.50 and as much as $100. Transfers (two allowed) deduct an additional 25¢ from the original fare and are valid for two hours on CTA "El" and bus routes.

Convenient **CTA Visitor Passes** allow unlimited travel for a set number of days; the one-day pass ($5) is good value, as are two-day ($9), three-day ($12), five-day ($18) and seven-day ($20) passes, which are valid for consecutive days of travel. You can buy passes at the airport on arrival, at any of the visitor information centers, as well as in Union Station and many of the currency exchange offices downtown.

The CTA also runs Chicago's **buses**, which accept Transit Cards, as well as coins and bills in exact change. Fares are the same as the El ($1.75), and for an extra 25¢ you can transfer between buses and trains within a two-hour window. Most bus lines operate daily; during rush hour and peak times, buses run every five minutes, every 8–12 minutes during off-peak hours. Service is sporadic between midnight and 4am, but the major bus lines run all night.

Chicago Transit Authority

For route information and timetables, as well as disabled access, for CTA trains and buses call ⓣ 12/836-7000 or log on to ⓦ www.transitchicago.com

For passes and other information call ⓣ 1 888/968-7282 or visit the above website.

Useful bus routes

#6 Jeffrey Express To get from downtown to Hyde Park.

#22 Clark Runs along Dearborn and Clark streets, and is one of the best buses for getting to Lincoln Park and the North Side.

#29 State Runs between the Loop and Navy Pier, on State St, Illinois St, and Grand Ave.

#36 Broadway Similar to the #22, it runs along Clark between the Loop and Lakeview, then jumps to Broadway for its long slog north.

#72 North A good shuttle along North Ave, between the lake and Bucktown and Wicker Park.

#73 Armitage Runs parallel to the #72, but four blocks north on Armitage Ave.

#146 Marine-Michigan Runs between Museum Campus, the Loop (via State St) and to Andersonvile (via Lake Shore Drive).

#151 Sheridan This Loop-Lincoln Park-Lakeview route runs along Michigan Ave, Stockton Ave (good for the Lincoln Park Zoo), and Sheridan Rd.

Metra

The commuter rail network run by **Metra** (information line: ⓣ312/322-6777 weekdays,

312/836-4949 evenings and weekends, Ⓦwww.metrarail.com) serves Chicago's suburbs, stopping at four main stations in the city: Union Station, Ogilvie Transportation Center, LaSalle Street Station (LaSalle Street and Congress Parkway), and Randolph Street Station (where Randolph Street meets the northern tip of Grant Park). You're not likely to need Metra unless you want to visit Hyde Park (and the Museum of Science and Industry) or McCormick Place. (See individual chapters for details on getting to these locations.)

Fares start at $1.85 and go up to $6.95, depending on the distance traveled. A weekend pass offering unlimited travel on Metra costs $5. Tickets can be bought from agents or vending machines at stations (or on the train if there's no ticket seller on duty at the station).

Taxis

Taxis are plentiful and are worth using if you're in a hurry or happen to be in areas that aren't well served by public transportation, especially late at night. If you know you'll be spending time in the more outlying areas like the South Side, it's a good idea to book a return cab in advance (see p.271 for a list of cab companies).

Fares are $2.25 to start the meter, $1.80 for each mile thereafter and $1 charge for a second passenger, $0.50 for each additional passenger. Most fares between the Loop and locations within a few miles of there (River North, N Michigan Avenue, the Gold Coast and Old Town, Museum Campus, Little Italy, and Greektown) will run from $6 to $11. For points farther out (ie Andersonville and Hyde Park), expect to pay at least $15–20. Bear in mind that the tip should be 15 to 20 percent of the fare.

Taxis can be hailed on the streets or use the taxi stands outside train and bus stations, and hotels. Finally, when you arrive at your destination, ask the driver for a receipt – if ever you leave something in the taxi, you'll have a way to track it down.

For a list of taxi companies, see "Directory," p.271.

Driving

There's not much reason to rent a car in Chicago, unless you want to explore outposts like Oak Park or admire the scenic route along Lake Shore Drive; public transportation will get you to most places fairly efficiently, while congestion and a dearth of parking spaces, especially in the Loop and the surrounding areas, can make for a harrowing experience.

If you absolutely need a car (see p.23 for rental agencies), be prepared to pay hefty overnight **parking charges** ($24+) to park your car at a garage or lot, or else pay close attention to street parking signs to avoid being ticketed, which will cost you a minimum of $50 for even a minor parking offense.

During peak hours, on-street parking can be impossible, while streets in the residential areas either have two-hour ($2) parking meters or require resident permits. In most cases, you're better off putting your car in a parking lot or garage (from $11/hr to $17 for four hours to $20+/day). In the Loop, try the cheap underground garages on the north end of Grant Park (enter through Columbus Drive or Michigan Avenue).

If your car is towed, expect to pay at least $150 to liberate it from the City of Chicago Auto Pound Headquarters (Ⓣ312/744-4444).

Bikes

Chicago is a bike-friendly city, with miles of bike lanes, plenty of bike racks, and some twenty El stations where riders can store their bikes indoors and hop on the train. Bikes are permitted on El trains, except during peak hours on weekdays (7–9am and 4–6pm). The popular, lakefront path provides twenty-plus miles of uninterrupted cycling through well-tended parkland, with many sightseeing attractions, shopping districts, and other diversions close by. For more information on biking in Chicago, visit Chicagoland Bicycle Federation's website at Ⓦwww.biketraffic.org.

Cyclist's protocol is taken very seriously in Chicago. When using the cycle lanes, especially along the lakefront, which can become very congested in the evenings and during the weekends in summer, always keep to the right. If you need to pass a pedestrian, rollerblader or cyclist, warn them by stating clearly "on your left" and overtaking accordingly.

Of the main **bike rental outfits**, Bike and Roll Chicago has locations at 600 N Lake Shore Drive (ⓣ773/327-2706) and Millennium Park, 239 E Randolph (ⓣ1-888/BIKE-WAY, ⓦwww.bikerental.com), where you can rent bikes for $10 per hour or $40 per day. Special offer discounts for a minimum four-day rental period start from $9.99 per day. The North Lakeshore one is open from May 1 to September 30, the Millennium Park store is open year-round.

City tours

Most tours of Chicago explore either architecture or the city's neighborhoods, though of course any number of smaller, specialized tours do exist, from ethnic food samplings and exploring financial exchanges to haunted house tours.

River tours and lakefront cruises are often the best way to get a feel for the city's size. There are a handful of companies that operate them, any of which will be sufficient, but the Architecture Foundation (see p.49) puts on the most detailed and comprehensive tours. For more leisurely sightseeing at slightly more expense, you might try the cruise lines that offer lunch and dinner trips up and down the lake, the latter often around sunset.

Bicycle tours

Bike and Roll Tours ⓣ773/327-2706 (North Avenue Beach) or ⓣ1-888/Bike-Way (Millennium Park), ⓦwww.bikeandroll.com. Three-to four-hour guided tours covering the lakefront, Lincoln Park, Grant Park, Chinatown, and Hyde Park's Osaka Garden, $30. Evening bike and boat tours also available, $45. Free self-guided tour maps also provided.

Bike Chicago Rentals and Tours ⓣ312/595-9600 (Navy Pier), ⓦwww.bikechicago.com. Tours of the lakefront and neighborhoods (June–Aug Mon–Fri).

Bus and trolley tours

American Sightseeing Tours ⓣ312/251-3100 or 1-800/621-4153, ⓦwww.americansightseeing.org/chicago. Two-to five-hour tours ($17–60) ranging from bus tours of all the major neighborhoods – the Grand Tour takes in most of the city – to river cruise and walking architectural tours to a "Roaring Twenties" dinner tour and bus tours to Oak Park; reservations required.

Chicago Motor Coach Company ⓣ312/666-1000, ⓦwww.chicagocharterexpress.com. Narrated double-decker bus tours (1hr+; $13) that cover the Historic Water Tower, Navy Pier, and the Sears Tower, among other stops. Purchase tickets on the bus, or at the Sears Tower.

Chicago Trolley Company Tours ⓣ312/663-0260, ⓦwww.chicagotrolley.com. One hour and forty-five minute hop-on hop-off tours (all-day pass $25, two-day pass $35) on motorized board-at-will trolleys (or double-decker buses), which make ten stops in the downtown area, including Sears Tower, Navy Pier, Museum Campus, and the Historic Water Tower.

Gray Line Tours ⓣ1-800/621-4153, ⓦwww.grayline.com. One of the better bus-tour companies offering a good variety of tours, from the four-hour citywide "Inside Chicago" tour ($30) to the seven-hour "Ship and Shore tour" ($66) taking in the entire city by bus, plus lunch and a cruise on Lake Michigan. Tours leave from the *Palmer House Hilton*, 17 E Monroe St.

Cruises and river trips

Chicago Architecture Foundation ⓣ312/922-3432, ⓦwww.cruisechicago.com or ⓦwww.architecture.org. Intelligent, remarkably extensive list of tours, many with an architectural slant. Highly recommended. See box on p.49 for further details.

Chicago from the Lake ⓣ312/527-2002, ⓦwww.cfl81.com. Ninety-minute, informative architectural river cruises and historical river/lake cruises operating from May through October, $27. Tours leave from River East Plaza, 465 E Illinois St. Between May and November, tours leave almost every hour.

Metro Ducks ⓣ312/642-3825 or 1-800/298-1506, ⓦwww.metroducks.com/chicago. Restored World War II amphibious landing vehicles first plunge into the Chicago River, then hit the city's roads for the usual sights. The ninety-minute tours ($20) leave from *Rock 'n' Roll McDonald's*, 600 N Clark St.

Odyssey Cruises ⓣ708/990-0800, ⓦwww.odysseycruises.com. Pricey brunch, lunch, dinner, and romantic midnight cruises ($43–101 per person) on a huge, super-sleek yacht, departing from 600 E Grand Ave at Navy Pier. Reservations are required.

Shoreline Sightseeing ⓣ312/222-9328, ⓦwww.shorelinesightseeing.com. Architecture cruises and thirty-minute sightseeing tours ($22) leaving from Shedd Aquarium, Buckingham Fountain, and Navy Pier.

Spirit of Chicago ⓣ1-866/211-3804, ⓦwww.spiritofchicago.com. Swanky harbor cruises, with bar and live music. Lunch and dinner cruises from $40 and $78; sunset cruises $28. Boats depart from 600 E Grand Ave at Navy Pier. Year-round.

Wendella Boats ⓣ312/337-1446, ⓦwww.wendellaboats.com. Well-run architecture and sightseeing cruises ($19), leaving from the pier near the Wrigley Building at 400 N Michigan Ave. Summer only.

Specialist tours and activities

Chicago Blues Tour ⓣ773/772-5506, ⓦwww.chicagobluestour.com. Twice-yearly tour ($30) of South Side blues clubs and the Blues Heaven Foundation, formerly Chess Records.

Chicago Ethnic Grocery Store Tours ⓣ773/465-8064, ⓦethnic-grocery-tours.com. Led by a guide with an encyclopedic knowledge of the city's ethnic food, these tours also offer the chance to sample food along the way ($60).

Chicago Neighborhood Tours ⓣ312/742-1190, ⓦwww.chicagocitytours.com. Four- to five-hour neighborhood ($25) and specialty tours ($50, including lunch) given year-round, though most are offered between May and November. Themes include "The Chicago Fire," "Literary Chicago," "Threads of Ireland," and "Hidden Murals."

Loop Tour Train ⓣ1-877/244-2246. Free forty-minute architecture and history tours co-sponsored by the Chicago Architecture Foundation, Chicago Office of Tourism, and the Chicago Transit Authority (May 4 to Sept 28). Departs from the Randolph/Wabash El station every Saturday at 11.00am, 11.40am, 12.25pm, and 1pm. Pick up tickets on the day of the tour at the Chicago Office of Tourism Visitor Information Center (see p.28).

Not Your Mama's Bus Tour c/o StreetWise, 1331 S Michigan Ave (a block south of Roosevelt Rd) ⓣ312/554-0060, ⓦwww.streetwise.org. Chicago as seen through the eyes of the underprivileged. Tours led by formerly homeless vendors of the *Streetwise* newspaper, who give personal reflections on life on the streets while you ride a bus through Cabrini Green and the West Side, covering roughly ten sights in over ninety minutes. Tours offered on Fridays at 6pm, sometimes Saturdays at 6pm (May–Nov; $20).

Untouchable Tours ⓣ773/881-1195, ⓦwww.gangstertour.com. Guides dressed as gangsters lead bus tours of Prohibition-era haunts and hideouts of Chicago gangsters in Chinatown, Pilsen, Little Italy, Greektown, and Lincoln Park ($20, children $15). Tours depart from the parking lot of *Rock 'n' Roll McDonald's*, at 600 N Clark St.

Walking tours

Chicago Architecture Foundation ⓣ312/922-3432, ⓦwww.cruisechicago.com or ⓦwww.architecture.org. Offers by far the largest, most extensive list of walking tours in Chicago, with well over fifty different routes and themes.

Chicago Tour Guides Institute ⓣ773/276-6683, ⓦwww.chicagoguide.net. Three-hour walking tours tailored for groups, offered in numerous languages (starting from $160 for three hours). You'll need to request transportation if you don't have your own, and tours must be paid for at least seven days in advance.

Opening hours and public holidays

We've noted specific opening and closing times for specific attractions throughout the Guide, but given that opening hours can change, it's always a good idea to call ahead.

Opening hours

Office hours are generally 9am–5pm. Stores open as early as 8am and can close as late as 11pm on weeknights; on weekends, stores may open an hour later and close an hour earlier, especially on Sundays. Most **museums** follow roughly the same hours, though a few have extended hours (8–10pm) one day during the week and one on the weekend. Public spaces – plazas, monuments, and such – are generally open 24 hours, but Chicago parks close around 11pm (or earlier, depending on the park) and reopen around 7am.

In the wake of the events of September 11, 2001, and subsequent security scares, some Chicago attractions – notably the Board of Trade no longer permit visitor access.

Public holidays

The following are public holidays on which banks, post offices, and many (although by no means all) shops and attractions will be closed:

Jan 1 **New Year's Day**
Third Mon in Jan **Martin Luther King, Jr.'s Birthday**
Third Mon in Feb **Presidents' Day**
Last Mon in May **Memorial Day**
July 4 **Independence Day**
First Mon in Sept **Labor Day**
Second Mon in Oct **Columbus Day**
Nov 11 **Veterans' Day**
Fourth Thurs in Nov **Thanksgiving**
Dec 25 **Christmas Day**

The media

Though by no means a news capital of the country, Chicago does have a nationally respected newspaper and television network, and is more or less the media center for most of the Midwest.

Newspapers and magazines

Chicago's **main newspaper**, the conservative *Chicago Tribune* (50¢; ⓦwww.chicagotribune.com), covers a mix of local, national, and international news in a tone that's less staid and, at times, breezier than that of its East Coast counterparts, the influential *New York Times* and *Washington Post*. With the death of famed Chicago writer Mike Royko and the controversial ousting of columnist Bob Greene from his post at the *Trib* (as the paper is known) in September 2002, the paper lost its nationally known writers; the ageing Pulitzer-winner Studs Terkel has resumed the title of the town's best chronicler – any account from him is sure to be among the city's best writing.

The city's other major newspaper, *The Sun-Times* (50¢; Ⓦwww.suntimes.com), tends to be more sensational in its coverage, focusing less on international news and more on local stories. The paper's lead film critic, Roger Ebert, is best known for his nationally aired TV show, *Siskel and Ebert*, on which he entertainingly sparred with *Tribune* film columnist Gene Siskel over the latest film releases for 23 years, until Siskel's death in 1999. Their signature thumbs up/thumbs down approach to movie viewing has survived relatively intact (though with a new co-host), as *Ebert and Roeper*, airing on WLS (Channel 7).

Besides the two major newspapers, there's the *Daily Herald* (Ⓦwww.dailyherald.com), Chicago's largest suburban daily paper – read mostly in the surrounding counties.

The **free weekly** *Chicago Reader* (Ⓦwww.chicagoreader.com) is indispensable for current arts and entertainment listings, and often has quirky editorials on a variety of topics. Other free papers have joined the scene but none comes close to cracking the *Reader*'s hold on the city. Chicago also has a few glossy monthlies, including the well-written and picture-heavy *Chicago* magazine ($4.99; Ⓦwww.chicagomag.com). You can find these in most downtown bookstores, as well as in cafés and bars.

Most downtown **newsstands and bookstores** sell a huge variety of national and international newspapers, the best of which is probably Borders, 830 N Michigan Ave, at N Pearson Street (Ⓣ312/573-0564).

TV and radio

Chicago seems to be in the middle of a television transformation: for a city that has been a fan of sports and local news, attention post- 9/11 has become much more focused on national issues such as terrorism and the global nuclear threat, bringing more sustained viewing interest in round-the-clock cable news than ever before, and pushing local news stations behind worldwide cable TV in popularity. You can still catch offerings from the four major networks (NBC, ABC, Fox, and CBS), as well as a respectable line-up of shows and news on the city's own two local channels – WGN (Ch 9) and WTTW (Ch 11) – plus the low-budget Cable CLTV (Chicagoland TV). Channel 11's homespun *Wild Chicago* show, airing every Sunday and Monday night, shouldn't be missed for its irreverent interviews and tours of Chicago's lesser-known areas.

Admittedly, local news programming is almost completely US-centric, and an unbroken run of success by the Chicago Cubs will air over, say, any major happenings in the British Parliament. For international news, you'd be better off sticking with the national cable channels (Fox News Channel, CNN, MSNBC).

Radio is a significant part of most Chicagoans' daily routines, given the amount of time they wind up spending in traffic. There are plenty of radio options up and down the dial for news and entertainment; see below for a list of stations.

Live talk shows

Although Chicago, unlike New York, is not somewhere you'd choose to seek out live talk shows, a few options do exist, if you want to be part of the studio audience. Oprah Winfrey, veritable queen of Chicago and national media personality, hosts **The Oprah Winfrey Show** from her West Side Harpo Studios, 1058 W Washington Ave. For more details, see p.132.

Known for his show's trashy brand of entertainment, **Jerry Springer** tapes his eponymous show here in Chicago at the NBC Tower, 454 N Columbus Drive, on the second floor (Ⓣ312/321-5365). Go if you must – it's sensational American TV at its worst.

In the same lurid vein, there's **The Jenny Jones Show**, also taped at the NBC Tower (Ⓣ312/836-9485). Shows tape twice a day on Tuesday, Thursday, and Friday (9.30am–1pm, 1.30–4pm).

Broadcast TV stations

Channel 2 (WBBM/CBS)
Channel 5 (WMAQ/NBC)
Channel 7 (WLS/ABC)
Channel 9 (WGN)
Channel 11 (WTTW/Network Chicago)
Channel 32 (WFLD/Fox)
Cable CLTV/Chicagoland

Radio stations

Local AM stations

WMAQ (670) Sports
WGN (720) Talk
WBBM (780) News
WLS (890) Talk and news
WMVP (1000) Sports

Local FM stations

WBEZ (91.5) Talk, music, and news (including National Public Radio programming)
WRT (93.1) Rock
WNUA (95.5) Jazz
WBBM (96.3) R&B
WLUP (97.9) Rock
WFMT (98.7) Classical
WUSN (99.5) Country
WKQX (101.1) Contemporary pop and rock
WKSC (103.5) Mainstream Top Forty
WJMK (104.3) Oldies

Crime and personal safety

For the most part, violent crime in Chicago is concentrated in a few areas, notably pockets of the South Side and West Side that see more homicides in a year than some US states. Tourists, however, have no real business venturing into these areas, and therefore shouldn't expect to encounter problems beyond what they would expect in any major city.

Overall, common sense should keep you out of trouble: stick to well-lit streets at night, and avoid parks, parking lots, and alleys. Always lock your car, keep an eye on the kids at all times, and know where you're going or at least give the impression that you do. Don't have expensive jewelry on view and don't carry nice cameras, bags, or any other items that might draw attention to you. Men should keep wallets in the front pocket, women should wear purses across the shoulder. When riding the subway at night (not advisable after midnight), have your wits about you and do not fall asleep – you'll be easy prey for any thief, or worse. Should you run into trouble and need emergency police assistance, find a phone and call ⓣ911 or hail a cab and ask the driver to take you to the nearest police station. (For non-emergencies, call ⓣ312/744-4000.)

If you're planning to explore Hyde Park, or others areas of the **South Side**, take special care: there are a few extremely dangerous sections sprinkled throughout – downtrodden communities where high-rise housing projects have become home base for gangs and drug trafficking. The same can be said of **Cabrini Green** just west of the Gold Coast, and larger stretches of the West Side, especially around the **United Center**. Never walk in these areas or drive through here at night.

Emergency numbers for lost cards and checks

American Express cards ⓣ1-800/528-4800
American Express checks ⓣ1-800/221-7282
Citicorp ⓣ1-800/645-6556
Diners Club ⓣ1-800/234-6377
MasterCard ⓣ1-800/826-2181
Thomas Cook/MasterCard ⓣ1-800/223-9920
Visa cards ⓣ1-800/847-2911
Visa checks ⓣ1-800/227-6811

Travelers with disabilities

Chicago is trying to be one of the better disabled-friendly cities in the US, but it still has a long way to go. Modernization issues plague many of Chicago's older buildings; however, ramps and other forms of access are being added to museums, sites, and sports facilities, and the city's public transportation system has facilities such as station elevators and buses equipped with lifts and ramps.

Inquire with the CTA (Ⓣ1-888/968-7282) to find out which stops are wheelchair accessible; maps showing these stations are online at Ⓦwww.transitchicago.com. For wheelchair-accessible taxis, call Ⓣ1-800/281-4466.

For general information on accessibility, contact the Mayor's Office for People with Disabilities (Ⓣ312/744-6673), the Department of Disabilities (Ⓣ312/744-2400) or the Department of Tourism (Ⓣ1-877/244-2246 or Ⓣ312/201-8847, TTY number for the hearing impaired is Ⓣ1-866/710-0294).

US and Canada

Access-Able Ⓣ303/232-2979, Ⓦwww.access-able.com. A one-stop shop for travelers with disabilities.

The Boulevard Ⓣ619/222-8735, Ⓦwww.blvd.com. Adaptive products, van rentals, accessible hotels worldwide, and many links.

Mobility International USA voice and TDD Ⓣ541/343-1284, Ⓦwww.miusa.org. Information and referral services, access guides, tours, and exchange programs. Annual membership ($35) includes quarterly newsletter.

Society for the Advancement of Travelers with Handicaps (SATH) Ⓣ212/447-7284, Ⓦwww.sath.org. Travel-disabled information available to members ($45, students $30).

Wheels Up! Ⓣ1-888/389-4335, Ⓦwww.wheelsup.com. Provides discounted airfare, tour, and cruise prices for disabled travelers; also publishes a free monthly newsletter.

UK and Ireland

Holiday Care UK Ⓣ0845/124 9971, Ⓦwww.holidaycare.org.uk. Resource for travel and holiday information for people with disabilities, focusing on accessible hotels and attractions.

Irish Wheelchair Association Ireland Ⓣ01/8186 400, Ⓦwww.iwa.ie. Information about traveling abroad with a wheelchair.

Tripscope UK The Courtyard, Evelyn Road, London W4 5JL Ⓣ020/8994 9294. National telephone information service offering free travel advice.

Australia and New Zealand

Australian Council for Rehabilitation of the Disabled Ⓣ02/6283 3200, Ⓦwww.acrod.org.au. ACROD provides lists of travel agencies and tour operators for people with disabilities.

Disabled Persons Assembly New Zealand Ⓣ04/801 9100, Ⓦwww.dpa.org.nz. Provides lists of travel agencies and tour operators for people with disabilities.

The City

The City

1

The Loop

Roughly encompassing the tongue of land south and east of the Chicago River and bordered by Grant Park, **The Loop**'s pre-eminence in commerce, culture, and city transport make it unmissable for all visitors, if not overwhelming to most locals. The north–south arteries of State, LaSalle, and Dearborn streets more or less define the Loop, while further east, flanked by the green expanses of Grant Park, the southern stretches of **Michigan Avenue** flaunt Chicago's cultural kudos with the world-class collections at the **Art Institute**, the classical **Fine Arts Building**, an historical artistic enclave, and **Orchestra Hall**, home to the much-vaunted Chicago Symphony Orchestra.

State Street is the Loop's commercial hub, filled with stores and thriving again after the city pumped substantial sums into a beautification project during the late 1990s: this is where you'll find the department-store goliaths of Marshall Field's, Carson Pirie Scott, and Sears. A walk along **Dearborn Street** reveals a fascinating visual architectural timeline. William le Baron Jenney's Manhattan Building, built in 1891, was the prototype for the Chicago School of Architecture (see "Architecture" color insert), while Mies van der Rohe's Federal Center Complex ushered in the age of modernism in the 1950s. The Bank One Center built by Spaniard Ricardo Boffil in 2003 is an iconoclastic statement that presents Chicago's embrace of experimentalism and grandiosity with a can-do confidence and lack of pretension. **LaSalle Street** is where the money's made – literally; it's the financial hub of the Midwest and home to the Board of Trade since Chicago's early days – it's here where you can really make, or lose, big money. To the west of the loop, where Wacker Drive skirts the river, the jaw-dropping **Sears Tower**, for many years the world's tallest building, dominates the Chicago skyline.

The Loop is also divided between the ground-dwellers and office workers. At street level, standing under the rattling train tracks or zigzagging through the hordes of people, it's easy to imagine Chicago in the nineteenth century, a

In the Loop

Though it's a widely held belief that the Loop was named after the elevated train lines encircling the district, the nickname actually preceded the arrival of elevated cars by fifteen years. In the 1860s, a cable-car line was set up to shuttle residents of the newly created suburbs on Chicago's South Side to and from downtown stores like Field, Palmer & Leiter (later Marshall Field's). The consensus is that **the Loop name** came from the circular turnaround where the cable car would reverse direction for the return journey.

bustling, no-nonsense place of factory hands and railroad workers. But looking out from the observatory deck of the Sears Tower, there's a sleek, silent grandeur to the city's skyline. The honking cars and rushing people are far away, and you'll be hurled ahead a hundred years into Chicago's future.

It should go without saying that the Loop is at its busiest and best during the **working week**, when restaurants and attractions are open, and when it's easiest to peek inside the many architecturally impressive buildings. The one strip that still buzzes in the evening is Randolph Street, the hub of Chicago's **Theatre District** and a good place to grab a coffee or snack outside office hours; while on weekends, if you wander away from the revitalized State Street strip, the Loop can be majestically deserted.

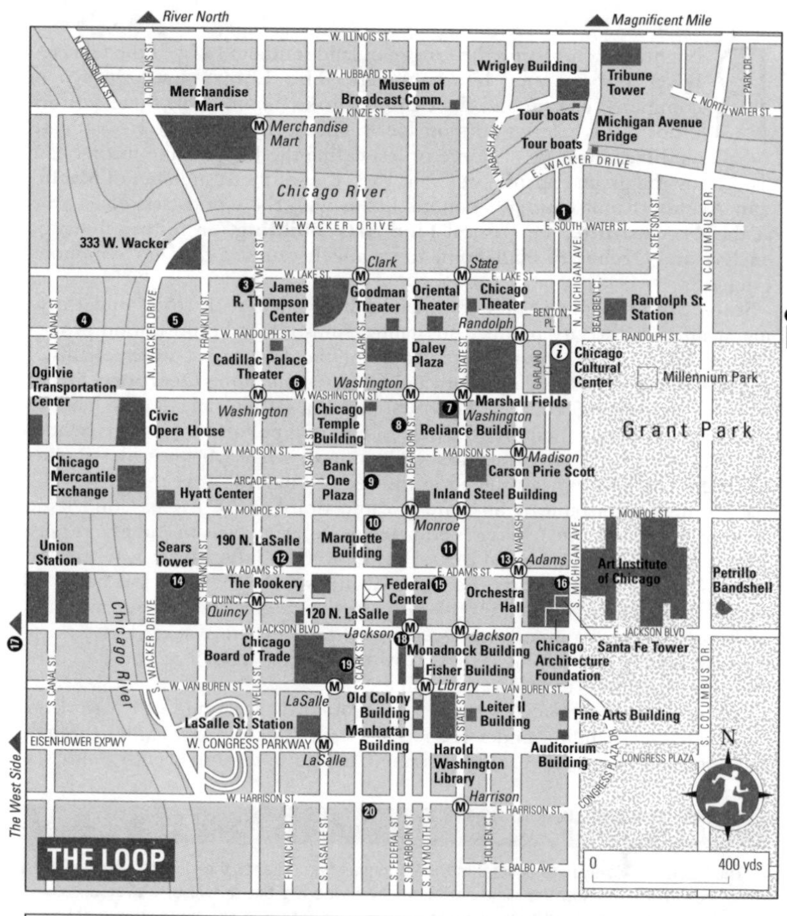

EATING						DRINKING			
Aria	2	Lou Mitchell's	17	Nine	4	Atwood Café	7	Cardozo's Pub	6
Berghoff	15	Miller's Pub	13	Orange	20	The Big Downtown (Palmer House Hilton's)	11	Cavanaugh's	18
Corner Bakery	1	Mrs. Levy's Delicatessen	14	Russian Tea Time	16			Monk's Pub	3
Everest	19	Nick's Fishmarket	9	Trattoria No. 10	8			Whiskey Blue	12
Giordano's	5			Vivere	10				

Some history

Chicago's oldest official settlement, **Fort Dearborn**, the major western military garrison, stood in the area now defined as the Loop from 1803 until 1812 when it was destroyed in the wake of an Indian uprising. A second fort was built in 1816 and was garrisoned intermittently according to the state of affairs with the Indians. In 1857, a fire destroyed virtually all that remained of the fort.

The city owes its current spectacular downtown to a mix of luck, both bad (the disastrous great fire of 1871) and good (the arrival of rule-breaking, visionary architects in its wake). With the rabble of wooden buildings wiped away by the blaze, men like **Louis Sullivan** (see "Architecture" color insert) were able to stretch their considerable design skills and, in the process, usher in the modern architectural age. Chicago was the cradle of the skyscraper – the first was built here in 1885 – and the city's enthusiastic welcome of new and often unusual buildings has helped it amass one of the world's best collections of modern architecture, from the prototype skyscrapers of the 1880s and 1890s – the Marquette Building built in 1885 by Holabird and Roche, and the Reliance Building, designed by Daniel Burnham and completed in 1895 – to more recent achievements like the breathtaking Sears Tower.

In recent years, downtown Chicago has been transformed into a paradigm of urban Renaissance. Since 1989, **Mayor Richard M. Daley** has spent over five billion dollars cleaning up the river and the alleys, transforming streets and sidewalks into attractively landscaped boulevards ablaze with flowering planter boxes, turning concrete plazas into public art spaces, replacing lampposts with classic European retro models, and erecting whimsical wrought-iron fencing. Daley's vision is to create a vibrant 24-hour downtown in the style of Manhattan and there are all the signs that his plans are coming to fruition. Office to condo conversions have become routine as more than one hundred thousand new tenants are expected to move downtown over the next twenty years. The downtown population has increased largely due to "empty nesters" returning

Tours of the Loop

A highly recommended and quick way to see the Loop is the exceptional ninety-minute **architectural river cruise** run by the Chicago Architecture Foundation (CAF), leaving daily at frequent intervals from the *Chicago's First Lady* dock located at Michigan Ave and Lower Wacker Drive (April 1–June 9 Mon–Thurs 3 trips, Fri, Sat & Sun 5 trips; June 10–Oct 2 Mon–Thurs 6 trips, Fri 7 trips, Sat 8 trips, Sun 9 trips; Oct 3–Oct 30 Mon–Thurs 5 trips, Fri, Sat & Sun 6 trips; Nov 4–Nov 20 Fri, Sat & Sun 3 trips; $25 Fri, Sat, Sun & holidays, $23 Mon–Thurs; ⓣ847/358-1330, ⓦwww.architecture.org or www.cruisechicago.com). The knowledgeable docents explain the history, significance, and architecture of all the riverfront buildings, including the Sears Tower, 333 W Wacker Drive, the Merchandise Mart, and the Wrigley Building. Reservations are always advised.

The CAF also runs excellent **walking tours** of the Loop: the "Historic Skyscrapers Tour" and the "Modern Skyscrapers Tour" ($12 each tour, $20 for both, discounts are available for seniors and students; 2hr). Although CAF has timed the tours so that you can do both in a single day, with the intensive walking you'll have to do, you're better off taking them over two days. An extensive program of highly engaging special-interest tours ranging from Frank Lloyd Wright tours of Oak Park to tours around buildings featuring Tiffany-designed interiors, are available. Leave from CFA's ArchiCenter, at 224 S Michigan Ave (ⓣ312/922-3432, ⓦwww.architecture.org). The website provides full schedule and prices. For more on tours of the Loop and the city beyond, see pp.38–39.

from the suburbs to enjoy the delights of a diverse, safe, and cultured metropolis, and the influx of talented and creative professional graduates who have flocked to the city on unprecedented levels since the mid-1990s.

Along Michigan Avenue

The area along Michigan Avenue immediately south of the river was, around a century ago, known as the city's prime entertainment district, and many of that era's grand structures preserve a sense of its unabashed artistic aspirations. The Neoclassical **Art Institute** (accorded its own chapter; see pp.66–67) is unmissable, presenting a monumental collection of nineteenth-century European art and an iconic body of twentieth-century American art. Musical inspiration comes in the form of the classical structure of **Orchestra Hall**, home to the revered Chicago Symphony Orchestra, and the Chicago School **Auditorium Building** built by Adler and Sullivan in 1889, which exudes turn-of-the-century grandeur, with ornate reliefs lavishly encrusted with gold leaf. The **Santa Fe building**, designed by Daniel Burnham in 1904, with a stunning atrium glistening with white marble and terracotta, is home to the **Chicago Architecture Foundation** (see box, p.49), whose excellent themed tours of the city are without peer.

The Chicago Cultural Center

Among the finest of Michigan Avenue's buildings is the **Chicago Cultural Center**, 78 E Washington Blvd, at Michigan Avenue, two blocks north of the Art Institute (Mon–Thurs 10am–7pm, Fri 10am–6pm, Sat 10am–5pm, Sun 11am–5pm; free; Orange, Purple, Brown, or Green Line to Randolph; ⊕312/744-6630 or 312/346-3278; for a weekly event schedule ⊛www.chicagoculturalcenter.org). An 1897 Beaux/Arts–style palace intended as the original Chicago Public Library, it's worth a visit alone to marvel at the opulence of the interior spaces. Based on classical Greek and Italian Renaissance models and exuding stately grandeur, the Washington Street lobby drips with Carrara marble and glimmers with mosaics of rare Favrile glass. In the Preston Bradley Hall on the fourth floor you'll see intricate mosaic scrolls and rosettes spanning the arches under a stunning, 38-foot **Tiffany dome** – the world's largest and estimated to be worth some $35 million.

In addition to being home to the **Chicago Office of Tourism** (see p.28), there are various galleries, touring exhibits, screenings, free lunchtime concerts, and a café. To explore the Cultural Center, either walk around yourself or take one of the **free tours**, which meet in the Randolph Street lobby and last an hour (Wed, Fri & Sat 1.15pm). Pick up a self-guided tour brochure at any of the first-floor welcome desks.

There are six art galleries: **Exhibit Hall** and **Sidney Gates Gallery** on the fourth floor, **Renaissance Court** and **Michigan Avenue Galleries** on the first floor, and **Chicago Rooms** on the second floor. The **Landmark Chicago Gallery** along the center's western corridor features black-and-white photographs of the city's landmarks which evocatively trace the development of Chicago's architectural persona, from the Carson Pirie Scott building (the first steel-framed department store; see p.54) to the Union Stockyard Gate and beyond.

Formerly located in the Chicago Cultural Center on Michigan Avenue, the sleek new **Museum of Broadcast Communications**, 400 N State St at W Kinzie (Ⓣ312/245-8200, Ⓦwww.museum.tv), is scheduled to open in July 2006. The museum's extensive archives, including grainy newsreels, old adverts, sepia-tinged photos, and programming artifacts provide a fascinating retrospective of radio and television history, organized into nine interactive genre-based exhibits: comedy, drama, music, news, talk, sports, game shows, children's shows,

△ The Sears Tower

and commercials. The MBC Television Center allows a peak at the on-air process, while the nostalgic Radio Hall of Fame presents the early days of radio when it was *the* broadcast medium. Also of interest, exhibits reveal the stories behind the innovators who created TV and radio broadcasting, and the media moguls who transformed the phenomenon into a global industry.

Orchestra Hall and Santa Fe Center

Heading south along Michigan Avenue, opposite the Art Institute, the 2600-seat **Orchestra Hall**, also known as Symphony Center, 220 S Michigan Ave, is a magnificent space that you can **tour** for free (for details call ⓣ312/294-3333) – or of course by purchasing a ticket to see the **Chicago Symphony Orchestra** (see p.230). Admire the early twentieth-century Burnham design, quite classical in nature, with a Georgian revival-style, symmetrical brick-and-stone facade in deep pink hues, bearing the names of the great composers – Beethoven, Bach, Mozart, Schubert, and Wagner – and inside a soaring Beaux/Arts–style auditorium space.

Right nearby, and easily recognized by its huge rooftop sign, the **Sante Fe Center**, 224 S Michigan Ave, houses the excellent **Chicago Architecture Foundation**, or CAF (Mon–Fri 9am–6pm, Sat 10am–6pm, Sun 10am–5pm; ⓣ312/922-3432, ⓦwww.architecture.org). This is the site where Burnham hatched his groundbreaking plan for the city in 1909. The center is named after the Santa Fe Railroad – the railway exchange stood here until construction began in 1903. Inside, a grand white-marble staircase descends into the elegant, sky-lit atrium where CAF has its office and tour center. The knowledgeable and enthusiastic staff can help you pick the right tour and direct you to the center's architecture exhibits; be sure to check out the impressive scale model of downtown Chicago. Skidmore, Owings and Merrill, Chicago's largest architecture firm, responsible for the John Hancock Center (1969) and Sears Tower (1974), also have their headquarters here.

One block south, at 17 W Adams St, is the historically significant **Berghoff Restaurant**. Built in 1872, it's one of only two buildings with cast-iron fronts in Chicago – cast iron was banned after the fire due to its flammability. It remains a Chicago institution for its old-world atmosphere and hearty German -American food (see p.183 for review).

The Fine Arts Building

Continuing south along Michigan Avenue, you'll come across the brownish-gray **Fine Arts Building**, at no. 410, a Neo-Romanesque structure built in 1885 by Solon S. Beman as a showroom for the Studebaker Company's carriages and wagons. A renovation in 1898 added several floors to the building and converted it into studio space, which fostered an artist's colony of sorts that included the likes of Frank Lloyd Wright (who had a drafting studio here) and Frank L. Baum (author of *The Wizard of Oz*). Little of the interior has changed since then – the spacious halls and open stairwells are still there, as are the original Art Nouveau murals that grace the walls on the tenth floor.

The Fine Arts Building hosts a collection of galleries, including, on the fourth floor, the FAB gallery that showcases mainly contemporary local artists (Wed–Sat noon–6pm; ⓣ312/913-0537, ⓦwww.fabgallery.com). Look out for the works of Roger Bole whose impressionistic, often bleak paintings of Chicago, ranging from "L" stops to anonymous rooftops, present the poetry and human drama of the city's everyday life. Take a ride up in the hand-operated vintage elevator for a whiff of Old Chicago.

The Auditorium Building

The stately Chicago School **Auditorium Building**, 430 S Michigan Ave, is best known for its 4000-seat **Auditorium Theatre**, whose entrance is at 50 E Congress Parkway (☎312/922-2110, Ⓦwww.auditoriumtheatre.org). The near-perfect acoustics and four massive, flamboyantly trimmed arches moved Modernist Frank Lloyd Wright to call it the "greatest room for music and opera in the world." The Auditorium Building itself was built by Sullivan and Adler in 1889 and included a hotel and office, but after less than a decade, the building had fallen into disrepair; at its lowest point it served as a recreation center for soldiers, who turned the stage into a makeshift bowling alley. Roosevelt University eventually bought the building in 1946, but it wasn't until the 1960s that the structure was fully restored and re-opened. In 1989, the Auditorium Building celebrated its one-hundredth birthday with the opening of *Les Misérables*. A comprehensive restoration project was initiated in 2001 with extensive paint analysis to bring back the original color patterns, stenciling detail, and a lovely mural that once graced the interior. In 2002, the theater's 113-year-old stage was removed and reconstructed in time to play host to the Bolshoi Ballet, which performed to sell-out crowds and received critical eulogy. Sullivan fans note: if you can't make a concert, then come for a tour (Mon–Fri, call for times; $5; ☎312/431-2389).

Along State Street

Immortalized by Frank Sinatra as "That Great Street" in his musical tribute to the city, the iconic **State Street**, one of the major north to south thoroughfares, remains one of the city's prime retail and entertainment corridors (though when it comes to glamour and glory, however, the Magnificent Mile, see p.75, has certainly usurped its status). Over the years State Street's fortunes have ebbed and flowed, from its apotheosis as a major shopping enclave at the turn of the twentieth century to a neo-urban wasteland in 1979 when Mayor Jane Byrne attempted to transform the street into a pedestrian mall. In 1996, Major Daley set about breathing life back into State Street, traffic flowed through once again, department stores that had relocated owing to flagging sales returned, sidewalks were widened, and planter boxes and vintage streetlamps brought light, color, and a new energy.

Throughout its history, State Street has set precedents on a grand scale. "Give the lady what she wants" was the concept for the original department store, **Marshall Field's**, while the **Carson Pirie Scott** building broke the classical norm with designer Louis Sullivan's maxim that "form follows function." Amid the bustle, the serene **Reliance Building**, the prototype skyscraper, was renovated in the late 1990s to become the suitably elegant *Hotel Burnham*.

The Leiter Building II

At Congress and S State Street, two blocks west of Grant Park, you'll come upon the blocky-looking **Leiter Building II** at no. 401, which was built in 1891 by William Le Baron Jenney (see box, p.279). The structure's skeletal exterior frame and spacious interior stories – with sixteen-foot ceilings and uncluttered by beams or fixed walls – were designed to maximize retail space. This seemingly small advancement was ideal for the Chicago department store Sears, Roebuck and Co, which occupied the building for many decades. Incidentally, the more primitive Leiter Building I, built in 1979, at the corner of Monroe and Wells, was demolished in 1972.

1 The Harold Washington Library

Anchoring the lower Loop at 400 S State St, is the nine-story, rust-colored **Harold Washington Library**, the city's main branch (Mon–Thurs 9am–7pm, Fri & Sat 9am–5pm, Sun 1–5pm; ⓣ773/542-7279, ⓦwww.chipublib.org). Its enormous granite slabs, five-story arched windows, and brilliant green hat of iron helped put it in *The Guinness Book of World Records* as the largest public library building in the world. Indeed, all sorts of numbers could be tossed out to impress: over two million volumes, 71 miles of books, and the largest **blues archive** in the country which features collections of audio, video, demo, and promotional recordings, not available commercially, from such blues legends as Willie Dixon, John Lee Hooker, and Buddy Guy. Casual visitors, however, will be more drawn to the hundreds of paintings on display throughout as well as readings, book-signings, and educational events.

Designed in Neoclassical style, the library was actually built in 1991 in honor of the city's first African-American mayor, Harold Washington (see p.278). It was designed by Thomas H. Beeby, whose vision won the widely publicized competition, launched in 1988.

On the north wall of the main lobby, look for the blue Jacob Lawrence **mosaic mural** depicting key moments from Washington's life. If you look down through the circular opening into the lower lobby, you'll see *DuSable's Journey*, created by Houston Conwill, a map that traces the routes of **Jean-Baptiste Point du Sable** – Chicago's first settler – through the waters he navigated between his homeland of Haiti and Chicago; the quotations around the map's edges are taken from Washington's inaugural speeches.

Carson Pirie Scott

At first sight, the **Carson Pirie Scott department store**, four blocks north of the Harold Washington Library, at 1 S State St, is a somewhat less glamorous sibling to Marshall Field's (see p.55). Inside, it's your average huge and soulless department store dedicated to conspicuous consumption; however, historically speaking, the building itself is an architectural landmark, an embodiment of visionary architect Louis Sullivan's revolutionary melding of function and form – the animated cast-iron geometric and naturalistic imagery on the first two stories is trademark Sullivan. Look out for his initials traced into the organic design above the main entrance. A twelve-story annex was completed in 1903 by Burnham and Root, based on Sullivan's original concepts and design. The entrance at the corner of Madison and State streets is the best vantage point for admiring the intricate ironwork.

The Reliance Building

Lauded as the forerunner of the glass-and-steel skyscrapers that sprung up everywhere in the middle of the twentieth century, the thin, cream-colored **Reliance Building**, 32 N State St, lies one block north from Carson Pirie Scott, on the corner of W Washington Street. It was designed by Daniel J Burnham in 1891 and construction was completed in 1895 by Charles B. Atwood. Preceding modern glass-and-steel towers by some sixty years, the pioneer of the Chicago School of Architecture appears to almost defy gravity; the entirely interior steel-frame construction supports wide flat and bay windows, flanked by moveable sash windows – a style subsequently referred to as "the Chicago window." By the 1960s, this historic treasure had fallen from glory and the City of Chicago began a thirty-million-dollar restoration. Exuding old-world grandeur, the European-style *Hotel Burnham* opened in 1999; step inside for a look at the lobby and decorative trimmings, or sip a cocktail in the charming *Atwood Café* (p. 206). For a review of the rooms, see p.168.

Marshall Field's

The flagship, enormous department store, **Marshall Field's and Co**, at 111 State St (Mon 9am–6pm, Tues–Sat 9am–8pm & Sun 11am–6pm; ⓣ312/781-1000, ⓦwww.marshallfields.com), is a Chicago institution, known for its lavish window dressings around the winter holidays. It's housed in a nine-story Neoclassical building that was built in stages between 1892 and 1914 by Daniel Burnham (see boxes, p.278 & p.281). While it may be unassuming compared to other Loop architectural highlights, there is no shortage of superlatives to describe the paradigm of the global department-store phenomenon. Taking up an entire city block, it's hard to miss, adorned by two huge, bronze (now green) clocks, one of which has been keeping time for over a century. The clock at the corner of State and Washington streets cemented its status as a Chicago symbol when a painting of it by Norman Rockwell landed on the cover of the *Saturday Evening Post* in 1945 (in which a repairman sets the time on the big clock using his pocket watch). Flanking the State Street entrance are two granite pillars, constructed in 1902, and only surpassed in height by the pillars on the Temple of Karnak in Egypt.

Even if you're not planning to shop, be sure to check out the glistening **Tiffany ceiling** inside the north atrium, the first ever built of Favrile iridescent glass (1.6 million pieces to be precise). Completed in 1907, the project took more than eighteen months to execute. Covering six thousand square feet, the ceiling is considered the largest Tiffany mosaic in existence.

At the time of writing Marshall Field's became a division of Federated department stores and despite controversy, is expected to switch over to the Macy's nameplate by fall 2006.

The Theatre District

Since the relocation of the Goodman Theater to Dearborn and Randolph in 2000, the city has been trying to re-create the **theater culture** that thrived here a century ago, refurbishing many of its early twentieth-century theaters and movie houses which, from the 1920s until the 1940s, played host to some of the country's legendary thespians. Following the Theatre District's 1940s apogee, fortunes waned and actors, writers, and producers began to garner their Chicago stage experience as a launch pad to move onwards and upwards, to Broadway.

Today, all initial signs of rejuvenation suggest success; the area immediately around the theaters is noticeably glitzy, with new hotels and restaurants springing up, each seemingly more expensive and crowded than the last. Once again, Chicago's unique confection of jewel-box and garage theaters, performing everything from all-star box-office Broadway-run hits to more avant-garde original productions, is gaining international recognition among actors, audiences, and critics for its superlative productions.

A quick look around should begin at the **Oriental Theatre/Ford Center for the Performing Arts**, 24 W Randolph St (☎312/977-1700), built on the site once occupied by the Iroquois Theater, where in 1903 a deadly fire killed six hundred people. After the fire, the Oriental Theatre produced plays for forty-odd years before closing down; fortunately, in 1996 an extensive renovation project breathed new life into the theater's famously bizarre interior – a riot of sculptured sea horses, goddesses, and elephants, all designed to resemble, however obliquely, an Asian temple.

The iconic vertical "C-H-I-C-A-G-O" sign and marquee of the **Chicago Theatre** at 175 N State St, is all but impossible to miss, as is the facade, styled after the Arc de Triomphe. The theater is better known, however, for its opulent interior – exquisite murals, crystal chandeliers, and bronze light fixtures, all modeled after Versailles. Forty-five-minute **tours** (year-round Tues noon & third Sat of each month 11am & noon; May 1–Sept 30 noon; $5; ☎312/462-6363), led by docents, cover all the highlights, including the theater's magnificent Wurlitzer pipe-organ – demonstrations are often given on the Saturday tours – as well as the stage and backstage dressing rooms.

One block west, at 170 N Dearborn St, the facade of the **Goodman Theatre** (☎312/443-3800, www.goodman-theatre.org), lit up in rainbow-colored lights, may bring to mind the flashiness of New York's Times Square. The state-of-the-art complex, which opened in 2000, puts on performances in its two auditoriums and outdoor amphitheater.

Two blocks west of the Goodman, the **Cadillac Palace**, 151 W Randolph St, whose staid and unbecoming exterior hides a gemlike interior, in look and feel like that of a French palace, right down to the huge mirrors, crystal chandeliers, and gold fixtures.

To see some of the grand interiors without seeing a show, try one of the Chicago Architecture Foundation's excellent ninety-minute **Theatre District tours** which take place several times a year only ($10, students and seniors $5; ☎312/922-3432); for details on shows or **ticket information**, see "Performing arts and film," p.266.

Along Dearborn Street

A striking array of structures political, theatrical, and historical punctuates the north to south artery of **Dearborn Street**. The showpiece of **Daley Plaza** and one of Chicagoans' most beloved landmarks, is the bizarre and untitled **Picasso sculpture**. The panoply of great and gifted innovators who built Chicago are well represented along Dearborn. A shrine to Modernism, Mies van der Rohe's starkly beautiful **Federal Complex** is a masterpiece of spatial composition. From the **Bank One Plaza**, whimsical mural by Chagall is eye-catchings and has the sublime **Marquette Building** with its prototype "Chicago style" windows and inside its glimmering bronze lobby an exquisite Tiffany mosaic.

Daley Plaza and around

At the corner of Dearborn and Washington, you'll come upon the concrete expanses of **Richard J. Daley Plaza**, crisscrossed by waves of office workers, whose focal point is the untitled cubist **Picasso sculpture**, on which – depending your orientation – will look like a giant angry bird, a woman's face, or, as one

△ The El train in the Loop

youngster told Chicago writer Studs Terkel, a giant red hot-dog. The fifty-foot creation was unveiled in 1967 and has transcended initial waves of derision to become one of the city's most beloved symbols. Picasso was 82 and living on the French Riviera when he completed the design model, which was later to be built by US Steel in Gary, Indiana. The artist never made it to Chicago to view the completed work. Picasso returned the $100,000 commission fee sent by Mayor Richard J. Daley – the father of current mayor Richard M. Daley, after whom the plaza was named – claiming it was a "gift for the people of Chicago." At various times during the year – check with the tourist office for a complete schedule – the space hosts **performances**, and around the winter holidays, an enormous twinkling Christmas tree.

Crash and Byrne

Daley Plaza provided the setting for the climactic scene of the quintessential Chicago movie, **The Blues Brothers** (1979). In a classic movie moment, misfit brothers Elwood and Jake, played by Chicago natives and Second City (see p.93) legends, Dan Aykroyd and John Belushi, drive their Bluesmobile across the plaza, smashing into the glass lobby of Daley Center. Belushi and Aykroyd had approached newly elected **Mayor Jane Byrne** to request the closure of the Daley Plaza for three days so they could shoot the scene. Having pledged during her campaign to quash the "Machine" of former mayor Richard M. Daley ("The Boss") (see p.286), Byrne saw the opportunity as highly symbolic. "I said, 'Be my guest,'" Byrne recalls. "I was fighting the Machine. I felt like 'Knock it all down.'"

Across Washington Street stands the **Chicago Temple Building**, home to First United Methodist Church of Chicago, among other tenants. Besides a French Gothic sanctuary on the ground floor, the building's main highlight is the **Chapel in the Sky**, located in the eight-story spire, which, from afar, looks like an elf's hat plopped onto a staid office-tower. The chapel, which tops out at 568 feet above street level, is the world's tallest church; the only way to see inside it, however, is on one of the **free tours** leaving from the church's office on the second floor (Mon–Fri 2pm, Sun after services, usually 9.30am and noon; ⓣ312/236-4548).

Beneath the Chicago Temple Building, you'll spot yet another piece of public art, this one a sculpture by Picasso's contemporary, **Joan Miró**. This 39-foot *Chicago* statue, made of concrete, steel, and ceramic tiles to represent a "great Earth mother," will perhaps bring to mind other ideas; what passes for a head looks more like a pitchfork.

From Bank One Plaza to the Marquette Building

Walk south on Dearborn Street until you reach **Bank One Plaza** (on your right), between Monroe and Madison, where, at the north end, the sixty-story **Bank One Building**, designed by C.F. Murphy and Associates, curves gracefully skyward with a stunning inward sweep that recedes 105 feet from its two -hundred-foot-wide base. Though it's one of the most photographed edifices in the city, most people come here to see Chagall's *Four Seasons* mosaic, a three thousand-square-foot wall of glass-and-stone tiles in two hundred and fifty different shades, all painstakingly applied to give shape to whimsical dancers, musicians, animals, and angels floating above cityscapes, as if carried by the wind.

Nearby, the rounded glass building at **55 W Monroe**, erected between 1977 and 1980, was also the work of C.F. Murphy and Associates, including young architect Helmut Jahn (see box, p.279), who drew on everything from the Carson Pirie Scott Building, post-war Modernism, and the exterior-frame innovations of the Inland Steel Building for inspiration. The result was a pastiche of a skyscraper – the first building to hide its structure with reflective glass; its surface, all aluminum and glass, curves sleekly round the corner of Dearborn and Monroe streets. There's not much to look at inside, except a handy branch of American Express (see "Currency exchange," p.270).

Some of the progress in office building can be charted as you continue on down the block. The **Inland Steel Building**, standing diagonally opposite at 30 W Monroe St, was completed in 1957. Breaking new ground on an international scale, it was the first skyscraper built on pilings (steel columns), and the first to use external steel beams for structural support. Like the Leiter Building II (see p.53), the exterior frame freed the interior of beams and fixed walls, thereby allowing the maximum amount of rentable space. The building was also the first in the world to have an underground parking garage and air conditioning.

The striking seventeen-story, 1895 **Marquette Building**, a block south on Dearborn Street, was, nevertheless, a prototype of the tall office building (especially for the massive panes of the Chicago-style windows). Its decorative features set it apart from much of its progeny. The bronze reliefs over the main door

Mies van der Rohe: From here to modernity

The pivotal force behind the post-war Chicago School (see "Architecture" color insert), and one of the greatest influences in redefining modern architecture, was **Mies van der Rohe** (1886–1969). His aphorisms, "Less is more" and "God is in the details" have become the basis for a plethora of contemporary design philosophies, and his influence on the architecture of his adopted city is keenly felt in the Loop.

Born in Aachen, Germany, Mies van der Rohe followed in the footsteps of his master stonemason father before becoming a draftsman, specializing in furniture. He joined the office of renowned architect Peter Behrens where his peers included Le Corbusier and Bauhaus-founder Walter Gropius. It was under Behrens that van der Rohe developed a design theory based on **solid structural techniques and material integrity**; despite his buildings' naked simplicity, van der Rohe was a perfectionist and used only the most luxurious materials for each construction.

In 1914, he opened his own office and was soon heralded as the exponent of **International Style Modernism**. Van der Rohe became the last director of the **Bauhaus school of design** in Germany in 1930, but as the Nazi regime tightened the straightjacket placed on advocates of Modernism, none of van der Rohe's designs were executed and the Bauhaus was disbanded in 1933. In 1937, van der Rohe accepted an offer from John Holabird to head the architecture school at the Armour Institute (later to become the Illinois Institute of Technology) and relocated to Chicago. Under his tutelage, the unification of technology and art revolutionized the institute's curriculum, and van der Rohe's theories found expression in his design for the campus. The campus centerpiece is Crown Hall, where one of van der Rohe's abiding architectural principles, "It is not the building that is the work of art, but the space," is apparent.

In the 1950s, van der Rohe's design reached its zenith with the construction of the **Federal Complex Center** (see p.60). Viewing the complex, it's clear that the composite of three buildings transcends functionality to become a sculptural expression. Each relate to one other with artistic synchronicity – the low-slung post office has two lobbies to replicate the features of the other two buildings and its flat roof almost seems to be floating above the plaza.

The deceptively simple **twin towers of 660–880 Lake Shore Drive**, built between 1949 and 1951, established the benchmark for high-rise post–World War II architecture. The precision of the glass and metal structure was not the only unique feature; in choosing his site, van der Rohe defined a precinct distinct from the hustle and bustle of urban life.

Van der Rohe's last American creation was the **IBM building** in Chicago, located on the river's north bank at 330 N Wabash, where ferocious wind downdrafts knock pedestrians off their feet, literally. Completed in 1971, two years after the architect's death, it is a classic "curtain wall" skyscraper, a steel structure draped with dark aluminum and bronze-tinted glass.

depict scenes from the 1674 expedition of Chicago's European discoverer Jacques Marquette, from the launching of his canoe to his local burial. But the exterior pales beside the glittering lobby, whose shimmering bronze fixtures are offset by a **Tiffany glass mosaic**, running around the atrium on the first floor. Designed by J.A. Holzer, it, too, retells the story of the French exploration of Illinois.

The Federal Center Complex

Between Jackson Boulevard and Adams Street, the triumvirate of black steel buildings that comprise the **Federal Center Complex** – a courthouse, government office building, and single-story US post office – are the work of Ludwig Mies van der Rohe, founder of the International Style of modern architecture (see box, p.59). The US General Services Administration commissioned the complex in 1959; budgetary strife resulted from the fifteen years of its painstaking construction.

Austere in the extreme, these buildings are the best early examples of Chicago architecture's leap from the Chicago School to Modernism; compare the federal buildings with neighboring Chicago School buildings like the Monadnock and Fisher, and you'll see the dramatic difference. All three governmental buildings are geometrically perfect and their steel frames brought to the surface, resulting in a highly linear and orderly construction that is beautiful in its simplicity. Stand in the plaza that joins them and the precision of the steel and glass proportions will jump out at you. Even the grid lines of the rectangular concrete blocks that form the plaza floor were carefully designed to line up with the building's vertical axis – hardly surprising for an architect who is said to have stood over the architectural model for hours, as if in meditative trance, before moving something an eighth of an inch in a flash of recognition.

In the plaza, providing a counterbalance to the "Miesian" aesthetics of almost religious exactitude is **Alexander Calder**'s inexplicably named *Flamingo* "**stabile**" ("static" and "mobile"). Standing 53 feet tall and painted in vivid vermillion, the steel sculpture was completed in 1974, just three years before the artist's death.

Lower Dearborn Street

The hulking **Monadnock Building**, at 53 W Jackson St, embodies the architectural shift from load-bearing masonry walls to skeletal steel frames. Built by Burnham and Root, the aptly named Monadnock (an Abenaki Indian term meaning a mountain standing alone) – was not only the tallest office building in the city when it was completed in 1891, but also one of the first commercial buildings with electricity. At sixteen stories – the tallest made entirely from stone – its walls are six feet thick to support the structure's immense weight. An addition, built two years later at 54 W Van Buren St, was constructed from steel frames that allowed thinner walls and created more room for glass windows.

In startling contrast, at 131 S Dearborn St, is the Postmodern glass and steel **Bank One Center**, completed in 2003. Inside the lobby there is a stunning limited-edition cast of one of the greatest masterpieces of Hellenistic Greek sculpture, the *Winged Victory of Samothrace* (190 BC). The original is on display in the Louvre in Paris.

Across W Van Buren Street, the 1896 **Fisher Building**, at 343 S Dearborn St, designed by Daniel Burnham in 1896, isn't as monumental or groundbreaking as some of the other buildings in the Loop, but it does represent an aesthetic change with an unusually whimsical depiction of eagles, cupids, snakes, and sea creatures (an allusion to the name of original owner Lucius G. Fisher) decorating the terracotta facade. The interior is lavishly decorated with elaborate mosaic floors and rich mahogany woodwork. Originally designed as offices, it has been converted into condominiums for residential use.

Just south, the seventeen-story **Old Colony Building**, 407 S Dearborn St, was the first structure to use portal arches at its corners to shield against the wind, which became increasingly problematic as buildings grew skyward. Rounded bay windows, also known as oriel windows, were added to the narrow steel-and-glass frame to increase natural light.

The bay-windowed **Manhattan Building** at 431 S Dearborn St, erected in 1891, was the quintessential Chicago School prototype. The world's first entirely iron-frame building, it was briefly – at sixteen stories – the tallest. It's also the oldest surviving building by William Le Baron Jenney, the man responsible for the Leiter Building II and whose revolutionary designs paved the way for the dozens of skyscrapers that came thereafter.

Along LaSalle Street

Chicago's Wall Street, the Midwest's financial Mecca, occupies the six blocks between Lake Street and Jackson Boulevard. For the most part, the area is a prosaic strip of moneymaking functionality. During peak rush-hour, swathes of office workers scurry from the bowels of the "El" to their high-rise office abodes, following a turbo-charged caffeine injection courtesy of the chain gangs of coffee shops and lunchtime eateries that pepper the area.

Most visitors' attention is focused upon the stunning Art Deco **Chicago Board of Trade** building, whose frenzied trading-pit has its origins in a central marketplace, which was opened in 1848 by about eighty merchants who needed an outlet to sell their products. Further north, the eye-catching Moorish exterior of **The Rookery** is complimented by the delicate naturalistic flourishes of the gold-leaf interior, which bears the hallmark of Frank Lloyd Wright; while one of the city's more recent architectural treasures, **190 S La Salle** by Philip Johnson, sports a gabled roof and lavishly gilded lobby which are quite breathtaking.

The Chicago Board of Trade and around

Half the world's wheat, corn, and pork-belly futures change hands here, at the world's busiest grain exchange amid the cacophonous roar of the **Chicago Board of Trade**, at 141 W Jackson Blvd at S LaSalle Street. Touring the building is no longer possible after the terrorist attacks of September 2001.

The building itself is one of the rare examples of Art Deco anywhere in the city. The gorgeous, 1930 monolithic tower is appropriately topped by a thirty-foot stainless-steel statue of *Ceres*, Roman goddess of grain. The thirteen-foot clock on the facade, high above the main entrance, can be seen from almost fifteen blocks away on LaSalle Street.

Heading south, you'll come to an irreverent Helmut Jahn building at **120 N LaSalle**. It's his last building to date, and though not nearly as wave-making as his Thompson Center (see p.62), it definitely has some of his flashy style. The convex facade, covered in reflective glass, bulges out over the street, while above the main entrance you'll see Roger Brown's colorful mosaic, *The Flight of Daedalus and Icarus*.

190 S LaSalle

The real Postmodern sight on LaSalle is the rather inappropriately prosaically named **190 S LaSalle**, Philip Johnson's only Chicago work. It's easily one of the more elegant and refined variations on the theme, best viewed from a few blocks away. Johnson teamed up with John Burgee Architects and built it during the late 1980s, almost completely mimicking the design of Root and Burnham's gorgeous 1892 Masonic Temple (demolished in 1939). This gives Johnson's masterpiece an opulent pre-1900 air. Everything about it has a beautifully classic feel, from the five-story red granite base, to the thousands of thin, vertical windows, which soar to the exquisite gables some forty stories skyward. Similarly, the grand, seemingly endless lobby is rich in Gothic splendor; millions of dollars' worth of gold leaf on the ceiling, individual elevator banks decorated in their own shades of marble, and the intriguing **bronze sculpture** on the lobby's north end (Alfred Carel's *Fugue*) bring to mind a secular cathedral, complete with an altar of sorts manned by the security guard at the lobby's south end. Hanging in the adjoining side room is a **tapestry** of Daniel Burnham's 1909 plan of Chicago, a chance to see the tremendous vision and plans he had for this city.

The Rookery

In startling contrast to 190 S LaSalle, the massive red granite building at 209 S LaSalle St, known as **The Rookery**, was built between 1885 and 1888, and was the tallest building in the world at the time of its construction. The seminal work of two leading Chicago architects, Burnham and Root, it is one of the city's most celebrated and photographed edifices. Its forbidding Moorish Gothic exterior, which looks as if it's been chiseled into a sophisticated office building, gives way to a wonderfully airy lobby, decked out in cool Italian marble and gold leaf in 1905 during a major remodeling by Frank Lloyd Wright and restored in 1992. The spiral cantilever staircase rising from the second floor must be seen to be appreciated. The building takes its name from the City Hall that occupied the site in the aftermath of the Great Fire in 1871 – it became a favored roost or "rookery" for pigeons. While **tours** of the building have been terminated indefinitely since September 11, 2001, you can still visit the stunning lobby independently or as part of a tour with the Chicago Architecture Foundation (see p.49).

The James R. Thompson Center

Four blocks north of the Rookery, resembling an oversized slice of cake, is the **James R. Thompson Center**, 100 W Randolph St, is the state's headquarters in Chicago. Helmut Jahn's iconoclastic building was completed in 1985, its bulging sides and exuberant color scheme standing out amid the neighboring office towers. In his early period German-born Jahn – who was described by many critics as "Flash Gordon" – reveled in his *enfant terrible* image. Inside, glass elevator-shafts shuttle office-workers between floors, past the silver, red, and blue-toned interior. More than fifty state agencies are housed here, as well as an art gallery, three floors of restaurants and shops, and the expected parade of gawkers.

Aside from aesthetic concerns, the government workers found it too hot in summer and too cold in winter, thanks to the building's 400,000-square-foot glass shell. (In the end, the solution was to freeze eight 100,000-pound ice blocks every night and let them slowly melt the next day for use as coolant in the air-conditioning system.)

The sculpture standing in the building's foreground, looking like a cross between an iceberg and a ten-ton plaything, is Jean Dubuffet's *Monument with Standing Beast*. The mass of white fiberglass and black trim was taken from the artist's "art brute series," an attempt to divorce art from culture. According to Dubuffet, the piece contains four motifs: an animal, a tree, a portal, and a Gothic church. Good luck finding them.

The Sears Tower and the river

While the Loop proper is defined by the circle of El tracks, the blocks just beyond this core hold plenty of interest, chief among them, east of the river on Wacker Drive, the vertigo-inducing **Sears Tower**, visible from just about anywhere in the city. The broad, double-decked **Wacker Drive**, which follows the river northward and then west, was designed in 1909 by Daniel Burnham as an elegant promenade lined with benches and obelisk-shaped lanterns. Though it was never completed, and despite the almost constant intrusion of construction works, the promenade makes for a pleasant stroll, affording superb views of the river and downtown skyline (the State Street Bridge being an especially good vantage point).

Above the Loop, along the river's south bank, you'll find several **cafés** beside the **riverwalk** between Lake Michigan and Michigan Avenue; further west, past the water taxis and tour boats, there's a recently resurrected stretch of the riverwalk following the river's western bank with gardens and more cafés.

At 71 S Wacker Drive, just north of Sears Tower, and providing a gateway to the Loop at the eastern end of Monroe Street, stands the striking 49-story **Hyatt Center**, designed by Harry Cobb. While its serene curves slicing through the skyline like a ship's prow form a graceful aberration, its blunt vertical-end walls imbue it with that formidable edge that defines the no-nonsense Chicago street-grid and skyline. Cobb, whose mantra is that a building needs to be a "good citizen," made the security features integral to the design; the planter boxes in the plaza are tough enough to protect the building's supporting columns from a truck bomb. This sense of fortification without compromising beauty has made the building one of the most prestigious office addresses in the city, and a symbol of architectural innovation since September 11, 2001. At a time when downtown office-vacancy rates have been increasing at unprecedented levels, the Hyatt Center had filled more than 75 percent of its 1.7 million-square-foot capacity in time for its ceremonial unveiling in July 2005.

The Sears Tower

East of the river, on S Wacker Drive at Adams Street, stands the 1450-foot **Sears Tower**, which was the tallest building in the world until 1997, when Malaysia's Petronas Towers controversially nudged it from the number-one spot by the length of an antenna. In 2004, the 1670-foot Taipei Tower trumped them all, but still hanging on to its superlatives, the Sears Tower remains the tallest building in the world in terms of inhabited space. In fact, the building grows an additional eight inches in summer, due to the steel's expansion.

Skidmore, Owings and Merrill completed the tower, a composition of nine square tubes, in 1973. It took only three years to build and was technologically innovative, especially in its step-back, framed-tube construction (allowing the wide base to support the narrower upper tower) and the heated walkway around its perimeter to help clear winter snow. The tower's vital statistics are staggering: more than 10,000 people work here, riding the more than one hundred elevators and looking out through 16,000 windows – all, thankfully, equipped with automatic window-washers.

Enter on Jackson Street through the specially marked door and descend to the lower level to reach the ticket office. Feel free to skip the cursory eight-minute movie and head straight for the ear-popping elevator ride, which takes about seventy seconds to reach the **103rd-floor observatory** (daily: May–Sept 10am–10pm, Oct–April 10am–8pm, closed occasionally due to high winds; $11.95, seniors $9.75, children $8.50; ⓣ312/875-9696, ⓦwww.thesearstower.com). Once there, you'll have good views of the city's east and north sides, though even on a clear day you'll be squinting to see the neighboring four states (Michigan, Illinois, Indiana, and Wisconsin), as touted in the tower's literature: call to check the visibility index before turning up – if it's under five miles, come another time. The handy touch-screen computers mounted on the rails will help identify what you see, and you can read fascinating stories from the city's history on the walls.

If the lines for the Skydeck Observatory are too long, keep in mind that you can get similar views atop the John Hancock Building in Near North (see p.78); in any case, the crowds typically thin out after 4pm.

The Chicago Mercantile Exchange

Three blocks north at 30 S Wacker Drive, precious metals, currencies, and commodities are bought and sold to the tune of some $50 billion a day at the **Chicago Mercantile Exchange** or "The Merc," a dazzling throwback to pre-computer days, when Chicago was the hub of the railways – and subsequently, the nation's trade.

Sadly, since September 11, 2001, the fourth-floor viewing gallery that afforded a breathtaking view of the trading frenzy has been closed. For those interested to learn more about the origins of the Exchange and its role in the global economy, in the lobby you will find the high-tech **Visitor Center** (Mon–Fri 8am–4.30pm; free; ⓣ312/390-8249, ⓦwww.cme.com) that opened in March 2004. Interactive and informative exhibits include a selection of artifacts, newspaper headlines, photos, and video footage dating back to CME's humble beginnings as a butter-and-egg exchange in 1895, to seminal moments in the CME's trading history and, for aspiring brokers, there is even a simulated trading game.

The Civic Opera House and around

The massive **Civic Opera House**, at 20 N Wacker Drive, just below Washington Street, is another splendid venue for highbrow entertainment, home to the Lyric Opera. Conceived as a monument to culture and commerce and completed in 1929, the Neoclassical building was designed with a grand two-story portico running its entire length, making it look like a giant armchair from the river. While it's worth taking a two-hour tour of the opera house, they're usually only given in either February or March and are booked up several months in advance; with the price for the 2006 tours expected to be $35–40, they're also pricey (☎312/332-2244, Ⓦwww.lyricopera.org). For further information on performances, see p.231.

Walking north from here to where the river bends eastward, you'll spot **333 W Wacker Drive** on your right, a wafer-thin building covered in a skin of reflective green glass. Built in 1983, it was designed to mimic the contour and color of the Chicago River, and is best viewed from the opposite bank, which also has a few of its own notable buildings, namely the fortress-like **Merchandise Mart**, the twin corncob towers of **Marina City**, and Mies van der Rohe's sleek, black **IBM Building** (for more information, see p.84).

2

The Art Institute of Chicago

One of the top museums in the country, the **Art Institute of Chicago**, 111 S Michigan Ave (Mon–Wed & Fri 10.30am–4.30pm; Thurs 10.30am–8pm, Sat & Sun 10am–5pm; suggested donation $12, seniors, students & children $7, Tues free; ⓣ312/443-3600, ⓦwww.artic.edu), is one of Chicago's must-see sights. Located within Grant Park (see p.97) at Michigan Avenue and Adams Street, the Institute boasts a renowned collection of Impressionist and Post-Impressionist paintings, and with an iconic collection of twentieth-century American art, the museum can easily soak up an entire day.

Constructed for the **World's Columbian Exposition** between 1893 and 1916 by Shepley, Rutan and Coolidge, the building oozes turn-of-the-century opulence, noticeable in its Corinthian columns, soaring archways, and Neoclassical limestone facade. Guarding the grand entrance are two bronze lions, Chicago's mascots, which have been known to wear Bulls' jerseys and festive decorations to commemorate special events.

While most visitors, once inside, head straight to galleries 201–206 upstairs for the big-money Impressionist pieces works, there are rich works to be found nearly

School of the Art Institute of Chicago

The Art Institute of Chicago started life as the **Chicago Academy of Design**, a small art school founded in 1866 by a group of artists who wanted to provide top-notch education in studio arts and showcase student works. After outgrowing several rented facilities and losing its first permanent home to the 1871 Chicago Fire, the school changed its name to The Art Institute and eventually settled into its current location at 37 S Wabash Ave, in a modern building adjacent to the magnificent Beaux-Arts pile that houses the school's now formidable art holdings.

Today, the SAIC is one of the largest independent accredited schools of art and design in the US with a fine academic reputation. Alumni include **Georgia O' Keeffe** and **Walt Disney** (although both failed to graduate), **Hugh Hefner** (who studied anatomy), and political satirist **Herblock**. Degree programs extend to creative writing, art education, and arts administration; courses open to the public are offered through its Continuing Education and Special Courses Department (ⓣ312/899-5130, ⓦwww.artic.edu). Student works are also frequently on display in the school's galleries.

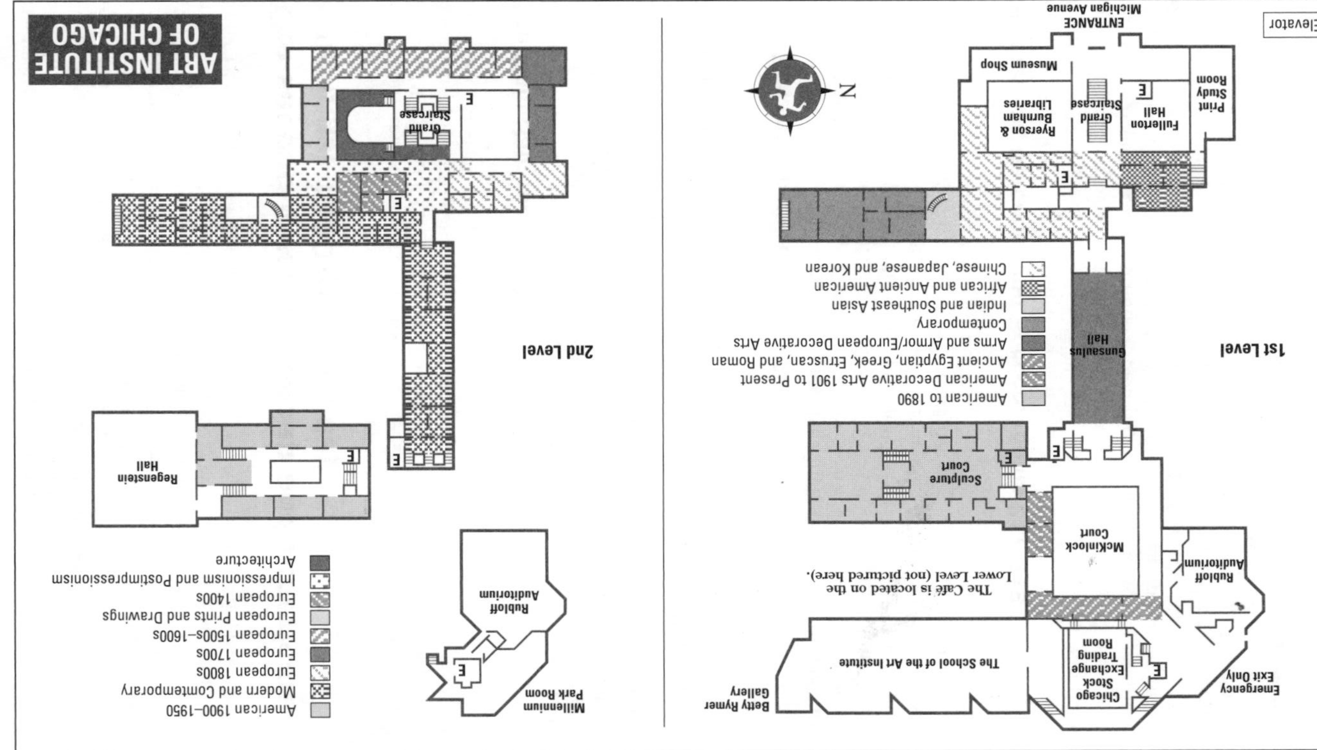
ART INSTITUTE OF CHICAGO
1st Level
E Elevator
Emergency Exit Only
Rubloff Auditorium
Chicago Stock Exchange Trading Room
McKinlock Court
The School of the Art Institute
Betty Rymer Gallery
The Café is located on the Lower Level (not pictured here).
Sculpture Court
Gunsaulus Hall
Print Study Room
Fullerton Hall
Grand Staircase
Ryerson & Burnham Libraries
Museum Shop
ENTRANCE Michigan Avenue
N
American to 1890
American Decorative Arts 1901 to Present
Ancient Egyptian, Greek, Etruscan, and Roman
Arms and Armor/European Decorative Arts
Contemporary
Indian and Southeast Asian
African and Ancient American
Chinese, Japanese, and Korean
2nd Level
Millennium Park Room
Rubloff Auditorium
Regenstein Hall
Grand Staircase
American 1900–1950
Modern and Comtemporary
European 1800s
European 1700s
European 1500s–1600s
European Prints and Drawings
European 1400s
Impressionism and Postimpressionism
Architecture

everywhere, and the museum has collections spanning a vast number of eras and featuring a variety artists. We've provided a room-by-room overview below – be aware that the museum constantly rotates its monumental holdings, so paintings may not correspond precisely to the room references. Also, bear in mind that the numerous wings (and the fact that the museum's bisected by the railway tracks) can make it tricky to find your way around, so take a **free map** or one of the excellent **audio tours** ($6) at the information desk in the main hall. There is also a **pocket guide** to the museum available for $3.95 in the bookstore: it's chatty and knowledgeable, but not laid out logically to follow the museum's displays.

The second level: European and American Paintings, 1300–present day

The paintings on this level are arranged in a rough chronology, although confusingly this scheme starts at rooms 207–225 and then cuts back through rooms 201–206 and 226. Twentieth-century pictures are split between the two wings, in two sequential arrangements, before continuing on to the first floor in rooms 134–139.

The Main Hall: room 200

Before diving into the galleries, pause in the stairwell as you enter. Here, you'll find a fine collection of architectural fragments, most of them salvaged from demolished buildings. There are chunks of cornices and framed windows: one of the most notable is Frank Lloyd Wright's **Avery Coonley Playhouse Window**, from the Riversdale, Illinois, home that he considered his masterpiece. Also be sure to stop by the ornately scrolled **Chicago Stock Exchange Elevator Grilles** by Adler & Sullivan. (For those titillated, there's also a full reconstruction of a trading room in room 153; (see p.73).

The Renaissance: rooms 207–209

Among the small yet thoroughly unmissable fifteenth-century **Italian and Flemish paintings** here, take a look in room 209 at **Lucas Cranach the Elder**'s lithe, tender, seductive *Adam and Eve* (1526) and **Jan Sanders van Hemessen**'s *Judith* (1540). The erotic, muscular, sword-wielding female subject, Judith, slayed the Assyrian general Holofernes in order to save the Jewish people, and the venerated portrayal of Judith is suggestive of Hemessen's moral ambiguity toward the evils undertaken for her cause.

Mannerism, Baroque, and Rococo: rooms 211–219

In room 211, Tintoretto's sensual *Tarquin and Lucretia* (1580/90) is a terrific example of Mannerism's obsession with distortion and *contrapposto* (the twisting of a figure on its own vertical axis). Incandescent light floods the painting, which depicts Prince Tarquin's violent rape of Lucretia, which led to her eventual suicide and the subsequent downfall of the Roman monarchy in 510 BC. Don't miss sixteenth-century Spanish master **El Greco**'s *Assumption of the Virgin* (1577) in room 215, which exemplifies the artist's religious preoccupations while showcasing his unique, distended style. Lauded as his finest work displayed outside Spain, it's one of seven paintings that was commissioned in Toledo for an altarpiece. El Greco's deft use of color imbues the canvas with a supernatural aura while the apostles and angels surround the Virgin as she ascends to heaven on a crescent moon.

The **Golden Age of Dutch painting** is the focus of room 216: it's rare to come across paintings by Rembrandt's talented pupil, Aert de Gelder, but the swollen psychological painting here, *Portrait of a Young Woman*, is eye-catching. Rembrandt's own *Old Man with Gold Chain* (c.1631) contrasts the craggy subject's furrowed face with his gleaming jewels (even so, the viewer's drawn first to the wrinkles around his eyes).

In room 218, the four paintings in **Giambattistta Tiepolo**'s sensual *Torquato Tasso* series (1740) is a paradigm of his dream-like technique, where it often seems like he's painting with pastel-colored ice cream. In the same room are several examples by Francesco Guardi of the *veduta* (meaning "view") style that was also popular at this time, portraying detailed city scenes. In room

△ The Art Institute of Chicago

219, Fragonard's sketch-like *Portrait of a Man* (1768) is arresting – his subject's reddish-tinted face looking almost like rotting meat.

Impressionism and Post-Impressionism; rooms 201–206, 226

This collection was mostly purchased (then donated) by **Bertha Honoré Palmer**, wife of Potter Palmer (see box, p.282), who was passionate about art (she purchased twenty-five Monet paintings in 1891) and reinventing Chicago, hitherto regarded as a cultural backwater. In 1893, she organized a seminal exhibition of Modern European Paintings at the World Columbian Exhibition (see pp.280–281), which is one of the finest Impressionist selections in the world, and undoubtedly the museum's best-known feature.

The definitive vanguard of the Impressionist movement is represented in room 201. The familiar loose brushstrokes flushed with vivid colors capture the subjective grace and joy of a fleeting moment, characteristic of Renoir, Monet, and Caillebotte. The immediate crowd-pleaser, forming the centerpiece of room 201, is **Gustave Caillebotte**'s striking masterpiece, *Paris Street, Rainy Day* (1887), which plays with focus and perspective using his careful mathematical techniques; the shimmering cobblestones almost glisten with wetness. On the south wall, you'll find **Renoir**'s *Acrobats at Circus Fernando* (1879), Bertha Palmer's favorite painting, and one she carried with her everywhere, even on trips abroad. You'll also see what is considered the first truly impressionist landscape, an early **Monet** from 1868, *On the Bank of the Seine, Bennecourt*, which has a free, bold energy that his calculated later pictures can lack.

In contrast to the brilliant hues of the outdoor scenes painted by his Impressionist peers, **Degas** preferred to focus on the intimacy of family life, composing indoor scenes that were artificially lit. The feeling of motion conveyed in the *Millinery Shop* (1884/1890), a painting cropped in such a way to give the viewer the perspective of a passerby looking into a shop window, reveals Degas' credo that we take in the minutiae of life through a rapid succession of impressions. In room 202, Degas' passion for the human body in motion is apparent in his meticulously composed sculptures, *Retiring* (1883), *Young Spartans* (1860), and *Spanish Dance* (1883).

Room 203 is filled with Monet canvases that provide an interesting contrast with **Camille Pissarro**'s *Woman and Child at the Well* (1882). While Monet's canvases focus on the primordial nature of the French countryside and are devoid of human figures, by the 1880s Pissarro had begun to place greater emphasis on capturing the human form. Here, experimenting with color and form, the landscape is secondary to the two women who dominate the painting. But, the showstopper in this section, in room 205, is surely **Georges Seurat**'s *La Grande Jatte* (1884). It took 28-year-old Seurat two years to paint this pointillist masterpiece, and that perfectionist instinct is evident even in the white frame, which he specially designed.

Shortly after Seurat exhibited *La Grande Jatte*, **van Gogh** came to Paris from Holland. In his painting *The Bedroom* (room 205), van Gogh employed Seurat's pointillist "dot" technique to create an energetic surface, which in van Gogh's own words demonstrated a "Seurat-like simplicity." In the same room, look for **Henri de Toulouse-Lautrec**'s famed *At the Moulin Rouge* (1892/95) and its lurid greenish-yellow face of May Milton. Monet resurfaces with two sequences in room 206: his seemingly psychedelic London paintings of Waterloo Bridge in which the smog and grime of nineteenth-century London appear to dissipate all traces of urban life, transforming the image into a timeless poetic vision. The fifteen canvases which form the calmer *Grain Stacks* series (1891) demonstrate Monet's fascination with temporality as he explores the emotional and visual consequences of capturing the light and atmosphere at different times of the day, month, and year.

Modern and Contemporary: rooms 231–249

Surrealist **Mark Chagall**'s *Praying Jew* (1923) is displayed in room 231. Jewish themes were recurrent in the Russian-born, French artist's work, and in this image the holy figure is none other than a nomadic beggar posing in the black-and-white prayer shawl that belonged to Chagall's father. The artist's signature fantasy and wit were never too far from even the most somber themes.

One of the best-known pictures from his Blue Period, **Picasso**'s melancholy *The Old Guitarist* (1903) is on view in room 234B. The guitarist's contorted features are representative of the growing artistic trend of the early twentieth century to convey the subject's mental state through his physical being. **Paul Gauguin**'s colorful evocations of the local scenery in Tahiti are also displayed in room 234B. Devoid of any allusion to modern civilization, they reveal Gauguin's emphasis of the intuitive over the intellectual, the primitive over the refined. **Edouard Vuillard**'s *Window Overlooking the Woods* (1899) is a monumental canvas with a lavishly textured surface that resembles a tapestry. Matisse's first original sculpture, *The Serf* (1900–1903), is also displayed here.

Passing across the spiral stairway, room 235 has two stunning **Rodin sculptures**: *Adam* (1881) and *Burgher of Calais* (1889). The latter figure formed part of a monument which served as an allegory for courage and sacrifice; it alludes to an episode from the Hundred Years' War when six citizens of Calais, who had been seized by the English, offered their lives in exchange for those of their fellow citizens. Perhaps the maddest Surrealist of them all, **Dalí**'s *Visions of Eternity* (1936) is displayed in room 236. The playful pictures of Magritte are well represented in the museum. *Time Transfixed* (1938) fulfils the characteristic Surrealist device of placing commonplace objects in unusual contexts. According to the artist, this image of a locomotive juxtaposed with a living-room fireplace was intended to stir in the viewer a meditation on the mysteries of thought.

Jackson Pollock and **Willem De Kooning** are exhibited in room 238A and 238B – don't miss Pollock's *Greyed Rainbow* (1953), painted just three years before the artist died in a car accident. The hypnotic, swirling arabesques of black-and-white paint splashes epitomize the style of the American Abstract Expressionist movement that Pollock pioneered. Pollock instigated the use of trowels and other implements instead of brushes, a style which is now referred to as "action painting." You'll find three of **Mark Rothko**'s color fields in room 239, and more kaleidoscopic explorations of color and form by Russian-born painter **Vasily Kandinsky**, one of the first abstract artists of the twentieth century, in room 240. The utopian visions of Bauhaus artist **Paul Klee** are displayed in room 241, fantastical, dreamy watercolors that defy classification, but express the introverted artist's overriding belief that art could bring about social change. **Matisse** takes up the lion's share of room 242 and 243. *Interior at Nice* (1919/1920) is acclaimed as the most accomplished variation of a series which was executed by the Fauvist leader at the *Hôtel de la Méditerranée*.

American 1900–1950: rooms 262–273

Far and away one of the institute's premier attractions is the newly expanded gallery of American art featuring some of the most iconic artworks of the nineteenth century. Start in room 262 with one of the museum's greatest treasures, **Edward Hopper**'s *Nighthawks* (1942). While the composition – three people lost in thought in an all-night diner in New York – suggests a narrative, Hopper's stated intent was to present a fleeting moment in time, "unconsciously, probably I was painting the loneliness of a large city."

Room 262 contains many pieces by **European surrealists** who came to the United States during and following World War II and were to have a profound influence on American artists. Also in room 262, you'll discover **Peter Blume**'s *The Rock* (1948), an almost magical-realist vision of post-war despair juxtaposed against hope. The workers depicted on the left are building Frank Lloyd Wright's "Falling Water" – one of the celebrated architect's most famous constructions that Blume believed represented the quintessential American vision of the future. The rock in the middle of the painting, scarred but enduring, is Blume's symbol of humanity's will and ability to survive. Before leaving room 262, note **Ivan Albright**'s two hauntingly macabre pieces, which encourage contemplations of the viewer's own mortality. Albright's life-long obsession with the ravages of time is epitomized in *The Picture of Dorian Gray* (1943), created for the film of that name. Albright renders with meticulous detail and lavish color the image of the protagonist as a haunting allegory of human decay – moral, spiritual, and physical.

Regionalism and a search for identity in the United States and Mexico is the underlying theme in room 263. The highlight here, and perhaps in the entire museum, is **Grant Wood**'s *American Gothic* (1930), in which his sister and dentist posed with a pitchfork to create one of the most reproduced (and parodied) images in American art. It's one of the best examples of Regionalism, a movement that rejected avant-garde European art in favor of simple rural themes. Room 245 is dedicated to Arthur Dove, the first American painter to experiment with abstraction, and the pioneering Modernist **Georgia O'Keeffe**. Look out for her ominous *Black Cross, New Mexico* (1929). On a visit to New Mexico, O'Keeffe recalled the great frequency with which she encountered mystifying crosses, which represented to her the "dark veil" of Catholicism. O'Keeffe looked to find the essential beauty in each object through reducing them to their elemental form. O'Keeffe worked right up to her death, aged 98, in New Mexico, where she had lived since 1949. Room 273 focuses on the theme of the Gilded Age and Expatriatism. The highlight here is **John Singer Sargent**'s portrait of *Mrs George Swinton* (1897), which defined the artist as the most desired portraitist among wealthy Europeans and Americans.

The first level: Contemporary Art

The **Contemporary Art** collection in room 136–139 is stunning, from its massive **David Hockney** canvas *American Collectors* (1968), all pinched profiles and pink kaftans bathed in dazzling California light in room 136, to the works of Cuban-American conceptual artist **Felix Gonzales-Torres**. In *Untitled Portrait of Ross in LA* in room 137, the Ross Laycock of the title was Gonzales-Torres' partner who died of AIDS in 1991. The 175lb mound of colorful candy (which corresponds to the ideal body weight) serves as a symbol for Ross and a reflection upon love and loss – help yourself to a candy, the installation's self-renewing nature (the candy is replaced constantly) symbolizes the triumph and endurance of art in a fragile, temporal world.

The monumental fifteen-foot *Mao* (1973) by **Andy Warhol** looms over room 136. The most influential and renowned of the Pop artists, Warhol used irony with aplomb to examine the impact of consumerism and the cult of personality – themes which have particular resonance in today's celebrity-obsessed societies. Warhol's larger-than-life portrayal of the Chinese totalitarian ruler, who died in

1976, reflects the iconography still in evidence across China. There's more Pop Art in this room from **Roy Lichtenstein**, whose *Brushstroke with Splatter* (1968) is one of a series in which the artist moves from comic-book-style parodies of popular culture to irreverent send-ups of fine art; the supposed spontaneity and intuitive nature of Abstract Expressionism is undermined by Lichtenstein's deliberate and precise evocation of the style's basic elements – the brushstroke and its splatter.

The **Rubloff building** at the back is normally home to the site-specific **American Windows** by **Marc Chagall**: these six dazzling stained-glass panels were produced by the artist in honor of America's Bicentennial. Unfortunately, due to the expansion of the gallery, the windows have been removed – construction work is scheduled for completion in 2009. On the other side of the courtyard, be sure not to miss the painstaking reconstruction of a trading room from Adler & Sullivan's old **Chicago Stock Exchange**.

3

Near North

While the Loop is more important as a center of business and finance, Chicago's **NEAR NORTH** has established itself as the most energetic downtown area, with its three very different districts – **the Magnificent Mile**, **Streeterville**, and **River North** – each offering very different reasons to visit, from the Mag Mile's world-class shopping district to Streeterville's family-friendly **Navy Pier**, and the blocks of **art galleries** in River North. Transformed almost overnight from an industrial area of low-rent factories by the building of the Michigan Avenue Bridge in the early twentieth century, Near North is actually where most visitors spend the bulk of their stays, either enjoying the family entertainment at Navy Pier or, more likely, maxing out their credit cards at the megastores lining N Michigan Avenue.

One of the most famous shopping strips in the world, the **Magnificent Mile**, along Michigan Avenue just north of the river, features a glitzy selection of stores that Chicago relentlessly pitches. As resistant as some visitors may be to buy into such hype, those who skip Michigan Avenue will miss out on one of the city's best attractions. The streets here are wide enough that they rarely feel crowded (save during the holiday season), there are parks and benches for a pause between stores, and its expansive openness is refreshing after the canyons of buildings and low-flying trains in the Loop. Even those allergic to shopping should find something to buy, thanks to the enormous selection; if you're determined not to spend a dollar, it's still worth dawdling here to look at neo-Gothic buildings like the **Tribune** and **Water Tower** as well as **Wrigley's** gleaming chewing-gum headquarters, which resembles a mammoth ivory wedding cake.

The area sandwiched between Michigan Avenue and the lake is officially known as **Streeterville**. Originally a dump (literally – see box, p.80 for more on its history), it is now one of the swankiest places in the city, home to high-rise, high-price condos and gleaming residential skyscrapers. The area is still mostly homes, hotels, and a smattering of restaurants spread out over a series of uninspiring industrial blocks, but recent visitor-friendly developments like the corporate funland of **Navy Pier** – one of Chicago's top tourist attractions – is drawing more foot traffic to the neighborhood.

River North is one of the most schizophrenic districts in the city. On the one hand, it's crammed with theme restaurants like the *Hard Rock Café* and the *Rainforest Café*, which cater to families and hapless tourists. On the other, it's Chicago's answer to New York's SoHo district: away from the main drags of Ontario and Ohio streets, you'll find a thriving, loft-heavy gallery district. The exhibits here on the whole are less avant-garde and more accessible than in similar neighborhoods in other cities.

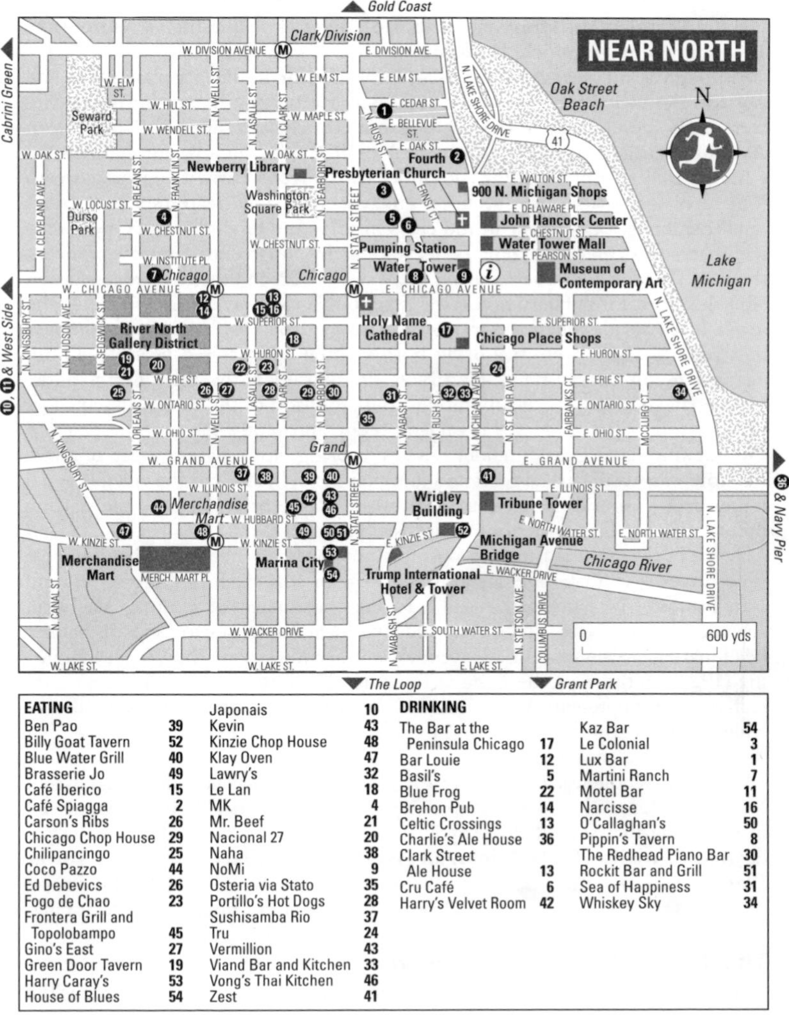

EATING			
Ben Pao	39	Japonais	10
Billy Goat Tavern	52	Kevin	43
Blue Water Grill	40	Kinzie Chop House	48
Brasserie Jo	49	Klay Oven	47
Café Iberico	15	Lawry's	32
Café Spiagga	2	Le Lan	18
Carson's Ribs	26	MK	4
Chicago Chop House	29	Mr. Beef	21
Chilipancingo	25	Nacional 27	20
Coco Pazzo	44	Naha	38
Ed Debevics	26	NoMi	9
Fogo de Chao	23	Osteria via Stato	35
Frontera Grill and Topolobampo	45	Portillo's Hot Dogs	28
Gino's East	27	Sushisamba Rio	37
Green Door Tavern	19	Tru	24
Harry Caray's	53	Vermillion	43
House of Blues	54	Viand Bar and Kitchen	33
		Vong's Thai Kitchen	46
		Zest	41

DRINKING			
The Bar at the Peninsula Chicago	17	Kaz Bar	54
Bar Louie	12	Le Colonial	3
Basil's	5	Lux Bar	1
Blue Frog	22	Martini Ranch	7
Brehon Pub	14	Motel Bar	11
Celtic Crossings	13	Narcisse	16
Charlie's Ale House	36	O'Callaghan's	50
Clark Street Ale House	13	Pippin's Tavern	8
Cru Café	6	The Redhead Piano Bar	30
Harry's Velvet Room	42	Rockit Bar and Grill	51
		Sea of Happiness	31
		Whiskey Sky	34

Be aware that away from Michigan Avenue, distances in Near North can be large, especially as you wander round River North: grab one of the **free trolleys** (see box, p.99) or head there on foot in comfortable shoes.

The Magnificent Mile

Walking along the wide swath of Michigan Avenue north of the Chicago River is the one thing that almost every visitor to the city will do. One of the world's most famous shopping districts, it's well stocked with mainstream retailers, from an enormous Virgin Megastore to a Niketown, as well as every major department store from Saks to Neiman Marcus (for more information on these and other stores, see "Shopping," Chapter 22). Equally as diverting are skyscrapers like the **Wrigley Building** and **Tribune Tower** as well as the views from the 100-story **John Hancock Building**.

Although S Michigan Avenue was an early addition to the city plan (1836) and was soon crowded with museums and civic institutions, its northern stretches were only developed in the early twentieth century after the **Michigan Avenue Bridge** was finally constructed in 1920, allowing expansion across the Chicago River. Inspired by the Alexander III Bridge in Paris, it's decorated with four forty-foot pylons, two at either end, each of which features a sumptuous relief depicting a key event in the city's history (the city's discovery by seventeenth-century French explorers, its settling by nineteenth-century pioneers, the Fort Dearborn Massacre during the War of 1812, and the city's regeneration after the Great Fire). This was also the first double roadway bridge ever built: the lower level was designed to service the *Chicago Sun-Times* and *Chicago Tribune* newspapers, which were originally both written and printed nearby, without disrupting commercial traffic flow. Note the two leaves that are raised to allow large boats to pass underneath: though the city took to the design quickly – it now has fifty such bridges – mastering them, apparently, took a little practice. On opening day, a bridge tender raised the bridge for a passing boat, unaware that four cars were parked on it and dumped the vehicles into the river. If you'd rather cruise around the river than dive into it, the bridge is now the starting point for many **bus and boat tours** (see p.49).

Developers continued to lure business northward by renaming hardscrabble Pine Street – at that time, an unpaved road of soap factories, breweries, and warehouses – N Michigan Avenue to take advantage of existing Michigan Avenue's cachet. Next, they persuaded two local businesses to establish banner headquarters at the grand new avenue's southernmost end: the Wrigley Building (1924) on the west, the Tribune Tower (1922) to the east. Still, it wasn't until real-estate entrepreneur Arthur Rubloff christened the strip "The Magnificent Mile," then set about making good this claim of magnificence, in the 1960s, that the area truly came to life.

With the wholehearted support of Mayor Richard Daley, the Magnificent Mile exploded with shops, and it hasn't looked back since. If you're interested in exploring that side of things, you may be drawn to any of the three major downtown **malls**: **900 N Michigan Ave**, **Chicago Place**, and **Water Tower Place**. There isn't much to choose between them, although 900 N Michigan is probably the swankiest, and Water Tower Place the most notable architecturally.

The Wrigley Building and around

Flanking the southern entrance to what locals refer to as the "Mag" Mile is the **Wrigley Building** at 400 N Michigan Ave, sometimes called the "Jewel of the Mile." The building is clad in 250,000 terracotta tiles, each of which is monitored in a computer database for ease of maintenance. Well over a thousand people work in the building, which is the home of the Wrigley chewing-gum company as well as advertising agencies, foreign consulates, and other companies. The building does indeed sparkle at night when hundreds of floodlights across the river bathe the creamy, glazed terra-cotta facade and huge clocktower. Modeled after the Giralda Tower of the Cathedral of Seville, the building has flourishes reminiscent of the French Renaissance. Though not quite as impressive, the building's interior, open during regular business hours, is noteworthy for its extensive brasswork.

Just north of the Wrigley Building, looking a bit out of place among the drab office buildings, is the pensive-looking statue of **Benito Juarez**, president of Mexico from 1861 to 1872, and a contemporary of Illinois native Abraham

Lincoln. Indeed, Juarez was often referred to as the "Mexican Abraham Lincoln," and the two shared a regular correspondence and friendship, perhaps owing to both having grown up poor, their backgrounds in law, and their similar paths to the presidency.

For a memorable bite to eat in the area, head down the stairs to the venerable grease-pit **Billy Goat Tavern**, tucked away beneath the statue and Michigan Avenue. Immortalized by John Belushi's "cheezborger" skit on *Saturday Night Live*, this smoky, subterranean dive is where journalists and tourists have been scarfing down burgers since it opened in 1934 (for a review, see p.189).

The Tribune Tower

Across the road from the Wrigley Building stands the **Tribune Tower**, 435 N Michigan Ave (Mon–Fri 8.30am–5pm; tours by appointment only; ⓣ312/222-2116, ⓦwww.tribune.com); despite the dozens of skyscrapers now crowding the downtown skyline, it still stands out, thanks to its ornate, neo-Gothic design. A great tower that rises like a cathedral from the riverbank, complete with flying buttresses and ornate scrollwork, it's one of Chicago's signature structures and, along with the Wrigley Building, it was meant to act as a flashy anchor for the newly accessible Near North district.

The tower was built in 1925 as headquarters for the *Chicago Tribune*, supported by the deep pockets of the newspaper's eccentric editor-publisher Robert "The Colonel" McCormick. Dapper McCormick and his scruffy co-publisher, Joseph Patterson, launched a contest in 1922 to mark the 75th anniversary of the founding of the *Chicago Tribune*, offering $100,000 in prizes to architects around the world willing to submit designs for a grand new headquarters. The winning entry was by American team John Mead Howells and Raymond Hood. The Colonel spared no expense on his masterpiece: it would cost a staggering $8.5 million to build.

Like Louis Sullivan, Howells and Hood were heavily influenced by Britain's Arts and Crafts movement, which rebelled against angular, mass-produced decoration; hence, most of the detailing features plants and animals, and likewise the figures from Aesop's fables, woven into the scrollwork in the stone screen

Fragments of history

The most famous feature of the Tribune Tower are the **fragments of famous buildings** dotting the facade; they include rocks from the Houses of Parliament in London, St Peter's in Rome, and the Forbidden City in Beijing. The tradition began with the Colonel himself who, while working as a war correspondent during World War I in France, grabbed a chunk of Ypres cathedral that had been knocked from the wall by German shells. Soon, the Colonel was instructing his far-flung network of newshounds to gather other notable rocks (by honorable means) to create a display that would underscore his claim that the *Trib* was the "World's Greatest Newspaper." Of course, many reporters chose to risk the wrath of local lawmakers rather than the anger of their ornery boss, so no one can be sure how many of the souvenirs were purloined rather than purchased. Their activities became so well known that one journalist arrived in Reims, France, to see the local newspaper blaring warnings about his intentions across its front page.

These days, new (legal) acquisitions are set aside for ten years to gauge their true historic value before being mounted on the walls – exceptions include a piece of the Berlin Wall added in 1990, and the Moon rock on long-term loan from NASA that's displayed in its own glass case. To identify the fragments, pick up one of the superb free **leaflets** available inside the main lobby.

above the main entranceway. Don't miss the **main lobby**, which has notable decorative features of its own: quotations serving as propaganda in support of a free press are chiseled over almost every inch of marble. There's a massive relief map of North America on the main wall; strangely, it's made from plaster mixed with old dollar bills, since tough currency paper enhances durability. The planned image included much of South America, too; but the slightly batty and very patriotic Colonel decided to make the United States more prominent by chopping two feet off the bottom of the design.

The *Chicago Tribune* is still housed here: look for the squat, later additions that were built to its north and east with the *Tribune*'s entry into radio and television. **WGN radio** (its call letters hark back to "World's Greatest Newspaper" – see p.42) still broadcasts from here, and you can watch the djs at work from the ground-level glass window on Michigan Avenue.

The John Hancock Building and around

Sleek and muscular, the **John Hancock Building**, 875 N Michigan Ave, is the street's dominant fixture, a quarter-mile-high construction of cross-braced steel, black aluminum skin, and bronze-tinted windows that rises nearly out of sight, tapering upward to be capped, eventually, by two massive spires. Though it appears imposing from its base, viewed from afar it's beautifully austere, heavily influenced by the Miesian School – except for the colorful band of light at the top, visible at night.

Though shorter than both the Sears Tower and the Empire State Building, the Hancock Building was, from its completion in 1969 until 1998, among the world's top ten tallest structures and offers – on a clear day – jaw-dropping 360-degree panoramic views of the city from its 94th-floor **observatory**. It also made history as the tallest mixed-use building in the world, its combining of commercial and office space with apartments being unusual for its time.

More than a thousand feet above Chicago, the observatory (daily 9am–11pm; last observatory ticket sold at 10.45pm; $9.50, children 5–12 $6; ⓣ312/751-3680, ⓦwww.hancock-observatory.com) has an open-air viewing deck where winds can force the building to sway as much as ten inches from side to side, though you probably won't even notice. Don't let this, or the somewhat steep ticket price, prevent you from taking the elevator up to the observatory; the views are truly staggering – like the Sears Tower, you'll see as far as Indiana, Michigan, and Wisconsin on a clear day. It's open later than the Sears Tower, and the lines are less gruelling, and if the views alone aren't diverting enough, you can listen to an audio tour ($3) or check out one of the talking telescopes that point out what you're seeing. There's a wall devoted to city history and a bit about the construction of the building itself.

If you just want the view, though, skip the observatory and head straight to the **Signature Room** on the 96th floor, where you can take in the scenery for the price of a drink. On the 95th floor, the view is the best thing about the *Signature Room* **restaurant**, which serves overpriced, uninspired American fare. At the base of the Hancock building, in a small store-lined courtyard, you'll find a branch store of the **Chicago Architecture Foundation** (see p.49), which can set you up with tours and literature on Chicago's famed designs.

Opposite the John Hancock Center is the English and French Gothic **Fourth Presbyterian Church**, at 126 E Chestnut St, built in 1914. Peek inside for a look at the elegantly understated interior or stop by the fountain in the peaceful courtyard – a quiet spot for a picnic just a stone's throw from Michigan Avenue.

Water Tower: a symbol of Chicago

For a city on the shores of one of the country's largest sources of fresh water, Chicago has a surprisingly long history with poor drinking water. The quality was so bad, in fact, that it caused many outbreaks of disease, a pattern that forced the city to depend on bottled liquids. All that began to change, though, on March 25, 1867, when the city broke ground for the new water tower at Michigan and Chicago avenues, and two years later, the **Chicago Water Tower and Pumping Station** was up and running, a boon for the city's health.

Though the Water Tower survived the devastating 1871 fire, its odd-looking appearance failed to impress Oscar Wilde, who visited Chicago in 1882 and described the tower as a "castellated monstrosity with pepper boxes stuck all over it." Though its looks have hardly improved over the years, and despite the efforts of local groups to replace it with more modern buildings, the homely tower has steadfastly held its ground – testament perhaps to its enduring legacy.

The Chicago Water Tower and Pumping Station

Chicago's past and present collide at the intersection of Michigan Avenue and Pearson Street, where the groundbreaking vertical mall **Water Tower Place** faces off against one of the last remnants of Old Chicago, the **Chicago Water Tower**. An awkward-looking structure surrounded by low turrets, the tower's limestone cladding withstood the Great Fire that engulfed the rest of downtown, turning the clumsy example of Victorian neo-Gothic into a stirring symbol of Chicago's survival.

Topped by a 100-foot tower that resembles a thick-stemmed tulip, the Water Tower was built in 1869 to house a standpipe that equalized the pressure of water from the **Pumping Station** across the street (see box above). Both were part of major sanitation projects undertaken by the city to supply safe drinking water to its swelling population, plans that centered on an ambitious tunnel that was built under Lake Michigan to tap into deeper, cleaner waters far from shore.

Today, the tiny interior of the Water Tower houses temporary photo exhibitions: you're more likely to dawdle in the grassy plaza to eat a sandwich or watch the endless stream of eager street performers. Though there is no public access to its pumping equipment, still in operation, the Pumping Station houses the **Chicago Water Works Visitor Center** (ⓣ1-877/CHICAGO, ⓦwww.choosechicago.com), whose knowledgeable staff can provide tons of maps and brochures, plus details on the latest cultural events in Near North. A recent addition to the building is a 270-seat theater that hosts productions by the Lookingglass Theatre Company (ⓣ312/337-0665, ⓦwww.lookingglasstheatre.org), an edgy group that boasts *Friends* star David Schwimmer as a founder and active member, and whose past productions include 2005's *Lookingglass Alice*, a twisted take on the Lewis Carroll classic, and the original staging of *Metamorphoses*, Mary Zimmerman's gorgeous 2002 Tony Award–winning play performed in and around a pool of water onstage.

Streeterville

Stretching north of the river and east of the Magnificent Mile to the lake, **Streeterville** was hardly a place to visit until the city revamped **Navy Pier** in 1995, creating the city's largest amusement park and one of its top attractions. The arrival of the **Museum of Contemporary Art** a year later helped

George Wellington Streeter

More than any Chicago neighborhood, Streeterville had a shaky start. The land east of Michigan Avenue and north of the Chicago River came into being through a bizarre set of circumstances. On July 11, 1886, **George Wellington Streeter**, a captain and a spitfire of a man, ran his makeshift boat aground on a sandbar some four hundred feet offshore of today's Streeterville. After obtaining permission from one of the landowners to let him keep his boat there, he persuaded city contractors to dump refuse around his boat. In a short time, the rubbish had filled in the space between his boat and shore and could be called "land," a circumstance that Streeter would use to great advantage. He declared this previously nonexistent plot of over a hundred acres the "Free District of Lake Michigan," a territory independent of both Chicago and neighboring Illinois, and then sold chunks of it to unscrupulous buyers. For the next three decades, Streeter guarded this illegal shanty area with dubious legal claims and a shotgun. Somehow he survived through all of this, but the courts eventually overruled him in 1918, paving the way for development to begin in earnest west of his plot.

raise the neighborhood's profile a notch, and nowadays even locals are likely to venture here for the swanky hotel bars and restaurants that dot the landscape. The **lakefront** (see p.9) makes for a pleasant stroll or a bike ride; the bike path running between Oak Street Beach and Olive Park (just north of Navy Pier) is accessible through tunnels at Oak Street, Chicago Avenue, Ontario Street, and Ohio Street.

The Museum of Contemporary Art

Everything you might imagine that's provocative, offbeat, seductive, and divisive, is at the **Museum of Contemporary Art (MCA)**, 220 E Chicago Ave (Tues 10am–8pm, Wed–Sun 10am–5pm; suggested donation $10, students and seniors $6, free 5–8pm on Tues; ⓣ312/280-2660, ⓦwww.mcachicago.org). This squat, boxy building lurking behind the Water Pumping Station was designed by German architect Josef Paul Kleihues and cost almost $50 million. The dominant feature of its facade is the steep, sweeping steps, which lead you to the main entrance on the second floor.

The museum is on four levels: the first floor is home to the shop and auditorium, while the main, second floor is where temporary exhibitions take place. Thanks to the museum's commitment to emerging artists, you'll often find intriguing unknowns showing alongside names like Andy Warhol and Dan Flavin. But whether you enjoy the temporary exhibits or not, you're apt to find plenty of interest on the upper two floors, where a rotating selection of the permanent collection is on display.

Modern-art stalwarts like Jasper Johns, Sol LeWitt, and even René Magritte are represented in the museum's holdings, as are the modernist mobiles of **Alexander Calder**; a local art collector has lent the museum fifteen of his bobbing, abstract sculptures on indefinite loan, among them the monochromatic *Black 17 Dots* and *The Ghost*, especially eye-catching given the sculptor's penchant for using rainbow colors. **Jenny Holzer**'s scrolling LED signs are mesmerizing, as are **Bruce Nauman**'s flashing neon slogans like *Life Death Love Hate Pleasure Pain*. Contemporary art's king of kitsch, **Jeff Koons**, is also well represented – look for his shiny chrome *Rabbit* – as is the deadpan work of minimalist **Donald Judd**, who specializes in step-like sculptures.

Chicago architecture

In an architectural prize-fight between America's biggest cities, there's little question that Chicago would win by a knockout, thanks to the sheer volume and variety of its grand buildings. Wandering around the labyrinth of downtown Chicago will leave you feeling dizzy, yet you'll soon be able to pick out distinctive landmarks. Unique structures ranging from the ancient-looking Water Tower to the sleek and futuristic IBM Building will give you an idea of the spectrum of architectural genius that has been cultivated here over the past 150 years.

The devastation of the Great Fire of 1871 stirred the dreams of every megalomaniac architect, and visionary and ambitious men flocked from around the world for the unlimited opportunities for innovation it afforded. The story of Chicago's buildings since the Great Fire – and of its leading role in world architecture – centers mainly on William Le Baron Jenney, Louis Sullivan, Frank Lloyd Wright, and Mies van der Rohe, although plenty of others were on hand to contribute. See the History section, p.279–280 for short bios and career highlights of each.

Carson Pirie Scott

Form follows function: **the Chicago School**

After the fire, Chicago was in need of rebuilding and willing to try out fresh designs to reflect the resilient spirit of its people. The revolutionary style it adopted became known, unsurprisingly, as **the Chicago School of architecture** and was helmed by Jenney, the "father of the modern skyscraper," who contributed the **Manhattan Building** to the urban skyline emerging in the Loop. Jenney was the first to employ a steel frame in the construction of his buildings, instead of heavy masonry.

While Jenney is considered the founder of the Chicago school, it was Louis Sullivan, one of his mentees, who single-handedly ushered in a new era of architecture under his motto "form follows function." Sullivan elaborated on Jenney's steel frame, adapting it to taller structures with more windows, which allowed for better interior lighting. Unlike his more commercially minded peers, Sullivan evinced a love of decoration, nature motifs, and intricate (and costly) scrollwork, best exemplified by the building he designed to house the **Carson Pirie Scott department store**.

Window dressing

The Chicago School of architecture is marked by its innovative window treatments that fused form with function. Oriel windows are a type of bay window that run the height of a structure to emphasize its verticalness, while Chicago windows contain three sections: a huge, fixed central pane and two smaller sashes on either side to allow more control of the heating and cooling of the building. Excellent examples of Chicago School windows are the Fisher Building and the Marquette Building.

Fisher Building (right)

Frank Lloyd Wright: **the Prairie style**

While his predecessors looked skyward **Frank Lloyd Wright** turned to the wide, flat grasslands and farm fields for inspiration, eventually inventing the **Prairie style**. Wright's low, horizontal buildings are nothing if not functional, with open interiors, long stretches of windows, and a connection to their surroundings, conjoining structure with nature, indoor with outdoor.

There are a clutch of Wright homes in **Oak Park**, including his home and studio, but the masterpiece of this movement is the **Robie House** (1910), in Hyde Park; its use of natural stone, low-pitched roofs, open floorplans, and extensive overhangs is quintessential Wright.

Robie House

Less is more: **the International style**

Until the 1938 arrival of German émigré **Mies van der Rohe**, Chicago's downtown was a hodgepodge of architectural styles ranging from the Neo-Gothic Tribune Tower to the Art Deco Board of Trade. Van der Rohe cultivated his groundbreaking new **International style**, which championed the modernist ideals of the first Chicago school and took them a step further, eliminating all historical references and ornamentation. Instead, he celebrated neutral, rectilinear forms of glass and steel. Two of Mies' most notable buildings are the **IBM Building** (1971), completed two years after his death, and **860-880 Lake Shore Drive** (1951), the first building to use an all glass and steel curtain wall – this would later be a trademark of the modern skyscraper.

Mies still looms large over Chicago, notably in the firm of **Skidmore, Owings & Merrill**, whose Miesian designs include the **John Hancock Building**. In contrast, the work of **Helmut Jahn**, who aggressively rejects Mies principles in favor of whimsical, oddball buildings like the **James R. Thompson Center**.

IBM Building

Chicago's best skyscrapers

◀ The Monadnock Building, the Loop (1893)
Look closely and you'll see how the tallest masonry building in the city captures the evolving architectural style of the times. The north half was constructed in the old style with a base of load-bearing, six-foot thick brick walls; the south portion is an essentially modern skyscraper with a steel skeleton and wide windows.

▶ The Reliance Building, the Loop (1895)
Precursor of the modern skyscraper, this fourteen-story steel-and-glass structure features narrow strips of ornately decorated terracotta and an almost entirely glass facade that makes the building seem as if it's floating.

◀ The Tribune Tower, Near North (1925)
Hard to believe this majestic Gothic building, headquarters of the *Chicago Tribune* newspaper, was modeled after Rouen Cathedral. Note the flying buttresses at its tower, which reaches a height of approximately 463 feet.

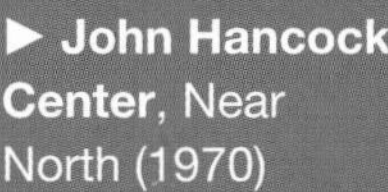

▶ John Hancock Center, Near North (1970)
This 100-story black steel frame building features exterior steel columns braced by innovative x-shaped steel diagonals, which effectively distribute windforce on all sides – a major concern as the buildings grew taller and the windstreams stronger.

The Sears Tower, the Loop (1973)
Granddaddy of them all, the sleek Sears Tower is the third largest building in the world. It's actually comprised of nine skyscrapers wrapped into one, each framed with a steel tube that joins with the others enabling the massive building to withstand high winds.

As for photography, the museum boasts an impressively wide-ranging collection of portraits by **Cindy Sherman** (in fact, MCA also owns a painting of Sherman by **Chuck Close**, in his customary passport-photo style) and works by the controversial **Andres Serrano** – the MCA has some of his *Morgue* series, in which deceased subjects are identified not by name but by the manner of death.

The chic on-site café, **Puck's at the MCA**, is run by ubiquitous restaurateur Wolfgang Puck; it's best visited in summer when there's outdoor seating on the secluded terrace.

Navy Pier

Navy Pier, located at E Grand Avenue, at the end of E Ohio Street, may be Chicago's top tourist attraction, and is certainly family-friendly, but it has the feel of commercialism gone amok – everything in sight is sponsored to within an inch of its life. Navy Pier could also be anywhere – aside from one museum, which touts its local connection, this pier makes little reference to its hometown or its history. Built as Municipal Pier No. 2 in 1916 under Burnham's Chicago plan (see box, p.281), it was quickly appropriated during World War I by the Navy, for which it was renamed in 1927. Navy Pier then served various civil and military purposes until the city decided to smarten up the ramshackle structure in the 1970s, and pumped massive investment into its refurbishment; it opened in its current incarnation in 1995. Note that it's fairly confusing to get around, thanks to the enormous concrete garage and convention center in its mid-section: stop at the information desk as soon as you enter through the main western doors and grab a **free map** – you'll need it.

Navy Pier practicalities

Navy Pier hours are Nov–May, Mon–Thurs 10am–8pm, Fri & Sat 10am–10pm, Sun 10am–7pm; June–Aug, Mon–Thurs & Sun 10am–10pm, Fri & Sat 10am–midnight; Sept & Oct, Mon–Thurs 10am–9pm, Fri & Sat 10am–11pm, Sun 10am–7pm. Admission to the park is free, but some attractions charge a fee. For further details, contact ⓣ312/595-PIER or 1-800/595-PIER or visit ⓦwwwnavypier.com.

Getting there and around

Getting to Navy Pier on **public transportation** is easy. Six bus lines stop at the pier's front entrance: #29 along State Street, #65 along Grand Avenue, #56 along Milwaukee Avenue, #66 along Chicago Avenue, and #120 and #121 from the Northwestern and Union Metra train stations, respectively.

There's also a convenient **free trolley** that runs between State Street and the pier (along Grand Avenue and Illinois Street) every fifteen minutes (Mon–Thurs 10am–9pm, Fri & Sat 10am–11pm, Sun 10am–8pm). Walking to Navy Pier is by no means cumbersome, but the free trolley will save you at least fifteen minutes.

If you're driving to Navy Pier, park at one of the three **parking garages** ($9.50 per hour), or if they're full, head to the additional parking spaces just west of Lake Shore Drive.

On the boardwalk, you'll pass by any number of **tour boat companies**: the Shoreline Sightseeing Co runs thirty-minute cruises along the lakeshore year-round ($12; weather permitting), while the more luxury-minded Odyssey Cruises runs two- to three-hour lake cruises year-round, starting from $39 (with brunch, lunch, or dinner, $50–$84). If you'd rather get around on your own steam, **Bike Chicago** rents just about anything with wheels and runs free lakefront tours. For contact details for these outlets, see p.250.

△ The Water Tower

Pier attractions

From the info desk, you can access the popular **Chicago Children's Museum** (Mon, Tues, Wed & Fri 10am–5pm, Thurs & Sat 10am–8pm; $7, free to 12 months and under; ⓣ312/527-1000, ⓦwww.childrensmuseumchicago.org). Children will enjoy this place, but it's less interesting for the older ones. Exhibits include a large archeology pit, where would-be fossil hunters can dig for treasure; the city of Chicago, resized for toddlers, so little ones can drive a local bus; and even a fourteen-foot-high model of the Sears Tower made from more than 50,000 Lego bricks.

More enjoyable for adults is the **Crystal Gardens**, a free giant hothouse on the upper level of the complex that's filled with exotic plants, as well as gravity-defying fountains that shoot semicircles of water into the air. It's pleasant enough and a good place for a picnic, but there's nothing especially compelling or unusual about any of the exhibits.

The Pier's main attraction, **Pier Park**, is a mini–amusement park further east of the Crystal Gardens. It's here that you'll find the soaring, 148-foot **Ferris wheel** (open during pier hours, weather permitting; $4), which offers great views of downtown – though it adds nothing much if you've already checked out the John Hancock Building on N Michigan Avenue(see p.78). Close by, there's an **old-fashioned carousel**, aimed at very young kids, with painted horses and the like (open weather permitting; $3).

Centrally located adjacent to the Pier's parking lot, the **Chicago Shakespeare Theater** (ⓣ312/595-5600 or 5635, ⓦwww.chicagoshakes.com) was ingeniously designed by its architects to host two terrific, intimate venues. The larger, with five hundred seats, has a thrust stage designed to replicate an Elizabethan setup, while the smaller studio space upstairs is a flexible venue that can accommodate up to two hundred. For further details, see "Performing arts and film," p.227.

Tiring as it may be, don't give up walking yet – by far the best attraction on Navy Pier is unceremoniously stuck back in the corridors on the southern side of the two Exhibition Halls. The free **Smith Museum of Stained Glass** (opening hours the same as Navy Pier; for tour information, call ⓣ312/595-5024) is an 800-foot-long gallery space that displays gorgeous stained-glass panels dating from 1870 to present day, grouped into four styles: Victorian, Modern, Prairier, and Contemporary. You'll be able to guess the windows' original purpose and location by the subject matter – in fact, many of those on display were produced and installed locally. Look for Louis Sullivan's octagonal ceiling panels, rescued from the original Chicago Stock Exchange building before it was demolished, and Frank Lloyd Wright's *Avery Coonley Pool House Window*; it comes from the home that Wright considered the most successful of his Prairie designs. Other notable pieces include the darkly erotic and dreamlike *Queen of the Elves* by Marie Herndl and the startlingly modern *Round Headed Window* from a local church. The latter, produced in 1887, has poppy aquamarine circles ringed with honey and caramel rectangles that wouldn't look out of place in today's trendier interior-design magazines.

Much of what's on offer at Navy Pier changes seasonally – in summer, for instance, check the website or call for details on outdoor concerts at the **Skyline Stage**; while in winter, there's a free **skating rink** in Navy Pier Park. Otherwise, for our pick of the stores, bars, and restaurants, see "Shopping," p.260, "Drinking," p.204, and "Eating," p.180.

River North

The once industrial wasteland of **River North**, due west of Streeterville on the other side of Michigan Avenue, has seen its fortunes rise ever since the 1970s, when artists first recognized affordable studio space in its abandoned warehouses and factories. The area around Michigan Avenue is heavily commercial, but you need only walk a few blocks further west to where the **art galleries** take over and the crowds almost disappear. In the past fifteen years, the area has thrived, and nearly all of the streets – Chicago, Kinzie, and Illinois notable among them – have benefited from the artistic spillover: you'll find everything here from art-supply stores and antique furniture shops to trendy restaurants, while the preponderance of velvet-rope clubs turns the area after sundown into a buzzing nightlife scene.

The Merchandise Mart

Though sights are thin on the ground, there are a few buildings worth noting along the north bank of the river. The monumental **Merchandise Mart**, 300 N Wells St at N Orleans Street (tours Mon & Fri 1pm; 90min; ☎312/527-7762; call ahead to confirm times), houses six hundred private showrooms of home furnishings, plus a culinary school, two floors of mall shops, and a food court that are all open to the public. Skip the building tour unless you're looking for interior design inspiration, as the Mart is most impressive from the outside, where you can fully appreciate its enormity. With 4.2 million square feet of space, it's the largest building in terms of floor area in the country besides the Pentagon and even has its own zip code (60654). It was constructed for Marshall Field in 1931 as a showroom and administrative headquarters. When the department store faced tough economic times after World War II, Kennedy patriarch Joe – who knew a good bargain when he saw one – snapped up the building for a fraction of its value simply by paying its back taxes. (Interestingly, the Mart is still owned by the Kennedys today and is the source of much of their wealth.) Joe's unmistakable – if oddball – 1953 addition to the building was the **row of eight bronze busts** on marble pillars at the Mart's main entrance, grandly titled "the Merchandise Mart Hall of Fame" and paying tribute to the patron saints of shopping, including F.W. Woolworth, Edward A. Filene, and, of course, Marshall Field himself.

Marina City, the IBM Building, and around

Walking three blocks east to Dearborn Street, you'll see the twin corncob towers of **Marina City** (entrance at 300 N State St), a monument to the combined power of late-1960s paranoia and the Chicago winter. Bertrand Goldberg designed the complex to be completely self-contained, offering everything you could need in your life (doctor, dentist, mall, even an undertaker) under one roof: in theory, you could be born, live, and die here without ever leaving the building. Since most residents do need to get out and about once in a while, the bottom twenty stories are used as parking garages: the cars peeking out at the edge of each floor look surreal and not altogether secured hundreds of feet high in the air. Most visitors to the city, though, will only stop by to check out the *House of Blues* nightclub (see Chapter 16, "Live music and clubs"), the adjacent *House of Blues Hotel*, or the wine restaurant *Bin 36*, all of which opened here as part of a massive modernization program in the late 1990s.

In contrast to the curvy Marina Towers, the **IBM Building** looming up behind them at 330 N Wabash Ave seems positively funereal. The near-black monolith was Mies van der Rohe's last American commission, and a variation of his seminal curtain-wall skyscraper – for better or for worse, the source of lesser imitations. You can ponder the building's aesthetic merits in the open forecourt at its base.

After years of discussions, planning, and back and forth between city officials and real-estate magnate Donald Trump, construction has finally begun on **Trump International Hotel & Tower** (Ⓦwww.trumpchicago.com), the 92-story, 1360-foot, $750 million hotel and residence complex on the north

The River North gallery district

River North's **gallery district** doesn't generate quite the excitement that it did during its heyday in the 1980s, now that some galleries have had to pack up and move to cheaper neighborhoods, but it still accounts for a sizeable chunk of the city's art scene, notably around Huron, Superior, and Wells Street, where you'll find some well-established places.

Galleries usually host receptions for new shows on Friday evenings (5–8pm), and there are often plenty of Chicago glitterati on hand for great people-watching. Two openings are worth noting: the second or third Friday in September kicks off the **Fall Gallery Season**, while on the second Friday in January, all of the galleries have coinciding openings. For information on current events and occasional free trolleys that run between the River North galleries and the Michigan Avenue museums, pick up a copy of the free Chicago Gallery News, available from most hotels and galleries. For additional gallery reviews, see chapter 18,"Galleries,".

side of the river just east of the IBM Building where the Chicago Sun-Times Building once stood. The chunky, low-lying (and much reviled) headquarters of the *Sun-Times* was demolished in early 2005 to make way for Donald's new tower, which, when finished in 2008, will stand as the city's (and the nation's) second-tallest building after the Sears Tower. The building will be not only tall, but truly swanky, with a 60,000-square-foot health club, and in-home dining and catering services.

Back on State Street, heading north for eight blocks or so will bring you to the **Holy Name Cathedral**, 735 N State St (tour information ☎312/787-8040), the seat of the Roman Catholic Archdiocese of Chicago. Built in 1875 to replace the original brick structure that was destroyed in the Great Fire, the grand, Gothic Revival church was designed by Patrick Charles Keely, who, by that time, had a remarkable six hundred churches and sixteen cathedrals under his belt. The interior of the church features several striking examples of contemporary spiritual art, from the sculpted resurrection crucifix suspended from the ceiling to the bronze-cast Stations of the Cross on the walls of the nave. Note the red decorations hanging high above the sanctuary – cardinals' hats (*galeros*), each one representing one of the city's past cardinals.

4

The Gold Coast and Old Town

At the northern end of the retail explosion of Michigan Avenue, sits the hushed, moneyed enclave, the **GOLD COAST**. It's one of the few snooty places you'll find in staunchly blue-collar Chicago, and for that reason alone seems almost refreshing – the quiet backstreets make a great haven from the crowds and noise of Near North. Although there's little to do in the area other than shop, eat, and drink, **Astor Street** is compelling for its collection of eye-popping mansions (the swankiest are at its northern end). It's also worth spending a little time at the chic boutiques along **Oak Street**.

Though just as residential, adjacent **OLD TOWN** is livelier and more down-to-earth, a modestly charming area of historic wooden homes and hip restaurants and shops. Casual visitors are most likely to take in a play at one of Chicago's most prestigious theatrical venues, the **Steppenwolf Theatre**, or a show at the legendary comedy club **Second City**. To the south and west of this neighborhood are the **Cabrini Green** public-housing projects, an area notorious for violence and gang activity that is best avoided.

Some history

Not long after the Great Fire, department-store magnate **Potter Palmer** and trendsetting wife **Bertha** made headlines in 1882 when they abandoned their swanky neighbors on the South Side to build a mansion in the middle of nowhere – on the site of the tower block at 1350 N Lake Shore Drive (sadly, the Palmers' house was demolished in 1950). Soon, their fashionable friends followed and the neighborhood now known as the Gold Coast gained the favored standing it enjoys today: you can still see the mansions built by the likes of **John Jacob Astor** more than a hundred years ago, even if they're being crowded out by row upon row of high-rise, door-manned buildings.

The Fire transformed Old Town, too, which was nothing but pasture for local cows until the blaze. Afterwards, thousands of German immigrants, displaced from their downtown homes, began to arrive, and the nickname "German Broadway" soon stuck. It was never a wealthy place – as is clear from the modest houses everywhere – but the government's decision in the 1950s to sweep away a run-down section in southwestern Old Town, proved to have

EATING

Ashkenaz Delicatessan	20
Adobo Grill	3
Dinotto Ristorante	5
Edwardo's Natural Pizza	15
Gibson's	25
Hugo's Frog Bar and Fish House	27
Kamehachi of Tokyo	7
Le Colonial	28
Morton's of Chicago	24
Oak Street Bistro	10
Old Jerusalem	8
Original Pancake House	23
Pump Room	B
Salpicón	9
Topo Gigio Ristorante	6
Twin Anchors	2
Vinci	1

DRINKING

Bella Lounge	14
Butch McGuire's	18
Coq d'Or	11
The Leg Room	19
Melvin B's Truckstop	21
Mother's	16
Old Town Ale House	4
P.J. Clarke's	17
Signature Room	12
Tavern on Rush	22
Whiskey Bar and Grill	26
Zebra Lounge	13

ACCOMMODATION

The Gold Coast Guest House	C
Hotel Indigo	D
Old Town Chicago B & B	A
Omni Ambassador East Hotel	B

dire consequences. The city's misguided plans for housing projects in **Cabrini Green** turned the area, almost overnight, into a violent no-go zone and caused many residents to flee to the suburbs. The resulting plummeting rents in Old Town attracted hippies and their hangers-on, who created a mini Haight-Ashbury in the late 1960s. Ironically, like their West Coast counterparts, they inadvertently started the process of gentrification that has peaked, along with the rents, here (except for the corner around Cabrini Green) – some of the highest in the city.

The Gold Coast

Bounded by Chicago Avenue, North Avenue, Lake Shore Drive, and LaSalle Street, the **Gold Coast** is focused during the day around the stylish boutiques along **Oak Street** and the eponymous beach on the lake – Chicago's most central (and style-conscious) patch of sand. After dark, the summertime crowds can be found in the myriad bars (see p.209 for reviews) of **Rush and Division streets**, where hordes of thirty-something singles congregate.

Above Division Street, the Gold Coast enters its most exclusive stretch; a stroll along Dearborn Street, State Street, and N Astor Street towards Lincoln Park will take you past some of the city's most palatial digs, like the elegant Philip B. Maher–designed Art Deco high-rise at **1260 N Astor St**, once home to famous Chicago names such as Potter Palmer II, Robert Hall McCormick III, and Morton Salt Company chairman Sterling Morton.

Getting here is easy by train or bus. Take the Red Line to Clark/Division and walk east towards the lake, or hop on the #151 bus to Division; head north on State to explore the neighborhood's mansions, or south to hit the commercial district at Oak Street.

Oak Street and around

On the border between Near North (see p.74) and the Gold Coast, you'll find Chicago's swankiest shopping strip, **Oak Street** – a designer row filled with ultra-chic shops like Prada and Jil Sander as well as salons that cater to the local ladies who lunch. After the Great Fire, when the city's prominent families moved north, Oak Street became the center of this wealthy new neighborhood and quickly became known for the best shopping in the city. While the biggest-name boutiques are on Oak, the district has spread to neighboring Rush, Bellevue, and Cedar streets, with countless spas and boutiques. (For our pick of the shops here, see "Shopping," p.260.)

At its eastern reaches, you'll find the **Oak Street Beach**, a small stretch of sand that's packed on summer weekends with residents from the high-rise condos along Lake Shore Drive. The beach evolved when this area was a resort – the famed **Drake Hotel** (for review, see p.174) opened in 1920 as a beachfront property, where guests could wander from the changing rooms on the arcade level out onto the sands. Since the construction of Lake Shore Drive, however, the beach has been cut off from the *Drake* and other hotels; it's now reachable by a pedestrian tunnel beneath the road. Expect to share the sand here with women who bought their expensive bikinis on Oak Street a few blocks to the west. There are full facilities by the water, including volleyball courts and the **Oak Street Beachstro** (May–Sept Mon–Fri 11am–9.30pm, Sat & Sun 8am–9:30pm; ☎312/915-4100), a restaurant right on the beach across from the *Drake* that offers a casual (albeit overpriced) menu along with stellar lake and skyline views.

If you find the neighborhood's vanity a tad oppressive, there's relief nearby at the Romanesque **Newberry Library**, 60 W Walton St (Tues–Thurs 10am–6pm; Fri & Sat 9am–5pm, except before a Monday holiday; free tours Thurs 3pm, Sat 10.30am; ☎312/943-9090, Ⓦwww.newberry.org). This sumptuously appointed research library, whose wide-ranging collection covers Western Europe and the Americas from the Middle Ages, includes a few oddities as well, such as the only bilingual text of *Popol Vuh*, the legend of an ancient Guatemalan tribe written down in 1515. The library often puts on exhibitions in the downstairs galleries, where you can linger over artifacts, photographs, and paintings from its collection.

Across from the library, **Washington Square Park** shows little sign of its colorful past. Known as "Bughouse Square" from the 1910s–1960s for the neighboring flophouses, the park became a famous public forum where everyone from established authors and editors to anarchists, struggling artists, hack writers, and street performers had their say on the soapboxes. The spirit of the soapboxers lives on in the Newberry Library's annual "Bughouse Square Debates," held every summer in conjunction with the library's book sale. (One lesser-mentioned, more sinister detail about the park's history: in the 1960s and 1970s, the park was a late-night cruising area for homosexuals, male prostitutes, and drug dealers; in 1978, it was revealed that several victims of the serial killer John Wayne Gacy were young men he had met in the park.)

The street life picks up by several notches a couple of blocks west on **Rush Street**, a touristy strip of landmark restaurants, bars, and shops, before reaching its culmination (or low point, depending on your view) with the testosterone-charged revelry of **Division Street**, home to a string of raucous bars vying for attention, notably *Mothers* and *Butch McGuire's* (for reviews of these and other bars in the area, see "Drinking," p.209).

North of Division Street

Wander the side streets – Astor, Dearborn, and State in particular – to take in the grandeur of one of Chicago's wealthiest and most desirable neighborhoods, the area north of Division Street. The **Three Arts Club**, 1300 N Dearborn St (ⓣ312/944-6250, ⓦwww.threearts.org), is one of the area's most accessible buildings, and a good place to start a stroll. Founded in 1912 by a group of socially conscious women, including Jane Addams (see p.134), the residence has housed women studying the arts since it first opened in 1912 (and still does), and the hefty brick and terracotta design has artsy touches, like the colorful Byzantine-style mosaics in the arches above the main entrance (representing painting, music, and drama) and classical sculpture set in the walls (note the replicas of the Jean Goujon panels of the *Fontaine des Innocents* in Paris). The pretty courtyard, where you can sit for a spell, hosts performances and art exhibits throughout the year. Note: A massive renovation and restoration project is set to begin in July 2006 with the building scheduled for reopening (complete with gallery space and a 110-seat theater) in September of 2007.

If you're dressed the part, head a block east to the **Pump Room**, in the *Ambassador East Hotel*, 1301 N State Parkway (ⓣ312/266-0360, ⓦwww.pumproom.com), for a taste of old-fashioned glamour. While the restaurant milks its movie-star associations for all they're worth – the foyer is covered with photos of celebrity patrons, from Humphrey Bogart and Frank Sinatra to Lauren Bacall and Elizabeth Taylor – it's still a fun place to linger over a drink and soak up the swank atmosphere.

Further up N State Parkway, the unassuming red-brick mansion at no. 1340 was once the famed **Playboy Mansion**, home and office of publisher and Chicago native Hugh Hefner, whose lavish parties for the glitterati are renowned. Hefner is long gone from here (he moved out in the early 1970s) as is the door plate inscribed "*Si non oscillas, noli tintinnare*" ("If you don't swing, don't ring"), and the mansion has since been converted into million-dollar apartments.

Charnley-Persky House and around

From the Playboy Mansion, walk a block north to W Schiller Street and take a right to N Astor Street, and you'll arrive at the **Charnley-Persky House** at no. 1365, an austere three-story building of brick and limestone – easily identified by the wooden-columned balcony on the second floor – considered a forerunner of modern residential architecture. Louis Sullivan and his then assistant Frank Lloyd Wright built the house between 1891 and 1892, adopting the low-lying, symmetrical style that would later become the hallmark of Wright's Prairie School architecture (see "Architecture" color insert) and herald the move away from Victorian design trends. Inside, the stairwell and mantelpieces feature beautifully carved woodwork, while the entrance is a skylit atrium paneled in burnished oak. The Society of Architectural Historians (1365 N Astor St ⓣ312/573-1365, ⓦwww.sah.org) runs **free tours** on Wednesday at noon and on Saturday at 10am, with an additional tour offered from April to November on Saturday at 1pm. The latter includes a guided walk along Astor Street and a visit to the nearby **Madlener House**, the work of architect Richard E. Schmidt and designer Hugh M. G. Garden.

A few blocks to the northeast at 1524 N Lake Shore Drive is one of the city's quirkier sights: the hidden gem, **International Museum of Surgical Science** (May–Sept: Tues–Sun 10am–4pm; Oct–April: Tues–Sat 10am–4pm; $6, students/seniors $3; tours included with admission Sat 2pm; ⓣ312/642-6502, ⓦwww.imss.org). Set in an historic 1917 mansion modeled after a chateau on the grounds of Versailles, the museum boasts a fascinating collection of 22 galleries devoted to the history of surgery around the world, plus a turn-of-the-century apothecary shop and even a polio exhibit featuring a rare working iron-lung from the mid-twentieth century.

A couple blocks west of here, just below Lincoln Park, the conspicuous octagonal tower, nineteen chimneys, and numerous gables, turrets, and dormers mark the Queen Anne–style red-brick Roman Catholic **Archbishop's Residence** at 1555 N State Parkway. The mansion was built in 1880 on the former site of a cemetery; soon after, the archdiocese sold off the surrounding plots of land to wealthy Chicago families, who proceeded to construct their dream homes in the neighborhood.

Old Town

Spreading west of LaSalle Street to North Avenue, **Old Town** has a much more lived-in look than does the dandified Gold Coast. The neighborhood boasts a broad ethnic and cultural mix. Many of the early, more-established immigrants fled to the suburbs during the post–World War II boom years; they were replaced by blacks and Italians, who moved into rooming houses and, later, the Cabrini Green housing projects (see box). While the neighborhood's refurbished century-old row houses and workers' cottages are prime real-estate today for yuppies, in the 1970s its then-shabby housing stock and derelict factories attracted a variety of creative types, from hippies to aspiring comedians and actors. Your best base for exploring is **Wells Street**, the main drag: note that, even forty years after the hippies landed in and livened up the neighborhood, Old Town still has its share of sketchy streets. Though Wells Street shows no signs of its hippie past, at least one survivor – the *Second City* comedy club – is still going strong. The rest of the neighborhood, which has benefited from the gentrification of neighboring Lincoln Park, is now crammed with a lively mix of bars, galleries, and barbecue joints, and makes for a diverting afternoon's wander.

Summertime sees Old Town at its liveliest, particularly during the neighborhood's **Old Town Art Fair**, a nearly 60-year-old fest held the second full weekend in June that's actually more a fun excuse to mingle with the crowds than for serious art buying (see p.257).

To **get here** take the Brown Line El train to Sedgwick, turn left out of the station, and turn right at North Avenue to Wells Street. It's worth staying on these main thoroughfares of Wells and North, especially at night, and to skip anywhere close to Cabrini Green (south and west of the train stop around Division Street between Sedgwick and Larrabee) entirely.

Wells Street and the Old Town Triangle

Old Town has little in the way of cultural sights, but the neighborhood's streets – Wells, Eugenie, and Willow in particular – are still worth exploring for their rows of Victorian homes and offbeat shops. Especially noteworthy on Wells is the **House of Glunz**, 1206 N Wells St, a family-owned wine shop with an eclectic selection, dating to 1888.

Farther up Wells Street above North Avenue begins the **Old Town Triangle**, a quaint little section of late nineteenth-century homes that have been preserved (to varying degrees of authenticity) thanks to an urban-renewal project in the 1940s to protect the district's narrow streets and distinctive architecture. Built in the years immediately following the Great Fire, these "workers' cottages" were built mostly in wood and designed with front-facing gable roofs, rectangular floor plans, and little ornamentation. Since then, property values have climbed precipitously with the onslaught of gentrification, which has brought with it restaurants, galleries, and shops.

The neighborhood's chief claim to fame, however, is the famed **Second City comedy club**, 1616 N Wells St, which has been turning out stars since its

Cabrini Green

Just a mile due west of the Gold Coast, roughly bordered by Division, Halsted, North, and Larrabee, the **Cabrini Green housing projects** have become synonymous in America with urban blight and gang violence – from the shooting of two police officers by a sniper in 1970 to the 1997 case of Girl X, a 9-year-old who was raped, beaten, poisoned, and left for dead in a stairwell (she survived).

Seventy-acre Cabrini Green is one of the saddest examples of misguided post-war urban planning, driven by the chronic housing shortage when returning WWII veterans and new immigrants overwhelmed the city's housing market. Originally opened in 1943, the planned complex included suburban-style row houses, with small, neat yards and private entrances. For a while Cabrini Green seemed to be a success, providing affordable housing for low-income residents, but migration from the Deep South continued, and soon city housing was again under strain. In 1958, the Chicago Housing Authority added the Cabrini Extension, fifteen tower blocks nicknamed "The Reds" (after their color) and designed to house seven thousand people, and eight more high-rises were added the following year – the William Green Homes, or "The Whites." Soon, however, like so many other high-rise public-housing projects, the area spiralled into decay, with frequent shootings, gang activity and drug deals, arson fires, graffiti-sprayed walls, broken lights and windows, and syringe-littered grounds.

Despite the lurid folklore about Cabrini Green (this is where the Nineties' horror movie *Candyman* was set), it's no myth that the area remains a dangerous, no-go zone, ridden with gangs and drug problems. The city may be trying to encourage development in the area (including a recently built shopping center), but there's absolutely no reason for a casual visitor to Chicago to stray inside.

doors opened in 1959 (see box opposite, p.229). The grizzled **Old Town Ale House,** across the street at 219 W North Ave, sees a share of *Second City* comics at the bar, but it's also a Chicago institution in its own right, a dignified old dive with book-lined shelves, bouffant-haired bartenders, and a motley crew of yuppies, old-timers, artists, and loners. Stop in after seeing *Second City* and you may end up rubbing elbows with the folks you just saw onstage (for review, see p.209).

St Michael's Church

Massive **St Michael's Church**, 1660 N Hudson Ave, rises up nearly 290 feet and marks the center of the old German Catholic community that existed here during the mid-to late 1800s. It was for years the tallest building in Chicago, even after the 1871 fire that left only the charred walls and belltower standing. Built in its place in 1873, the new church is a handsome example of the Romanesque style, with ornate murals, stained-glass panels, and steeply pitched gables, continues to be a focal point for the community, with several summer and fall festivals (including the popular Oktoberfest in late September) which raise funds to preserve the building.

△ St. Michael's Church

The Second City

"To be, to be... sure beats the shit out of not to be."

John Belushi as Hamlet, *Second City*, Chicago, 1971

John Belushi may not have taken these words to heart, considering his premature end in 1982, but **The Second City improv club** that launched his career is still going strong, enjoying the kind of success expected of a First City venue. Taking its name from a biting *New Yorker* profile about Chicago's second-rung status, the club has been the last word on comedy in Chicago for forty-plus years, delivering a steady stream of quality acts on its two stages. Alan Alda, Alan Arkin, and Ed Asner, followed by the likes of Bill Murray, Gilda Radner, Dan Aykroyd, and John Belushi in the 1970s, Bonnie Hunt, Mike Myers, and Chris Farley in the 1980s, and blossoming comics Amy Sedaris, Tina Fey, and Stephen Colbert in the 1990s all had their start here, many becoming household names on TV's long-running *Saturday Night Live*.

The Second City evolved from a drama troupe formed by students at the University of Chicago (*The Graduate* director Mike Nichols and *Tootsie* writer Elaine May among them), becoming the improvisational Compass Players, who later settled into the club's present location in 1959. Since then, the company has expanded to include two theaters (the mainstage and the adjacent *Second City etc.*), plus training centers in several locations across the continent, including LA, Toronto, Las Vegas, and Detroit, where comedians-in-training are schooled in the unique mix of improvisation and writing of smart, satirical sketches that have become the company's trademark.

Many of the club's alumni have gone on to star in feature films that have capitalized on *The Second City's* humorous blend of satire and slapstick, from *National Lampoon's Animal House* (Belushi) and *The Blues Brothers* (Aykroyd and Belushi) to *Caddyshack* (Murray) and *Wayne's World* (Myers). Though *The Second City* may have lost some of the manic energy of its heyday in the 1980s, it's still the best place to catch improv comedy in Chicago. For a review, see p.229.

5

South Loop and Near South

The lakefront portion of the **South Loop**, which extends south from Congress Parkway to Roosevelt Road, and from Lake Michigan to Halsted Street, is one of the swishest parts of the city. A triumvirate of superb attractions, including the unmissable **Field Museum**, the **Adler Planetarium**, and the **Shedd Aquarium** can all be found here, each housed in beautiful classical buildings that gracefully extend south along lakefront. Known as **Museum Campus**, the area was created in the late 1990s, when Chicago finally rerouted Lake Shore Drive to the west so that culture-hungry tourists wouldn't risk their lives scampering between these attractions. Often referred to as Chicago's front yard, **Grant Park** was built on landfill in the 1920s, a legacy of Daniel Burnham's revolutionary plans for Chicago, and is now used for many of the city's open-air festivals. **Millennium Park**, the lakefront's latest incarnation, was unveiled in July 2004. A glitzy techno-Baroque theme park, opening four years behind schedule, it remains, to some degree, a work in progress.

Much of South Chicago was built on two industries: railroads and printing. In the late nineteenth century the area around S Dearborn Street, between Congress Parkway and Polk Street, hummed to the sound of the printing works, giving rise to the name **Printers Row**. Now, of course, the presses are long gone and the gigantic buildings that once housed them have been largely converted into condos, creating mini, self-contained communities dotted along the strip. In recent years, the South Loop has become a rapidly developing upscale residential zone. It's estimated that from 2004 to 2007 more than two thousand residential units will be built annually, bringing in their wake a burgeoning supply of restaurants and shops to inject nocturnal zeal into an area habitually transformed into an urban wasteland after the exodus of evening rush hour.

The **Near South,** extending from Roosevelt Road to the Stevenson Expressway, is the first clear sign most visitors will see of Chicago's urban problems, thanks to the swaths of unkempt housing projects that begin here and continue on throughout the South Side. Aside from the historic **Prairie Avenue Historical District**, which preserves the palatial mansions of Chicago's former elite, the one safe, intriguing outpost out this way is Chicago's **Chinatown**, filled with markets and restaurants – it's a great place for a cheap meal.

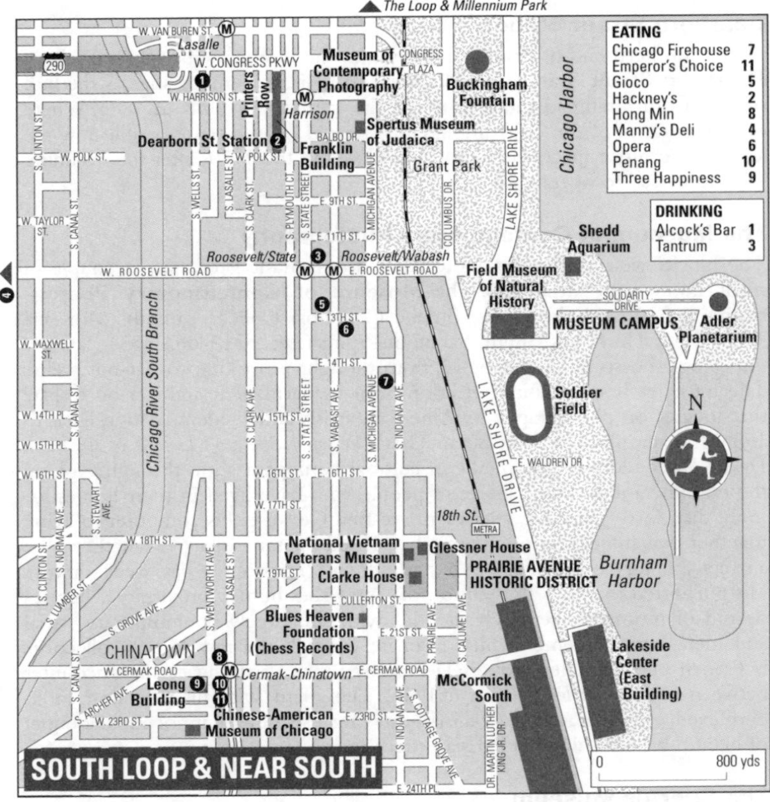

Though the South Loop is safe for visitors, be aware that the area surrounding Chinatown is still rather iffy: take public transportation and you should be fine, but make sure not to wander outside the district's ten or so buzzing blocks.

Printers Row and around

For years an industrial wasteland, **Printers Row** was the last stop on most railroad lines and strewn with derelict warehouses and beer joints left over from its heyday as the center of the Midwestern printing industry. Like most other neighborhoods within a stone's throw of the Loop, however, it has been revitalized with a proliferation of loft apartments flanked by cafés, shops, and restaurants, ranging from hole-in-the-wall stalwarts – a symbol of grittier days gone by – to sleek and chi-chi newcomers like *Orange* and *Opera* (see "Eating" p.192). This short stretch manages to pull in more visitors with each passing year, especially in June during the lively **Printers Row Book Fair** (see p.256).

The area's literary connections are still evident from the terrific **bookstores** here, as well as the numerous publishing offices (for a list of bookstores, see "Shopping," p.260). Look out for the terracotta panels on the **Franklin Building** at 720 S Dearborn. Designed by renowned muralist Oskar Gross they present the history of the publishing industry, which once defined this neighborhood.

Dearborn Street Station

At the southern end of Printers Row stands the Romanesque Revival pile of **Dearborn Street Station**, a monument to Chicago's importance as the hub of the nation's railroad industry when the station was built in 1885. Where once thousands of the city's immigrants stepped off the trains, you'll now see a renovated office space; the station was closed in the 1970s after the declining railroad ceased to operate here.

The Museum of Contemporary Photography

The blocks west of Printers Row, across from Grant Park, have a couple of small, noteworthy attractions. The **Museum of Contemporary Photography** at 600 S Michigan Ave on the Columbia College campus (Mon–Fri 10am–5pm, Thurs until 8pm, Sat noon–5pm; free; ⓣ312/663-5554, ⓦwww.mocp.org) boasts exhibits ranging from thought-provoking to flat-out weird. The museum has a rotating selection from its permanent archives on display that focuses on photography by American artists and residents dating back to 1936. Indiana photographer Susan Carr's *Personal Spaces – Details of American Homes Series* addresses the theme of cultural homogenization through evoking the idiosyncratic personal spaces of people who have lived in their homes for more than forty years. New Jersey native Ben Gest uses his computer to bring together two subjects in one frame that shared the same space – whether it be a street, a library, or a staircase – but at different times of the day, week, or year. His purported theme is the tension that underlies human proximity when it's devoid of intimacy. Seemingly at odds with the largely contemporary social and metaphysical themes which resonate through the rest of the collection, is French photographer Robert Doisneau's more classically comic encounter between *le Garde et les Balloons* (c.1946). The guard, with his rifle aloft, looks perplexed, even threatened, by a man carrying a seemingly innocuous bouquet of helium balloons down a Parisian street.

The Spertus Museum

Some 3500 years of Jewish history, art, tradition, and ethnology is presented a few doors down, where the **Spertus Museum**, 618 S Michigan Ave (Mon–Wed & Sun 10am–5pm, Thurs 10am–7pm (Jan & Feb until 5pm), Fri 10am–3pm; $5, students and seniors $3, Fri free; ⓣ312/322-1700, ⓦwww.spertus.edu), houses the largest collection of Jewish art and artifacts in the Midwest, including Torah scrolls, jewelry, textiles, and the **Zell Holocaust memorial** – a list of names of those lost in the Holocaust. Among the seventeenth- to nineteenth-century ritual objects and textiles presented in the **Judaica exhibit**, there are some highly evocative pieces executed by renowned twentieth-century artists including **Friedrich Adler** and **Moshe Zabari**, as well as a unique German Ark textile set.

The nineteenth- and twentieth-century Fine Art collection is a must-see; look out for the work of **Leon Golub**, whose poignant material forms a metaphysical commentary upon the fear of a culture in crisis. However, the consistently impressive temporary exhibits are the main draw. **Kids** needn't feel left out: in the basement is the Rosenbaum ARTiFACT Center's **archeological site**, where they can dig up dusty finds. After a "how-to" demonstration by a member of the museum's education center, kids can spend an hour pretending to be real-life archeologists, digging for replica artifacts, decoding ancient alphabets, and experiencing what Middle Eastern culture must have been like around 520 BC. (Note: it's not a drop-off and kids require parental monitoring.)

In 2007, the museum will move to a new site just north of its current location on Michigan Avenue. The new building will accommodate the ever-expanding library archives, incorporate new high-tech educational facilities, feature a new theater, kosher café, and provide a more sophisticated environment for the museum's permanent collection and temporary exhibitions.

Grant Park

East of the Loop, **Grant Park** (daily 6am–11pm) provides a welcome but not entirely complete break from the downtown urban grid – wide strips of high-speed road and railroad slice through it, so casual rambling can be frustrating. The whole two-hundred-acre swath, stretching from Randolph Street south to Roosevelt Road, is sprinkled with sculptures and monuments, from a stern Lincoln to a proud Plains Indian on horseback.

The northern half of the park has been redefined by the flamboyant, undulating, stainless-steel ribbons of the **Jay Pritzker Pavilion**. Unmistakably the work of Frank Gehry, it forms the centerpiece for the striking **Millennium Park**. Heading four blocks south, just east of the Art Institute, is the immense **Buckingham Fountain**, sitting amid colonnades of trees and thousands of rose bushes. Grant Park's major attractions are gathered in the southern half of Grant Park, in something known as **Museum Campus** (☎312/409-4178, Ⓦwww.museumcampus.org), where three excellent museums, the **Field Museum**, **Adler Planetarium**, and **Shedd Aquarium** are set among sculptures and terraced walkways.

Some history

During the late 1800s, the land that makes up today's Grant Park was being snapped up for rail expansion and future high-rises, but two men – **Daniel Burnham** and **Montgomery Ward**, the latter known for establishing the world's first mail-order business – were busy trying to protect the lakefront east of the Loop. Ward's prolonged battle to save the area from development actually had its roots as early as 1852, when the Illinois Central Railroad built a trestle in Lake Michigan so that trains could reach the river. Ungainly as it was, the trestle buffered Michigan Avenue and its mansions from both floods and violent storm-driven waters, and over the years, the land between the rail tracks and the shore gradually filled in, especially after debris from the fire of 1871 was dumped here and the area named Lake Park. Its condition became so disgusting that Ward, nicknamed the "watchdog of the lakefront," fought for its renovation, much to the disbelief of local businessmen and city officials who considered the land fit for development and a source of revenue for the city.

Summer festivals in the park

Nearly every weekend in summer sees a musical festival in Grant Park (be it gospel, blues, country, jazz, or classical), held in the area around the Petrillo Music Shell, and on Wednesday, Friday, and Saturday evenings at the Jay Pritzker Pavilion in Millennium Park. Every Tuesday during July and August, Grant Park hosts one of Chicago's favorite summertime rituals, the free **Movies in the Park**. In early July, the **Taste of Chicago** festival attracts some four million people to a weeklong feeding frenzy, garnished with concerts and other live entertainment (for details on park events, see "Festivals and events," p.254).

Thanks to Ward's continuing legal fight, however, the land was left largely undeveloped (though McCormick Place was built in the 1950s), and in 1901, the patch of green was renamed Grant Park. In time, Daniel Burnham's plan for the massive reconstruction of the city, which changed street grids and property lines, saved the lakefront "for the people." Though Burnham's ideas took decades to be fully realized, thanks to his initial plan the lakefront park now stretches from Grant Park south to 67th Street.

Millennium Park

The lakefront area that spreads south from Randolph to Monroe streets, west to Michigan Avenue and east to Columbus Drive forms the 24.5-acre **Millennium Park**. Officially opened in July 2004, four years after the millennium, and three times the allotted budget of $4.75 million, it's an arresting display of contemporary architecture and design.

Lauded by *New York Times* architecture critic Paul Goldberger as "one of the great new models for a kind of urban park," it has been less reverentially described by passing Chicagoans as "a sculpture garden on steroids." When viewed facing east, from the bowels of the Loop's broody Gothic streets, it's a surreal sight, the physical embodiment of a visionary, ambitious city that always thinks Big.

The **Jay Pritzker Pavilion**, an open-air concert hall, is the park's anchor. It's trademark Frank Gehry, a 120ft-tall whimsical steel confection superimposed against the soaring, austere planes of the Chicago skyline. Billowing ribbons of shimmering steel form the stage's "headdress," while interlacing trellises of steel pipes support the state-of-the-art sound system. There are concerts throughout summer (Wed & Fri 6.30pm, Sat 7.30pm; free; ⓣ312/742-7638, ⓦwww.grantparkmusicfestival.com). Gehry also designed the snaking, stainless-steel BP Bridge, which connects Millennium Park to Daley Bicentennial Plaza, just east, and is the only Gehry-designed bridge in the world. Alongside Gehry's pavilion, the shiny, kidney-bean-shaped **Cloud Gate**, designed by sculptor Anish Kapoor, is nicknamed the "Bean" by Chicagoans – Kapoor was so late in naming the piece, the moniker had already stuck. Inspired by liquid mercury, the sculpture was forged from 168 polished steel plates that reflect the city's skyline, which provides in the words of Kapoor, "a gate to the city, a poetic idea about the city it reflects." One of the largest sculptures of its kind in the world, it weighs 110 tons and measures 66ft in length and 33ft in height. The sculpture was concealed beneath a tent for much of 2005; hastily unveiled in time to meet Millennium Park's inauguration, welding grooves were still visible on what should have been a smooth, reflective ellipse. Escalating costs have brought *Cloud Gate*'s total expense to over $17 million, to the chagrin of many Chicagoans.

Walking south through Millennium Park, at 55 N Michigan Ave, you'll come to **McCormick Tribune Plaza**, which doubles as a 16,000ft **ice rink** from November to March (free, rental skates available for $4–5; ⓣ312/742-5222) and a tourist-oriented, **open-air bar/restaurant** in summer. In the southwest corner of the park, two 50ft-glass towers facing one another across a granite plaza form **Crown Fountain**, the work of renowned Spanish architect Jaime Plense. Kaleidoscopic video images project one thousand Chicagoans from digital LED screens enclosed within the towers, and, intermittently, water spurts from the puckered lips of the pixilated image to the glee of frolicking children.

Also in the northern section of the park, on the corner of Michigan and Randolph, Wrigley Square is dominated by **Millennium Monument**. With a serene row of Doric columns, it's a replica of the peristyle that stood here between 1917 and 1953.

In the southeast corner, the **Lurie Garden** is a more hushed statement: the "contemplative" space needs a few more years to mature and is still rather too reminiscent of an artist's model. There are over two hundred perennials, trees, shrubs, atmospheric lighting, and a 15ft-high "shoulder hedge" – a nod to Carl Sandburg's immortalized poem *Chicago* which included the iconic line, "Stormy, husky, brawling, City of the Big Shoulders."

Buckingham Fountain and around

Southeast of Millennium Park and the Art Institute, **Buckingham Fountain** was donated to Grant Park in 1927 and modeled after a fountain at Versailles. An ornate pile of stacked pink marble, the fountain provides a spectacle from May to October when it shoots more than a million gallons of water up to 150 feet in the air. It also plays host to popular light and water shows daily from dusk to 11pm.

A few statues nearby are worth noting: across Columbus Avenue to the west of the fountain is the seated **Lincoln statue,** surveying the park from atop a pedestal. Like its counterpart in Lincoln Park, the statue, created by Augustus Saint-Gaudens, was unveiled in 1926, though it's more subdued. Flanking Congress Parkway near Michigan Avenue, **The Bowman and the Spearman** is an impressive pair of seventeen-foot-high bronze Indian warriors, created by sculptor Ivan Mestrovic.

The Field Museum of Natural History

Ten minutes' walk from Buckingham Fountain, the **Field Museum**, 1400 S Lake Shore Drive at Roosevelt Road (daily 9am–5pm, last admission at 4pm; $12, students and seniors $7, discounted tickets available Jan & Feb, Sept 19–Dec 20 Mon & Tues, free tours Mon–Fri 11am & 2pm, Sat & Sun 11am & 1pm; Orange, Red, or Green line to Roosevelt, then CTA bus #12; ⓣ312/922-9410, ⓦwww.fieldmuseum.org), is yet another legacy of the 1893 World's Columbian Exposition (although the current, updated building dates from 1921). The museum was created as a permanent home for many of the natural history exhibits that had been displayed at the exhibition and was endowed by millionaire Marshall Field. These days, despite a few careworn exhibits, it's a fascinating museum collecting natural history's greatest hits, and vies with the more gimmicky Museum of Science and Industry in Hyde Park (see p.141) as the best way to captivate a child for an afternoon, if not longer.

The enormous, Greek-temple-like building is set on three floors, and is filled with over twenty million objects across six acres; don't let that daunt you, as

Museum Campus transport

Plenty of **free trolleys** link the Field Museum, Shedd Aquarium, the Adler Planetarium, and the surrounding parking lots, though distances are small enough that you could easily walk them. In summer, Shoreline Marine Sightseeing (frequent departures 10am–6pm; $6 each way, $5 seniors & $3 children; ⓣ312/222-9328, ⓦwww.shorelinesightseeing.com) runs **water taxis** between Shedd Aquarium and Navy Pier, as well as half-hour **lake cruises** from the aquarium on the weekend and from Navy Pier during the week. Alternatively, a cab ride from the Loop will set you back around $7.

with comfortable shoes and a plan of the museum (available at the information booth), it's easily navigable.

On the main floor, on the building's north side, is the *Tyrannosaurus rex* **Sue** (see box), the premier attraction of the Field Museum's collection, the most complete *T-rex* fossil ever found, missing only one foot, one "hand," and a few back bones. Paleontologists speculate that Sue's (actually, her gender is officially undetermined) body was most likely buried by an avalanche or mudflow, which kept her bones intact for millions of years. Take the stairs to the second floor to see Sue's skull; too heavy to mount, the one you see in context on the main floor is a replica cast. There's also a virtual journey inside Sue's head, and touchable bone casts that reveal the life-threatening wounds inflicted upon the great flesh-devouring monstrosity some 65 million years ago. On the upper level, the excellent **Life Over Time** exhibition, scheduled to reopen in May 2006 with a sleek, high-tech display that will take in 3.8 billion years of evolution – from the dawn of Earth to the arrival of man – will feature an expanded Dinosaur Hall, or **Dinozone**, which will allow kids to play the role of a paleontologist, using interpretive screens to examine a dinosaur's anatomy.

On the main floor, aside from Sue, stop by **Inside Ancient Egypt** for its tomb of Unis-ankh, son of a fifth-dynasty pharaoh; the limestone chunks were brought here and reassembled by the museum's first president, Edward Ayer. A dedicated Egypt enthusiast, he also purchased many of the mummies and coffins on display in the lower part of this exhibit; don't miss the re-creation of a 2450 BC marketplace at the end for its lively evocation of daily life in ancient Egypt; cut-out figures re-enact the centuries-old bartering process and glass displays present the valuable artifacts from the period. On the ground level is the trippy **Underground Adventures** exhibit. Upon entering, visitors are "shrunk" to one hundredth of their size and set on a pathway under the earth, surrounded by soil, giant roots, and oversized, fiberglass insects, including a Cadillac-sized crayfish. Also downstairs is, the preserved figure of **Bushman**, a 6ft-tall lowland gorilla. Once one of the museum's most popular displays, Bushman has been

△ Sue, the *Tyrannosaurus Rex*

T-rex Sue and the custody battle of the century

Sue's discovery on a Cheyenne River Sioux Indian reservation in the badlands of South Dakota by fossil hunter Susan Hendrickson in 1990 was the spark for one of the greatest custody battles in the history of paleontology. The reservation property was held in trust by the government for a Sioux Indian, **Maurice Williams**, who was paid five thousand dollars by fossil hunters to renounce all claims.

The government soon got wind of the discovery and in 1992 the US Justice Department quickly dispatched FBI agents to seize the skeleton pending a decision on ownership (the *T-rex* was found, after all, on government land). Eventually, the court ruled in Williams' favor – the 1906 Antiquities Act doesn't cover fossils. Thus, **Sue's bones** were auctioned off to the highest bidder at Sotheby's in New York in October 1997; thanks to the combined corporate muscle of McDonald's and Disney, the Field was able to outbid its rivals for the skeleton – to the staggering sum of $8.4 million. On May 17, 2000, after two and a half years spent assembling the 13ft-tall, 14ft-long fossil, the Field Museum revealed to the world the crown jewel of its collection.

virtually forgotten thanks to the frenzy surrounding Sue. The massive gorilla from Lincoln Park Zoo was so well known at his death in 1950, that he was laid in state for several days so that mourners could pay their respects. He looks faintly ridiculous now, trapped in an eternal glower inside a glass case that he would have shattered with one fist when alive.

The Shedd Aquarium

On the shores of Lake Michigan, the **Shedd Aquarium** (summer: daily 9am–6pm; rest of year: Mon–Fri 9am–5pm, Sat & Sun 9am–6pm; $8, $6 seniors & children, Aquarium and Oceanarium $18, $14 seniors & children, All Access Pass $23, $16 seniors & children, Sept–Feb Mon & Tues Aquarium section free, Oceanarium and Wild Reef discounted tickets $15, $10 seniors and children; ⓣ312/939-2438, ⓦwww.shedd.org), is the largest indoor aquarium in the world. The 1920s structure is rather old-fashioned, but, for the most part, displays are informative and entertaining.

The central exhibit, set in an octagonal space, is a 90,000 gallon re-creation of a **Caribbean Coral Reef**, complete with sharks and thousands of rainbow-colored tropical fish. The undisputed star is the green sea-turtle **Nickel** – named after the 1975-nickel coin found lodged in her esophagus when she arrived at Shedd in 2005 from Clearwater Marine Aquarium in Florida. Injured in a motorboat incident, the scar is still visible on her carapace. Surrounding the Caribbean reef, the **Amazon Rising** exhibit reveals the impact of the changing seasons on one of the world's most ecologically diverse environments. Look out for the red-bellied piranhas, green anacondas, and wattled jacanas (the feminist icons of the bird world, defending huge swathes of territory and being entertained by a harem of up to five males, who kindly take care of the incubation and parental care after hatching). The otherwise lackluster **Waters of the World** exhibit features an **endangered blue iguana** from Grand Cayman (less than thirty remain in the wild), the largest lizard in the Western Hemisphere.

Designed to replicate a rocky Pacific Northwest coastline, the **Oceanarium** provides an enormous contrast, with its modern lake-view home for marine mammals such as Pacific dolphins, beluga whales (which consume nearly six hundred pounds of seafood daily), and delightfully playful sea otters – seventy to eighty percent of the world's sea-otter population is to be found in Alaska. The

Oceanarium also functions as a carefully disguised amphitheater for demonstrations of the animals' "natural behavior," such as jumping out of the water and fetching plastic rings. Performances are four times daily (Mon–Fri 10.30am, noon, 1.30pm, 3.30pm) but at other times you can watch from underwater galleries as the animals cruise around the tank, and listen to the clicks, beeps, and whistles they use to communicate with each other.

The aquarium's latest addition is **Wild Reef**, featuring twenty-six interrelated habitats housed in an underground wing. A re-creation of a Philippine coral reef, it boasts more than five hundred breeds of fish and live coral, with engaging educational information panels. There are more than fifty kinds of shark– one of the most diverse displays in North America of this maligned oceanic predator – such as bamboo, zebra, and sand bar. There are species of ray, including mangrove rays and blue spotted stingrays (their keen sixth sense allows them to detect electrical impulses). Note that this is not one of the best-value Chicago experiences; the basic admission price doesn't cover the Oceanarium – a highlight for most visitors and especially popular with children. Look out for specified **discount ticket** days, which change annually, and consult the website for updated information.

The Adler Planetarium

At the eastern end of the Museum Campus, and jutting out into Lake Michigan, is the expanded, renovated, and more technologically advanced **Adler Planetarium** (daily: summer 9.30am–6pm; winter: 9.30am–4.30pm; first Fri of each month until 10pm; $20, $19 seniors $18 children, including choice of 2 shows or $16, $15 seniors, $14 children including 1 show, each additional sky show $5; Jan 10–March 1 & Sept 12–Dec 20 admission only, free Mon & Tues; CTA bus #146, #127, #12; ⓣ312/922-7827, ⓦwww.adlerplanetarium.org), whose permanent exhibits include **Dawn of the Space Age**, a history of space exploration, and **Bringing the Heavens to Earth**, an examination of the impact of astronomy on ancient cultures. Recent state-of-the-art additions include **CyberSpace**, where "Cyberclassrooms" linked by high-velocity broadband networks enable two-way telecasts with NASA, whose "feeds" project breaking space-related news across plasma displays. In the main gallery, you can have a 3D experience of a Martian landscape through interactive viewing stations.

As part of its 75th anniversary in 2005, American space hero Captain James A. Lovell contributed his personal collection to Adler, including personal space artifacts, documents, and memorabilia. Lovell became a national icon in 1970, when he and his crew successfully modified the Apollo 13 lunar module into a lifeboat when the oxygen system failed (the mission's thrilling feat was given the Hollywood treatment in the 1995 Oscar-winning movie *Apollo 13*, starring Tom Hanks). The planetarium's new focus on human space exploration will include an interactive exhibition, scheduled to be unveiled in 2006, featuring the restored Gemini 12 spacecraft, one of four spacecraft flown by Lovell.

The Adler houses two planetariums that put on half-hour shows several times daily. When there isn't a show on, it's cool for a look at the clear night sky projected on the dome by the Zeiss projector. On the lower level, the 360-degree **StarRider Theater** is a virtual-reality, interactive, digital movie theater that, like the Sky Theater, offers excellent shows of the explore-the-universe type, but with some added excitement – using "controls" in your armrest, you can participate in flight-simulation shows. SonicVision (Fri & Sat 7pm, 8pm, 9pm, 10pm; $8, $6 students) is StarRider's psychedelic extravaganza, where hallucinogenic images are set to a musical montage, featuring Goldfrapp, Moby, and Queens of the Stone Age. It is a visually compelling experience if you happen to be in the area when a performance is scheduled.

Outside, from the planetarium's front steps you'll have great views of the **downtown skyline**.

Soldier Field

Just south of Museum Campus, the 100ft Doric colonnades of oversized **Soldier Field** (tours 9am–5pm by reservation only; $15, $7 seniors, $4 children; ⓣ312/235-7244, ⓦwww.soldierfield.net) marked it as a sports palace of a bygone age before its controversial renovation in 2002. Designed by Holabird & Roche, who pioneered the Chicago School, the original seven-acre stadium was built in the 1920s as a memorial to American soldiers who died in battle. Since then, the stadium has been the stage for many famous sporting events, including the 1927 heavyweight boxing rematch between Jack Dempsey and Gene Tunney that ended with the famously polemical "long count." (Dempsey knocked down Tunney but lost five precious seconds by heading to the wrong corner before the referee started his count. On the count of nine, Tunney staggered to his feet and proceeded to beat Dempsey.)

Home to the Chicago Bears since 1971, Soldier Field closed in 2002 for a $600-million facelift. The new stadium was unveiled on Sept 29, 2003, and was received with scorn and derision by an overwhelming number of Chicagoans. The design's attempt to merge the classical colonnades of the original stadium with a modern structure, while still maintaining a historical essence has resulted in a jarring eyesore. Despite the addition of new memorial features, including the 1930s *Doughboy* statue representing a World War I infantryman, moved from Garfield Park, and a 280ft green granite memorial waterfall that lines the stadium's north entrance, Soldier Field's looming lakeshore presence is a contextual failure, compared to the low-slung treasures of the neighboring Field Museum and Shedd Aquarium. When all is said and done, though, the Bears will remain, everyone will continue to get the name wrong (not Soldier*s*), and die-hard fans will keep braving the arctic winds off the lake (notice the teams of loud barechested men, seemingly numb to the sub-zero temperatures).

The Prairie Avenue Historic District and around

The city's first elite neighborhood, **Prairie Avenue**, was for a brief time the most expensive street in America outside New York's glitzy Fifth Avenue. Some of Chicago's first homes were built around Prairie Avenue in the mid-eighteenth century, and it came to be known as "Millionaire's Row" – the most coveted property in town. George Pullman (see p.280), creator of the Pullman railroad car, and some twenty industrial magnates settled here following the Chicago Fire, building extravagant mansions along S Prairie Avenue. Though a handful of their homes have survived, only **Glessner House** and **Clarke House** are open to the public, providing a glimpse of Chicago's Gilded Age.

By the beginning of the twentieth century, the rich had moved on to the lakefront north of the Loop to join millionaire Potter Palmer (see p.282), and the area around Prairie Avenue plunged into decades of seediness, helped along by the saloons and brothels that had sprung up nearby following the success of the railroads leading into the South Loop. In recent years, the city has made

Walking tours of Prairie Avenue

Walking tours, put on from June through October by Prairie Avenue House Museums, point out the avenue's prominent residents, the architecture of the homes, and the history of the district's decline and renewal.

The only way to see inside **Clarke House** and **Glessner House** – the most visited of the bunch – is on a guided tour, which leaves from the Tour Center (the Glessners' former stables) on the 18th Street side of the house (Wed–Sun, tours of Clarke House noon, 1pm & 2pm, tours of Glessner House 1pm, 2pm & 3pm; $15, $12 seniors & $8 children for both houses, $10, $9 seniors & $5 children for one house; free Wed; ⓣ312/326-1480, ⓦwww.glesserhouse.org. Tours (one hour in each house) are on a first-come, first-served basis and are limited to twelve people for Glessner House, seven for Clarke House. To see both houses, be sure to show up at the Tour Center no later than 2pm.

considerable strides in transforming what was previously an unsafe and down-at-heel semi-industrial area into a fashionable loft neighborhood. The blocks around Michigan and Prairie avenues are attracting young professionals with spruced commercial and leisure amenities ranging from prosaic chain-stores and fast-food restaurants, to health clubs, outdoor cafés and bars, and convenient downtown access.

You're best off **getting here** by cab, bus, or train, as the route from downtown is confusing. It's about a $6 cab ride from the Loop, or a short hop on the Michigan Avenue CTA buses (#1, #3, and #4), all of which stop at the corner of 18th Street and Michigan Avenue, in front of the Prairie Avenue House Museums (see box above).

Clarke House

Built in 1836, **Clarke House**, 1855 S Indiana Ave, is Chicago's oldest house and seems more suited to a New England town than a masonry-heavy city like Chicago. Even as far back as the 1850s, the house was reason enough to make an excursion here; city-dwellers used to come by carriage to see this white, timber-frame Greek Revival house with its white colonnade, built in what was then a forest. Later, the house spent many years as a community center before being gussied up as a minor museum of interior decor in the late 1970s.

Although the house has moved twice to avoid demolition (it's now just two blocks from its original location), the interior has faithfully re-created the Clarke family home. All of the interior decoration, from the wallpaper to the furniture, is faithful Victorian reproductions – none of the originals survived. Guided tours amply evoke the pioneer existence during the early days of industrialization and the American migration west.

The neutral sandstone color of the Greek Revival exterior is attributed to the taste of the wealthy classes during the 1850s who eschewed the conspicuousness of bright white in favor of more earthy tones that would complement the surrounding landscape.

The Glessner House Museum

One of the few structures to have survived the neighborhood's decline is the Romanesque 1886 **Glessner House**, standing sentry on the southwest corner of Prairie Avenue and 18th Street. It is Chicago's only remaining house designed by one of the most important architects of the nineteenth century, Henry Hobson Richardson, whose Romanesque-revival features inspired both

Frank Lloyd Wright and Louis Sullivan. Commissioned by John and Frances Glessner, its unadorned structure was a departure from the more decorative traditional Victorian architecture, causing outrage among the neighbors, especially industrialist George Pullman (see p.280). "I do not know what I have ever done," he reportedly said, "to have that thing staring at me in the face every time I go out my door." Behind the forbidding facade, the house opens onto a large garden court, its interior filled with Arts and Crafts furniture, swathed in William Morris fabrics and wall coverings, and generously paneled in oak. Today, it exists almost entirely furnished as the Glessners left it, crammed with the family's collection of ceramics, delicate Art Nouveau and Venetian glass, plus intricate hand-carved furniture and ornamental pieces by Chicago artisan Isaac Scott.

Between Glessner House and Clarke House, the **Chicago Women's History Park** makes for a nice little walk along a curving path lined with a hundred plaques commemorating Chicago's famous women.

The National Vietnam Veterans Art Museum

Next door to the Glessner House, the **National Vietnam Veterans Art Museum**, 1801 S Indiana Ave (Tues–Fri 11am–6pm, Sat 10am–5pm, Sun noon–5pm; $10, students $7; ⓣ312/326-0270, ⓦwww.nvvam.org), focuses on the war from a personal point of view. Opened in 1981, the only museum of its kind in the United States, it contains more than five hundred works by 125 American Vietnam veterans of the war, and to a lesser extent, soldiers from Australia and North and South Vietnam. The somber and, at times, wrenching exhibits include a mix of paintings, photographs, sculptures, drawings, diaries, and other artifacts.

One of the most powerful works hangs from the ceiling above the front desk: *Above and Beyond*, a 10ft by 40ft sculpture consisting of 58,000 dog tags representing Americans killed in the war. Each stainless-steel tag is imprinted with a soldier's name, branch of service, and casualty date, and hung in chronological order. The solitary black dog-tag hangs in memory of soldiers who died from their injuries after the war.

Veterans are on hand to lead discussions for the visiting school groups; join one of these groups, if you can, and experience a powerful firsthand account.

The Blues Heaven Foundation

The rather cold-looking, steel-and-glass monstrosity southeast of the museum, at 2301 S Lake Shore Drive, is **McCormick Place**, a sprawling convention complex designed by Helmut Jahn. As there's really not much to see here, you are better off heading five blocks west to the **Blues Heaven Foundation** museum at 2120 S Michigan Ave, inside the building that once housed the legendary **Chess Records**, the greatest of all blues labels.

Started in 1957 by brothers Leonard and Phil Chess, the studio launched so many top blues musicians – everyone from Willie Dixon and Bo Diddley to Muddy Waters, Koko Taylor, and even Chuck Berry – that it became a shrine of sorts, nowadays run by the Willie Dixon Blues Heaven Foundation for the preservation of the blues. The Rolling Stones, who took their name from a Muddy Waters tune, even cut an album here and commemorated the place in their song *2120 South Michigan*.

You can take a **tour** of the renovated studio, though unless you're a blues aficionado or simply want to say you've been to the site, you're better off skipping it altogether – you won't see much beyond a sterile recording studio and there's little in the way of informed commentary by guides. Tours last a half-hour to 45 minutes (it's best if you call ahead to book a place) and end with a short *Keepin' the Blues Alive* video (Mon–Fri noon–3pm, Sat noon–2pm; $10 donation; ⓣ312/808-1286). For more on Chicago blues music, see Contexts, p.289.

Chinatown

A mile west of McCormick Place, and best accessed on either the Red Line to Cermak-Chinatown or bus #24 to E Cermak Road and S Wentworth Avenue, the narrow, ten-block area of Chicago's **Chinatown** has maintained a decidedly authentic feel. The distinctive green and red **gate** at Wentworth Avenue and Cermak Road marks the beginning of the district, and once through here you could just as well be in downtown Hong Kong as central Chicago.

Chicago's first Chinese immigrants began arriving in the 1870s, after the completion of the first transcontinental railroad when many of them found themselves out of work and without a place to live. They soon carved out an area around Cermak Road and Wentworth Avenue, two miles south of the Loop, though in time overcrowding threatened to strain the budding neighborhood's infrastructure, and construction of city highways in the area restricted further growth. Even so, Chinatown has managed to survive and remains almost entirely Chinese.

There's nothing in the way of traditional sights around here, except the **On Leong Building**, 2216 S Wentworth Ave, easily identified by its large green and red pagodas – formerly the Chinese city hall and long the heart of the bustling commercial district. Today it houses, among other things, the only indigenous Chinese shrine in the Midwest. In 2005, the **Chinese-American Museum of Chicago** opened at 238 W 23rd St (Fri 9.30am–1.30pm, Sat & Sun 10am–5pm; $2, $1 children, seniors & students; ⓣ312/949-1000) and uniquely aims to evoke the history of the Chinese population in the Midwest through paintings, photographs, textiles, and documents. At the time of writing, the museum had yet to establish a permanent collection.

Chinatown Square is an offshoot just to the northwest, with more shops, restaurants, plus the Chamber of Commerce. It's fun to poke around the little groceries filled with exotic spices, myriad teas, medicinal herbs, and exotic-looking vegetables, but the real attraction here is the food: you'll be spoiled for choice among the more than forty **restaurants** serving inexpensive Mandarin, Szechuan, Shanghai, and Cantonese cuisine; *Emperor's Choice* on Wentworth Avenue and *Three Happiness* on W Cermak Road are among the best. For reviews of these and other restaurants in the area, see "Eating," p. 192.

A few boisterous **festivals** also make the neighborhood worth checking out if you are in town: July boasts the popular Lantern Festival and February sees the vibrant Chinese New Year Festival take over the local streets (for more on these happenings, see "Festivals and events," p.254).

6

Bucktown, Wicker Park, and the Ukrainian Village

The districts of **BUCKTOWN** and **WICKER PARK**, around three miles northwest of the Loop, are among Chicago's most progressive, home to a lively alternative music scene, numerous thrift stores, and a thriving bohemian culture of cafés and clubs. The **UKRAINIAN VILLAGE,** the districts' younger sibling further south, is grittier and less affected, but not by much: though still dominated by the Eastern European immigrants who settled here a hundred years ago, it too is in the midst of a massive gentrification process by young hipsters and condo dwellers.

While there are no big-ticket sights in any of these locales, you'll find a couple of rewarding pockets, such as the quiet streets of the **Wicker Park historic district** (especially Hoyne and Pierce avenues), lined with some of the city's finest examples of Victorian-era architecture and a striking contrast with the modern, concrete low-rises on the neighborhood's main drags; many of these old houses have been superbly, if a little self-consciously, restored.

The best way to see these neighborhoods, however, is after dark; the **nightlife** here is, hands down, the best in the city, centered on the boisterous "six corners" intersection of **Milwaukee**, **North**, and **Damen** avenues. The other commercial hubs – **North Avenue, Division Street**, and **Chicago Avenue** – run east–west and serve as the informal dividing lines for Bucktown, Wicker Park, and the Ukrainian Village, respectively. Be on alert for some **gang activity**, especially in Wicker Park west of Western Avenue; stick to the main thoroughfares (and don't cross Western Avenue) and you should have few problems.

Some history

While today Milwaukee Avenue is the central artery of these three neighborhoods, in the early 1800s it was an unpaved Indian trail that ran from Chicago to Milwaukee, Wisconsin. The area was sparsely populated by **Polish immigrants**, many of them farmers. After the Great Chicago Fire of 1871, homeless Chicagoans started moving here in large numbers, and the Polish population

EATING				DRINKING			
Bongo Room	25	Letizia's Natural Bakery	26	California clipper	30	Marie's Rip-Tide Lounge	10
Café Absinthe	15	Margie's Candies	6	Celebrity	16	Nick's Beergarden	24
Café de Lucca	13	Meritage Café and Wine Bar	5	Club Lucky	19	Northside Café	14
Earwax Café	22	Spring	17	Gold Star Bar	29	Pontiac Café	21
Hilary's Urban Eatery	27	Thyme Café	20	Hideout	12	Quencher's	2
Hot Chocolate	4	Toast	9	Holiday Club	23	Rainbo Club	28
Iggy's	16	Vienna Beef Factory	1	Leopard Lounge	11	Subterranean	18
La Bonita	3			Map Room	7		
Le Bouchon	8						

continued to swell, augmented by an influx of **Ukrainians**. These Eastern European communities were largely centered on the area's many churches, the most influential of which was (and still is) the looming **St Stanislaus Kostka Church**, which exerted such influence over the area that locals initially referred to the neighborhood as "Stanislawowo" and later, in the twentieth century, as the slightly more anglicized "Kostkaville."

After World War II, many Poles moved to less-crowded areas further northwest up Milwaukee Avenue (still a Polish stronghold today), and this area of the city became more ethnically diverse, attracting large numbers of **Latinos** (mostly Puerto Ricans). In the 1960s and 1970s, a rise in gang activity and violence led to the abandonment of the neighborhood by many residents, and the area fell into disrepair. Factories closed, arson fires raged, and drug addicts and prostitutes roamed the streets.

The process of urban renewal began in Bucktown, the northernmost of the three areas, and has gradually bled south over the past twenty years. Largely ruled by Latino gangs since the 1960s, Wicker Park remained a staunch no-go zone until the housing prices in Bucktown skyrocketed and displaced artists made the leap south over the railroad tracks at North Avenue and established homes in Wicker Park. Today, much of the original Polish community, along with the more recent Hispanic residents, has been pushed north and west, to the other side of Western Avenue. With gentrification edging ever westward, it's a safe bet that this will be the next boundary to be crossed.

Bucktown

Much like many of the city's inner suburbs, **Bucktown** began life as an immigrant hub: Germans, Poles, and other Eastern Europeans who arrived in the mid-nineteenth century settled on and around Milwaukee Avenue. In the 1800s, the area was dominated by open fields where Polish settlers raised goats; the male goat is called a buck, which is how the neighborhood most likely got its name.

Bucktown spreads just north of the six corners, bounded on either side by the Kennedy Expressway and Western Avenue. Above this sprawling intersection are a bevy of restaurants and cafés, plus a few galleries, located mostly on Damen and Milwaukee avenues, south of Armitage. Of special interest are the *Northside Café*, a bustling **burger joint and bar** with a roomy outdoor patio, at 1635 N Damen Ave, and neighborhood classic *Club Lucky*, a short hop away at 1824 Wabansia Ave, where the former Polish banquet hall and bar has been restored to its 1930s glory and currently packs 'em in as a casual Italian joint. Stop by old-fashioned **ice-cream parlor** *Margie's Candies*, a few blocks west on Western Avenue, which has been churning out delicious home-made concoctions since 1921; its quaint booths have seen everybody from Al Capone and Sinatra to the Beatles and Princess Di – the Smashing Pumpkins even wrote a song about tables six and seven.

Restaurants and bars aside, it's worth a wander around Bucktown's quieter streets for a look at the variety of architecture. The stretch of Wabansia Avenue from Milwaukee to Ashland has a good representation of Chicago **housing styles** – be it contemporary or Victorian, single or multi-family residences, coach houses, flats, or lofts. The cornerstone of Bucktown's development sits just west of here at no. 2300. The handsome, four-story, red-brick and glass building housing the **Clock Tower Lofts** was built around 1900, and originally occupied by curtain makers and tailors. The building was entirely gutted in the early 1990s and converted into airy lofts, and within a few years their value had doubled, with waves of development spreading from here in all directions.

Concord Street and around

Skip over to **Concord Street**, where many of the houses were built from stone by wealthy, late nineteenth-century industrialists, and so have weathered well. The only thing disrupting the old-world, suburban calm is the El, which now rumbles along the street's eastern reaches. Look out for the graphic, stained-glass features in the windows of **no. 2140**. Also note the houses that have suffered stylistic alterations, from the stone cladding that smothers **no. 2121** (the original detailing is still visible above the dormer window) to the Queen Anne mansion, **no. 2138**, whose rounded turret windows have been replaced by flat panes to save money.

Be sure not to miss the wonderful building at **2041 North Ave**, at Milwaukee, behind whose delicate white terracotta facade once stood the 1923 **Luxor Bathhouse**, a relaxing haven for Turkish and Russian immigrants. This structure has since been converted into the upscale restaurant *Spring* (see p.194), but the fish reliefs above each window bear witness to its original use.

Wicker Park

While slightly truer to its Eastern European roots than nearby Bucktown, **Wicker Park** is also facing head-on the encroaching forces of urban renewal. Immigrant communities coexist with the artsy types who've been driven here by rising rents elsewhere in the city, creating an eclectic mix of artists, elderly women in babushkas, and black-clad youth, all sharing the sidewalk en route to the café, deli, Polish Roman Catholic church, or the nearest poetry slam. Though yuppies have started to move in (bringing with them a few generic sports bars that horrify longtime locals), the neighborhood retains an anti-establishment feel. In 2001, when MTV filmed its popular series, **The Real World** here, the producers faced protests from angry locals upset at the area's commodification.

Though it's not much to look at, there is an eponymous **park** here, just south of the six corners, named for brothers Joel and Charles Wicker, who donated it in 1870. In its heyday the park held a small swan pond and a shelter, but the pond was long ago filled in and there's just a plain-looking fountain breaking up this little patch of green. Writer **Nelson Algren** (see box) once lived in one of the pretty Victorian homes south of the park – but beware: after sundown it's best to steer clear of the park, as it's known as a haven for drug dealers.

In a city full of ornate churches, the **St Stanislaus Kostka Church**, 1351 W Evergreen Ave (☎773/278-2470), west of Wicker Park, still stands out. Towering more than two hundred feet tall, the church has a stunning Baroque interior, complete with chandeliers and stained-glass windows, which you can view by appointment. Built in 1876, the church was for many years the stronghold of the city's Polish Catholic community, once the heart of "Stanislawowo" and later "Kostkaville." As the area became increasingly gentrified and with the building of the Kennedy Expressway, much of the Polish community moved

The Wicker Park historic district

Chicago's architectural blockbusters, whether pioneering skyscrapers or modern engineering marvels, tend to be crammed into the Loop, but the northwest district of Wicker Park has its own immaculately maintained gems – nineteenth-century Victorian homes spared Chicago's wrecking ball to become a designated **historic district**.

This area, bounded by N Damen Avenue and N Leavitt Street, stretching from Caton to Division streets (a sliver of it falls in neighboring Bucktown), is one of the most stringently gentrified segments of this up-and-coming area.

Start a walking tour of the area on **N Hoyne Avenue**, once known as "Beer Baron Row" for the number of brewing tycoons who built their homes here in the late 1800s. Of the many eye-catching old buildings, the two most prominent are **nos. 1407** and **1521**. The former is set on the corner of Schiller Street, its onetime grandeur evident from the adjoining coach-house and enormous octagonal tower, though sadly, it's one of the worst preserved on the street. The latter (a block north) is in better condition: note the elaborate, wrought-iron scrollwork and table-leg columns, as well as the massive ornamental canopy over the entranceway. The Queen Anne period house, topped by a turret with a witch's-hat roof, also preserves the expensive curved glass that was made possible late in the nineteenth century by industrial innovations. It's also worth stopping by **no. 1558**, at the junction with North Avenue, whose elaborately restored exterior features ironwork on its tower, leaded windows, and lime paint with dark green contrasts.

Head back to **W Pierce Avenue** for more fine Victorian homes. The most famous is the **Paderewski House** (no. 2138), built in 1886 and one-time residence of the Polish consulate; the house was renamed in honor of the famed Polish pianist after he gave a performance on its porch. Today, it's still one of the grandest in the area, a double-fronted mansion with a veranda even outside its dormer windows. Across the street is the unmistakable **Gingerbread House**, at 2137 W Pierce Ave, so named for the look of its intricate, machine-cut moldings. Built in 1888, this late Victorian masterpiece is painted in an eye-popping gold, ochre, and blue color scheme – a far cry from the sober paint that would have graced it when it was built. **Nos. 2118** and **2046** farther down are also notable: the former for its faux-Gothic decorative elements above the upper windows, the latter for its rounded-glass bay windows.

away; these days, masses are given in English and Spanish as well as Polish, reflecting the area's changing make-up.

Division Street and around

A once dangerous expressway, **Division Street** was made famous by Studs Terkel's *Division Street America* (see box), a penetrating portrait of Chicago's hardscrabble urban life. In recent years, the street's rough reputation has been softened somewhat with the arrival of lounge-style restaurants and lower crime rates, but there's still enough grit left here to merit caution – from empty storefronts to shady alleyways – especially after dark. Division and the surrounding side streets are not particularly well lit, and pedestrian traffic thins out after 10pm.

For a one-of-a-kind Chicago experience, head to the **Division Street Russian Bathhouse** at no. 1916 (Mon–Thurs 8am–10pm, Fri & Sat 7am–10pm, Sun 6am–10pm; $22 for all-day admission, massages start at $25 for 30min; ⓣ773/384-9671), a throwback to Chicago's stockyard days, when residential indoor plumbing wasn't as common as it is today. One of the few remaining *schvitz* (Yiddish for "sweat") places left in the country, the humble bathhouse has traditionally seen folks from all walks of life unwind in its blistering 180°F steam rooms, ice-cold pools, massage rooms, and showers including more than a few celebrities, from Jesse Jackson to Mike Ditka (check out the signed photos on the wall). A separate women's side of the bathhouse offers waxing, facials, massages, and a eucalyptus-scented wet sauna. Afterwards a stop at **Letizia's Natural Bakery**, just up Division at no. 2146, will replenish whatever you've sweated out.

While the six corners area south of North Avenue has more commercial attractions than you'd ever wish to visit, a few are worth noting for their lively scene or historic value. Along Milwaukee Avenue, south of North Avenue, look out for *Earwax*, 1561 N Milwaukee Ave, an enormous carnival-themed **coffeehouse-cum-video store**; the hugely popular *Bongo Room*, 1470 N Milwaukee, known for its mouth-watering **brunch** menu and long waits. More bars and clubs are clustered along this stretch of Milwaukee Avenue just south of North Avenue, and also along Damen Avenue in the two blocks north of North Avenue. Shoppers will find the best stores – from vintage to records – along these same stretches. For more information, see the "Eating" (Chapter 14), and "Drinking" (Chapter 15).

The Ukrainian Village

South of Wicker Park, the **Ukrainian Village** has been home to Chicago's Polish and Ukrainian communities since the late 1800s, when a steady stream of Eastern

Division Street's literary legacy

Two of Chicago's most beloved native sons, writers **Nelson Algren** (1909-1981) and **Studs Terkel** (1912-), found inspiration on **West Division Street**. Having grown up poor on the South Side, Algren lived in Wicker Park (at 1958 W Evergreen St.) for nearly twenty years after studying journalism in college and serving in the Army. At that time, the neighborhood wasn't just a bit rough around the edges, as it is today – it was a veritable skid row for drunks, pimps, prostitutes, and hoods. Algren was fascinated by the city's underbelly, and wrote about it eloquently in controversial works like, *Chicago: City on the Make*, and *The Man with the Golden Arm*, which depicted a man's descent into heroin addiction and was subsequently made into a 1955 movie starring Frank Sinatra and Kim Novak. After Algren's death in 1981 at the age of 72, the City of Chicago renamed Evergreen Street Algren Street – but soon changed it back after complaints from local residents.

For Terkel – who was one of Algren's closest friends – Division Street epitomized life in the United States, with people of all walks of life, all ethnic backgrounds, and all classes coming together in one neighborhood. A popular TV actor and radio host in the 1940s, Terkel turned to writing after being blacklisted in 1953 for refusing to co-operate with Joseph McCarthy's House Un-American Activities Committee. Intrigued by the lives of the "anonymous millions," the writer set out to preserve the oral history of normal, everyday citizens, interviewing seventy city residents for his 1967 book *Division Street: America*. Terkel talked to immigrants, ambitious locals, and street-wise kids, compiling their views and beliefs to show that, across lines of class and race, each subject had "pertinent comments to make on urban life in the twentieth century." Now in his '90s, Terkel is still on the job, conducting interviews, writing books, and acting as the Distinguished Scholar-in-Residence at the Chicago Historical Society.

European immigrants settled west of Damen Avenue between Chicago Avenue and Division Street. These days, the neighborhood is more of a melting pot, with yuppies joining the city's growing Hispanic community in the developing area as the Eastern European influence dwindles. But stroll along Chicago Avenue, and you'll still pass delis selling pillowy *pierogi* (stuffed dumplings) and hear local Poles chatting in their native tongue (you may hear them refer to the Village as *Helenowo*, after the area's sizeable Polish Roman Catholic parish). Off the main drag, rows of simple red-brick two-flats are centered on the orthodox **churches** that are still the centers of the community. The neighborhood celebrates its heritage at the annual **Ukrainian Village Fest**, held in September and featuring a beer garden, live music, traditional dancing, food, and games.

△ St. Nicholas Ukrainian Cathedral

St Nicholas Ukrainian Cathedral and around

The dominant feature of the low-rise skyline of the **Ukrainian Village** is the ornate, onion-domed roofs of **St Nicholas Ukrainian Catholic Cathedral**, 2238 W Rice St, at N Oakley Boulevard (tours by appointment, call ⓣ773/276-4537, ⓦwww.stnicholaseparchy.org), which was built in 1913 when the surrounding area was little more than pasture. Almost one hundred years later, the church remains the hub of the local Ukrainian community and all services, except one on Sunday, are held in the native language.

The cathedral is a scaled-down model of St Sofia in Kiev, with thirteen rather than the original's 32 domes, but it's a magnificent replica nonetheless, all beige brick and greenish copper. The mosaic in the main loggia above the entranceway was installed in 1988 to commemorate the 1000th anniversary of Christianity's arrival in the Ukraine, and features the king who ushered in its acceptance, St Volodymyr. It's well worth calling ahead to arrange a tour of the dazzling, Byzantine-style **mosaics** in the interior, as well as the largest **chandelier** in North America (holding a blinding 480 bulbs).

More modern but less intriguing than the neighboring cathedral, stands the squat and monumental **Sts Volodymyr and Olha Ukrainian Catholic Church** (ⓣ773/276-3990), 739 Oakley Blvd on the southeast corner of Chicago Avenue. The sapphire-blue and ochre-yellow ceiling murals in the interior are striking, but the real reason to stop by is the enormous, glittering mosaic above the main entrance, which depicts the church's namesake saints, St Volodymyr and his mother St Olha, accepting Christianity into the Ukraine.

The Polish Museum of America

Preserving the heritage of the city's more than one million Poles, the longstanding **Polish Museum of America**, 984 Milwaukee Ave, at Augusta Boulevard (Mon–Wed & Fri–Sun 11am–4pm; $3 donation; ⓣ773/384-3352, ⓦpma.prcua.org), has an eclectic mix of art and artifacts, mainly from Poland but relating to Polish Americans as well, and is worth a visit for those intrigued by the Polish-American experience. Known for its holdings of the personal effects of renowned pianist, statesman, and former Polish prime minister Ignacy Paderewski, the collection also features several exhibits sent from Poland for the city's 1939 World's Fair (for which the museum's striking, thirty-foot-high stained-glass window was made) but stranded here when the country was invaded during World War II. Other displays feature Polish folk costumes, military uniforms, hand-carved Easter eggs, and religious relics; be sure to check out the huge painting in the Great Hall of Revolutionary War hero Casimir Pulaski.

Another hidden neighborhood gem, the small **Ukrainian Institute of Modern Art**, 2320 W Chicago Ave, at Western Avenue, (Wed–Sun noon–4pm; free; ⓣ773/227-5522, ⓦwww.uima-art.org), highlights the works of contemporary Ukrainian and Ukrainian-American artists, from religiously themed oil paintings to abstract sculptures in forged steel.

7

Lincoln Park

Snooty hipsters deride **LINCOLN PARK** as a yuppie haven, filled with weekend rollerbladers working up a sweat before grabbing a latte. It's certainly true that the area is upscale, middle-class, and rather mainstream, but its gorgeous namesake park is a powerful lure for any visitor, as are the verdant avenues of the surrounding neighborhood. The one offbeat section exists in Lincoln Park's northern reaches around **DePaul University**: this enormous Catholic institution, better known for hard partying than devout prayers, has created a small but funky scene in the surrounding blocks.

Originally filled with orchards supplying produce to the city farther south, the Lincoln Park area was converted into Chicago's first cemetery in the mid-nineteenth century. The local dead rested in peace for only a few years before city bigwigs had their bodies moved elsewhere to make room for a massive, prairie-inspired greenspace fit for the unofficial capital of the Midwest. **The park**, established in 1864 and named in honor of President (and Illinois native) Abraham Lincoln, is a staggering slab of greenery, stretching more than 1200 acres and home to one of America's last free zoos.

It would be a hundred years before the surrounding neighborhood reached the same chic desirability of the park. An immigrant enclave that fell into disrepair through under-investment and lack of city interest, the **Lincoln Park neighborhood** was transformed in the 1970s after local institutions like DePaul University and the Lincoln Park Conservation Association successfully agitated for attention (and dollars) – more than $300 million was pumped into a forcible gentrification project that's left the area as it is today: clean, green, and just a tiny bit bland.

You'll find plenty of bars, clubs, and restaurants here – especially along **N Halsted Street** and the diagonal arteries of **N Lincoln Avenue** and **N Clark Street**. Expect to rub shoulders with the Midwestern college graduates and upwardly mobile twentysomethings who've flocked here to nest alongside young families, despite the soaring rents. Not surprisingly, Lincoln Park is one of the safest places in the city. Getting to the neighborhood is easy, thanks to a thorough network of buses and trains running through the area (see box; over).

The park

Extending some six miles from North Avenue to Hollywood Avenue along the lakefront, **Lincoln Park** is much larger and more user-friendly than the urban Grant Park (see p.97) to the south. Lush and conspicuously devoid of commercial development, the park offers some of the most dramatic views of the downtown skyline. The park's main attractions are the **Lincoln Park Zoo** and the **Lincoln Park Conservatory** along with the newly renovated

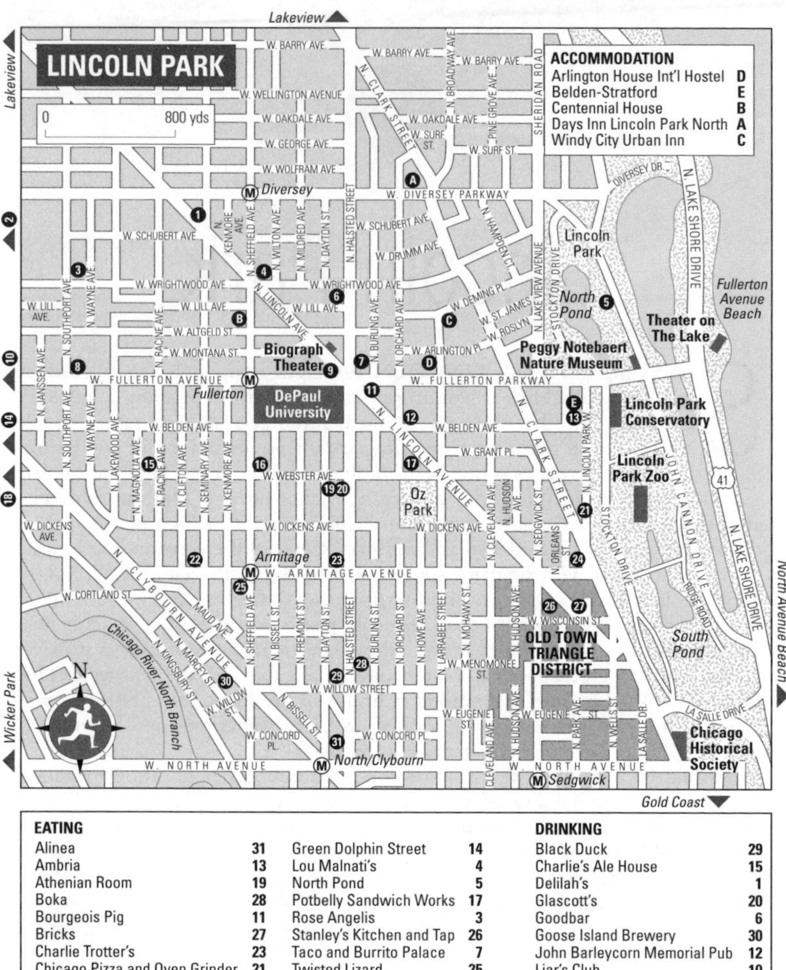

EATING	
Alinea	31
Ambria	13
Athenian Room	19
Boka	28
Bourgeois Pig	11
Bricks	27
Charlie Trotter's	23
Chicago Pizza and Oven Grinder	21
Dee's Mandarin Restaurant	22
Geja's Café	24
Green Dolphin Street	14
Lou Malnati's	4
North Pond	5
Potbelly Sandwich Works	17
Rose Angelis	3
Stanley's Kitchen and Tap	26
Taco and Burrito Palace	7
Twisted Lizard	25
Via Carducci	8

DRINKING	
Black Duck	29
Charlie's Ale House	15
Delilah's	1
Glascott's	20
Goodbar	6
Goose Island Brewery	30
John Barleycorn Memorial Pub	12
Liar's Club	10
McGee's	16
Red Lion Pub	9
Walsh's Shubert Inn	2
Webster's Wine Bar	18

Chicago Historical Society, but it's probably best experienced for its natural delights; thanks to the lake's natural regulation of air temperature, it makes for a comfortable place to laze through a hot summer's day, notably at the beaches, where throngs of locals come to sunbathe, swim, and play volleyball.

Running the length of the park is the scenic **lakefront path**, excellent for running, rollerblading, and biking, and the easiest way to reach many of the park's beaches, playgrounds, tennis courts, and ball fields. In fact, Chicago's reputation as one of the most bike-friendly cities in the country is due, in large part, to the extensive network of bike paths here. For details on rental outfits, see box, p.250.

Although the wide streak of Lake Shore Drive cuts the park off from the water, you'll have plenty of chances to cross it via pedestrian tunnels and bridges.

Getting there and around

Getting to the Lincoln Park neighborhood is a breeze: just hop on the Brown, Red, or Purple El lines to the Fullerton stop, and you'll be in the middle of DePaul University. The park itself is about a half-mile east and is more easily accessed by the #151 bus (also get off at Fullerton). For park programs and general information, contact the Chicago Park District at ⓣ312/742-7529 or visit their website, ⓦwww.chicagoparkdistrict.com.

Driving is strongly advised against, since **parking** in this very crowded neighborhood is scarce – even pay-lots are few and far between – especially after 6pm. Cycling is a better option; the **Bike Chicago booth** at the **North Avenue Beach boathouse** rents bikes for $10 per hour and $35 per day; they also rent in-line skates (see p.250). Between May and September, you can rent **paddleboats** on Lincoln Park's South Pond, outside *Café Brauer* (2021 N Stockton Drive; $10/half-hour or $15/hr). Boat rentals are from 10am to dusk. For more on these and other activities, see "Sports and outdoor activities," p.246.

The Chicago Historical Society and around

At the park's southwest edge, the red-brick and glass **Chicago Historical Society**, 1601 N Clark St (Mon–Wed noon–8pm, Thurs–Sat 9.30am–4.30pm, Sun noon–5pm; $6, free Mon; ⓣ312/642-4600, ⓦwww.chicagohs.org), holds an exhaustive record of the city's growth from its frontier days, either on display in its permanent and temporary exhibits or archived in its research center.

On the **first floor**, costumed staff bring the Illinois pioneer days to life, demonstrating chores such as spinning flax and weaving yarn. A miniature Conestoga wagon is a minor highlight of the section devoted to the US garrison Fort Dearborn and Chicago's early days as a fur-trading center. Among the interactive exhibits, "The Great Chicago Fire: The Web of Memory" stands out, with online essays, eyewitness accounts, photographs, and galleries of items rescued from the blaze (hours vary on weekdays, Sat 11am–4.30pm, Sun noon–4.30pm).

The bulk of the **second floor** is taken up by the American History wing. Many of Abraham Lincoln's personal effects can be viewed in the exhibit "A House Divided: America in the Age of Lincoln," a trenchant, detailed look at slavery and the Civil War through a wealth of artifacts. Chief among these are Lincoln's famed correspondence with General Ulysses S. Grant, the table on which he wrote the Emancipation Proclamation, and his deathbed. Elsewhere on the floor, the "We the People" exhibit looks back at the American Revolution, focusing on the unsung heroes and lesser-known personalities who helped shape the nation between 1765 and 1820.

Only serious history buffs should head up to the third-floor **research center**, which holds thousands of newspaper-clipping files and more than 1.5 million images of Chicago dating from the early nineteenth century, as well as paintings, sculptures, recordings, and costumes. Particular highlights are the Studs Terkel Oral History Archives, where you can listen to fifty years' worth of radio interviews conducted by Chicago's renowned historian, and the Charles F. Murphy Architectural Study Center, a huge collection of drawings, photographs, and models contributed by Chicago's major architects. To commemorate the museum's 150th anniversary in 2006, the space is undergoing extensive renovation of its galleries, adding audiovisual presentations, a children's gallery, and more. The center will remain open throughout. The new galleries will be unveiled in the fall of 2006.

On a grassy flat just north of North Avenue and just east of the Historical Society, you'll find the white **Couch Mausoleum**, the last remaining sign of the park's past life as a cemetery. The Couch family refused to move the mausoleum to make room for the park, a case that went all the way to the Supreme Court.

Nearby **The Standing Lincoln**, by renowned artist Saint-Gaudens, depicts the sixteenth president. Standing in front of an ornate claw-foot chair, head slightly bowed in humble reflection, Lincoln appears poised to address a congregation. A replica of this original statue – considered the highlight of Saint-Gaudens' career – stands in Lincoln's tomb in downstate Springfield.

During the warmer months, volleyball tournaments and jugglers keep things lively at **North Avenue Beach**, a patch of sand two blocks east of the Historical Society, where Chicagoans come to sun and be seen (for more details, see p.252). The center of activity here is the 22,000-square-foot **North Avenue Beach House**, which resembles an ocean liner and features outdoor showers; a lifeguard station; rental offices for bikes, chairs, and volleyball equipment; and the rooftop hangout *Castaway's Bar & Grill* with great views of the city skyline and a low-key menu.

The Lincoln Park Zoo and around

In the heart of the park sits the renowned **Lincoln Park Zoo**, which you can enter at 2200 N Cannon Drive, just west of Lake Shore Drive at the Fullerton Parkway exit (Nov–March 9am–5pm; April–Oct 9am–6pm; Sat until 7pm in summer; zoo grounds close one hour after last ticket sale; free; ⓣ312/742-2000, ⓦwww.lpzoo.com). The zoo is the oldest in the country, as well as one of Chicago's last major freebies (although the hefty parking charge [$12] tends to negate that deal somewhat), and welcomes more than three million visitors annually. Opened in 1868 with the gift of two swans from New York's Central Park, Lincoln Park Zoo's sylvan 35-acre lakefront site is home to more than one thousand animals, divided between four trails, marked blue, red, gold, and green, that snake past different groupings of animals (primates, birds, reptiles etc.) through its grounds. The zoo is best known for its collection of great apes, and now houses them in the state-of-the-art new **Regenstein Center for African Apes**, boasting 29,000 square feet of indoor and outdoor living space, dozens of trees, and 5000 feet of artificial vines for climbing. Monkey-lovers should check out the **Primate House** for the smaller lemurs and howler monkeys. Other highlights are the **Kovler Lion House**, with its impressive collection of big cats and the interactive **Farm-in-the-Zoo**, aimed squarely at little ones, a five-acre replica of a Midwestern farm, where kids can milk cows, churn butter, and groom goats. Another new attraction for kids is the **Pritzker Family Children's Zoo**, with interactive exhibits that teach toddlers about bears, wolves, beavers, and otters through engaging exhibits that emphasize play and discovery – one station lets kids climb a mesh-enclosed "treetop canopy" – and also giving kids a peek at the animals themselves.

Things have not all been rosy recently at the zoo, which came under intense scrutiny in the spring of 2005 with the deaths of several animals – including three langur monkeys, a gorilla, and all three of the zoo's African elephants – occurring in less than a year and a half. After extensive investigation, the zoo was found to not be at fault, and zoo officials insist that they are dedicated to keeping the animals happy and healthy. Regardless, the zoo remains one of the city's top attractions, and is still a great place to visit for both children and adults.

Faintly reminiscent of London's Crystal Palace on a far smaller scale, the **Lincoln Park Conservatory** stands just south of Fullerton Parkway on

Stockton Drive (daily 9am–5pm; free; ⓣ312/742-7736, ⓦwww.chicagoparkdistrict.com). Built in the early 1980s, this steamy indoor oasis is divided into four areas (Palm House, Show House, Orchid House, and Fern Room), and has thousands of exotic plants on display. There's nothing spectacular in its collection, but this part of the park does afford great views of the city.

Across Fullerton Parkway, you'll find the sophisticated **Peggy Notebaert Nature Museum**, 2430 N Cannon Drive (Mon–Fri 9am–4.30pm, Sat & Sun 10am–5pm; $7; ⓣ773/755-5100, ⓦwww.naturemuseum.org), centering on an enormous glass enclosure housing an artificial rainforest full of hundreds of exotic **butterflies**; there's also an exhibit on the butterflies' life cycle and migration patterns, with knowledgeable staff on hand. Although the rest of the exhibits are better suited to school field trips, there's plenty of compelling stuff here for nature buffs, including a "wilderness walk" through simulated prairie, savannah, and dune environments, and a 17,000-square-foot rooftop garden that demonstrates eco-friendly "green" technology.

North of the zoo

Though attractions are scarce in Lincoln Park's northern reaches, there are a few activities that can make a jaunt up here worthwhile. The narrow, sandy strip at **Fullerton Avenue Beach**, 2400 N Lake Shore Drive (daily from Memorial Day through Labor Day 9am–9.30pm) is less of a scene than the North Avenue and Oak Street beaches to the south (see p. 252 and p.88). Nearby, the red-brick **Theater on the Lake** hosts annual summer performances by top local theater groups like Steppenwolf and Second City (for more on these companies, see Chapter 17, "Performing arts and film").

About two miles north of the theater, off Waveland Avenue, the crowded, nine-hole **Sydney R. Marovitz Golf Course** (see p.253) has good views of the city, but if you're looking to hit a few balls you're better off heading elsewhere (like, say, the **driving range** at 141 W Diversey Parkway, which is tucked a block east of the intersection of Diversey and Sheridan; for details, see p.253). Beyond here, there's more rolling park and space for a few outdoor pursuits, such as **archery** on Belmont Harbor Drive, and **birdwatching** at the **Magic Hedge**, an area of trees and shrubs at Montrose Point to the far north. The "hedge" sits at the tip of a curled sliver of land off the shores of Lake Michigan and lies in a migration corridor where sightings of more than three hundred species of birds have been recorded on this sandy hill. The best time to visit is during spring and fall migrations, but on any given day you're likely to spot up to fifty-odd species, including warblers, swallows, and falcons; especially eye-catching are the thousands of purple martins that flock here in early August. The Magic Hedge is only accessible **by car**; from Montrose Avenue, east of Lake Shore Drive, take a right on Montrose Harbor Drive, then follow the first curve in the road to the small hill to the east.

The Lincoln Park neighborhood

Loosely bordered by North Avenue (1600N), Diversey Parkway (2800N), Damen Avenue (2000W), and the lake, Lincoln Park was first settled in the early to mid-1800s by German immigrants who took to farming the area's land. The neighborhood boomed after the Great Chicago Fire, attracting German and Irish immigrants who toiled to construct thousands of homes to accommodate the waves of new residents moving north from downtown. Today, visitors to the neighborhood will find little to remind them of this ethnic heritage aside from the Irish pubs that proliferate here. The best way to see the Lincoln Park neighborhood is to walk, and the streets around DePaul University are as good a place to start as any. On **Armitage** and **Webster** avenues, you'll pass upscale boutiques and shops of every kind, from women's fashion to outdoor-equipment stores; while **Halsted Street** is the focus of the area's nightlife, with countless bars overflowing with Abercrombie & Fitch-clad twentysomethings and their girlfriends – cheerfully preppy lasses who are disparagingly referred to by jaded locals as "Lincoln Park trixies." **Lincoln Avenue** and **Clark Street** – the two main commercial thoroughfares – cut diagonally through Lincoln Park from southeast to northwest and are dotted with secondhand bookstores, music shops, and vintage-clothing stores, becoming more eclectic the further north you walk. Away from these streets, the area is pleasantly residential and tranquil.

While the neighborhood isn't known for any sight in particular, it is home to a notable institution or two. Below Fullerton Avenue, **DePaul University** begins its 36-acre sprawl, though its campus holds little of interest for casual visitors. Founded in 1898, the school's 20,000 students make it the largest Catholic university in the country, and recent *Princeton Review* surveys found them to be the "happiest" students in the country, thanks to a diverse student body, small class size, and continued improvements to the campus such as a three-level student center completed in 2002.

Just above Fullerton Avenue, at 2433 N Lincoln Ave, the 1915 **Biograph Theater** marks the site where bank robber John Dillinger met his end in a shootout with the FBI in 1934. Dillinger was also known to frequent the back rooms of what's now the *John Barleycorn Memorial Pub*, just down the street (for a full review, see p.212). Declared a national landmark in 2001, the building was recently purchased by **Victory Gardens Theater** and is in the midst of a renovation process that will add a 299-seat mainstage theater, a black box space, and disability access. The theater, named the **Zacek-McVay Theater**, is set to open in fall 2006.

Following N Lincoln Avenue south to Webster Avenue, you'll arrive at leafy **Oz Park**, replete with a yellow-brick road and three sculptures by John Kearney: a shiny Tin Man made entirely of chrome car-bumpers, and a bronze

The St Valentine's Day Massacre

One of the bloodiest moments in Chicago's gangland history took place in Lincoln Park on February 14, 1929, when five men – three dressed as cops, two as civilians – visited the garage of **Al Capone**'s rival **Bugs Moran** at 2122 N Clark St, surprising seven of his henchmen. Announcing a bust, the men in uniform promptly lined Moran's men up against the back wall of the garage, gunned them down execution-style and sped off into the night, an event that came to be known as the **St Valentine's Day Massacre**. The "cops" were widely believed to be Capone's men in disguise, sent to avenge the deaths of two of Capone's heavies as well as the theft of his booze shipments from Canada. Although Moran had taken cover at the first sight of the "cops" and escaped unharmed, the massacre effectively put him out of business.

While the police could never pin the deed on Capone (in fact, no one was ever charged for the crime), who was vacationing in Florida at the time, the FBI arrested him for tax evasion a few years later and shipped him off to Alcatraz. The garage was demolished in 1967; these days, there's just a patch of lawn and a few trees where the garage once stood, though spooked passers-by have claimed to hear screams and machine-gun fire in the vicinity. For more on Capone, see p.284.

△ Tin Man statue in Oz Park

cowardly lion and scarecrow, the last of which was dedicated in the summer of 2005. Named after Frank Baum's mythical land (Baum wrote *The Wonderful Wizard of Oz* while living in nearby Humboldt Park), the thirteen-acre park is a great place to shoot hoops, play volleyball, or just take a break from shopping.

8

Lakeview and Andersonville

While the North-Side area of **LAKEVIEW** was long little more than the poor man's version of its southern neighbor Lincoln Park, in recent years, rising real-estate prices and increased congestion have turned the area into a similar yuppie haven, although some of its rough-around-the-edges appeal remains. Though there isn't much to see or do here besides window-shop and hang out in cafés, it's still pleasant to browse **Clark Street**, the main thoroughfare, on a weekend afternoon or stroll along the lakefront parkway.

Incorporated as a town in 1865 by a group of German celery-farmers, Lakeview takes its name from the long-since-vanished *Lakeview Inn*, a local hotel with sweeping vistas of Lake Michigan. This chunk of land north of Fullerton Avenue remained a separate town (much like Hyde Park on the South Side, annexed by Chicago at around the same time) until 1889, when it was swallowed whole by the growing city. As the settlement rapidly grew, its neighborhoods took on individual identities, none more so than **Wrigleyville**, which in 1914 became home to the newly built Wrigley Field, stadium of the Chicago Cubs. Sandwiching the ballpark are Chicago's two most gay-friendly neighborhoods. To the south, the "pink triangle" of **Boystown** occupies the blocks between Halsted Street, Broadway, and Belmont Avenue. Once a haven for silent-movie makers and speakeasy patrons, **Uptown**, north of Boystown, still has a few traces left of its Jazz-Age past. Further north, **ANDERSONVILLE** is a former Swedish settlement that, while holding onto its Scandinavian roots, has become another center for the city's gay and lesbian community.

Transport links here grow spottier the farther north you travel; the best option is to hop on the Red El line train that bisects the area. And remember to check the sports schedules before planning a trip – during home games, Wrigleyville transforms into a boozy, frat boy–packed nightmare, where it's often impossible to find **parking** (or a seat, for that matter). As there are no major highways around these parts, and virtually no parking to be found, the El trains to the Red Line Addison stop nearby become moving sardine-cans.

Wrigleyville

The neighborhood surrounding Wrigley Field, **Wrigleyville**, got its name from savvy developers, hoping to trade on the park's immense popularity to

EATING

Acqualina 10
Ann Sather 26
Café 28 11
Henry's 1
Intelligentsia 28
Le Creperie 32
Magnolia 9
On Common Ground 12
Penny's Noodle Shop 23
Rise 22
Southport Grocery 18
Southport Lanes and Billiards 24
Swedish Bakery 2
Tango Sur 13
Taste of Lebanon 6
The Wiener's Circle 33
Victory's Banner 21

DRINKING

Cubby Bear 19
Cullen's Bar and Grill 15
Duke of Perth 30
Ginger Man 14
Green Mill 8
Hopleaf 7
Hye Bar 16
The Irish Oak 20
Jack's/404 wine bar 31
Jet Vodka Lounge 34
Pops for Champagne 29
Redmond's 25
Resi's Bierstube 3
Sheffield's Wine and Beer Garden 27
Simon's Tavern 5
Tiny Lounge 17

sell the new houses they were building nearby. During baseball season, the area is overrun by **Cubs fans**, loyally bedecked with blue-and-white team paraphernalia and crowding into the many local bars, spilling out into the streets and even onto the rooftops. It quiets down some during the off-season, but not much – on weekends, the neighborhood's twentysomething residents pack into **sports bars** on the stretch of Clark Street between Addison and Roscoe, and the stadium itself has become a sort of Mecca: even in the dead of winter, tourists will hop off the train at Addison to stand outside and contemplate the coming baseball season.

Wrigley Field

At the center of it all, ivy-covered **Wrigley Field** itself remains one of the best places to get a real feel for baseball – the Cubs are so traditional that it fought the installation of floodlights until 1988. Even if you know nothing about baseball, there are few more pleasant ways to spend an afternoon than drinking beer, eating hot dogs, and watching the Cubs struggle to win a ball game (they haven't won a World Series since 1908).

Built in 1914 and named for Cubs owner and chewing-gum bigwig Philip Wrigley, the stadium has been extensively renovated in its ninety-odd years, but some things haven't changed: the field is still the smallest in the league, the ivy planted by the outfield walls in 1937 is still there, and the scoreboard continues to be operated by hand. Equally enduring is the tenacious loyalty of its fans; despite heavy losses the Cubs manage to sell out nearly every game. The "Bleacher Bums," a contingent of raucous fans, have been a fixture ever since they first staked their claim to the outfield bleachers back in 1966. One of their traditions is to toss home-run balls hit by the opposing team, back onto the field. For more information on the Cubs and seeing a game, see p.247.

If you can't make it to the ballpark during a game, there's a ninety-minute **tour** of the stadium that will take you through the clubhouses, suites, dugouts, press box, bleachers, and playing field (call for schedule; tickets are $15 and must be purchased in advance; ⓣ773/404-2827).

Alta Vista Terrace

Nicknamed the "Street of Forty Doors," this charming oddity, tucked away northwest of the stadium, is well worth a detour. In the 1890s, after a trip to London's chic Mayfair district, local real-estate developer Samuel Eberly Gross decided to create his own version of the area's stately townhouses back home in Chicago. It took him four years to build his vision, **Alta Vista Terrace**, a single block of row houses wedged between N Sheridan Road and N Grace Street, but by 1904, they were complete and have remained refreshingly untouched ever since. Indeed, thanks to the close-set homes' unique, high-Victorian style and the unusual narrowness of this one-way street, Alta Vista is unlike any other road in Chicago.

Architecturally, the houses may seem eclectic and far from uniform at first; doorways are painted a variety of colors, from bright red to slate gray, and the buildings feature various ornate gables and windows that set them apart from one another. Look more closely, though, and you'll notice a curious thing: each house on the block has an identical twin that is diagonally opposite it across the street. With only minor variations, these houses were designed to be exactly the same, from the shape of their ornate gables and garland molding to the striking round bay windows that adorn several on the block.

Graceland Cemetery

The final resting place of Chicago's old-time elite, the lush **Graceland Cemetery** (8am–4.30pm) makes for a pleasant ramble across its 120 rolling acres, which spread from W Irving Park Road to Montrose Avenue. Opened in 1860, Graceland was created to replace the overcrowded municipal cemetery in what's now Lincoln Park (see p.115), a move brought on by fears that the lakeside cemetery posed a serious health risk. The main entrance is at Clark Street and Irving Park Road, where you can pick up a map as well as a copy of the Chicago Architecture Foundation's *A Walk Through Graceland Cemetery* ($9.95), though only fanatics looking to search out every marker might find need for this.

You'll spot a wide variety of memorials here, everything from fussy Gothic graves to veritable temples, all laid out among a lush landscape of giant oak, elm, and maple trees. Socialites **Potter and Bertha Palmer** (see p.86) lie inside a massive Neoclassical mausoleum held up by sixteen columns. Less ostentatious are steel tycoon **Henry Getty**'s grave – a subdued stone cube designed by Louis Sullivan – and the headstone of **Daniel Burnham**, which sits on a small island linked to the shore by a narrow walkway.

Two of Chicago's most influential architects have surprisingly unremarkable tombs: **Ludwig Mies van der Rohe** lies beneath a polished stone slab set into the ground, while **Louis Sullivan**'s is only slightly more conspicuous. Sullivan, in fact, died in 1924 in poverty and lacked a gravestone for several years.

Chicago shopping magnate **Marshall Field** is commemorated here with the Daniel Chester French–designed monument *Memory*, a contemplative seated figure that bears more than a passing resemblance to the Lincoln Monument, which French also designed. One of the more whimsical gravesites is that of **William Hulbert**, founder of professional baseball's National League, who is memorialized with a large baseball-shaped marker. Other don't-miss sites include the tomb of wealthy hotelier **Dexter Graves**, whose grave is marked by the eerie, hooded bronze figure *Eternal Silence* (also known as the "Statue of Death"), which stands in front of a polished black-marble slab; the pyramid-shaped mausoleum of Prussian-born brewery owner **Peter Schoenhofen**, guarded by a male sphinx and a female angel holding a bronze key; and the Plexiglas box-enclosed, life-sized statue of 6-year-old Inez Clark, who, local ghost stories attest, can sometimes be seen walking through the cemetery in nineteenth-century garb.

To **get here**, take the Red line to the Sheridan stop and walk a few blocks west on Irving Park Road.

Boystown and around

The buff bodies and rainbow-colored Art Deco pylons lining Halsted Street let you know you're in **Boystown**, the hub of Chicago's sizeable gay community. Along with the Castro in San Francisco and Chelsea in New York, Boystown is one of the most welcoming, gay-friendly districts in the US. The neighborhood is most alive during the summer, when events like the **Gay Pride Parade** in late June and **Northalsted Street Market Days** in early August draw thousands upon thousands of gay, lesbian, bisexual, and transgendered folks to party in the streets (for more information see "Festivals and events," Chapter 21). With its excellent restaurants and lively cafés, the street life buzzes mostly on **Halsted Street** and **Broadway** between Belmont Avenue and Irving Park Road – among them *tchotchke* shops, rare-book stores, and leather markets. Recent years have seen something of an exodus to Uptown and Andersonville to the north, but the intersection of Roscoe and Halsted is still ground zero for the city's queer set.

Most of the action centers on the long-standing bars here – *Sidetrack* and *Roscoe's Tavern* in particular, both classics (see p.243 for review); on busy weekend nights, lines snake out of both bars. In the 1980s, the neighborhood had a seedy feel, with men openly cruising each other on Halsted and soliciting for sex on the side streets (particularly Elaine Place a block east), but, for better or for worse, ubiquitous condo development and rising real-estate prices have transformed the 'hood into another polished yuppie corridor. A few blocks just east of Wrigley Field, the much-anticipated **Center on Halsted** is set to open in late 2006. The first facility of its kind in the Midwest, the center will cater to the city's gay, lesbian, bisexual, and transgender community, with gay youth programs, mental health and community services, galleries, and recreational and social space. See "Gay and lesbian Chicago," p.239, for more information.

Outside its specific neighborhoods, Lakeview holds a few pockets of interest along its commercial thoroughfares. One of the more popular strips is **N Southport Avenue** between Belmont Avenue and Irving Park Road, along which cluster shops, restaurants, and bars, minus the crowds and sales gimmicks. One of the strip's long-standing novelties is **Southport Lanes**, at no. 3325, a four-lane bowling alley that opened in 1922 and still uses human pinsetters to this day – one of the posted rules says "Remember, if you see legs, don't bowl!" Several blocks north, it's hard to miss the large pink neon sign and old-fashioned marquee of the **Music Box Theatre**, at no. 3733, a refurbished movie house built in 1929. Step inside to see the twinkling stars on the ceiling – worth a look (and accessible), even if there's not a show on (see p.231 for details).

Some of the **restaurants** around Belmont Avenue are worth going out of your way for. The Lakeview branch of *Ann Sather*, at 929 Belmont Ave, is always packed and sells the chain's signature treats – gooey Swedish cinnamon rolls – while *Giordano's*, at no. 1040, is one of the best places for Chicago-style deep dish pizza. You'll also find a clutch of excellent dining options along N Clark Street, notably *Mia Francesca*, at 3311 N Clark St, which serves some of the city's most popular Italian food (if you don't mind the long wait). For reviews, see "Eating," Chapter 14.

Uptown

The curtain of nondescript high-rises between Lakeview and Andersonville forms the backdrop for **Uptown**, once the playground of Prohibition-era mobsters and pre-Hollywood-era filmmakers (see box p.128). Mostly untouched until the late 1890s, the area was swampy and undesirable. As wealthy Chicagoans continued to move north, though, this "suburb" became more attractive, and by the early 1900s Uptown was one of the city's fastest-growing neighborhoods, with dozens of high-rise apartment buildings, hundreds of shops, and an active nightlife centered around the area's many restaurants and speakeasies. Inexpensive, plentiful housing helped Uptown become one of the city's most diverse ethnic neighborhoods; growth continued until the 1960s, as more and more residents relocated to the suburbs and the neighborhood began a swift decline that led to arson, violence, and neglect that Uptown still struggles with today. In recent years, the recovering district has become a center of the city's Vietnamese, Korean, and Native American communities; the big news these days is the onward progress of gentrification in the area, with a new *Starbucks*, Borders bookstore, and a slew of reasonably priced, newly gutted and rehabbed properties drawing young professionals to live in the midst of halfway houses and Section Eight housing. Most of the action happens around the intersection

△ Music Box Theatre

of Broadway and Lawrence; **to get here**, take the Red Line to Lawrence and walk a block west to Broadway.

Uptown's colorful past survives at *The Green Mill* (see p.221 for review), a former speakeasy that was once Al Capone's favorite watering hole and still Chicago's best **jazz club**. Just north of *The Green Mill* is one of the neighborhood's greatest monuments, the ornate **Uptown Theater**, at 4816 N. Broadway, a majestic movie and stage palace. The theater was built in 1925 in the Spanish Revival style, with elaborate roof parapets, twisting columns, and terracotta ornamentation; with seating for 4300 people it was the second-largest movie palace in the country after New York's Radio City Music Hall. Shuttered in the 1970s, the theater was designated a Chicago landmark in 1991; local civic groups have pressured the building's current owners to renovate and reopen the theater, but the structure remains closed for the foreseeable future.

A little over a mile to the west in Lincoln Square, the **Old Town School of Folk Music**, at 4544 N Lincoln Ave, hosts hundreds of concerts a year, which reflect the school's exhaustive course offerings – everything from blues guitar to the Djembe and Aztec ceremonial dances. Take the Ravenswood El line to Western Station, then walk east to Lincoln Avenue and turn south to the school or else catch the Lincoln (#11) or Western (#49) bus lines to their Wilson Avenue stops and from there walk south on Lincoln Avenue.

Andersonville

Perched north of Lakeview and Uptown, **Andersonville** is as small-town as Chicago gets, with independent shops and cafés, a friendly, neighborly feel, and a lingering Scandinavian heritage. Beginning in the 1840s, many Swedes began to immigrate to Chicago to escape overpopulation in their home country. After the Great Fire, wooden homes were outlawed in Chicago, so the Swedish poor moved north of the city, transforming a cluster of celery farms into a bustling center along **Clark Street** between Foster and Bryn Mawr, still the commercial heart of the neighborhood today.

Hollywood in Chicago

Back in the early 1900s during the heyday of silent movies, the epicenter of the film industry wasn't LA or New York – it was Chicago, whose Uptown-based **Essanay Studios** was a powerful force in bringing cinema to the masses.

Founded in 1908 by **George K. Spoor** and actor **G.M. "Bronco Billy" Anderson**, Essanay ("S and A") was based in a warehouse at 1333–45 W Argyle St. It was in this building's studios and outdoor courtyard that the pair made hundreds of silent films starring Anderson (who created the first cowboy hero in Bronco Billy), legendary actress **Gloria Swanson**, and, most famously, **Charlie Chaplin**, who made *His New Job*, *A Woman*, and the classic short *The Tramp*, for the studio. The studio was a bona-fide smash, and Spoor and Anderson soon set up Essanay-West in Los Angeles, where the industry was gaining a foothold thanks to more reliable weather and an infinite pool of star talent.

Soon, though, the tides turned on Essanay: Chaplin defected to Metro Films (soon to become MGM), and disputes between Spoor and Anderson led to the collapse of the studio in 1917, less than ten years after it was established. Eventually, Anderson and Spoor would go on to win honorary Academy Awards in 1948 and 1958, respectively, for their contributions to the development of film. The studio warehouse itself was declared a Chicago landmark in 1996, and the company's logo – a terra cotta Native American head – is still visible over the entrance of the building, now home to St Augustine College.

Although Swedes continued to emigrate here well into the twentieth century, by the 1960s their community had begun to disperse, many returning to their homeland or moving to the suburbs. Despite the exodus, Andersonville still has one of the highest concentrations of Swedes in the US, and Clark Street does still boast several thriving Swedish shops, bakeries, and a museum. Preserving that heritage becomes ever more challenging, though, in the face of a burgeoning influx of professionals (including a sizeable gay and lesbian community) moving north to escape the escalating costs of Lakeview and Lincoln Park.

While public transportation to the area can be time-consuming, it's probably the best way to **get here** as taxi fares from neighboring Lakeview can be over $10. Take the CTA Red Line to Berwyn or Bryn Mawr or hop on bus #22 (Clark), #36 (Broadway), or #92 (Foster).

Clark Street and around

Lined with shops, restaurants, and bustling cafés, **Clark Street** is the heart of Andersonville, and everything worth visiting in the neighborhood is on or nearby it in the few blocks north of Foster Avenue. Chief among these is the engaging **Swedish American Museum Center**, 5211 N Clark St (Tues–Fri 10am–4pm, Sat & Sun 11am–4pm; ⓣ773/728-8111, ⓦwww.samac.org), devoted mainly to Chicago's Swedish-American heritage but with enough broad appeal to please anyone interested in the immigrant experience. Officially dedicated in 1976 by Swedish king Carl Gustaf, the museum began as a modest storefront with collections of family histories; three decades, a move, and several renovations later, the collection encompasses several floors of historical and cultural exhibits, from displays of works by contemporary Swedish artists to maps, artifacts, and a hands-on children's museum that teaches kids about the immigration experience using a 20ft model steamboat and a replica of a Swedish farmhouse.

During the winter holidays, residents of nearby states make the pilgrimage to Andersonville for the **Swedish food**: traditional *rosette* and *spritz* cookies,

Swedish meatballs, Göteborg sausage, and pickled herring. Any of Clark Street's handful of establishments devoted to Swedish cuisine are worth a try, particularly cozy café *Svea*, 5236 N Clark St; *Erickson's Delicatessen & Fish Market* at no. 5250 (whose owner is also a trove of information about the history of the neighborhood); and *The Swedish Bakery* at no. 5348, where customers routinely wait an hour for fabulous marzipan, *limpa* bread, and other sweet treats.

One of the last great **city taverns**, *Simon's*, at 5210 N Clark St, is thick with dark, divey atmosphere and history, helped along by the worn mahogany bar, the steamship motif, and the Viking paraphernalia. During the 1930s, the original owner began a free check-cashing service for Swedish laborers, throwing in free sandwiches to boot – an ingenious idea, as most of the money he doled out to his workers never left the bar. If you're lucky, the present owner will show you the bullet-proof check-cashing station under the stairs or the original basement door to the speakeasy, which was run on the premises during Prohibition.

Around the corner from Simon's at the intersection of Ashland and Foster is the **Neo-Futurarium**, where fringe theater group the Neo-Futurists have staged their play Too *Much Light Makes the Baby Go Blind* every weekend night since December of 1988, making it the longest-running show in Chicago today (see p.229). A cult favorite for college students, the production features thirty plays performed in sixty minutes, and admission price is determined by the roll of a die (5153 N Foster Ave ⓣ773/275-5255, ⓦwww.neofuturists.org).

Away from Clark Street, the neighborhood holds little of interest, though the quiet, narrow side streets to the east are lined with rows of charming early twentieth-century brownstone houses and make for a pleasant stroll.

9

The West Side

Comprising the neighborhoods of Greektown, Pilsen, Little Italy, and the West Loop, Chicago's **WEST SIDE** was the gateway for Chicago's myriad ethnic groups, who flocked to the city during its late-nineteenth-century boom years and congregated in its now distinct neighborhoods. Since then, many of the Greek, East European, and Italian residents have moved to the suburbs or been displaced by large-scale development (notably the campus of the University of Illinois-Chicago), a shift especially evident in **Greektown**, where these days you'll struggle to find many Greek Americans other than those running the local restaurants.

Little Italy, conversely, is one of the few immigrant communities that *is* flourishing, as young hipsters move in alongside older residents. Chicago's Mexican-American community is booming as well; the city has one of the largest Hispanic populations in the country, found in pockets across the city but clustered most heavily in the former Eastern European neighborhood of **Pilsen**, whose buildings are covered with brightly painted murals and tile mosaics paying homage to important Mexican and Chicano figures, from Frida Kahlo to Carlos Santana.

Between these residential areas and downtown stands the **West Loop**, where warehouses thrown up in the nineteenth century have been converted into trendy loft apartments a hundred years later. Aside from these and the popular restaurant row along W Randolph Street, the West Side is a solid, working-class area with few official sights – a visit here is more about soaking up ethnic flavors (and sampling a few at local restaurants, too), than hopping between museums.

The best **public transport** option to reach these neighborhoods is the El Blue Line, which hugs the Congress Expressway; but make sure to stick to main streets, especially at night. Pilsen especially is a safe enclave stuck amid blocks of urban blight: get off at the 18th Street stop or just grab a cab.

The West Loop

Crossing the Chicago River from the Loop into the **West Loop**, the first thing you'll notice are the gleaming new office towers and the tips of construction cranes poking into the sky, all signs of economic spillover from the Loop. This is where the West Side proper begins, bounded by Ashland Avenue to the west, the river to the east, Grand Avenue to the north, and 16th Street to the south, a sprawl of tired-looking low-rises that continues on, flat and unchanging, for miles.

Close to the river are the city's two main train stations. You can get a whiff of the grand days of train travel inside **Union Station**, at 500 W Adams St, through which almost every cross-country Amtrak train passes. During the 1940s and 1950s, more than 100,000 people filed across the pink marble floors

of the Great Hall daily or sat under its airy, vaulted ceilings on the wooden benches; now that number has been halved, and most travelers bypass the hall and buy their tickets on board the trains instead. The climactic baby carriage shootout scene in the movie *The Untouchables* was filmed on the marble steps.

The more contemporary **Ogilvie Transportation Center**, also known as North Western Station, serves the Metra commuter-rail network three blocks north at 500 W Madison St. The train station is housed beneath the striking **Citicorp Center tower** – the blue glass of Helmut Jahn's Postmodern skyscraper cascades down its north and south sides like a waterfall.

Around the train stations, you'll find the city's oldest church standing a couple of blocks west of Union Station, at 700 W Adams St: **Old Saint Patrick's** has fifteen magnificent stained-glass windows inspired by Celtic art from the

Columbian Exposition and the *Book of Kells*. Each July, the restored Romanesque building, completed in 1856, hosts the self-styled "World's Largest Block Party," a fundraiser that doubles as a singles' event (see p.257). Just west of North Western Station you'll find **Claes Oldenburg**'s playful *Batcolumn*, a slender 100-foot cage shaped to resemble an oversized baseball bat planted in front of the Social Security Administration Building, at 600 W Madison St. A short walk northwest of here will bring you to the area's top **restaurants**, who've set up shop on artsy-industrial W Randolph Street; for reviews, see "Eating," p.199.

The only other place of note around the West Loop is **Harpo Studios**, at 1058 W Washington Blvd (Mon–Fri 9am–5pm; ⊕312/633-1000), a former armory where the enterprising **Oprah Winfrey** tapes her phenomenally popular talk shows. **Tickets** to the shows are free. They're generally made available one month at a time and are snapped up within days, so check the website (®www.oprah.com) for updates on schedules and availability. Keep in mind that on the day of taping, you'll have to stand outside until the doors open, and it will likely be cold, given that the show takes June to August off.

Greektown and around

The first Greek immigrants arrived in Chicago in the mid-1800s, mostly seamen whose plan was to work, save money, and then return to the homeland. Many did indeed return to Greece and spread the word about the opportunities available in Chicago (particularly after the Great Fire), resulting in new waves of immigrants to the city. By the 1900s, a full-fledged **Greektown** had grown up around Harrison and Halsted streets around the former intersection with Blue Island Avenue. Known as "the Delta," the area had developed into a bustling little community by the 1950s, but the building of the Eisenhower Expressway and the UIC campus eventually pushed Greektown a few blocks north to its present location, centered on the intersection of Halsted and Madison streets.

Today, the surrounding neighborhood has been transformed into a yuppie haven of lofts and high-end restaurants, but the stretch of Halsted Street between Madison and Van Buren is still staunchly Greek. Despite the tacky Greek temples and pavilions on the street corners – misguided attempts to beautify the neighborhood for the 1996 Democratic National Convention – this pocket of the city has avoided becoming too touristy, and you'll still hear the mother tongue spoken in the area's shops, cafés (*tavernas*), and boisterous restaurants, where families and large groups chatter away and cries of "Opa!" fill the air as plates of *saganaki* (flaming cheese) are set alight.

The highlights of the neighborhood calendar are the annual **Greek Independence Day Parade** in late March and a weekend in August when the tempting aromas of the **Taste of Greece** festival fill the air.

The United Center

The polished **United Center**, at 1901 W Madison St, replaced the old Chicago Stadium in 1995, a famously loud space that saw just about every kind of event, from hockey and basketball to Elvis concerts and speeches by Franklin D. Roosevelt (the phrase "New Deal" was first uttered here). Home to the **Bulls** and ice hockey's **Blackhawks**, the new stadium has been called "the House that Michael Built," after the Bulls' Michael Jordan, who led his team to dominate the NBA during the 1990s (for more about the sports teams, see pp. 247–248).

There's nothing special about the stadium to make the one-hour backstage **tour** worthwhile (for groups of 15–40 only, by reservation; $20, includes lunch;

☎312/455-4500), but if you're here for a game or a concert, be sure to check out the **bronze statue** of Jordan out front. Bear in mind that the surrounding neighborhood is gang-ridden, desolate, and **dangerous** (particularly west of here on Madison Street and on nearby Damen Avenue), so take a cab there. If you have a car, the stadium has plenty of monitored parking.

The Garfield Park Conservatory

Unfolding across 185 acres four miles west of Greektown, **Garfield Park** has exotic flower gardens and a lagoon, as well as facilities for all kinds of sports (tennis, basketball, soccer, baseball), a playground, and a pool. Inside the park is one of Chicago's least-known and most underrated attractions, the **Garfield Park Conservatory**, 300 N Central Park Ave (Fri–Wed 9am–5pm, Thurs 9am–8pm; $3 suggested donation; ☎312/746-5100, Ⓦwww.garfield-conservatory.org; Green Line to Conservatory–Central Park), sister to the Lincoln Park Conservatory but the bigger and better of the two. Billing itself as "landscape art under glass," the current conservatory sits in the surrounding park. It was built between 1906 and 1907 to replace the original glasshouse designed by William Le Baron Jenney (see box, p.279), which fell into disrepair and was demolished.

Spend a few hours here, wending your way through various rooms devoted to plant groups, past primeval-looking ferns and mosses, giant agave (the source of tequila), and other striking cacti, towering banana trees, and waterfalls. Kids will enjoy the hands-on displays in the **children's garden**, turning a crank to guide a giant "bee" into a flower, among other things. There's also an outdoor sensory garden where you can hold and smell fragrant flowers and fruits. Visitors can take self-guided **tours** (guided tours are for members only) through the well-marked and easily navigable gardens, which are almost never crowded.

Little Italy and around

Many of Chicago's first Italian immigrants came to the city in the 1890s as temporary workers, intending to return home with money earned from hard graft on the railways, but those who settled in this poor enclave quickly turned it into **Little Italy**, a lively, restaurant-packed community. Now, the charming old row houses that fill most of the backstreets like Aberdeen and Carpenter – as well as the construction of fancy new condominiums and lofts where run-down housing projects once stood – have seduced young professionals into moving here. The neighborhood's relative seclusion (it's tucked away in a pocket just west of Interstate 90/94 and south of Interstate 290) has thus far protected it from the rapid-fire development that has taken over much of the rest of the city.

To catch the full flavor of Little Italy, you'll need to amble down Taylor Street, from Halsted to Ashland. Look out for *Mario's Italian Lemonade*, the little red, green, and white shack at 1068 W Taylor St, which has been selling delectable **Italian ices and lemonade** for more than thirty years. Among the last of Little Italy's old-fashioned, family-owned businesses, *Mario's* draws long lines in summer that give the place a friendly, block-party atmosphere. Across the street at no. 1079, *Al's Number 1 Italian Beef* has been doing similarly brisk business since 1938. For pure Chicago-style gluttony, their "dipped" **Italian beef sandwiches** are hard to beat (see p.199).

If you're here during the day, the neighboring streets make for a pleasant stroll; head for the blocks around **Arrigo Park**, a patch of green just north of the intersection of Taylor and Loomis streets, which has some lovely turn-of-the-century townhouses at its northern end. The park has a baseball field and is a popular gathering spot for local Ultimate Frisbee players.

For the record, the place where Mrs O'Leary's poor cow supposedly kicked over a lantern and started the massive **fire of 1871** (see p. 278) was in a barn at what's now the intersection of Jefferson and Taylor streets, just short of a mile from the center of Little Italy, and east of the John F. Kennedy Expressway. There's really nothing to see here, other than the ironically situated **Chicago Fire Academy**, where trainee firefighters learn to extinguish smaller blazes.

The Maxwell Street Market

If you're in Little Italy on a Sunday, poke around the **Maxwell Street Market**, a couple of blocks away at the intersection of Roosevelt Road and Canal Street. This giant **open-air flea market** happens every Sunday, rain or shine, from 7am to 3pm, and boasts **live blues music**, sketch artists, around 500 vendors who hawk everything from all sorts of fresh **produce** and ethnic food to antiques and clothing.

Locals still moan that it's only a shadow of the original Maxwell Street Market, which held court on Maxwell Street from the late 1800s till 1994, when the city forced the market to relocate to its current location. The naysayers may be right, but you can still come away with a bargain or two, or sample from the wide variety of food stalls that sell everything from Polish sausages, tacos, and empanadas to thick, tortilla-like Salvadoran *pupusas*.

Jane Addams Hull-House Museum

Just west of Little Italy, you'll run smack into a concrete sprawl known as the campus of the 25,000-strong **University of Illinois-Chicago** (UIC). The university, which made headlines in the 1960s when it started building locally, brought much-needed money into the area, but at the same time displaced many of the residents, and altered the West Side's landscape for good. You will, however, find a piece of the area's history preserved in the form of the **Jane Addams Hull-House Museum**, 800 S Halsted St, at Harrison Street (Tues–Fri 10am–4pm, Sun noon–4pm; free; ⓣ312/413-5353), which makes for a rewarding visit if you're in the area.

Hull-House was an innovative settlement house (or neighborhood social welfare agency) founded in 1889 that provided much-needed services to children, women, and immigrants on Chicago's struggling West Side, where many of them lived in appalling conditions. **Jane Addams**, a social reformer who went on to win the Nobel Peace Prize, founded the house with fellow reformer Ellen Gates Starr after being inspired by a visit to Toynbee Hall, an influential settlement house in London's East End. By 1907, Hull-House had grown to fill several buildings, with day-care programs for the children of working mothers, employment centers for immigrants, an art studio and gallery, a labor museum, a public kitchen, and even a coffeehouse.

The organization, still a force for social welfare in the city, has moved on to headquarters in the Loop. Two of the original Hull-House buildings have survived, though, and are owned and run by the university: both Hull Mansion and the dining hall have been restored to their original appearance. Inside Hull Mansion, you'll see some of Addams' original furniture, paintings, and photographs, plus rotating exhibits and memorabilia from famous supporters and Hull-House visitors such as Carl Sandburg, Ida B. Wells, Frank Lloyd Wright, W.E.B. Dubois, Clarence Darrow, Gertrude Stein, and William Butler Yeats, among others. On the second floor of the dining hall, a fifteen-minute slideshow explains how Hull-House tackled the West Side's deplorable social problems.

For an excellent firsthand account of Hull-House, read Addams' *Twenty Years at Hull-House* (see p.300).

Pilsen

In summer especially, you could easily mistake **Pilsen** for a neighborhood on the outskirts of Mexico City, with radios blaring mariachi music from apartment windows and residents congregating around the *fruterías* (produce markets), *panaderias* (bakeries), and Mexican restaurants. The bustling center, focused a mile south of Little Italy along 18th Street, west of Racine Avenue, is home to the city's large Latino community and, since the 1960s, has been a haven for local artists. The authentic **Mexican cuisine** to be found in the area's restaurants – many along 18th Street between Racine and Ashland avenues – is reason enough to come here, as is the **Mexican Fine Arts Center Museum**, the largest Latino cultural institution in the US. Much art can be found out of doors as well, courtesy of local muralists who have covered the walls of local buildings with tributes to Mexican culture. Good examples of this artwork can be found at the Blue Line 18th Street El station at 18th and Paulina, as well as at 1645 W 18th St, where the Jose Clemente School is alive with **colorful mosaics**.

The first **Mexican immigrants** began arriving in Chicago in the mid-1800s, their numbers growing steadily until World War I, when labor shortages in the US brought thousands of Mexicans to Chicago seeking work. Many found jobs in the steel mills, railyards, and stockyards, and settled on the near West Side, where the immigration services of Hull-House (see p.134) did much to ease their way. However, much like the West Side's Greek and Italian communities, urban renewal and the building of expressways eventually forced the Mexican immigrants to settle here, a neighborhood originally settled by **Czech émigrés** in the early 1800s, who named it after the town of Plzen in West Bohemia in 1870 (the neighborhood of Pilsen East, centered on eighteenth and Halsted streets, still retains some Czech flavor). Today, roughly one million Mexicans live in Chicago, and census figures estimate that by 2010, Mexicans will be the largest ethnic group in Chicago.

Getting here on public transportation is possible, though in most cases time-consuming. On weekdays, take the Cermak Branch of the Blue El Line to the 18th Street stop; bear in mind that this branch doesn't run on weekends. Your best bet on weekends is to take a taxi. The buses that run along Halsted Street, Blue Island Avenue, and the other main streets into Pilsen are slow and irregular.

The Mexican Fine Arts Center Museum

Pilsen's main attraction is the engaging **Mexican Fine Arts Center Museum**, at 1852 W 19th St and Wolcott Avenue (Tues–Sun 10am–5pm; admission free; ⓣ312/738-1503, ⓦwww.mfacmchicago.org), dedicated to the arts of Mexico as well as US Mexican communities. The small but wide-ranging exhibits are presented in five rotating galleries, with thoughtful captions in both Spanish and English. On display is a history of Mexican art from ancient times to the present day, shown through pre-Columbian artifacts, charming Talavera de Puebla pottery (glazed Spanish-influenced earthenware), and contemporary photos of the Mexican experience in Chicago. You might also spot a few sketches by famed muralist Diego Rivera, as well as etchings by Jose Clemente Orozco, and the politically charged work of David Alfaro Siqueiros.

The museum is known locally for its annual, month-long **Day of the Dead exhibit** – the nation's largest – which commemorates the holiday with paintings,

△ Day of the Dead Festival exhibit at the Mexican Fine Arts Center Museum

folk art, sculpture, and mixed-media pieces that explore the theme of death and dying (for more on the festival, see p.259). The museum also puts on performing arts festivals twice a year, in the spring and fall.

Free guided **tours** of the Main Gallery are offered to groups of ten or more in English or Spanish. There's also a **gift shop** stocked with distinctive black Oaxacan pottery and hand-woven rugs, silver jewelry, and a wide selection of posters and books. The museum's only drawback is its somewhat remote location on the lower West Side; you could make a day of it by combining a visit here with a trip to nearby Chinatown (see p.106) or to the historic homes further east on S Prairie Avenue.

10

The South Side and Hyde Park

No neighborhood better illustrates the urban contrasts marking modern Chicago than the **SOUTH SIDE**, which encompasses the neighborhoods of Hyde Park and the University of Chicago, Kenwood, and Bronzeville. You can wander through the hushed, neo-Gothic quadrangles of the University of Chicago, famous for snagging Nobel Prizes, then – mere blocks away – find yourself in the most dangerous and run-down districts of the city, swaths of low-rise streets, where windows are boarded up, garbage is scattered across wasteland, and a sense of hopelessness predominates.

The story of **HYDE PARK**, the main target for most visitors heading to the South Side, is intertwined with Chicago's apogee in the 1890s, when it was the site of the city's two greatest civic projects. The first, the **University of Chicago**, was grafted onto the newly annexed area of Hyde Park by the city in 1892 and quickly achieved academic fame; it's perhaps best known as the site of the first nuclear reaction (for more on this, see p.286). A year after the university was founded, Hyde Park was selected as the site of the **World's Columbian Exposition**, a mammoth civic scheme that was arguably Chicago's finest moment: remnants from that spectacular success include the building that houses the **Museum of Science and Industry** and the Midway Plaisance greenspace. Hyde Park also holds one of the hands-down most important (and most intriguing) structures in the city, Frank Lloyd Wright's **Robie House**.

Flanking the western fringes of the university campus is **Washington Park**, expansive and rugged, with good sports and aquatic facilities, a refreshing change from the city's more manicured parks. The historic district of **Kenwood**, located north of Hyde Park Boulevard stretching to E 47th Street, is full of turn-of-the-century grandeur, with an eclectic display of Gothic, Tudor, and Queen Anne–style homes designed by Frank Lloyd Wright and other great twentieth-century American architects.

Outside Hyde Park and Kenwood, the South Side is a predominantly African-American neighborhood, and one all but forgotten by the city's (largely white) government: racial tensions run high and many locals feel that the area's been unfairly left to decay while white districts like Lincoln Park have been aggressively smartened up. However, the **Bronzeville** neighborhood, a cradle of opportunism during the 1940s, when it was birthplace to legendary jazz musicians, civil rights leaders, and entrepreneurs, contains enough vestiges of its former vibrance to reward a visit.

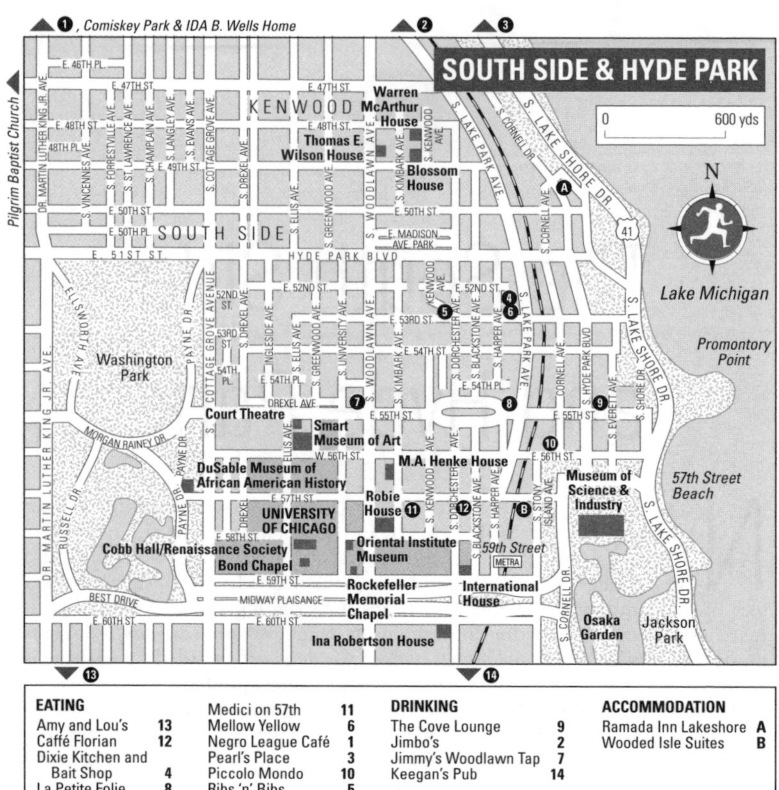

To **get to** Kenwood, take the Metra to 47th Street and for Hyde Park, take the Metra to 55th, 56th, 57th, or 59th street stations or the #6 Jeffrey Express bus; avoid the Green Line El. For the South Side sights and entertainment we've highlighted outside Hyde Park and Kenwood, the safest option is to take a cab.

Some history

The South Side has seesawed between swanky mansions and gritty industry since Chicago first exploded in the mid-nineteenth century. It was home to many of the local railway and manufacturing magnates until Potter Palmer decamped to the Gold Coast (see Chapter 4, "The Gold Coast and Old Town") in the 1880s and the rest of the elite followed. The South Side was also the site of the city's heavy industry, including the monumental slaughterhouses known as the **Chicago Stockyards**, whose stench wafted over the area until the 1950s.

But the South Side is best known as the crossroads between black and white Chicago. Labor shortages in the early twentieth century forced owners to look to African-American workers from the South to fill their factories. The newly arrived employees then settled close by their jobs, in Chicago's South Side. The South Side's African-American population grew, partly owing to the city's **segregation policy** (see p. 283), which sequestered most African Americans along a southerly strip of State Street. Isolated geographically, politically, and

Comiskey Park and the 1919 World Series

The thoroughly modern and desperately sterile **Comiskey Park Stadium** straddles the Dan Ryan Expressway in the unpolished South Side neighborhood of **Bridgeport**. It was here in 1919 that the most famous scandal in baseball history occurred. Despite having some of the best players ever assembled on one team – one that outclassed the rest of the league in regular season, en route to a 110-win season – the White Sox played uncharacteristically sloppily in the final game of the **1919 World Series**, which they were heavily favored to win, losing 10–5 to the Cincinnati Reds. Suspicion fell on eight of the White Sox players, who were soon accused of throwing the game in exchange for cash. Although all eight players, notable among them, star **Shoeless Joe Jackson**, were ultimately acquitted of criminal activity after a lengthy investigation. However, they were banned from baseball for life, and the team itself was disgraced with the nickname **"the Black Sox."** John Sayles' evocative film *Eight Men Out* (1988) offers a good introduction to the incident.

For information on the current – and untainted – Chicago White Sox, see p.247.

culturally from the city as a whole, Chicago's black community developed a singular identity – and its association with blues music and jazz clubs was truly cemented, especially in the entertainment district known as **The Stroll** (see p.284), which began at S State and 31st streets.

While a distinct African-American culture was developing here, so was a simmering resentment of local whites' treatment of blacks – there were six consecutive days of **race riots** across the city in July 1919 that resulted in the deaths of twenty-three African-Americans and fifteen whites. This anger only worsened as the largely white local government paid little attention to the economic impact Chicago's crumbling industrial backbone had on the South Side. The neighborhood has never truly recovered from the incident, and a casual trip by car down S Stony Island Drive will take you past low-rise buildings covered in barbed wire, piles of old furniture dumped on the streets, and heavy iron grilles on most shop windows.

Bronzeville

South of the McCormick Place Convention Center at 26th Street lies the primarily African-American neighborhood of **Bronzeville**. During the late nineteenth and early twentieth centuries, Bronzeville was a thriving "Black Metropolis," a land of opportunity for African Americans who had fled the South during the "Great Migration." Lively streets lined with stately homes, Art Deco theaters, jazz clubs, and blues bars nurtured musical icons, legendary activists, and pioneers of the twentieth century: Andrew "Rube" Foster, founder of the Negro National Baseball League; Ida B. Wells, a civil rights activist, journalist, and organizer of the NAACP; former Nation of Islam leader Elijah Muhammad; Bessie Coleman, the first African-American woman pilot; and Louis Armstrong, the legendary trumpeter. By 1929, Bronzeville's population had generated over $100 million in real estate and the Regal Theater, Savoy Ballroom, and Metropolitan Theater all ranked alongside the city's most prestigious entertainment venues. Nowadays, the story is very different, a depressing landscape of run-down streets, vacant lots, derelict buildings, segregation, and urban blight.

While resentment simmers that Mayor Daley has neglected the South Side in favor of "vanity" projects like Millennium Park, there are signs that with investment and local initiatives Bronzeville is making a comeback. Around 47th Street, restaurants, cafés, galleries, and bookstores are opening and attracting visitors from other neighborhoods. The eye-catching **Harold Washington Cultural Center**, unveiled in 2004 at 4701 S Martin Luther King Drive (box office 8am–4pm, ⓣ773/924-5156, ⓦwww.haroldwashingtonculturalcenter.com), has since become the focus of plans to develop the Bronzeville community. A swish arts, music, and educational complex, with a staircase that looks like a winding piano, the Cultural Center plays host to the occasional jazz legend (for review).

There are a few other sights of minor note, but it's really Bronzeville's historical resonance that provides the area's interest. The **Bronzeville Walk of Fame**, on Martin Luther King Drive between 25th and 47th streets, features ninety-one bronze plaques engraved with the names of Bronzeville's famous residents. Close by, the 15ft-statue, **Monument to the Great Northern Migration** (1996), depicts a travel-worn man pointing north, his feet resting upon a mound of soles, symbolizing all those who fled the South in search of the northern "Promised Land." One of the oldest African-American churches in Chicago, built by Louis Sullivan in 1890, the **Pilgrim Baptist Church**, 3301 S Indiana at 33rd Street is a gospel-music landmark, and aficionados should attend services on Sundays at 10.45am (dress respectfully). At 35th Street and Martin Luther King Drive, the **Victory Monument** pays tribute to the Eighth Regiment of the National Guard, an African-American unit that fought in France during World War I. Further south, at 3624 S Martin Luther King, is the former home of **Ida B. Wells**, who lived here between 1919 and 1930.

Note that violent crime rates are very high in the area. Care should be taken at all times. Take taxis everywhere and avoid the area at night.

Hyde Park

Seven miles south of downtown, **Hyde Park** is an island of middle-class prosperity surrounded by urban poverty, the most attractive and sophisticated South Side neighborhood. Fitting into less than two square miles between 51st Street and 61st Street and from S Cottage Grove Avenue to the lake, it's also one of the most racially integrated areas of the city, strikingly evident in its array of ethnic eateries and its mix of low-income housing and mansions. It's also among the more erudite, with the **University of Chicago** at its center and the popular **Museum of Science and Industry** in Jackson Park.

For a glimpse of collegiate Hyde Park – and a smattering of terrific second-hand bookstores – head for **57th Street**: it bisects the main campus and passes the **Robie House** on the way. Otherwise, Hyde Park's commercial hub is **53rd Street**, where there are traces of the urban blight that looms outside the area, with cheap cafeterias standing alongside chic houseware shops. Though the area is mostly safe, **crime rates** are still somewhat high, and you should try not to walk alone during the day and never at night, especially along the main drags of 53rd, 55th, and 57th streets, where racial tensions are still palpable.

Kenwood

The historical district of **Kenwood** extends east from S Drexel Boulevard to S Blackstone Avenue, and south from E 47th Street to Hyde Park Boulevard. When Kenwood became part of Chicago in 1889, the city's business, scholarly, and fashionable elite made Kenwood their suburban oasis, building grandiose homes along its leafy tree-lined boulevards; Kenwood exuded classical grandeur. Meatpacker Gustavus Swift, lumber merchant Martin Ryerson, and Sears Roebuck executive and philanthropist Julius Rosenwald, were the kings of Kenwood, and they commissioned the city's visionary architects to build their castles in a flamboyant array of styles. By the 1920s, many homes had been subdivided into multi-family apartments and new monolithic high-rises began to dilute its vintage aura.

It's not worth going out of your way, but if you happen to be in the area, there is a crop of landmarks here, including two of Frank Lloyd Wright's "bootlegged" houses (For more information on Wright, see "Architecture" color insert). **Blossom House**, at 4858 S. Kenwood, was built in 1892 in Queen Anne style; all buttercup yellow with a neat white trim and Palladian windows, it may not be signature Wright, but the fluid interior (access not permitted) betrays some Prairie School influence. Next door, the Dutch-style colonial house at **4852 S Kenwood** was commissioned by manufacturer Warren McArthur in 1892. Built with a gambrel roof and featuring a dado with Roman brick to create a horizontal plane, it was the first time that Wright used leaded windows.

Howard van Doren Shaw, described as, "the most rebellious of the conservative and the most conservative of the radical," built some twenty-one homes in the Hyde Park and Kenwood areas. His eclectic style ranged from Tudor Gothic to Georgian and beyond. Examples include the **Mrs. Ina Robertson house** at 6042 S. Kimbark; the **Thomas E. Wilson** house at 4815 Woodlawn, and the **M.A. Henke house** at 5620 Kimbark.

Promontory Point

For a change from Hyde Park's busy storefronts and crowded sidewalks, you can visit the small headland at the east end of 55th Street, **Promontory Point**. This open, grassy spot on the rocky shores of Lake Michigan usually teems in summertime with picnicking families, sunbathers, and joggers, all of whom come for the spectacular view northward to downtown Chicago. (The view south of industrial Indiana is much less appealing.) A dip in the lake around the Point is refreshing, but take care to avoid swimming in the generally unclean and crowded 57th Street Beach to the south.

The Museum of Science and Industry

The monumental **Museum of Science and Industry**, 57th Street and Lake Shore Drive (Mon–Sat 9.30am–4pm, Sun 11am–4pm; $9, $7.50 seniors, $5 children, free Mon & Tues Jan 3–March 15, Sept 12–Nov 24, Dec 24, "Campus week" (usually second week in June); ⓣ773/684-1414, ⓦwww.msichicago.org), is a textbook example of how terrific fun can be integrated with higher learning; it will entrance even the most reluctant child, thanks mostly to the genuinely enthusiastic and question-friendly staff. The Beaux-Arts building itself was originally designed as the Palace of Fine Arts for the World's Columbian Exposition in 1893; the only structure salvaged at the exhibition's end, it was painstakingly dismantled before a stone frame was rebuilt around its steel skeleton. A massive refurbishment in 1997 has made the place more navigable:

visitors now enter through the subterranean entrance hall, surfacing under the main rotunda, and can plan a visit from there. You'll still need a map (free), though, to get around the three sprawling levels.

On the main floor, whatever you do, don't miss the **Coal Mine**: here, hardhat-sporting staffers take you through a thirty-minute coal-miner training session, which includes a rickety ride on an underground trolley (expect long lines on the weekend). Close by, there's also the mesmerizing **Chick Hatchery**, divided into two habitats. In one, you can watch fluffy chicks running around and eating; in the other, you can witness the damp, awkward-footed baby birds pecking their way out of a shell and then slumping down to rest after all the effort. Also on this floor, the **Great Train Story** is a wonderful reincarnation of the museum's original model railroad that for over sixty years had re-created the journey between Chicago and Seattle. Imaginatively and ingeniously, the new train travels over steel trusses, through the Rocky Mountains, over the Grand Canyon, and past cotton gins, coal mines, and lumber mills.

Continuing the train theme, **All Aboard the Silver Streak** is a tour of the pioneering *Zephyr* train, which completed the longest and fastest non-stop railroad run in 1934. Traveling from Denver to Chicago, it averaged 77.6 miles per hour, slashing twelve hours and forty minutes off the previous record. Known as "shovelnose" streamline trains, nine others were built between 1934 and 1939.

△ Parakeets in Hyde Park

Hyde Park parakeets

Perhaps the neighborhood's most unique populace is the local flock of some hundred *Myiopsitta monachus* – better known hereabouts as Hyde Park **parakeets**. Native to Argentina and Brazil, these bright-green monk parakeets, sporting gray underbellies and blue wing feathers, were first sighted in the area in the 1970s nesting in huge tangles of twigs in the treetops or electrical poles. Unlike their South American counterparts, the Hyde Park parakeets aren't considered agricultural pests, but are known for their loud, high-pitched squawking.

How these tropical birds came to trade their sultry southern homeland for Hyde Park is not known, though it's commonly thought that the birds escaped from a cage at a Chicago airport. Despite the bitingly cold winters here, they have managed to thrive; threats of elimination by the US Department of Agriculture in the late 1980s eventually faded after local protests.

Nicknamed "Parrot Park," the corner of **Harold Washington Park** at Lake Shore Drive and 53rd Street is the most popular nesting site for the birds.

Other popular stopoffs on the ground floor include the enormous, exhaustively detailed dollhouse known as the **Fairy Castle**, created by Hollywood star Colleen Moore in 1928. The actress employed movie set designers and art directors to create her fantastical vision. No expense was spared: there's Royal Doulton china in the kitchen, Viennese tapestries in the dining room, platinum chairs encrusted with diamonds and emeralds, and a mother-of-pearl floor in the Princess' bedroom.

There's a fifteen-minute "captained" tour ($5) of the **U-505 Submarine**, captured from Germany in 1944 by forces led by a Chicago native. New interactive features, simulated sound effects, and atmospheric lighting make the experience feel very immediate as you maneuver through the warren-like spaces of the engine room, captain's quarters (whose bed was just thirty inches wide), and the torpedo room. Claustrophobics should steer clear.

Upstairs on the balcony, check out the **HIV exhibit**, which explains the virus in easy-to-understand, comic-book style, and the walk-through **human heart.** As you make your way through the museum, make sure to take the **blue stairs** at least once, which hold perhaps the most startling exhibit of all – a pickled human being, sliced into wafer-thin sections using a band saw in the 1930s, preserved in formaldehyde, and wedged between sheets of glass.

The Robie House

Perched on the edge of the University of Chicago, the **Robie House**, 5757 S Woodlawn Ave (access by tour only; $12, $10 age 7–18 years & seniors, children under 7 free; ☎708/848-1978, Ⓦwww.wrightplus.org), is one of Frank Lloyd Wright's masterpieces, and its location in Hyde Park makes it a more convenient alternative to his better-known homes in Oak Park west of Chicago (see pp.151–153). Commissioned by local businessman Frederick Robie in 1906, the red-brick house is a prime example of Wright's **Prairie School style** (see "Architecture" color insert). Drawing inspiration from the flat Midwestern prairie, and attempting to carve out a distinctly American style, Wright gave Robie an overwhelmingly horizontal house. The cantilevered roof seems to levitate over the building and extends 20ft from its supports. The main floor is a fluid space with no walls or partitions; the fireplace serves as a "screen" between the living and dining room areas.

Sacrificing practicality to achieve aesthetic consistency, he didn't even include downspouts in the building's drainage system, which resulted in ninety years' worth of water damage to the pavements. Wright wanted every element unified – which meant that he designed everything: building, plants, light fittings, chairs, even the clothes the Robies' two children would wear – and was known to show up unannounced at any time to make sure that all the furniture was still in its proper place. (The Robies learned to hold him off at the door, rearrange the rooms, and then invite him in.)

The house passed through several families' hands in quick succession after the Robie family lost its fortune. In 1926, the house was bought by the Chicago Theological Seminary, which promptly converted it into student accommodation. As if the damage this caused wasn't enough, by 1957 the Seminary had raised enough money to carry out its original plan of demolishing the building completely. It took the philanthropy of another businessman, William Zeckendorff, to save the house, which he then donated to the University of Chicago in 1963.

Though the Frank Lloyd Wright Preservation Trust completed work on the exterior in 2003, a further $4 million is still needed to finish the interior renovations, scheduled for completion in 2007. If you want to take a look inside, join one of the regular **tours**.

The University of Chicago

Perhaps the top institution in the Midwest, the **University of Chicago** is interested in proving itself worthy to the East Coast Ivy League crew: the intensely studious 13,000-strong student body is one symptom, as are T-shirts sold in the campus bookstore that read "The U of C: Where Fun Comes to Die." Previous alumni include Saul Bellow, Nobel Prize–winning author of *Herzog*; Nobel Laureate Milton Friedman, hailed for his study of monetary policy; Nathanial Kleitman, who identified REM sleep; Dr Alf Alving, who developed malaria prevention medication; and John Hope Franklin, the country's most esteemed scholar of African-American history.

For the most impressive introduction to the university, either walk or drive west down the **Midway Plaisance**, a long green strip that was the site of the World's Columbian Exposition. The Midway was then filled with full-sized model villages from around the globe, including an Irish market town and a mock-up of Cairo complete with belly dancers. These days, it's used mainly by joggers and students tossing Frisbees.

To explore the campus, consider taking one of the student-led **tours** that depart from the Office of College Admissions, 1116 E 59th St (March–Nov Mon–Fri 10.30am & 1.30pm; Dec–Feb Mon–Fri 10am; Sept 25–Nov 22 9am & 11am; ☎773/702-8650). Intended primarily for prospective students and their parents, these one-hour walking tours cover the entire campus and offer some campus history and architectural commentary, as well as some quirky anecdotes.

The Rockefeller Memorial Chapel and around

If you'd rather see things on your own, a good place to start is the **Rockefeller Memorial Chapel**, at 5850 Woodlawn Ave, philanthropist John D. Rockefeller's last, and major, architectural, contribution to the university. Dedicated in 1928, the austere limestone chapel's most impressive feature is its tremendous size, which you can take in by walking its length all the way to the altar, taking in the stained-glass windows and numerous religious figurines.

The chapel is, fittingly, home to the world's second-largest musical instrument – the tuned bells of the Laura Spelman **Rockefeller Carillon**. If you have the time and the gumption to climb the 274 steps of the stone spiral staircase for the complete carillon tour, you will be rewarded with a spectacular view of the city and Lake Michigan, plus the chance to stand inside one of the larger bronze bells and even pound out a couple of notes on the keyboard that will be heard for blocks. A single person controls the carillon's 72 bells by pressing large oak keys with his or her fists, as well as using foot pedals. **Tours** are offered during the academic year by appointment only (9am–4pm; ⓣ773/702-9202, ⓦwww.rockefeller.uchicago.edu). The carillon is played weekdays at 6pm and at noon on Saturdays.

Across the street from the chapel's entrance, book lovers cherish the **Seminary Co-op Bookstore**, housed in the cozy basement of the Chicago Theological Seminary at 5757 S University Ave. Reminiscent of an over-crowed small-town library, the store has over 100,000 volumes of academic and mainstream books on religion crammed in its cellar (see pp.262–263 for other Hyde Park bookstores).

The Oriental Institute

Just north of the chapel, the **Oriental Institute**, 1155 E 58th St (suggested donation $5; ⓣ773/702-9514, ⓦwww.oi.uchicago.edu), is well worth an hour's visit for its superb collection of artifacts from the ancient Near East, notably Egypt, Mesopotamia, Iran, and Anatolia. It's not a museum in the traditional sense, but a research institute that shows off just a fraction of its world-class holdings. The institute has recently unveiled its new galleries, including **Empire in the Fertile Crescent: Ancient Assyria, Anatolia, and Israel**. The institute's archeological teams excavated most of the Fertile Crescent artifacts seen here.

One of their greatest finds is a collection of bronze figurines discovered in Tell Judaidah in southeast Turkey. Dated 3000 BC, they are considered the earliest bronze artifacts discovered in the world. Other noteworthy artifacts include a fragment of the Dead Sea Scrolls – one of the few fragments of the ancient Hebrew manuscript, hidden around 100 AD, in the US. Another exhibit presents the finds from the institute's dig at **Megiddo** (the place referred to in the Bible as Armageddon and considered the cradle of archeology in Israel): don't miss the beautifully carved Megiddo ivories, dated 1300 BC. Especially worthwhile is the **Egyptian Gallery**, which houses more than 30,000 artifacts, one of the largest collections in the US. The most impressive piece is the "Colossal Statue of King Tutankhamun," which dates from 1334 BC (though it's hardly colossal, it's still pretty tall at seventeen feet). Also look out for the elaborately decorated "Mummy and Coffin of Meresamun," which shows scenes of the hoped-for afterlife.

Many of the artifacts in the **Persian Room** were excavated by the Oriental Institute during the 1930s, when the U of C was at its peak in the field of archeology. Among the highlights is the robust-looking "Colossal Bull Head" from Iran, one of a pair of beautifully carved stone statues dating from 486 to 424 BC. There is also a lavish collection of Achaemenid art, found during excavations at **Persepolis** (the ceremonial capital of the Persian empire from 612–330 BC) in the 1930s.

The Quads

At the heart of the university, between 57th and 59th streets and Ellis and University avenues is the **Main Quadrangle**, or "The Quads." Surrounded by neo-Gothic offices and libraries, its footpaths and lawns are the busiest part of the campus, usually buzzing with students heading to and from classes. The best ways to enter the quadrangle are from the east at the intersection of 58th Street and University Avenue or through the gate directly across from Regenstein Library on 59th Street. In the southeast corner, you'll find the peaceful **Social Science Quad**, which makes for a good spot to contemplate the periodic sounding of the bells.

Lying in the shadow of the much grander Rockefeller Chapel is the quaint but unremarkable **Bond Chapel**, in the Classics Quadrangle in the southwest corner of The Quads. The chapel is frequently the site of small weddings, perhaps owing to the rather high marriage rate among its alumni.

Just west, at 5811 Ellis Ave, the English Gothic–style **Cobb Hall** is the University's oldest building, built in 1892 by Henry Ives Cobb. The hall is home to the **Renaissance Society** (Tues–Fri 10am–5pm, Sat & Sun noon–5pm; free; ⓣ773/702-8670), which presents some of the country's most provocative contemporary art. Founded in 1915, the society gained an international reputation in the 1930s for its displays of avant-garde European art, including paintings by Picasso and Miró sourced directly from the artists' studios. In 1934, the society held the first solo exhibition of Alexander Calder's "mobiles," and it was the first Chicago gallery to exhibit Bruce Nauman and Julian Schnabel in the 1980s.

Cobb Gate, at the north end of the quads, forms the gateway to the University. Also designed by Henry Ives Cobb, the gargoyles that adorn the ornate Gothic gate are said to represent the progression of every University of Chicago student; the gargoyles at the bottom represent the impeding figures of the Admissions Counselor and Examiner, while the figures at the top symbolize the fourth-year students who have successfully climbed the ivory tower.

If only for its sheer oddity, pass by Henry Moore's bronze *Nuclear Energy* sculpture, located on the east side of S Ellis Avenue between 56th and 57th streets. The university was the site of the Manhattan Project research, and the heavy, mushroom-shaped work commemorates the moment that "…man achieved here the first self-sustaining chain reaction and thereby initiated the controlled release of nuclear energy."

The small, scholarly collection at the **Smart Museum of Art**, 5550 S Greenwood Ave (Tues, Wed & Fri 10am–4pm, Thurs until 8pm except during summer break, Sat & Sun 11am–5pm; free; ⓣ773/702-0200), is where the majority of the U of C's art collection – which spans more than five thousand years and contains more than nine thousand pieces – is stored and displayed. Perhaps because of the museum's modest size, there's a lot of attention paid to detail, from the impeccable displays and unique themes down to thoughtful captions and quotes from artists. Though you'll find a little bit of everything here – Old Master paintings, Frank Lloyd Wright's dining-room furniture, and twentieth-century paintings ranging from Rothko to Diego Rivera – the museum is perhaps best known for its works by the Chicago Imagists. Emerging from Hyde Park during the 1960s, the Imagists created playful neon, cartoon-like art which referenced non-Western and Surrealist art as well as drawing on images from popular culture. Look out for the work of the late Ed Paschke (1934–2004), one of the genre's leading exemplars. A graduate from the Art Institute of Chicago, Paschke was influenced by the photo-based works of Andy Warhol. Further highlights in the **Modern Art and Design** section (room 1)include the painting *Money is The Reason for Work* (1949) by French Dada artist Francis Picabia, and *Je m'arche* (1949), by Chilean artist Roberto Matta Echaurren, who whipped the New York art world into a frenzy during the 1940s by stating that emotions could be expressed through an abstract vocabulary.

Round out your U of C tour by grabbing a beer or a greasy lunch just north of campus at **Jimmy's Woodlawn Tap**, at 1172 E 55th St, a shabby, 50-year-old local bar that has seen the likes of Dylan Thomas, Margaret Mead, and Saul Bellow. Its literary days are clearly over and it remains to be seen whether it will survive the urban renewal under way in the area around 55th Street.

Washington Park

One of the social linchpins of the Southside, the rugged expanses of **Washington Park**'s 372 acres stretch west from Cottage Grove Avenue between 51st and 60th streets. The park was laid out by Frederick Law Olmsted (1822–1903) in the 1870s. The "Father of American landscape architecture," Olmsted is best known for landscaping New York's Central Park. During the 1920s, racial tensions soared in Washington Park when the area's population changed dramatically from mostly white to mostly African American. Despite the threats and intimidation by white gangs, semi-professional African-American baseball teams continued to play on the baseball fields at Washington Park during the 1920s.

Daniel Burnham's firm designed several buildings in the park, including the **Refectory**, at Morgan and Martin Luther King Drive, built in 1881, and the limestone **Roundhouse Stables**, built in 1880, in the southeast corner of the park; currently undergoing a multi-million-dollar renovation, the stables will form the expanded galleries of the **DuSable Museum of African American History** (see Chapter 21, "Festivals and events").

At the west end of the Park, don't miss Lorado Taft's sculpture **Fountain of Time**, based on poet Austin Dobson's lines: "Time goes, you say? Ah no, Alas, time stays, we go." The fountain is composed of the figure of Father Time watching over the flow of humanity in the form of one hundred human figures. It took Taft twelve years to complete the sculpture, which also contains a reflecting pool integral to the sculpture's symbolism. The Chicago weather and piecemeal restoration have done little to allow the sculpture to steal time and a massive restoration project was completed in 2005.

Washington Park is one of the South Side's social anchors, providing a range of sports amenities and hosting many festivals and events during summer (see p.258). The city's only public **cricket field** is here and on Sunday mornings, six teams of Washington Park residents can be seen decked out in their spick-and -span cricket whites, playing in Chicago's only organized cricket league. The park is full of facilities including basketball courts, racquetball courts, baseball diamonds, children's playground areas, and a lagoon. In 2003, a mini-arboretum was created between 51st and 55th streets and Martin Luther King Drive and Payne.

The **neighborhood** of Washington Park, west of the park stretching west from Cottage Grove to Wentworth Avenue and south from 51st Street to 63rd Street, holds little of interest for the visitor. It's one of Chicago's poorest neighborhoods; more than fifty percent of the houses are derelict.

DuSable Museum of African American History

On the west edge of Hyde Park and a ten-minute walk from the center of the U of C campus, the **DuSable Museum of African American History**,

740 E 56th Place (daily 10am–5pm, Sun from noon; $3, seniors & students $2, children age 6–13 $1, children under 6 free, free on Sundays; ⓣ773/947-0600, ⓦwww.dusablemuseum.org), is the oldest American institution devoted to collecting and preserving the heritage of Africans and African Americans. With such an ambitious mission, it's almost impossible for the museum not to fall short – which it does on several fronts – but there's still enough here to make a visit worthwhile if you're in the area; it's not necessarily something you'd journey out specifically for.

Start by picking up a map at the entrance and head past the bust of **Jean-Baptiste Point DuSable** (see p.275), the museum's namesake, to reach *The Ames Mural* (also known as *The Roots Mural*) – Robert Ames' mural of carved oak (1965), which powerfully brings to life the African-American struggle by way of key scenes and figures from history, from Harriet Tubman to civil-rights marches on Washington.

In a small corridor in the main leg of the museum, you'll find traditional African art displayed in the **Africa Speaks** exhibit, mostly carved pieces such as stools, dolls, and combs from early West African kingdoms; the Mossi dance masks are especially playful and ornate. The nearby **Trial to Triumph** exhibit, however, is disappointing: the news clippings, pictures of lynchings, and the meager display of handcuffs don't pack as much of a wallop as they could.

Things pick up across the hall in a room devoted to **the first African Americans in aviation**. Of special interest are the pilot license issued to the first African-American pilot, Bessie Coleman, and a photographic tribute to the Tuskegee Airmen, an all-black US Air Force team who distinguished themselves in combat during World War II.

The **main hall**, the largest space of all, is usually reserved for upbeat temporary exhibits. Beyond the main hall is a re-creation of the office of Harold Washington, Chicago's first black mayor.

A $25 million expansion, scheduled for completion in 2007, will see further exhibition space, cultural amenities, and research facilities housed in the Roundhouse building, a former limestone horse-stable and Historic Landmark, designed by Daniel Burnham.

11

Oak Park

Chicago's most famous suburb, **Oak Park**, ten miles west of the Loop, is the prime excursion in the outlying area, easily accessible by public transport. Reveling in the moniker of the "largest village in the world," its leafy, tidy streets are renowned as a cradle for artistic genius: Booker–Prize nominee Carol Shields (1935) and Ernest Hemingway (1899), the apotheosis of American individualism, were both born here and have injected their birthplace with a healthy shot of literary verve. The **Ernest Hemingway Home** where Big Ern's erudite and corporeal qualities were nurtured can be visited along with a small but satisfying **museum** dedicated to one of America's greatest twentieth-century writers. Don't expect a spirit of decadent bohemia – Oak Park, which Hemingway famously referred to as a "place of wide lawns and narrow minds," is a bastion of Midwest conservatism. It feels rather like Main Street USA, a safe, wholesome place with prettified Victorian homes, fronted by manicured gardens. It should come as no surprise that Ray Kroc, who founded *McDonald's*, lived here from the age of five.

The stunning collection of all-American architecture makes for a compelling visit: there are dozens of private homes designed by **Frank Lloyd Wright** here. Registered as National Landmarks they reveal Wright's signature Prairie-style architecture that reached its apogee in Oak Park. Many of the residences can now be viewed as part of a historic walking tour. The highlight of any visit to Oak Park, however, is a tour of the **Frank Lloyd Wright Home and Studio** where he lived from 1889–1909. Wright's concept of sacred space is embodied in the divine **Unity Temple**, while **Pleasant Home** provides one of the earliest and most opulent examples of the Prairie style.

It's a very pleasant place to spend the day, wandering around squirrel-filled backstreets, musing in the arty cafés, and perusing the old-fashioned bookstores, cobwebby boutiques, and parochial galleries. Still, modernization has been gradually taking hold: amid the mock-Tudor tearooms and winding alleys in downtown's shopping district, there's now a branch of Benetton and a large concrete parking garage, for instance – but by and large this twitchy-curtained community looks much as it did one hundred years ago.

Oak Park is very easy to navigate on foot, with most of the main sights and the **visitor's center** located between a four-block radius that extends north–south from Chicago Avenue to Lake Street and east–west from Forest Avenue to Oak Park Avenue. The downtown area is a kernel of activity just a few blocks further west with most of the main shops located around the Harlem Avenue and Lake Street nexus. Though it's highly recommended for a day-trip, there isn't much reason to spend the evening – nightlife largely comprises upscale restaurants aimed at the well-heeled, slightly older locals.

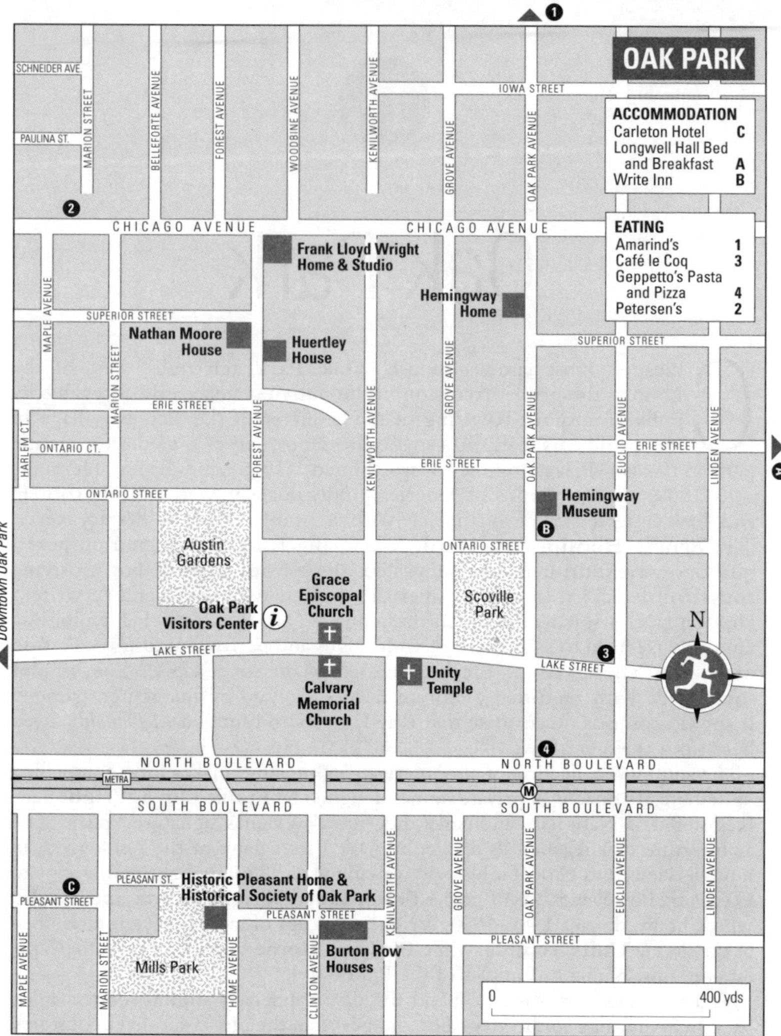

Some history

Oak Park was founded by an Englishman, **Joseph Kettlestrings**, who arrived with his wife and children in 1832. First known as Kettlestrings Grove, the town remained small, with a population of around five hundred for nearly twenty years. It was then nicknamed Oak Ridge after the oak trees that covered the high ground nearby. In 1872, it was renamed Oak Park after its servicing post office – another Illinois town had already assumed the mantel of Oak Ridge.

But when the railroad arrived in 1848, everything changed: the train allowed people to live locally but commute to jobs in the grimy city. Anxious to develop a wholesome locale, Kettlestring pitched Oak Park as a place for "good people who were against saloons and for good schools and churches." He needn't have bothered, as many fearful Chicagoans decamped to the suburbs, especially comparatively swanky neighborhoods like Oak Park, after the Great Fire in 1871. One of those newer arrivals was **Frank Lloyd Wright**, who moved here in 1887 with his mother, after she separated from her husband. Her young and talented son was eager to launch his architectural career and the rapid rebuilding that was going on in Chicago during that era provided the perfect opportunity for him to do so (for more on Wright, see box, p.152). Soon after moving to Oak Park, he was commissioned by many wealthy, suburban businessmen to construct houses for them.

Those wealthy clients were typical local residents and by the turn of the century the town was a prosperous, church-oriented enclave, where alcohol was banned for many years and movies weren't shown on Sundays until the early 1930s. The town has resisted Chicago's advances for years, determined to stay independent and with enough local wealth to ensure it can. In fact, Oak Park has changed little in a hundred years due to a combination of traditional residents and stringent zoning. Rest assured, though, at least now you can buy a beer or two.

Arrival and Information

To reach Oak Park by **car**, take the Eisenhower Expressway (I-290) west from downtown to Harlem Avenue and exit north. If you don't have a car, don't worry, as the town's well served by public transportation. Both the Green and Blue **El** lines stop here: the Green Oak Park stop is marginally more convenient, as it lets you off closer to downtown and the **visitor's center**. You'll find the latter at 158 N Forest Ave, hidden next to a massive concrete car park (daily: Oct–April 10am–4pm; May–Sept 10am–5pm; ⓣ708/848-1500 or 1-888/OAK-PARK, ⓦwww.visitoakpark.com). Free maps are available here, as well as an exhaustively informative **self-guided Heart of Oak Park audio tour** round town that takes approximately two hours (daily; 10am-3.30pm; $9, $6 youth & seniors, combined ticket available for Unity Temple, Hemingway Home and Museum, Pleasant Home, Historical Society of Oak Park, and Heart of Oak Park self-guided audio tour, $20). Illogically, it's more efficient to reverse the itinerary and work backwards if you want to see inside most sights (descriptions can be programmed in any order); the Pleasant Home (see p.155) has fewer tours available than the Frank Lloyd Wright Home & Studio and it's better to hit that first. An excellent way to get your bearings is to take the **free shuttle service** that connects all of the main sites on an hour-long looped route. Beginning at the El Green Oak Park station, shuttles run daily, every thirty minutes, between 10am and 5.30pm (ⓣ708/615-1830).

Frank Lloyd Wright Home & Studio and around

The slick operation at the **Frank Lloyd Wright Home & Studio**, 951 Chicago Avenue at Forest Avenue (guided tours only, Mon–Fri 11am, 1pm & 3pm, Sat & Sun every 20 min 11am–3.30pm; $12, $10 age 7–18 years & seniors; ⓣ708/848-1976, ⓦwww.wrightplus.org), adopts the officious approach of its former owner: visitors are frequently warned to touch nothing. If you can resist the temptation, you'll be rewarded with an informative trip around a sumptuously restored turn-of-the-century home. If you prefer to go it alone, there are **self-guided audio tours of the Historic District** that provide interesting background on the

Frank Lloyd Wright

The building as architecture is born of the heart of man, permanent consort to the ground, comrade to the trees, true reflection of man in the realm of his own spirit. His building is therefore consecrated space where he seeks refuge and repose for the body, but especially for the mind.

Frank Lloyd Wright

Without a doubt the most influential American architect of the twentieth century, **Frank Lloyd Wright** influenced generations of architects with his philosophies concerning space and interior design and the harmonious relationship between interior and exterior. Wright's signature **Prairie style** is evident in over twenty-five private residences that he designed in Oak Park between 1889 and 1915. Perhaps the best example of his style is **Robie House** (1908), at the University of Chicago campus in Hyde Park (see p. 143), where low horizontal lines, projecting eaves, and ribbons of art glass blend seamlessly with the landscape.

Born in June 8, 1867, in Richland Center, Wisconsin, Wright studied engineering at the University of Wisconsin before moving to Chicago in 1887 to work as an apprentice on a building commissioned by his uncle, who was a Unitarian pastor. After his apprenticeship with J. Lyman Silsbee, he joined the firm of Adler & Sullivan, working for **Louis Sullivan**, the genius whose maxim "form follows function" would pave the way for the pioneering Chicago School of architecture (see the "Architecture" color insert for more information). After signing an exclusive five-year contract, Wright began designing **the Auditorium Building** on S Michigan Avenue (see p.53).

In 1894, Wright opened his own office in the Schiller Building of downtown Chicago, but in 1898 his Oak Park home was expanded to form his studio (see p.151). The "bootleg" projects, including **Blossom House** and **Warren McArthur House** (privately owned), can be seen in Kenwood (see p.141).

Wright was the first architect to use concrete for non-commercial structures, the first to create open-plan interior spaces, and the first to view interior design as integral to the construction; at the Dana Thomas House in Springfield, Illinois, one of the best preserved of the Prairie-style constructions, there are more than one hundred pieces of Wright-designed white oak furniture. Wright's desire for total control over his buildings' interiors is even said to have extended to the dress code of his clients' children.

Wright's pioneering views of "organic architecture," the idea that a building is never really completed but an integral part of the setting, is embodied in the design of the **Frank Lloyd Wright Home** in Oak Park, where a willow tree formed an integral part of the building's design by connecting the hallway of the house to the studio. Sadly, the willow tree, not known for their longevity, died several years ago and a simulated replacement doesn't quite provide the natural effect.

25 homes designed by Frank Lloyd Wright (Mon–Fri 10am–3.30pm; $12, $10 youths age 7–18 years & seniors). There are also guided tours on the weekend (March–Nov 11am–4pm every 20 mins; Dec–Feb noon, 1pm & 2pm).

Wright's home and studio, where he lived and worked from 1889 to 1909, is a poster child for the development of the revolutionary **Prairie style**. It was here that Wright's architectural philosophy was defined and where he raised six children with his wife Catherine Tobin. Wright borrowed $5000 from his boss Louis Sullivan to build the house in 1889 and it enabled Wright to put into unfettered practice his theories that a building should not just be a shell, but an environment – that traditionally boxy Victorian interiors should be opened up. The home reads somewhat like a footnote to his more mature Prairie style works (for more information on Wright's Prairie style, see "Architecture" color insert); it only hints at his later, more beautiful designs. For a stunning, more accomplished example of Wright's residential architecture, head over to the Robie House in Hyde Park (see p.143).

Notice the earthy tones, wide verandas, and the tree growing through the passageway to his studio – all devices to blur the boundaries between man and nature, outside and inside. The house was pre-wired for electricity, even though there was no power line extending to Oak Park at the time it was built. Commuting to work in downtown Chicago, Wright knew that the revolutionary new power source would soon stretch out to the suburbs and wanted his house to be ready when it arrived.

The Home & Studio is worth stopping by as part of a larger tour of Oak Park, but given that the building shows only flashes of Wright's later genius (not to mention the schoolmarmish approach of those running the show), you're better off spending more of your time at the nearby Unity Temple (see p.154). South along N Forest Avenue, which is lined with gaudily restored Victorian mansions, two Wright buildings display the contrast between the architect's pre- and post-Prairie styles: the **Huertley House** (1902), at no. 318, and the **Nathan Moore House** (1895; rebuilt 1923), directly opposite on the corner of Superior Street. The former, a low-slung, heavily horizontal, brown brick home is a proto-Prairie building. The latter, a mustard-colored mock Tudor monstrosity, is a rare instance of the ornery architect following a client's brief rather than his own designs (justifiable however, given that it was one of Wright's first independent commissions and he couldn't kick and scream to get his way as he later would).

The Hemingway Home and Hemingway Museum

Ernest Hemingway, ardent lover of women, blood sports, revolution, guns, and cocktails, seems out of place in quaint, chocolate-box Oak Park, but the **Hemingway Home**, 339 N Oak Park Ave (home & museum Thurs, Fri & Sun 1–5pm, Sat 10am–5pm; $7, $5.50 students & seniors combined ticket; ⓣ708/848-2222, ⓦwww.ehfop.org), three blocks east of the Frank Lloyd Wright Home and Studio, where he was born and lived with his grandfather until the age of six, has been lovingly transformed into a period shrine to the writer.

In re-creating the Hemingway Home, the attention to detail is extraordinary. The Ernest Hemingway Foundation bought the property in 1992 and following ongoing restoration work it was finally opened to the public in 2001. Over one million dollars were spent in faithfully and atmospherically re-creating the home as it was when the Hemingway family resided there over a century ago. Restorers traveled to Florida to rescue cypress logs that were used in the original floorboards and Nottingham lace drapes were shipped from England, to recreate the home's appearance during the Victorian era

As an opulent re-creation of a Victorian home, the house is worth a visit but beyond random anecdotes from the tour guides and a few family possessions – taxidermied animals on the first floor and Ernest's first "book" penned at age two and a half – there is little of real interest to be gleaned about Hemingway's childhood. Not surprisingly, Hemingway's bristling relationship with Oak Park is conveniently glossed over, both in his childhood home and in the museum.

The small but engaging **museum**, two blocks south at 200 N Oak Park Ave, is housed in an old Christian Science church. The exhibits inside are excellent: picture-heavy panels trace Hemingway's life from birth to Paris to Havana, and there's a rotating temporary space or themed shows. The photographs from the

Hemingway family album are especially revealing – look for the 1910 image of 11-year-old Ernest showing his love of nature by feeding a nut to a squirrel (look closer, and you'll notice the squirrel's stuffed).

The Unity Temple

The **Unity Temple**, 875 Lake St at N Kenilworth Avenue, (March–Nov Mon–Fri 10.30am–4.30pm, Sat & Sun 1–4pm; Dec–Feb daily 1pm–4pm; guided tours Sat & Sun 1pm, 2pm & 3pm; $7, $5 seniors & students, children under 5 free; ⓣ708/383-8873, ⓦwww.unitytemple-utrf.org), is one of Frank Lloyd Wright's lesser-known masterpieces. Though Wright himself wasn't especially

△ Unity Temple

religious, his mother was a Unitarian, and helped her son snag the commission through her friendship with the local minister, to build this church for the Unitarian congregation in Oak Park. Wright's intent was to create a space of purity and simplicity, reminiscent of an ancient temple. Built from concrete, the design was an evolution in ecclesiastical architecture and represented a seminal moment in Wright's career; some fifty years after the building's completion Wright expounded upon his theories: "Unity Temple is where you will find the real expression of the idea that the space within the building is the reality of that building."

From the outside, the temple resembles a forbidding column-encased concrete box; Wright deliberately made it hard to find an entrance, so that worshippers would have to "interact" with the building as soon as they arrived. Slipping through the doors on Kenilworth Avenue, you find yourself in an atrium that leads, through a low-ceilinged passageway, into the main auditorium.

The sanctuary is illuminated from above – symbolizing the divine ideal – by a crown of leaded-glass windows, which extend around the building beneath the projecting roof, and by recessed amber skylights beneath a glass ceiling. The exposed electrical cords of ornate Japanese-style hanging lights are wrapped in gold silk, an early example of Wright's intent to express function without compromising luxury. The temple appears to be bathed in a heavenly, golden glow; Wright ensured that the predominant yellow hue would diffuse the earthy palette of greys, browns, and greens.

Wright created a serene space in the center of the square room, filled with pews; each of the two balconies overlooks this area and assures a sense of intimate community, despite its seating capacity of more than four hundred. By enclosing the stairs, the two balconies appear to be floating bridges that flow into the windows producing a fluid horizon of light and space. Another feature that fosters a sense of community is the placement of the exit doors: unlike most traditional churches, where the congregation turns its back on the pastor to leave, Wright wanted worshippers to pass the pastor as they left (and chat with him) – hence the hidden doors on either side of the pulpit through which you must leave.

If the clunky pews seem out of place, that's not unexpected – Wright designed his own, but as the cost of the building spiralled to one and a half times its projected budget, the congregation opted for cheaper alternatives. Note, too, the radiators everywhere: Wright's ingenious, but short-lived, forced-air heating system broke down almost as soon as the building was put to use and these radiators had to be grafted onto the building to keep worshippers warm. One feature that still functions beautifully is the auditorium's superb acoustics: fund-raising concerts are regularly held here; highly appropriate given Wright's belief that designing a building is similar to composing music.

Historic Pleasant Home and south Oak Park

It's a shame that poor, neglected **Pleasant Home**, 217 S Home Ave, located in Mills Park, south of the Metra train line, is so often eclipsed by its starry neighbor, Wright's Home & Studio (see p.151), as a visit here is every bit as interesting, enhanced by the friendly, passionate docents (March–Nov tours only, Thurs–Sun 12.30pm, 1.30pm & 2.30pm; $5, $3 students 5–18 years, children under 5 free; ⓣ708/383-2654, ⓦwww.oprf.com/phf).

The enormous thirty-room building was designed by Prairie School architect **George Maher** in 1897 for investment banker and philanthropist John Farson. Farson died soon after in 1910, and the house was sold to Herbert Mills, the inventor of vending and slot machines; in turn it was sold to the local park service in 1939 for use as a community center. A few years ago the home was reclaimed and slow restoration continues.

There's not much furniture inside yet, other than the monolithic dining table Maher designed (and that was too heavy to ever move), but the rooms themselves are an intriguing, early hint of how the Prairie style would evolve. Unconstrained by walls, the rooms flow into one another (a signature Prairie motif), while the huge windows open onto a wraparound porch (blurring the line between indoors and outside). In the library, the gigantic, curved-glass sash windows – which recede six feet into the wall above when lifted – underline the money-is-no-object opulence of the place. Maher was also determined to achieve balance in design, whatever the obstacle: see the fake door to the left of the onyx fireplace in the Great Hall; it's only there to even out the entranceway to the right. If the docent is willing, ask to stop by the women's bathroom on the first floor, which contains one of Maher's original marble sink designs, complete with built-in, shell-shaped soap dish.

Tours spend time on the second floor at the small, ragtag museum of the **Historical Society of Oak Park**: it's small, but there's a detailed room dedicated to the history of the area and filled with old photographs.

The final architectural pit-stop on a tour round Oak Park is just east of here, where you'll find the heaviest concentration of preserved **Victorians** in town, along Pleasant Street between Clinton and Oak Park avenues. The five **Burton Row Houses**, on the corner of Pleasant and Clinton, show how developers here were anxious to offer affordable housing to middle-class refugees from the city: the shared partition walls lessen privacy as well as price.

12

Rogers Park and the North Shore

Nearly ten miles north of the Loop at the northeast corner of the city, the tree-lined, residential neighborhood of **ROGERS PARK** is Chicago's most diverse neighborhood, with more than eighty languages spoken among the area's sixty-odd thousand residents. Home to the Jesuit-affiliated **Loyola University**; active Indian and Pakistani communities; and an increasing number of young professionals claiming condos along the city's last stretch of affordable lakeside housing, this neighborhood welcomes a hodge-podge of ethnic and economic backgrounds – though not many visitors, as there is little for tourists to see or do.

Cross north over Juneway Terrace and you've entered the entirely different world of **THE NORTH SHORE**, a series of homogenous lake-side suburbs that are also some of the nation's most affluent, home to a mix of CEOs, college professors, and wealthy financiers. From the college town **Evanston** (home of **Northwestern University**) to picturesque **Wilmette** with its breathtaking **Baha'í Temple**, the streets of these idyllic suburbs are lined with beautiful houses, manicured lawns, and luxury-car-filled driveways – it's no wonder director John Hughes used these houses for the settings of his 1980s teen movies *Ferris Bueller's Day Off* and *Sixteen Candles*. There's not much in these sleepy, comparatively stodgy burgs to appeal to out-of-town visitors; still, if you happen to be on the far north side of the city, lakeside **Sheridan Road** does make for a pleasant drive, lined as it is with the multi-million-dollar mansions of local CEOs and other corporate bigwigs. The sheer grandeur of some of these complexes makes for an intriguing glimpse into how the other half lives, and a striking contrast with adjacent Rogers Park.

Getting there

This region of Chicago is best visited by car. The best **public transport** option to reach Rogers Park is the El Red Line Loyola stop, at Loyola University; from here, you can take the #155 bus to explore Devon Avenue (the neighborhood is safest during the day). To visit Evanston, drive north on Sheridan Road from Chicago, or take the El Purple Line to the Davis or Foster stops; for Wilmette, continue north on Sheridan or get off at the last Purple Line stop, Linden.

Rogers Park

Eight miles north of the Loop, **Rogers Park** was established in the mid-1800s by Irish, German, and Luxembourgian immigrants, and that diversity has been one of the neighborhood's marked characteristics ever since. From Jamaican and Korean to Vietnamese, Latino, Peruvian, and African, this area north of Devon Avenue (6400N) and east of Ridge Boulevard (1800–2200W) to the lake is a true melting pot. Aside from the few small **beaches**, there are no real sights to speak of here; the main north–south drags are **Clark Street** to the west and the lake-hugging **Sheridan Road** to the east, both with a smattering of ethnic cafés and shops, from Peruvian restaurants and burrito counters to bike shops and run-down video arcades. Fans of Indian food should make tracks to **West Devon Avenue**, a treasure-trove of authentic Indian and Pakistani fare.

The neighborhood also has a significant student population, courtesy of the Jesuit-affiliated **Loyola University**, whose grassy, pleasant main campus covers several city blocks at the intersection of Sheridan Road and Broadway. The area is safe for the most part, but **gangs and drug dealers** are still active in this part of the city, particularly near the Red Line Howard stop, which should be avoided after dark.

Loyola University

One of the nation's foremost Catholic colleges, **Loyola University**, located at 6525 N Sheridan Rd, was founded in 1870 by the Society of Jesus, a Catholic order reputed for its passion for academics and intellectual curiosity. Spread out over a few blocks overlooking the lake, the picturesque campus is a mixture of architectural styles, from the hushed beauty of the Art-Deco **Madonna della Strada Chapel**, which overlooks the lake at the campus's eastern end, to the new **Joseph J. Gentile Center** basketball facility in the center of campus. A quiet oasis in the middle of a busy neighborhood, the campus makes for a relaxing stroll away from the noisy traffic racing by on Sheridan Road. If you're looking for action in this neighborhood, though, the couple blocks of Sheridan north of Devon Avenue is home to a few college hangouts, as is the stretch of **Broadway** south of Devon.

Rogers Park beaches

Though they'll never be mistaken for the expansive swaths of sand at Oak Street or North Avenue, Rogers Park also boasts several **beaches** that draw crowds of neighborhood families for sunbathing and swimming. The largest and most popular of these is at **Loyola Park**, a 21.5-acre facility stretching from Pratt Boulevard to Chase Avenue with a baseball field, a fieldhouse, a walking trail, and a tennis court as well as a fine – if crowded – stretch of beach.

Most of the neighborhood's other beaches are small, facility-less affairs at the eastern end of residential streets, like **North Shore Beach Park**, at 1040 W North Shore Ave, and the tucked-away **Rogers Avenue Beach and Park**, just south of Evanston at 7800 N Rogers Ave.

Along West Devon Avenue

Chicago's thriving **South Asian community** – the largest in the US after Jackson Heights, in New York – buzzes less than two miles west of Loyola University on Devon Avenue. Here, centered on Western Avenue (2400W), the street is lined with Indian and Pakistani shops: video stores hawking the latest Bollywood films, colorful saris draped in the front windows of traditional clothing stores, and the heady smell of curry wafts through the air from the doors of the neighborhood's many restaurants.

However, the street has always attracted a diverse ethnic and religious mix. In the mid-nineteenth century, it was a center of commerce for Chicago's Jewish community, and later attracted a number of Croatian Catholics; since the mid-1960s, though, West Devon has become a haven for a burgeoning Hindi, Muslim, and Sikh population from India and Pakistan, benefactors of the abolishment of racial quotas in immigration laws. Sights are few and far between along the strip; West Devon is worth visiting mostly for the authentic South Asian sounds and smells, and, of course, for the excellent **restaurants** see p.203 for reviews, which serve the best Indian food in the city, if not the Midwest.

Evanston

Follow Sheridan Road north from the city as it winds through Rogers Park, and you'll shortly end up in lakeside **Evanston**, best known as the home of **Northwestern University**. With its wide, shaded streets and grand, early twentieth-century homes, the town has a prosperous, small-town feel and a comparatively tranquil atmosphere. Casual but lively with families, thirtysomething condo-owners, and local college and high school students, the several blocks that make up **downtown Evanston** are a charmingly relaxed alternative to downtown Chicago's hectic shopping and dining scene.

As gentrification moves ever further north, though, Evanston has come to feel more like an extension of the city. Its charming **shopping** district, centered around Church and Davis streets, bustles with bookstores, clothing shops, and movie theaters, plus several notable **restaurants**. The city also boasts several lovely **beaches** just off Sheridan Road, as well as an active **arts** scene, including the highly regarded **Evanston Arts Center** and **Noyes Cultural Arts Center**, as well as the **Mitchell Museum of the American Indian**.

Evanston is easily accessible via the CTA's Purple Line; get off at the Davis stop for the downtown shopping district, or Noyes for Northwestern University.

Northwestern University

Continue along Sheridan Road, passing by the multi-million-dollar mansions dotting Sheridan Road in Evanston, and you'll eventually wind up at sylvan **Northwestern University**, whose lovely green campus rests on 240 acres of Lake Michigan shoreline. The campus itself is a hodgepodge of architectural styles, from the handsome Italian Renaissance columns and ornate balustrades of **Lunt Hall** at 2033 Sheridan Rd to the boxy reinforced concrete of **Nathaniel Leverone Hall**, just south at 2001 Sheridan Rd. While not quite as prestigious as its collegiate counterpart in Hyde Park, the University of Chicago (see p.144), NU is still considered one of the Midwest's elite universities. The campus buzzes with activity, but it's not the hard-partying place you might expect of a Big Ten school. That may well be because of the school's stellar academic reputation; a more likely explanation, though, is the fact that in 1855 – not coincidentally, the year the university was founded – the state's general assembly passed an amendment making it illegal to sell alcohol within four miles of the new school's campus. The city and university went "dry," and the amendment stayed on the books until it was overturned in 1972 by the town's city council. More than thirty years later, the campus is still comparatively quiet, and there are only a handful of bars dotting the main drags of the downtown area.

Among its several prominent schools are the CEO-breeding grounds of the Kellogg School of Management as well as the nationally renowned Medill School of Journalism. In addition, the Communication program has turned out countless stage and screen stars, from Ann-Margret, Warren Beatty, and Charlton Heston to current celebs like *Friends*' David Schwimmer and Tony Award–winners Denis O'Hare (*Take Me Out*) and Mary Zimmerman (*Metamorphoses*). With its many winding paths, ivy-covered buildings, and picturesque setting, the campus itself makes for a lovely lakeside stroll. To fully explore the campus, take one of the ninety-minute **tours** offered once or twice daily Monday to Saturday during the school year, and three times daily Monday to Friday during the summer. Intended primarily for prospective students and their parents, tours leave from the Office of Undergraduate Admissions, 1801 Hinman Ave (call ☎847/491-7271).

The Shakespeare Garden

One campus highlight is the **Shakespeare Garden**, 2121 Sheridan Rd, a formal English Tudor–style garden designed by renowned Prairie-style architect Jens Jensen in 1915 to commemorate the 300th anniversary of the death of Shakespeare. The intimate 70-by-100-foot plot is surrounded by two rows of hawthorn trees, and the garden itself is comprised of eight flower beds filled with more than fifty plants common in the Bard's day, including rosemary, hyssop, lavender, thyme, and lemon balm. In 1929, a fountain was added to the garden, featuring a bronze relief of Shakespeare's head designed by Hubert Burnham, son of legendary architect Daniel H. Burnham. The garden was added to the National Register of Historic Places in 1989.

The Mary & Leigh Block Museum of Art

A ten-minute walk to the southeast on campus, one of Evanston's finest museums hugs the lake. The free **Mary & Leigh Block Museum of Art**, 40 Arts Circle Drive (ⓣ847/491-4000; Tues 10am–5pm, Wed–Fri 10am–8pm, Sat & Sun noon–5pm), has an impressive collection – more than 4000 works of art in all – that dates from the thirteenth century to the present. Of particular interest are the museum's German Expressionist prints; twentieth-century American photography by Roland Freeman and Alan Cohen; and twentieth-century American and European sculpture, one of the finest collections in the Midwest, with 22 pieces showcased in the museum's outdoor **sculpture garden**. Among them are prized works like Joan Miró's *Constellation*, a free-swinging flattened sphere embedded with a golden pearl; Henry Moore's sexy, sinuous *Interior Form*; and pieces by Jean Arp, Lynn Chadwick, and Chicago-born Northwestern alumnus Irwin Kremen. **Free tours** of the sculpture garden are offered on Sundays at 2pm.

Downtown Evanston and around

Much of the action in **downtown Evanston** happens in the vicinity of Church and Davis streets between Maple and Hinman avenues, close to the Davis CTA stop. Here you'll find grad students bent over books in funky cafés, couples pushing strollers along brick-lined sidewalks, and a surprisingly sophisticated **dining scene**, with vegan and vegetarian hot spots as well as several high-end restaurants that match up well with the best in the city.

Shopping and entertainment is the focus of this area, but there are several worthy cultural sites nearby as well, thanks mostly to the city's active arts scene. The **Evanston Art Center** (ⓣ847/475-5300; Mon–Thurs 10am–10pm, Fri & Sat 10am–4pm, Sun 1–4pm; suggested donation $3), at 2603 Sheridan Rd, presents frequent exhibitions of local and Midwestern artists working in paint, photography, sculpture, and other media. Near the Noyes train station at 927 Noyes St, the **Noyes Cultural Arts Center** (ⓣ847/448-8260; Mon–Sat 10am–7pm, Sun 10am–6pm) is the center of the city's artistic community; the complex features two art galleries showcasing the work of area artists plus a 190-seat theater space, and also acts as the headquarters for several local arts organizations, including Light Opera Works, the Actors Gymnasium Circus and Performing Arts School, and Piven Theater and Workshop, whose alumni include John and Joan Cusack, Lili Taylor, Jeremy Piven, and Lara Flynn Boyle.

A couple miles to the northwest of downtown, the **Mitchell Museum of the American Indian** (2600 Central Park Ave ⓣ847/475-1030; Tues, Wed, Fri

& Sat 10am–5pm, Thurs 10am–8pm, Sun noon–4pm; suggested admission $5) offers an in-depth look at the history and culture of Native American tribes of the Woodlands, Plains, Southwest, and Northwest coasts. The collection includes more than 3000 objects, from an authentic full-sized birchbark canoe to glass beads, quillwork, carved bowls, and even a twentieth-century walrus-intestine parka from western Alaska. Each gallery includes a "touching table" with artifacts and raw materials – caribou fur, snakeskin, and buffalo skin among them – that visitors can handle. Not worth going out of your way for, but a popular stop for Native-American-history buffs.

Wilmette

Curving beyond Evanston, Sheridan Road hugs the lake and arrives in **Wilmette**, a quiet, affluent suburb of expansive lawns and even larger lakefront mansions. There are few attractions to make the trek this far north worthwhile to the average visitor, but those who do will be rewarded with the breathtaking sight of the majestic **Baha'í House of Worship**. Cyclists, too, will want to explore the paved, well-maintained **Green Bay Trail**, which extends nine miles north toward the **Chicago Botanical Garden**. To **get to** Wilmette, follow Sheridan Road north of Evanston, or take the El Purple Line to its final stop (Linden).

The Baha'í House of Worship

Rising 135 feet in the air, the pristine, ivory-hued **Baha'í House of Worship** (100 Linden Ave ⓣ847/853-2300; daily 7am–6.30pm, visitor's center daily 10am–5pm; free) is a breathtaking – if unexpected – lakeside sight in this quiet North Shore suburb. The oldest such temple still standing (six others exist around the world, with a seventh planned for Santiago, Chile), the structure is the North American center of the Baha'í faith, a religion that emphasizes racial unity, gender equality, a strong family unit, and world peace. Completed in 1953 and made entirely of cast concrete, the nine-sided, domed temple resembles a mosque: its dome is covered in ornate, lace-like ornamentation, with two levels of elaborate spires that emphasize the building's height, and the temple is surrounded by fountains, gardens, and broad lawns – ideal for quiet reflection. For more active pursuits, there's the nearby **Gillson Park**, a 60-acre lakeside recreation area with tennis and volleyball courts, grilling equipment, and a beach for swimming (beach pass $3.25 for residents, $6.50 for visitors).

The Chicago Botanic Garden and around

Spreading over 385 acres (much of it wooded), the **Chicago Botanic Garden** (1000 Lake Cook Rd, Glencoe; daily 8am–sunset; free; ⓣ847/835-5440) features twenty-six beautifully landscaped gardens, from a secluded, romantic English garden and a rose garden brimming with more than 5000 rose bushes to a Zen-like Japanese garden set on three islands. These lush displays are wild with dahlias, daylilies, sunflowers, coneflowers – well over two million plants in all – and attract nearly 800,000 visitors each year. The best way to explore is by taking a **tour** via motorized tram. Options include a general tour of the grounds (every half-hour 10am–3.30pm daily); a more focused tour of the main island (hourly 10.15am–3.15pm daily); and, during July and August, an evening tour (Sun–Thurs 5, 6 & 7pm; Fri & Sat 7 and 8pm). All tours are 35 minutes and cost $5 (children $3).

An excellent route to the Chicago Gardens is the **Green Bay Trail**, a favorite destination for Chicago cycling enthusiasts. This nine-mile, asphalt and crushed-stone trail meanders through Wilmette and the similar northern suburbs of Winnetka and Kenilworth and past Ravinia to downtown Highland Park. The entrance to the trail is located west of the park, just north of Lake Street on Green Bay Road.

Listings

Listings

13

Accommodation

With nearly thirty-two million visitors passing through Chicago each year (and growing), the city maintains an abundance of **accommodation**; indeed, there are more than 100,000 rooms in the metropolitan area, though, in truth, many of these are in large, rather anonymous hotels catering to business travelers and conventioneers. Even so, you shouldn't have too hard a time finding reasonable and affordable, if often unexciting, options in the city center. Most basic accommodation (save hostels and perhaps B&Bs) will run you a minimum of $100 a night, especially if you need a room at the last minute (rooms at better hotels average $150–175 per night).

A preponderance of hotels is concentrated in just a few pockets around downtown, the largest of which is **Near North**, where several dozen expensive hotels cluster in River North and around N Michigan Avenue. The more business-oriented **Loop** has a few pricey hotels, but also the city's best hostel, as well as some mid-range boutique options. Besides being close to many of the downtown attractions, the Loop offers easy access to O'Hare International Airport (40min by El train) – a cumbersome trip from other parts of the city unless you're willing to shell out around $40 for a taxi.

Outside the most central areas, accommodation choices thin out considerably, though there's more variety in terms of B&Bs versus business hotels, and rates are generally lower. Most of the city's B&Bs and guesthouses are located in **Old Town** and **Lincoln Park**, while **Lakeview** has some budget options and arty-boutique hotels, as well as gay-friendly accommodations (see p.240). Staying this far north may not be practical for extended downtown exploration – but all will do if you want to get a better feel for the city's residential neighborhoods. **West and south of the Loop**, you'll find few big-name chains, but again, these aren't areas where you'd choose to stay unless you're planning to spend most of your time in Greektown and Little Italy, or McCormick Place and Hyde Park. We've also included a list of **airport hotels**, which are worth considering only if you need to catch an early-morning flight.

Even in a major city like Chicago, where you'll find some of the top hotels in the country, it's still possible to find excellent rooms at drastically reduced prices, either through one of the popular **booking agencies** like Hot Rooms (Ⓣ773/468-7666 or 1-800/468-3500, Ⓦwww.hotrooms.com) or an **Internet search site** like Ⓦwww.orbitz.com, Ⓦwww.expedia.com, or Ⓦwww.hotels.com. In fact, unless you want to stay at a B&B or one of the hostels, you should do your pre-trip bargain hunting **online**. Many hotels offer Web-only specials or guarantee that their online rates are the lowest out there; if you find a great rate at a discount site, chances are the hotel's website will match or beat it. Since there are so many hotels in the city, even the top hotels are forced to slash rates

Best bargains

Best Western River North p.174
Hostelling International p.178
The Raphael p.173
Red Roof Inn Chicago p.173

during the week and at off-peak times, with many offering package deals for couples with tours and meals included. All in all, it's generally easy to find a $300 room at luxury places like the *W* hotels, or at the *Drake* for under $200.

Alternatively, going through a **B&B service** like Chicago Bed and Breakfast or At Home Inn Chicago (see box, p.170) will get you a room, or a full apartment, in a private residence or guesthouse, priced from around $85 to usually not more than $175, unless the B&B is exceedingly precious, historic, or otherwise. Corporate **discounts** and those for AAA (American Automobile Association) members can bring down the price significantly, so make sure to inquire about them before making your reservation. Keep in mind, however, that all Chicago hotels will add a 15.4 percent room **tax** to your bill. It's also wise to arrange for a room ahead of your visit, especially around holidays and in spring and summer; note that Chicago can also get overrun by conventions, some of them big enough to fill every available room in the city.

If you're arriving by car, **parking** at the Loop and Near North hotels will be unavoidable and costly ($20–35 per night).

Hotels

The Loop

Allegro 171 W Randolph St, at N LaSalle St ⓣ312/236-0123 or 1-866/672-6143, ⓕ312/236-0917, ⓦwww.allegrochicago.com; all lines to Clark St. This chic, recently restored 1920s business hotel, right in the Theatre District, has almost 500 rooms that blend contemporary decor – striped, upholstered headboards, walls painted in bold reds and oranges – with Art Deco accents, and offer amenities like flat-screen TVs and Aveda bath products. The staff's professionalism is a selling point and there's a free wine hour every evening (5–6pm), as well as an on-site fitness center and access to a nearby pool. $149–179

Hotel Burnham 1 W Washington St, at S State St ⓣ312/782-1111 or 1-877/294-9712, ⓕ312/782-0899, ⓦwww.burnhamhotel.com; Red or Blue Line to Washington; Brown, Green, Orange, or Purple Line to State/Lake. Located in one of the world's first glass-and-steel skyscrapers, the *Burnham* is an intimate boutique hotel where everything – from the romantic ambience to the exemplary service – strives to create a luxurious oasis amid the heavily trafficked business hotels of downtown. The one hundred rooms and twenty-odd suites all come with turn-down service and twice-daily housekeeping. There's a free wine reception in the lobby (daily 5–6pm), plus free coffee and tea (6–9.30am). Prices fluctuate wildly depending on availability, but Internet prices, last-minute and package deals (dinners, tours) can make this place affordable even if it's out of your immediate range. The excellent *Atwood Café* is located on the first floor (see p.206). $169–189

Congress Plaza Hotel 520 S Michigan Ave, at W Congress Parkway ⓣ312/427-3800 or 1-800/635-1666, ⓕ312/427-2919, ⓦwww.congressplazahotel.com; Red Line to Harrison; Blue Line to LaSalle; Brown or Orange Line to Library-State/Van Buren. Huge hotel (over 800 rooms) and convention center that was built for the 1893 World's Columbian Exposition and has seen better days. Many of the rooms tend toward the small and are sometimes rough around the edges but afford great views of Buckingham Fountain and Lake Michigan. The hotel is a decent alternative to some of the better-restored and modern boutique hotels in the Loop, which are generally the first to fill up. $139–159

CENTRAL CHICAGO ACCOMMODATION

Hotel	No.
Amalfi Hotel	21
Best Western Grant Park	38
Best Western River North	18
Cass Hotel	14
Comfort Inn	19
Congress Plaza Hotel	33
Crowne Plaza	29
Drake Hotel	1
Essex Inn	37
Fairmont Hotel	25
Fitzpatrick Hotel	12
Four Seasons Hotel	2
Hard Rock Hotel Chicago	26
Hilton Chicago and Towers	36
Holiday Inn and Suites Downtown	34
Hostelling International–Chicago	32
Hotel Allegro	27
Hotel Burnham	28
The Hotel Monaco	24
Hotel Inter-Continental Chicago	20
House of Blues Hotel	22
Ohio House Motel	17
Omni	13
The Palmer House Hilton	30
Park Hyatt Chicago	10
Peninsula Chicago Hotel	11
The Raphael	7
Red Roof Inn Chicago	15
Ritz-Carlton	9
Seneca Hotel	8
Sofitel Chicago Water Tower	5
Swissotel Chicago	23
The Talbott	6
Travelodge	35
W Chicago City Center	31
W Chicago Lakeshore	16
Westin	3
Whitehall Hotel	4

Bed-and-breakfast finders

If you're after a more congenial and personal experience than you might expect at a faceless business hotel, check out **Chicago Bed and Breakfast** (ⓦwww.chicago-bed-breakfast.com) or **At Home Inn Chicago** (ⓣ312/640-1050 or 1-800/375-7084, ⓦwww.athomeinnchicago.com); the former lists about a dozen proper B&Bs in the city, while the latter features a few dozen properties – mainly guesthouses and private homes. All are within about five miles of downtown, scattered about various neighborhoods.

Prices vary greatly for a night's stay ($85–295, plus tax), as does the quality of the rooms, apartments, and B&Bs, so be sure you know what you're getting and check the photos on the agency's website.

Many B&Bs have a two-night minimum stay, with weekdays almost always cheaper, which is not the case at some city hotels.

Crowne Plaza 10 S Wabash Ave, at W Madison St ⓣ312/372-7696 or 1-888/303-1746, ⓕ312/372-7320, ⓦwww.crowneplaza.com; Blue or Red Line to Monroe, all other lines to Madison. This recently remodeled, ten-story business hotel, inside the 1897 Daniel Burnham–designed Silversmith Building, has simple but tasteful rooms. The bright, cheery (though sometimes small, given the hotel's age) rooms come with a CD player and coffeemaker, and there's also a fitness center. Close to the Loop sights and a few blocks from the river and the Mag Mile. $189

Fairmont 200 N Columbus Drive, at E Lake St ⓣ312/565-8000 or 1-800/257-7544, ⓕ312/856-1032, ⓦwww.fairmont.com; Red Line to Lake; Brown, Green, Orange, or Purple Line to Randolph/Wabash. In addition to luxurious rooms and suites, the *Fairmont* features a pleasant art-filled lobby, two swank ballrooms, and a fitness club. The food and service are top-notch, and while not as splashy as the *Peninsula* or the *Park Hyatt*, it's just as plush and provides a somewhat more personalized touch. $209–369

Hard Rock Hotel 230 N Michigan Ave, at E Lake St ⓣ312/345-1000 or 1-877/ROCK-HOTEL, ⓕ312/345-1012, ⓦwww.hardrockhotelchicago.com; Red Line to Lake; Brown, Green, Orange, or Purple Line to State. The Loop's landmark 40-story Art-Deco Carbide and Carbon Building has been transformed into the city's hottest new hotel, which opened in 2004. The location is convenient – walking distance from Millennium Park, the Mag Mile, the Art Institute, and the Theater District – and the rooms and suites are stylishly appointed, with sweeping city views, 27-inch flat-screen TVs, and complimentary high-speed Internet access. Downstairs, live djs spin nightly in the *BASE* bar and a beautiful crowd gathers in the pricey but impressive Asian-fusion restaurant *China Grill*. $219–299

Monaco 225 N Wabash Ave, at E Lake St ⓣ312/960-8500, ⓕ312/960-1883, 866/610-0081, ⓦwww.monaco-chicago.com; Red Line to Lake; Brown, Green, Orange, or Purple Line to State/Lake. Plush boutique hotel decorated in French Art Deco style and close to the Mag Mile. Though some of the amenities like the "companion" goldfish – which guests who are missing their pets can take to their rooms – are gimmicky, the hotel itself is far nicer than any of the nearby business hotels charging similar prices. The rooms, some of which come with Jacuzzis, are stylish, and there are even some special "Tall" rooms, with longer-than-average beds and raised showerheads. Prices vary depending on availability; your best bet is to check their website for promotions and last-minute discounts. $249–299

The Palmer House Hilton 17 E Monroe St ⓣ312/726-7500, ⓕ312/917-1707 or 1-800/445-8667; Red or Blue Line to Monroe, all other lines to Adams/Wabash. The oldest continuously operating hotel in the US and the sister hotel to New York's famed *Waldorf-Astoria*, the *Palmer* is a good bet if you want to be in the Loop but close to the Mag Mile. There is an enclosed shopping arcade, a health club, small indoor pool, and four restaurants, including *Trader Vic's*, an iconic Tiki bar-restaurant. The rooms are generally smallish, but kept to Hilton standards. Though the larger rooms and suites can be pricey, it's possible to book one of the smaller rooms

Airport hotels

Hilton O'Hare Airport O'Hare International Airport, directly across from the terminals ⓣ773/686-8000, ⓕ773/601-2873, 800/445-8667, ⓦwww.hilton.com/hotels/CHIOHHH; Blue Line to O'Hare. This busy, 900-room hotel is nice enough and reasonably priced. Facilities include restaurants, a sports bar, and a health club. $107–215

Hyatt Regency O'Hare 9300 W Bryn Mawr Ave, Rosemont ⓣ847/696-1234, ⓕ847/698-0139, ⓦohare.hyatt.com; take the free hotel shuttle from baggage claim at O'Hare. The most likely reason you'd stay here is if you're stranded at O'Hare and the comparable, but slightly less expensive *Hilton* is full. The hotel has a pool and fitness center. $119–165

Sofitel O'Hare 5550 N River Rd ⓣ847/678-4488, ⓕ847/678-4244,1-800/221-4542, ⓦwww.sofitelchicagoohare.com; take the free hotel shuttle from O'Hare. Three miles from O'Hare, this plush hotel, with 300 immaculate rooms, includes a superb restaurant, a pool, sauna, and fitness center (all with 24hr access), a bakery, reasonable parking ($16/night), and free shuttles to the airport every 20 minutes, 24 hours a day. Rates are almost always cheaper on weekends. $135–155

Wyndham O'Hare 6810 N Mannheim Rd ⓣ847/297-1234 or 1-877/999-3223, ⓕ847/297-5287, ⓦwww.wyndham.com/hotels; take the 24hr shuttle from baggage claim at O'Hare. Two miles from O'Hare, the *Radisson* is the best value among the airport hotels, with basic rooms, indoor and outdoor pools, plus a small fitness center. $89–149

▽ *The Palmer House Hilton*

Rooms with a view

The Drake p.174
Park Hyatt Chicago p.173
Ritz-Carlton p.173
Swissotel Chicago p.171
W Chicago Lakeshore p.173

at highly discounted rates (as low as $120) that can work out to be cheaper than some budget chains. Free morning paper delivered to your door. $170–239

Swissotel Chicago 323 E Wacker Drive, at N Columbia Drive ⓣ312/565-0565 or 1-800/637-9477, ⓕ312/565-0540, ⓦwww.swissotel.com; Red Line to Lake; Brown, Green, Orange, or Purple Line to Randolph/Wabash. Stylish and better run than most other business hotels in town, the towering *Swissotel* has superb city views from its location on the Chicago River and Michigan Ave, and a 42nd-floor health club with pool. Each of the rooms has marble bathrooms and are fairly spacious. There's also a nine-hole golf course next door. Rooms with the better views cost $10–30 more, and like other business-minded hotels, rates tend to go down on weekends. $159–249

Travelodge 65 E Harrison St, at S Wabash Ave ⓣ312/427-8000 or 1-800/578-7878, ⓕ312/427-8261, ⓦwww.travelodge.com; Red Line to Harrison. No-frills chain in the South Loop near Grant Park that's clean and has comfortable enough beds and bathroom furnishings, but overall a bit lackluster. Basic amenities include coffeemaker, complimentary paper, and high-speed Internet access. $90–95

W Chicago City Center **172 W Adams St ⓣ312/332-1200 or 1-877/946-8357, ⓕ312/917-5771, ⓦwww.whotels.com; Red or Blue Line to Jackson; Brown, Orange, or Purple Line to Quincy.** Ultra-chic chain hotel in the heart of the Loop, with beautifully decorated and comfortable rooms. The lobby – a two-story space called "The Living Room" – is sumptuously ornate and equipped with its own dj. Best to ignore published prices and search for deals online instead. The second-floor hotel bar, *Whiskey Blue*, is a slick, retro after-work hot spot (see review, p.206). $219–299

Near North

Amalfi **20 W Kinzie St, at State St ⓣ312/395-9000 or 1-877/262-5341, ⓕ312-395-9001, ⓦwww.amalfihotelchicago.com; Red Line to Grand.** This sleek, new 215-room hotel with great city views just north of the river has spacious rooms, 316-thread-count Egyptian cotton linens, multi-head showers, and complimentary high-speed Internet in every room. Concierge-like "Experience Designers" can help with theater tickets and tough dining reservations. Pets welcome. $189–289

Best Western River North **125 W Ohio St, at N LaSalle St ⓣ312/467-0800 or 1-800/937-8376, ⓕ312/467-1665, ⓦwww.bestwestern.com/rivernorthhotel; Red Line to Grand; Brown or Purple Line to Merchandise Mart.** This refurbished *Best Western*, in a great River North location close to many attractions but off the main tourist drag, is the only downtown hotel that provides guests with free parking. Rooms are spacious, while facilities include a fitness center and an indoor pool on the roof. Close to transportation. $119–139

Cass Hotel **640 N Wabash Ave, at E Ontario St ⓣ312/787-4030 or 1-800/799-4030, ⓕ312/787-8544, ⓦwww.casshotel.com; Red Line to Grand.** No-frills hotel for budget travelers only that gets by on its low rates and central Near North location. Rooms are spartan and on the dingy side, and the lobby is usually thick with smoke – though the *Sea of Happiness* hotel bar is a wonderfully tacky dive. Tends to book up on weekends. $69–89

Comfort Inn **15 E Ohio St, at N State St ⓣ312/894-0900 or 1-888/775-4111, ⓕ312/894/0999, ⓦwww.chicagocomfortinn.com; Red Line to Grand.** Basic high-rise budget chain hotel – though with a more glamorous-looking lobby than most – but with amenities such as a fitness room, whirlpool, and sauna. Suites feature wet bar, microwave, and refrigerator, and an extra area with a sleeper sofa and desk. $140–190

Fitzpatrick Hotel **166 E Superior St, at N Michigan Ave ⓣ312/787-6000 or 1-800/367-7701,ⓕ312/787-6113, ⓦwww.fitzpatrickhotels.com; Red Line to Chicago.** Sumptuous hotel with a subtle Irish theme (think mini-shamrocks and expat staff) and a cozy pub done up with photos of Irish athletes and historical figures. The rooms, converted from apartments, are huge and well designed, with comfortable beds, and the location in Streeterville, one block east of Michigan Ave, is a major plus. $219–249

Four Seasons Hotel **120 E Delaware Place, at N Michigan Ave ⓣ312/280-8800 or 1-800/819-5053, ⓕ312/280-1748, ⓦwww.fourseasons.com; Red Line to Chicago.** The service is unbeatable at this majestic 343-room hotel, which offers sumptuous rooms with superb views, a spa, fitness club, skylit pool, and top-notch restaurants and lounges. You pay for what you get, and you'll rarely find a reduced rate here. $430–555

Hotel Inter-Continental Chicago **505 N Michigan Ave, at E Illinois St ⓣ312/944-4100 or 1-888/303-1758, ⓕ312/944-1320, ⓦchicago.intercontinental.com; Red Line to Grand.** Originally built in 1929 as a luxury men's club, this classic hotel features over 800 festively decorated rooms on 42 floors, as well as a junior Olympic pool. Best to stay in the Tower as opposed to the lower floors, despite the slight extra cost, as the views are impressive. The recently renovated rooms are impressively modern, with mini-bar, coffeemaker, and terry bathrobes. Hotel amenities include laundry valet service and a gorgeous, Olympic-sized swimming pool. Rates vary widely; best to check for deals on the website. $145–229

Ohio House Motel **600 N LaSalle St, at W Ohio St ⓣ312/943-6000 or 1-866/601-6446, ⓕ312/943-6063, ⓦwww.ohiohousemotel.com; Red Line to Grand; Brown or Purple Line to Merchandise Mart.** If you're on a tight budget, this two-floor roadside motel is usually available, though its down-at-the-heels air makes it a last-resort budget option. That said, it's probably the best cheap hotel in the downtown area for its location and great rates. $90–115

Omni 676 N Michigan Ave, at E Erie St ⓣ312/944-6664 or 1-800/843-6664, ⓕ312/266-3015, ⓦwww.omnihotels.com; Red Line to Grand. The spiffier, newer cousin to the *Omni Ambassador East* (see p.174), the *Omni* (used by the *Oprah Winfrey Show* for its guests) is pricey but worth the money. Each of the rooms features complimentary Internet access, two TVs, and plush terry robes. Health-conscious travelers can check into one of their "Get Fit Rooms" which feature a treadmill, dumbbells, and healthy snacks. There's also an indoor heated pool and two rooftop sundecks. $249–289

Park Hyatt Chicago 800 N Michigan Ave, at Chicago Ave ⓣ312/335-1234, ⓕ312/239-4000, ⓦwww.parkchicago.hyatt.com; Red Line to Chicago. Professional but not obtrusive, sophisticated, and perhaps a touch arrogant, the *Park Hyatt* is one of the newer entries to vie for the title of top Chicago luxury hotel. The list of amenities goes overboard – each room has CD and DVD players, four phones, and Mies van der Rohe–designed chairs – and the prices tend to as well. Hard to find reduced rates here, as occupancy remains high in its 200 rooms. Has a magnificient gourmet restaurant, *NoMi* (see p.189), that faces onto Water Tower Park. $355–445

Peninsula Chicago Hotel 108 E Superior St, at N Michigan Ave ⓣ312/337-2888 or 1-866/288-8889, ⓕ751-2888, ⓦwww.chicago.peninsula.com; Red Line to Chicago. Everything you've ever wanted from a hotel and then some is available at the hip *Peninsula Chicago*. The over 300 plush guest rooms are equipped with every conceivable amenity, including TVs beside the bathtubs. The spa on the 19th and 20th floors offers spectacular views of Lake Michigan and N Michigan Ave, while *The Bar* is popular with the martini-drinking set. $390–415

The Raphael 201 E Delaware Place, at N Mies van der Rohe Way ⓣ312/943-5000 or 1-800/983-7870, ⓕ312/943-9483, ⓦwww.raphaelchicago.com; Red Line to Chicago. Just behind the John Hancock building in Streeterville, this superbly located boutique hotel offers nice, larger-than-average rooms, affordable rates that include continental breakfast, and friendly service. $119–169

Red Roof Inn Chicago 162 E Ontario St, at N St Clair St ⓣ312/787-3580 or 1-800/733-7663, ⓕ312/787-1299, ⓦwww.redroof-chicago-downtown.com; Red Line to Grand. Better than you might expect from a budget motel chain, the *Red Roof*'s rooms are close to the Mag Mile, and the River North galleries and restaurants. Though slightly worn, the motel is a solid budget pick for the area, often going for $100 or less. Weekends generally see a moderate increase in rates. $96–140

Ritz-Carlton 160 E Pearson St, between N Michigan Ave and N Mies van der Rohe Way ⓣ312/266-1000, ⓕ312/266-1194, ⓦwww.fourseasons.com/chicagorc; Red Line to Chicago. Connected to Water Tower Place and a block from the Mag Mile, this is the place to stay if you want to feel like royalty. *The Ritz* has giant and richly appointed rooms, several top-notch restaurants, a health club, lap pool, and spa. The airy café off the lobby makes for a great place to soak up the luxurious atmosphere. $430–515

Seneca 200 E Chestnut St, at N Mies van der Rohe Way ⓣ312/787-8900 or 1-800/800-6261, ⓕ312/988-4438, ⓦwww.senecahotel.com; Red Line to Chicago. Plush boutique hotel, next to the John Hancock building, with spacious rooms for those wanting to stay near N Michigan Ave, but away from the crowds. Frequent special deals (standard room, full breakfast included) make this a sensible option. All rooms have free wireless Internet access. There are two excellent restaurants: the romantic *Saloon Steakhouse* and *Chestnut Grill & Wine Bar*. $109–179

Sofitel Chicago Water Tower 20 E Chestnut St, at N Rush St ⓣ312/324-4000, ⓕ312/324-4026, ⓦwww.sofitelchicago.com; Red Line to Chicago. This sleek glass tower is one of the more striking hotels in Chicago. The 400-plus rooms are minimally decorated yet chic, the service is impeccable, and many of the rooms – especially the suites – have lake views. Equally stylish is the street-level hotel hangout *Le Bar*. $235–295

W Chicago Lakeshore 644 N Lake Shore Drive, at E Ontario St ⓣ312/943-9200 or 1-888/W-HOTELS, ⓕ312/255-4411, ⓦwww.whotels.com; Red Line to Grand. The lakefront location is this chic hotel's biggest asset, followed by rooms with down-stuffed beds and high-end amenities. The luxurious first-floor lounge and bar are immensely popular with Chicago's crowd, as is the rooftop bar, *Whiskey Sky*. One of the closest hotels to Navy Pier and an infinitely more relaxed setting than its sibling in the Loop (see p.172). $249–289

Westin 909 N Michigan Ave, at W Delaware Place ⓣ312/943-7200, ⓕ312/397-5580, ⓦwww.starwoodhotels.com; Red Line to Chicago. Over 700 rooms in this large-chain luxury hotel right across from the John Hancock. The recently renovated rooms are plush, with *Westin's* signature pillow-top Heavenly Beds, and great views of the area. Has a pricey and excellent steakhouse (*The Grill on the Alley*) on the first floor. Can't beat it for location, and they often have discounted rates, especially in winter. $179–219

Whitehall 105 E Delaware Place, between N Rush St and N Michigan Ave ⓣ312/944-6300 or 1-800/948-4255, ⓕ944-8552, ⓦwww.thewhitehallhotel.com; Red Line to Chicago. Boutique hotel just off Mag Mile that achieves a sort of non-snooty European ambience. Guests have use of the fitness center as well as complimentary car service within a two-mile radius of the hotel. One of the top choices for those who want to stay in the area but try to avoid the chains. $139–249

Gold Coast and Old Town

See map on p.87 for hotel locations.

The Drake 140 E Walton Place, at N Michigan Ave ⓣ312/787-2200 or 1-800/55-DRAKE, ⓕ312/787-1431, ⓦwww.thedrakehotel.com; Red Line to Chicago. If it didn't occupy the most coveted piece of property in the city and have such history, Chicago's elegant *Drake* might have been surpassed years ago by its high-powered competitors. Across from Oak Street Beach and with outstanding views of Lake Shore Drive and Lake Michigan, the hotel has 535 renovated rooms, which still feel a bit aged and are smallish, especially compared to some of the newer hotels in the area. Some rooms start from $400 a night, but most cost half that, and a few rooms even less (check the hotel website for the best deals). $179–319

▽ *The Drake*

The Gold Coast Guest House 113 W Elm St, at N Clark St ⓣ312/337-0361, ⓕ312/337-0362, ⓦwww.bbchicago.com; Red Line to Clark/Division. This converted 1873 row house, run by a wonderful host, includes continental breakfast and evening refreshments in their rates and usually requires a two-night stay on weekends. Each of the four guest rooms comes with air conditioning and private bath – a couple even have a whirlpool – and bed sizes vary by room. There's also a charming garden outside and the lake is just a ten-minute walk away. No smoking. $119–189

Hotel Indigo Chicago – Gold Coast 1244 N Dearborn Parkway, at W Goethe St ⓣ312/787-4980 or 1-800/245-1258, ⓕ312/787-4069, ⓦwww.goldcoastchicagohotel.com; Red Line to Clark/Division. Bright, cheerful, completely renovated hotel that's a great deal in one of the city's most expensive neighborhoods. Very central – a few blocks from the lake and near the Mag Mile, as well as dozens of restaurants and bars. Rooms are well appointed but on the small side. $169

Old Town Chicago B&B Inn 1442 North Park Ave, at Schiller St ⓣ312/440-9268, ⓕ312/440-2378, ⓦwww.oldtownchicago.com; Brown or Purple Line to Sedgwick. Lavishly decorated wing of a multimillion-dollar Art-Deco town house in Old Town. The four guest rooms, all suites with luxurious queen beds, each come with private bath and cable TV, and breakfast as well as 24hr snacks are included in rates. There's also a nice roof deck. A three-night minimum stay is generally required for weekend stays reserved more than a week in advance. One of the nicer B&B options in the city. $160–200

Omni Ambassador East Hotel 1301 N State Parkway, at W Goethe St ⓣ312/787-7200 or 1-800/843-6664, ⓕ312/787-4760, ⓦwww.omnihotels.com; Red Line to Clark/Division. Great hotel in a prime Gold Coast location, offering surprisingly affordable room rates for the area. Considering its age, the rooms are very spacious, comfortable, and well kept-up. Built in the 1920s, the *Ambassador* was a favorite haunt of Frank Sinatra and the Rat Pack during the 1950s, and its famed *Pump Room* bar is still here, though it's lost the sheen of its glory days. $139–229

The Talbott 20 E Delaware Place, at N State St ⓣ312/944-4970 or 1-800/825-2688, ⓕ312/944-7241, ⓦwww.talbotthotel.com; Red Line to Chicago. Striving for (and mostly achieving) old English country club style, the *Talbott* is a small Gold Coast boutique hotel built in 1927. The rooms are small but comfortable, the service impeccable, and the lobby with its leather armchairs and dark-wood walls a wonderful escape. Just steps off Michigan Ave but utterly relaxing. $149–229

South Loop and Near South

See map on p.95 for hotel locations.

Best Western Grant Park 1100 S Michigan Ave, at E 11th St ⓣ312/922-2900 or 1-800/472-6875, ⓕ312/922-8812, ⓦwww.bestwestern.com/grantparkhotel; Green, Orange, or Red Line to Roosevelt. Located in the South Loop near the Museum Campus, this chain hotel has 173 rooms – all devoid of any sort of style, yet clean enough – an outdoor pool and sundeck, and complimentary coffee and newspapers. Popular with convention and tour groups; weekends tend to book up. Lake-view rooms fetch $10–20 more. $99–139

Essex Inn 800 S Michigan Ave, at E 8th St ⓣ312/939-2800 or 1-800/621-6909, ⓕ312/922-6153, ⓦwww.essexinn.com; Red Line to Harrison. Fifteen-story, 255-room South Loop hotel that's favored by many travelers for its cheap rates, clean (if somewhat spartan) rooms, and convenient location to Loop attractions. $109–119

Hilton Chicago and Towers 720 S Michigan Ave, at E Balbo Drive ⓣ312/922-4400 or 1-800/465-4329, ⓕ312/922-5240, ⓦwww.hilton.com; Red Line to Harrison. Unless you need to be here for a convention or want to stay near Grant Park, you might not find much reason to stay at this 1500-room hotel. Still, the rooms are kept up well enough, there are stunning lakefront views, and rates are more reasonable than Loop hotels. There's an indoor pool, fitness room, and all the business-traveler amenities you'd expect. $143–229

Holiday Inn & Suites Downtown Chicago 506 W Harrison St, at S Canal St ⓣ312/957-9100, ⓕ312/957-0474, 1-888/465-4329, ⓦwww.hidowntown.com; Blue Line to Clinton. A good, but not great, value chain-hotel just southwest of the Loop, near the Sears Tower, the two main Metra train stations, right underneath the inn. Easy access to Greektown and Little Italy. Rooms are spacious, staff are pleasant, and there's a small restaurant on site, as well as a fitness room and outdoor pool. $123–163

Hyatt Regency McCormick Place 2233 S King Drive, at E Cermak Rd ⓣ312/567-1234 or 1-800/633-7313, ⓕ312/528-4000, ⓦwww.mccormickplace.hyatt.com; bus #35. The place to be for conventioneers, this handsome hotel towers incongruously over the empty acres just west of the convention center. Although it's a bit isolated, it's possible to find some good deals here when there's not a huge convention in town. The 800 rooms are colorfully decorated and each offers complimentary high-speed Internet access. There is also an impressive array of on-site services like printing, shipping, and computer work stations. $149–179

Wheeler Mansion 2020 S Calumet Ave, at E 18th St ⓣ312/945-2020, ⓕ312/945-2021, ⓦwww.wheelermansion.com; Metra 18th St. Probably the city's most luxurious B&B, housed in a beautifully restored 1870s mansion, with the amenities of a small luxury hotel (Egyptian-cotton sheets, towels, and robes, turndown service). Popular with conventioneers meeting at McCormick Place, the B&B is also just a block from the historic Glessner House (see p.104) and the rest of S Prairie Ave. Rates include breakfast, and there's a classy first-floor dining room where you can order in food and dine in the evening. Minimum stays usually apply on weekends, and you can choose from standard rooms ($230–285), and junior and master suites ($265–365); prices include tax. $235–365

Wicker Park

See map on p.108 for hotel locations.

House of Two Urns 1239 N Greenview Ave, at W Division St ⓣ773/235-1408 or 1-877/896-8767, ⓕ773/235-1410, ⓦwww.twourns.com; Blue Line to Division/Milwaukee. Charming, quiet B&B in Wicker Park with five creatively decorated and unusual rooms (the "Alice

Room" has a Lewis Carroll vibe, with a jewel-toned, custom-made bed set high atop a stack of painted mattresses, a la *The Princess and the Pea*. Amenities go beyond the usual B&B offerings to include DVD rental, private phone lines, and answering machines. Take in some spectacular views of the downtown skyline from the roof deck. The only drawback is that most guest rooms share a bathroom with another guest room. Advance bookings usually require a minimum two-or-three night stay. A 10–15 percent discount is usually offered in January and February. $150–185

The Wicker Park Inn 1329 N Wicker Park Ave, at N Wood St ⓣ773/486-2743, ⓕ312/278-3802, ⓦwww.wickerparkinn.com; Blue Line to Damen. Three-room B&B in a two-story 1890s row house, a few blocks from the El. It's nothing extraordinary, and not as quaint as *Two Urns* (see p.175), but it does book up quickly – for weekend stays, call ahead two months. Rooms are bright but small – think your first post-college apartment. Breakfast is included and is served daily in the small dining area. Smoking is not permitted, and cats are on the premises. The inn charges a flat rate and accepts most major credit cards as well as travelers' checks. $115–135

Lincoln Park

See map on p.116 for hotel locations.

Belden-Stratford 2300 Lincoln Park West, at W Fullerton Ave ⓣ773/281-2900 or 1-800/800-8301, ⓕ773/880-2039, ⓦwww.beldenstratfordhotel.com; bus #74. One of the city's most elegant old hotels, this landmark inn and residence building in the heart of Lincoln Park boasts a gorgeous lobby with gold chandeliers and a painted sky-motif ceiling, plus stylish rooms and suites with nine-foot ceilings, plush carpeting, and comfortable furnishings. Other amenities include a rooftop sundeck, beauty salon, spa, and two stellar on-site restaurants, the four-star *Ambria* and the casual, buzzing *Mon Ami Gabi*. Great location overlooking the lake close to Lincoln Park Zoo. $189–209

Centennial House 1020 W Altgeld St, at W Fullerton Ave and N Sheffield Ave ⓣ773/871-6020, ⓕ773/871-0412, ⓦwww.bnblist.com/il/centennial; Red, Brown, or Purple Line to Fullerton. Small, cute B&B consisting of two apartments furnished in nineteenth-century European antiques – best for groups of 5–15. A two-night minimum stay is required and the apartments tend to book up well in advance. Breakfast and free local phone calls included. $115–185

Days Inn Lincoln Park-North 644 W Diversey Parkway, at N Clark St ⓣ773/525-7010, ⓕ525-6998 or 800/654-7871, ⓦwww.lpndaysinn.com; Brown or Purple Line to Diversey. A budget-friendly place to crash in accommodation-starved Lincoln Park. Not necessarily the most inspired atmosphere, but rooms are bright and clean, and rates include complimentary continental breakfast (6.30–11am), as well as passes to Bally's health club next door, which has an indoor track, lap pool, sauna, and whirlpool. $100–131

Windy City Urban Inn 607 W Deming Place, at N Clark St ⓣ773/248-7091 or 1-877/897-7091, ⓕ773/529-4183, ⓦwww.windycityinn.com; Red, Brown, or Purple Line to Fullerton. Cozy and friendly B&B in a restored Victorian mansion, with charmingly decorated rooms and suites named after local literary lights (Saul Bellow, Studs Terkel, Ernest Hemingway), none of which seem to have much to do with the author chosen. All rooms have private bath and rates include a breakfast buffet. Weekends tend to book up quickly. $115–255

Lakeview and Andersonville

See map on p.123 for hotel locations.

Best Western Hawthorne Terrace 3434 N Broadway, at W Hawthorne Place ⓣ773/244-3434 or 1-888/860-3400, ⓕ773/244-3435, ⓦwww.hawthorneterrace.com; Red Line to Addison; Red, Brown, or Purple Line to Belmont. Located in Boystown, one block from the Lincoln Park lakefront, this budget option – formerly a hotel for transients, though you'd never know it – has about sixty clean rooms (including some junior suites) that come with complimentary continental breakfast and newspaper. Facilities include a fitness center with a sauna and whirlpool. Two-night minimum stay on some weekends in high season. $139–169

City Suites 933 W Belmont Ave, at N Willow Ave ⓣ773/404-3400 or 1-800/248-9108, ⓕ773/404-3405, ⓦwww.cityinns.com; Red, Brown, or Purple Line to Belmont. A smallish, old-fashioned hotel on busy Belmont Ave, perfect for younger people who want to explore the area's bars and stagger home or to just walk around some of the city's less-explored neighborhoods. Rooms (double rooms and office suites) are basic but clean, and it's a dependable option in a non-touristy location. $139–179

Majestic 528 W Brompton Ave, at N Lake Shore Drive ⓣ773/404-3499 or 1-800/727-5108, ⓕ773/404-3495, ⓦwww.cityinns.com; Red Line to Addison. This old business hotel in Wrigleyville, with country-manor decor, has charming features like vintage elevators and radiators. A solid choice in an area not exactly overflowing with hotels and close to Lakeview's nightlife. Note, however, that it's a bit of a hike from downtown. $139–179

The Willows 555 W Surf St, at N Broadway ⓣ773/528-8400 or 1-800/787-3108, ⓕ773/244-3475, ⓦwww.cityinns.com; Brown or Purple Line to Diversey. Well-kept and affordable boutique hotel, located in a border zone between Lincoln Park and Lakeview, and just two blocks from Lake Michigan. Renovated in nineteenth-century French-country style, the hotel's rooms and suites have an easy elegance, with antique furniture, patterned wallpaper, and soothing peach and light green colors. Complimentary breakfast is included in rates. Sister to the *Majestic* and *City Suites* hotels (see above and p.176), the *Willows* is the most romantic of the three. $139–189

The West Side

See map on p.131 for hotel locations.

Crowne Plaza Chicago – Metro 733 W Madison St, at S Halsted St ⓣ312/829-5000, ⓕ312/795-6668, ⓦwww.ichotelsgroup.com; Green Line to Clinton; Blue Line to UIC/Halsted. Stylish, contemporary new hotel close to Greektown and the United Center and not far from the Sears Tower – a smart option for those wanting to be near the Loop and the West Side, but not wanting to pay Loop prices. The 398 rooms and 42 suites are done up in rich taupes and reds, with CD players and flat-screen TVs. Fitness center and restaurant on site. Valet is steep at $35, but worth it in this fairly gritty neighborhood. Pets welcome. $126–162

Hyde Park

See map on p.138 for hotel locations.

Ramada Inn Lakeshore 4900 S Lake Shore Drive, at E 51st St ⓣ773/288-5800 or 1-888/298-2054, ⓕ773/288-5819. Four-story no-frills motel in Hyde Park, with an outdoor pool and sweeping views of the lake. Affordable and good-sized rooms – if you're visiting the University of Chicago, and one of the only hotels in the area. Offers a direct shuttle to airports, a lifesaver for a hotel this far south. $99–140

Wooded Isle Suites 5750 S Stony Island Ave, at E 57th St ⓣ773/288-6305 or 1-800/290-6844, ⓕ773/288-8972, ⓦwww.woodedisle.com; bus #28. Simple, pleasantly furnished vintage studios and suites in a lovely, central Hyde Park location within walking distance of 57th Street Beach, the University of Chicago, and Museum of Science and Industry. All rooms include and (Memorial Day through Labor Day only), cable TV, and phone with answering machine; suites feature a fully equipped kitchen. $163–193

Oak Park

See map on p.149 for hotel locations.

Carleton Hotel 1110 Pleasant St, at Harlem Ave ⓣ708/848-5000 or 1-888/CARLETON, ⓕ708/848-0537, ⓦwww.carletonhotel.com; Green Line to Oak Park. Built in 1928, this charming boutique hotel in downtown Oak Park features about a hundred comfortable, spacious rooms and suites, most in the main hotel, with a couple dozen in an adjacent motor inn. Most rooms include kitchen area with microwave and refrigerator. $90–128

Longwell Hall Bed & Breakfast 301 N Scoville, at Chicago Ave ⓣ708/386-5043, ⓦwww.oakparknet.com; Green Line to Oak Park. English-style B&B around the corner from the Ernest Hemingway birthplace home and close to Frank Lloyd Wright homes in the historical district, offers three modestly sized but comfortable rooms decked out with Laura Ashley wallpaper and antique furnishings. No smoking/pets. $65–100

Write Inn 211 N Oak Park Ave, at Lake St ⓣ708/383-4800, ⓕ 383-4875, ⓦwww.writeinn.com; Green Line to Oak Park. Located in the heart of the Oak Park Historic District, with 66 renovated rooms and suites furnished with antiques and accessories from the 1920s, plus 45 short- and long-term rental apartments. Suites include mini-kitchens with fridge, sink, and microwave. Check the website for online discounts. $79–118

The North Shore

See map on p.158 for hotel locations.

Best Western – University Plaza 1501 Sherman Ave, at Oak Ave Evanston ⓣ847/491-6400 or 1-800/EVANSTON, ⓕ847/328-3090, ⓦwww.bestwestern.com; Purple Line to Davis or Dempster. Convenient to Northwestern University and Lake Michigan, this reliable chain hotel in the heart of downtown Evanston offers standard rooms at reasonable rates. Amenities include exercise room, seasonal outdoor heated pool, steam room, and sauna. $109–139

Margarita European Inn 1566 Oak Ave, at Oak Park Ave Evanston ⓣ847/869-2273, ⓕ869-2353, ⓦwww.margaritainn.com; Purple Line to Davis. Formerly used as housing for young working women in the early twentieth century, this stately brick and limestone hotel has 42 rooms, mini-suites, and suites, some with shared bath. Wireless Internet access available in the inn's common areas. Rates include continental breakfast; the hotel's first-floor restaurant, *Va Pensiero*, is one of the top Italian spots in the Chicago area. $79–160

Hotel Orrington 1710 Orrington Ave, at Church St, Evanston ⓣ847/866-8700, ⓕ866-8724, ⓦwww.hotelorrington.com; Purple Line to Davis. After a $34 million facelift, this recently reopened downtown Evanston hotel offers the most deluxe accommodations on the North Shore, with over 250 newly decorated, contemporary rooms and suites that boast plush bedding, in-room safe, "power shower" heads, and free high-speed Internet access. The property also has a fitness center and 24-hour self-serve business center. $129–189

Hostels and budget housing

Arlington House International Hostel 616 W Arlington Place, at N Geneva Terrace, Lincoln Park ⓣ773/929-5380 or 1-800/467-8355, ⓕ773/665-5485, ⓦwww.arlingtonhouse.com; Red, Brown, or Purple Line to Fullerton. Lincoln Park's only hostel is basic and not much else – stay only if you can't afford anything else. Dorms have up to seven beds; private rooms are available. Within walking distance of the Lincoln Park Zoo and Conservatory and the neighborhood's nightlife, and close to public transportation. Unlike many hostels, it's open 24hr, with no curfew. See map on p.116 for hotel location. $24–68

Chicago International Hostel 6318 N Winthrop Ave, at W Rosemont Ave, Edgewater ⓣ773/262-1011, ⓕ262-3632, ⓦwww.chicagointernationalhostel.com; Red Line to Granville or Loyola. You'll almost always find a spot at this very basic 125-bed hostel near Loyola University just south of Rogers Park. Beds cost $20 per night, with dorms sleeping four to eight and sharing two unisex bathrooms. A few private doubles ($48) and triples ($69) – with bath – are also available, and stays of ten days get one night free. The hostel, recently renovated and under new management, has a kitchen, laundry, luggage storage, and free parking. Accepts travelers' checks, Visa, and MasterCard, and requires a photo ID showing permanent residence outside Chicago. See map on p.158 for hotel location. $20–48

Hostelling International – Chicago (J. Ira and Nikki Harris Family Hostel) 24 E Congress Parkway, at S Wabash Ave, Loop ⓣ312/360-0300 or 1-800/909-4776, ⓕ312/360-0313, ⓦwww.hichicago.org. Red Line to Harrison; Blue Line to LaSalle; Brown or Orange Line to Library-State/Van Buren. Well run and meticulously clean, this modern, 500-bed hostel on the Loop's southern edge has dorms sleeping six to ten, most of which have adjoining bathrooms. Close to all El lines and within walking distance of Loop attractions, the lake, Grant Park, and Museum Campus. Facilities include a full-service kitchen, laundry room, and luggage storage, plus Internet access, Ping-Pong tables, and even a library. Open 24hr. Accepts cash, travelers' checks, Visa, and MasterCard. $34.50–37.50

International House of Chicago 1414 E 59th St, at Blackstone, Hyde Park ⓣ773/753-2270, ⓕ753-1227, ⓦwww.ihouse.uchicago.edu; Metra: 59th St. Simple housing for University of Chicago students that's open to the public. Right on campus and a block from the Metra at the University of Chicago/59th St train station, the 100-room building also has a little café, open on weekdays.

The front desk is staffed 7am–11pm, and check-in is not possible after 11pm; there is, however, no curfew. Discounts are available for double rooms or on stays of a month or more. Accepts travelers' checks and credit cards – you'll need the latter to make a reservation. Note: The House underwent extensive renovations beginning in the summer of 2005, with the east wing set for completion in spring of 2006. See map on p.138 for hotel location. $52–84

14

Eating

If there's something that Chicago does with aplomb, it's food. **Dining out** is a huge part of the city's culture – more relaxed and down-to-earth than in other major US cities, something reflected in the proliferation of reasonably priced restaurants. That's not saying there aren't plenty of world-class establishments here to give New York a run for its money, where you could easily spend well over a hundred dollars a head. At the other extreme, some of the things Chicago does best (notably pizza, steak, and hot dogs) can be had for less than $5. Sampling something from each part of the spectrum is ideal.

Upton Sinclair's 1906 *The Jungle* memorably exposed the disgusting conditions at the mythically vast slaughterhouses and meatpacking facilities that sprawled over the South Side. While conditions are much more hygienic these days, the industry's legacy left Chicago with an awful lot of meat and a large immigrant population to feed. A century later, fast food for the masses still reigns supreme across the city, testified in the proliferation of **hot-dog stands** like *The Wiener's Circle*, *Portillo's*, *Superdawg*, and others (don't even try the sacrilege of putting ketchup on your hot dog here), as well as numerous **Italian-beef joints**. Not to mention, of course, a plethora of brawny **steakhouses**, several outstanding barbecue and ribs joints, and a number of incredible burger places.

In a city where size matters and big is definitely better, local food portions are not just sizeable but extreme. Servers at many restaurants, especially Italian eateries, will make sure to ask you, "Did you want the *full* portion, or just the half?" When in doubt, go with the half, at worst you will still have room for dessert. Steaks are typically gargantuan, the **deep-dish pizzas** (see color insert) can easily defeat even the most dedicated trenchermen, and Italian beef sandwiches are piled high and slopping out all over the place: it's a rare Chicago diner who thinks they didn't get their money's worth.

While the cow may be king in the Midwest, **vegetarians** needn't feel excluded from the feeding frenzy. An eclectic crop of Italian and Asian restaurants along with all sorts of New American fusion cuisine, and everything in between, serve a medley of meat-free dishes. The much-vaunted *Green Zebra* is indicative of the trend towards inventive and flavorsome vegetarian-friendly

Steakhouse favorites

Blue Water Grill, Near North p.185
Chicago Chop House, Near North p.185
Gibson's, Gold Coast p.190
Harry Caray's, Near North p.186
Kinzie Chop House, Near North p.187
Lawry's, Near North p.189
Morton's of Chicago, Gold Coast p.191
Nine, the Loop p.184

Pizza favorites

Chicago Pizza and Oven Grinder, Lincoln Park p.195
Giordano's, the Loop p.183
Lou Malnati's, Lincoln Park p.196
Edwardo's Natural Pizza, Gold Coast p.190
Gino's East, River North p.186

delicacies served in a hip environment with no tie-die and no nut-roast in sight. Close to the city center most everything is available; for the high points in **ethnic cuisines**, you may have to venture further afield.

Relaxed weekend **brunches** are something else the city does well; the best places (see box, below) will have lines out the door and down the block, but there are any number of spots that will do in a pinch.

With the **Loop**'s residential allure rising, the paucity of restaurants and cafés in the area, beyond the prosaic chains, is set to change. Still, there are currently a clutch of stellar eating choices worth seeking out: the French haute cuisine at *Everest* or a classic Chicago breakfast at *Lou Mitchell's*. However, for the most part, Chicagoans will eat dinner in local neighborhoods rather than the Loop even if they are heading downtown for their post-dinner entertainment. In general, the further you venture from the tourist spots and into the neighborhoods, the better, more local, and more interesting your culinary experience will be.

Most visitors stay in the **River North/Magnificent Mile** area, where a great number of the city's finest restaurants are located, like *Frontera Grill* (considered by many the best Mexican food in the US), the fashionable *Blue Water Grill*, and some of the best steaks in town at the *Chicago Chop House*. Just west of the Magnificent Mile's Water Tower is the packed restaurant row of Rush Street, locally known as the "Viagra Triangle" for its older expense-account crowd, and unashamedly macho steakhouses. Just north, the appropriately named **Gold Coast** neighborhood, the youthfully eclectic Wells Street in **Old Town** and, a little further north, Halsted Street in **Lincoln Park**, cater to all tastes and tendencies with cuisine spanning everything from the sublime *Charlie Trotter's* to cozy Italian trattorias, sleek sushi lounge bars, and old-school American diners.

For further ethnic fare, quick jaunts to **Greektown**, around Halsted Street and Jackson Boulevard, and **Little Italy**'s Taylor Street, are relatively easy and more than worthwhile, though recent decades have seen them grow more commercial and less authentic; further out, **Pilsen** on the southwest side has some excellent **Mexican** fare. Further west, **Chinatown** boasts a few no-frills but authentic restaurants that are the only reason some Chicagoans ever make the journey. Further south on 57th Street, the **Hyde Park** area is your best bet for Southern soul food.

Wrigleyville and **Lakeview** – notably eclectic Clark Street – have perhaps the most Chicago-style eateries, which is to say, artery-hardening combinations of sausages, ribs, and other anomalous greasebombs. North along the youthfully hip (or, as some would note, homogenous) Southport

Brunch-spot favorites

Bongo Room, Wicker Park p.193
Orange, the Loop p.183
Southport Grocery, Lakeview p.197
Toast, Wicker Park p.193
Victory's Banner, Lakeview p.198

Quintessential Chicago

Avenue, from Lincoln Avenue, stretching west along Roscoe to Damen, there has been a gastronomic explosion. Sleek restaurants nudge up against kitsch breakfast joints, delis, pizza chains, old-fashioned ice-cream parlors, Irish-themed taverns, and sophisticated wine bars. And, overlooking it all, is a venerated Chicago institution: *Southport Lanes and Billiards* (see p.251), serving killer burgers. Further north, Viking delicacies, like potato pancakes topped with lingonberries, pickled herrings, and meat balls, are on offer in the Swedish enclave of Andersonville, and just west, the six blocks along **W Devon Ave** form "Little Bombay," where you will find the city's most authentic Indian cooking.

The listings in this chapter are arranged **geographically** and correspond more or less to the breakdowns in the Guide. Each neighborhood is in turn split into two divisions: **Cafés, and light meals**, which emphasizes spots for breakfast, lunch, or a quick bite any other time; and **Restaurants**, for slightly more formal dining, typically at dinner. However, there is certainly crossover between the two, and many diner-type places, found in the first category, can be useful for inexpensive meals at dinnertime too. And numerous upscale restaurants also serve lunch, often at a lower price than dinner menus. Note too that it's always good to have a **reservation** at the pricier establishments; if it's essential, we've said so in the review.

At the end of each restaurant review is a **price category**, rather loosely structured as a benchmark for the average meal of two courses plus a drink. However, it's easy to overshoot each category by factoring in multiple drinks, coffee, and desserts, and so on. The four categories are: **inexpensive** (below $15), **moderate** ($15–25), **expensive** ($25–40), and **very expensive** (over $40). Tax and tip are not factored in.

The Loop

Cafés and light meals

Corner Bakery 360 N Michigan at Wacker ⓣ312/236-2400; Orange, Purple, Brown, or Green Line to Randolph. It's getting so that you can barely turn a corner in downtown Chicago – especially the Loop – without running into a *Corner Bakery*. Forgive the faux-homely look and the often infuriatingly slow and confusing lines, and focus instead on the baked, buttery panini, gooey desserts, great coffee, and plethora of fresh-baked breads. Inexpensive.

Lou Mitchell's 565 W Jackson Blvd, at Clinton; T312/939-3111; Red Line to Jackson; Blue Line to Clinton. Started in 1923, this is Chicago's first diner, one block from Union Station. The menu has hardly changed, and the lines are long, but it's worth it to the businessmen who pack in for the monumental omelets, served with a mound of hash browns and thick, buttery slabs of toast. Free Milk Duds and donut holes ease the wait. Inexpensive.

Mrs Levy's Delicatessen Sear's Tower, 233 S Wacker Drive, at Adams ⓣ312/993-0530; Brown, Purple, or Orange Line to Quincy. Given the location, it's no surprise that the sandwiches here aspire to being the tallest in town. Deli creations (average $8) include an open-faced turkey sandwich stacked on

Classic hot dogs

Portillo's Hot Dogs, Near North p.184
Vienna Beef Factory Store & Deli, Bucktown p.193
The Wiener's Circle, Lakeview p.198

a challah roll then smothered in gravy and cranberries and served with potato; or go for the NY-style "A.T. Bernstein" (pastrami and corned beef drizzled with mustard and served on an onion roll). There is also a huge "garbage salad," pot roast, and the usual breakfast offerings. Despite the overriding "chain" feel, it has more charm than most, perhaps due to the cordial welcome often proffered by Mrs Levy herself. Open weekdays only 7am–3pm. Inexpensive.

Orange 75 W Harrison ⓣ312/447-1000; Red Line to Harrison. The second branch of this excellent and novel breakfast café (the original is in Lakeview at 3231 N Clark), a shiny, happy, sunny place with orange potted plants and citrus-soaked color scheme, whips up a wonderful left-of-field brunch. Steak and eggs Benedict, "frushi" (sushi rolls filled with fruit instead of fish), French-toast kebabs soaked in coconut and skewered with fruit, and gooey jelly-donut pancakes draw the salivating masses. *Orange* also serves lunch, but you won't need it. There are long lines on the weekend, but there's orange-infused coffee while you wait. Inexpensive.

Restaurants

Aria in the Fairmont Hotel, 200 N Columbus Drive, at Lake, ⓣ312/444-9494; Brown, Green, Orange, or Purple Line to Randolph. One of the most globetrotting menus in town features Middle Eastern, Latin American, Asian, Indian, and Mediterranean dishes (average entree $27) served in a thoroughly modern, but relaxed setting. From the ever-changing menu you could find anything from pad thai, to tuna *al escabeche*, to Vietnamese lotus root salad, *chicken tajine*, or Brazilian *vatapa*. The huge prime cuts of Midwest beef appeal to the homeboy diner. One of *Aria*'s star attractions is its delicious naan bread cooked in the centerpiece tandoori oven. You can also munch on tandoori flatbreads in the bar. Expensive.

Berghoff 17 W Adams St, at State ⓣ312/427-3170; Brown Line to Jackson. Century-old tavern that survived Prohibition by selling food and root beer. Unbeatably nostalgic scene, especially the oak-panelled walls, black-and-white photographs, and veteran wait staff. The satisfying, if heavy, German food is of the Wiener schnitzel variety, but there are lighter dishes; broiled salmon, chicken, and Alaskan halibut, but it's not *Berghoff*'s strong point. They also brew their own decent beer. Oktoberfest here is not to be missed. The recent café addition, good for a lunch on the run, has crowd-pleasing deli sandwiches, salads, and pasta. Moderate to expensive.

Everest 440 S LaSalle St, at W Van Buren ⓣ312/663-8920; Brown or Orange Line to LaSalle. It's a dizzying view from this high-flying, exclusive French restaurant located on the 40th floor of a Loop skyscraper and acclaimed chef-owner Jean Joho's food is no less dazzling, the prices no less soaring. There's pheasant wrapped and braised in Alsace-style cabbage and filet of wild sturgeon with Alsace Pinot Noir among the delectable offerings. Average bills per diner are in excess of $130. Far less wallet-raiding, however, is the pre-theater dinner, Tuesday–Friday 5.30pm, Saturday 5pm and 5.30pm, three courses $54. Closed Sunday and Monday. Very expensive.

Giordano's 223 W Jackson Blvd ⓣ312/583-9400; Brown Line to Jackson; 310 W Randolph St ⓣ312/201-1441; Brown, Green, Orange, or Purple Line to Randolph. Some consider this the town's best deep-dish pizza and while it's definitely top contender, the sheer number of locations has helped dilute this brand's consistency, especially in the Loop. A large fourteen-inch stuffed pizza starts at $16.95. Thin-crust pizzas are also available. Inexpensive.

Miller's Pub 134 S Wabash, at Monroe ⓣ312/645-5377; Brown, Green, Orange, or Purple Line to Adams. A Chicago institution, within these walls – covered in autographed celebrity photos – you can find some of the best ribs in town, as well as excellent steaks and seafood at unbeatable prices. The welcoming atmosphere, undeniable charm, and priceless people-watching make it worth stopping for a drink at the very least. Moderate.

Nick's Fishmarket One Bank One Plaza, 51 S Clark at Monroe ⓣ312/621-0200; Blue Line to Monroe. Popular with pre-theater crowds and one of the few decent seafood options in the Loop. A lot has been said about chef Jose Bernal's Asian flavoring of the menu – especially items like tuna sashimi and black and blue *ahi*. There is also an exotic Hawaiian influence; try the zesty Maui Wowie salad, as well as traditional entrees (average $30), Dover sole, Maine lobster and Alaskan salmon, all touching down daily. *Nick's Grill* upstairs has a more casual, less expensive, menu. Closed Sunday. Very expensive.

Nine 440 W Randolph St, at Canal ⓣ312/575-9900, ⓦwww.n9ne.com; Green Line to Clinton; Brown, Orange, or Purple Line to Washington. This sleek steakhouse serves prime cuts and contemporary American fare. Tempura rock shrimp with Asian dipping sauces, and the trio of caviar cones are the signature appetizers. Entrees (starting from $25) include 22oz porterhouse steaks, roasted sea bass, lamb chops with parmesan crusts, and veal shanks. Just in case it's all too flashy, keep it real and make your own campfire smores for dessert. If you didn't go broke ordering dinner, have a pricey martini at the popular and ultra-modern *Ghost Bar* upstairs. Closed Sunday. Very expensive.

Russian Tea Time 77 E Adams, at Wabash; ⓣ312/360-0000; Brown, Green, Orange, or Purple Line to Adams. Friendly, popular pre-theater spot near the Art Institute with an infectiously civilized old-world ambience. The broad menu (average entree $18) features caviar, blinis, Ukrainian borscht, *latkes* (potato pancakes), lamb *samsa* (an Uzbekistan puff-pastry dish), and more classic dishes to the tune of beef stroganoff, cherry quail, and salmon. The vodka list is extensive; begin the evening with a pomegranate martini and round off with a piquant shot of horseradish vodka. Moderate to expensive.

Trattoria No. 10 10 N Dearborn St, at Madison ⓣ312/984-1718, ⓦwww.trattoriaten.com; Brown Line to Washington. Classic but not stuffy Italian fare at this homely local favorite. Begin with a braised-rabbit salad for appetizer ($6-9) or dive straight in with a bowl of creamy risotto or a plate of home-made ravioli ($15–19); the *farfalle* with confit of duck is recommended. The entrees ($14-29) include veal wrapped in prosciutto and seared barramundi. Closed Sunday. Moderate.

Vivere 71 W Monroe, at Wabash ⓣ312/332-4040; Brown Line to Monroe. Perfect for a pre-theater repast (it's right by the LaSalle Bank Theatre), *Vivere* is the most worthwhile of the three family-owned restaurants in the Italian Village mini-complex here. The colorful decor and lighter, snazzier take on Italian fare attract more of a local crowd. Moderate.

River North

Cafés and light meals

Ed Debevic's 640 N Wells St, at Ontario ⓣ312/664-1707; Brown or Purple Line to Chicago. Sure, it's one of those wacky, 1950s-style diners where the waitstaff sing, dance on the tables, and serve up malts, burgers, and fries, but the catch here is that the staff is also insulting, obnoxious, and just plain rude. Not for masochists only, the food is actually quite tasty, and kids love the chance to talk back to adults. Inexpensive.

Mr. Beef 666 N Orleans St, at Erie ⓣ312/337-8500; Brown or Purple Line to Chicago. The little shack looks ready to fall over, held together only by will and the love of the diet-hating locals and celebrities. Jay Leno froths over the giant Italian beef sandwiches, dripping with juice and peppers. No credit cards. Open 8am–5pm weekdays, 10.30am–2pm on Saturday, closed Sunday. Inexpensive.

▽ *Mr. Beef*

Portillo's Hot Dogs 100 W Ontario St, at N LaSalle ⓣ312/587-8910; Red Line to Chicago. With more than 28 locations in the Chicago area, this flagship establishment, somewhere between a fast-food place and a tacky novelty restaurant, draws salivating locals, tourists, taxi drivers, and cops

Vegetarian favorites

for unbeatable hot dogs and, according to many Chicagoans, the best burgers in town. The Italian beef (thin-sliced beef piled into a hoagy and slathered with gravy and peppers) is a tangy delight. Inexpensive.

Restaurants

Ben Pao 55 W Illinois St, at Dearborn ⓣ312/222-1888; Red Line to Grand. Dark, lavish decor mixed with a well-rounded pan-Asian menu (average entree $19) that's got a little more pop to it than you'd expect for a non-Chinatown spot. The satays are particularly nutty and the piquant Kung Pao chicken, seven-flavor beef, and cherry bomb shrimp all pack a punch. There is also a great bar – try the sake flights – and a discriminating pre-theater menu. Moderate-expensive.

Blue Water Grill 520 N Dearborn ⓣ312/777-1400; Red Line to Grand. Following in the footsteps of its New York counterpart, this flamboyant American grill draws the after-work crowds and ageing hipster urbanites to its huge Baroque-industrial space in the hip gallery district. The menu (entrees $19–41) focuses on grilled fish and meat in a range of sauces – anyone as yet unchallenged by the Chicago portion size, should try the signature Tomahawk, an almighty 28oz rib-eye steak in a Bordelaise sauce. There is also a raw bar, sushi bar, and amongst a decadent dessert menu, the reinvented "Pop-Ums," ricotta fritters served with syrup, almond custard, and chocolate ganache. Reservations advised. Expensive to very expensive.

Brasserie Jo 59 W Hubbard St, at Clark ⓣ312/595-0800; Red Line to Grand. Upscale French brasserie, notable for its rather striking giant clock, the authentic zinc bar, and well-executed fish and steak dishes. The menu here emphasizes more rustic French fare like *steak frites* and onion tarts but alternates them with fusion dishes like shrimp and vegetables served inside a filo-dough pouch. There is an outstanding beer selection and an outdoor terrace in summer. Wear a hat on Thursdays and you will get a free dessert. Moderate to expensive.

Café Iberico 739 N La Salle St, at W Chicago Ave ⓣ312/573-1510; Red Line to Grand. This used to be considered one of the best places for tapas in town, and it still packs in families and gangs of co-workers passing their small dishes ($6–15) back and forth and pounding drinks. Nowadays, the draw is the convivial atmosphere rather than the food (fine but nothing special) courtesy of the huge jugs of sangría passed around on weekends and the uplifting live Spanish music. Moderate.

Carson's Ribs 612 N Wells St, at Ontario ⓣ312/280-9200, ⓦwww.ribs.com. Homesick ex-Chicagoans get ribs from *Carson's* shipped to them all over the world. This representative location – there are several in the area – is pretty plain and the service is tired at best, but the baby back-ribs, drenched in the sweet house sauce with a treacly texture (tasting like molasses), keep the place packed, especially on weekends. A tough call between this and *Twin Anchors* (see p.191) as for who has the better ribs. Expensive.

Chicago Chop House 60 W Ontario St, between N Dearborn and N Clark streets ⓣ312/787-7100; Red Line to Chicago. Housed in an old brownstone right near the *Hard Rock Café/Excalibur* tourist nexus, this classic steakhouse with a piano bar is heavy on Chicago memorabilia with wall-to-wall photos of the city's mayors, mobsters, and meat merchants. Always packed, it remains one of the best spots in town for prime-cuts of steak and chargrilled ribs. Casual attire and attitude. Expensive.

Chilipancingo 358 W Ontario St, at Orleans ⓣ312/266-6428; Brown or Purple Line to Chicago. This festive Mexican spot, decorated with the works of well-known Mexican artist Oscar Romero, serves gourmet Mexican dishes ($15–25) with a twist; including corn

Sushi favorites

masa boats and jalapeño peppers crammed with pork. But it's deservedly famous for its variety of deep-flavored *mole* dishes. Choose your tequila chasers from a selection of over 170 bottles. Moderate to expensive.

Coco Pazzo 300 W Hubbard St ⓣ312/836-0900; Red Line to Grand. Authentic Tuscan-style roasted meats and delicious pasta dishes served in classy surroundings – the rabbit-ragout pasta is superb. The restaurant's little sister, *Coco Pazzo Café* in Streeterville (636 N St Clair St), offers much the same quality at half the price, in a more informal setting. Moderate.

Fogo de Chão 661 N LaSalle St, at W Erie ⓣ312/932-9330; Brown or Purple Line to Chicago. All-you-can-eat Brazilian international chain restaurant where the servers wander the dining room wielding giant skewers of fifteen varieties of succulent meat, and slice up the ones you choose; a colored-disc system lets you control the pace. At $43 a head, it's only worth the splurge if you have a huge appetite. For non-carnivores, the salad bar is a fantastic compensation, with myriad vegetables, cheese, and fish. It's all best washed down with refreshing, but lethal, *caipirinhas*, Brazil's signature drink. Expensive.

▽ Dining room at *Topolobampo*

Frontera Grill and Topolobampo 445 N Clark St, at W Illinois St ⓣ312/661-1434; Red Line to Grand. Two top Mexican restaurants under one roof deservedly regarded as the best in the country. The more accessible and highly recommended *Frontera Grill* is more fun and casual but constantly packed due to its restricted reservation policy; a limited number of day-of reservations are available and groups of more than six can also reserve. Try the signature Topolo Margarita, while you wait in the bar and the time will merrily pass by. The menu changes frequently but the appetizer platters, which combine a sample of a handful of appetizers, are always a wonderful introduction. The guacamole is a must, the *moles* sublime. The smarter, more formal *Topolobampo* grills a mean ostrich but is almost impossible to get into with less than a couple weeks, notice. There's so much to choose from that the five-course tasting menu is the best bet for first-timers. Both restaurants are closed on Sundays and Mondays. *Frontera* is expensive, *Topolobampo* very expensive.

Gino's East 633 N Wells St, at Ontario ⓣ312/943-1124; Brown or Purple Line to Chicago. Incongruously packed into an ex-*Planet Hollywood* location, *Gino's* manages to maintain the unashamedly tacky, graffiti-strewn interior of the cramped old location over on Ontario. Avoid the house beer but dive into a hefty deep-dish pie with its slightly sweet, polenta crust loaded up with spicy sauce and gooey cheese. Though not the best in town, it's satisfying none the less. A large eight-slice pizza will set you back upwards of $19.50. There are also thin-crust pizzas, stromboli, pasta, and salads. Inexpensive.

Green Door Tavern 678 N Orleans St, at Erie ⓣ312/664-5496; Brown or Purple Line to Chicago. A former speakeasy and grocers, built in 1872, just after the Chicago fire, this precariously tilted structure is now home to a museum-piece tavern which has Chicago memorabilia strewn across the bar. It's a comfortable place to linger and soak up the gritty 1920s aura. The tavern serves over a dozen varieties of burger laden with all manner of your chosen topping from spicy mustard to blue cheese or bacon, and at least 30 beers. Inexpensive.

Harry Caray's 33 W Kinzie St, at N Dearborn St ⓣ312/828-0966; Red Line to Grand. The legendary former announcer for the Cubs lives on in his Italian-styled steakhouse, chock-full of sports memorabilia, that has weathered the years and turned out, unlike most sports-personality-run joints, to actually be a really enjoyable place to have a 23oz porterhouse steak and watch a game. Other classic favorites (average $23) are the chicken vesuvio, filet mignon, and a pepper-encrusted seared-tuna appetizer. Expensive.

House of Blues **329 N Dearborn St, at Kinzie ⓣ312/923-2000; Red Line to Grand.** The dark, kaleidoscopic interior lends a dramatic tint to an otherwise serviceable Southern menu. A lot depends on the choir performing that day, but the Sunday Gospel Brunch (usually 10.30am and 12.30; $38 per person; reserve in advance) can be one of the best in town, heavy on the seafood, meats, jambalaya, *étouffée*, sweets, and soul food. Complimentary champagne is served at noon. Expensive.

Japonais **600 W Chicago ⓣ312/822-9600; Brown Line to Chicago.** With a slick interior design and bold Japanese cuisine with French influences, this is one of the most hyped scene restaurants in town. Behind the marble revolving door, the original industrial shell has been lavishly embellished with tones of blood-red and gold and a shimmering glass-backed waterfall. The black-clad staff sashay through the aisles serving platters of nigiri, sashimi, *maki*, and house specials including kobe prime rib, panko-breaded salmon, and maple-smoked duck. For great people-watching, have a martini in the lounge bar – all low sofas, ottomans, and attitude–or outside on the patio in summer. Expensive.

Kevin **9 W Hubbard ⓣ312/595-0055; Red Line to Grand**. If you can live with the aloof ambience and fickle service, the Asian-French hybrid cuisine at *Kevin* lives up to the hype. The Asian-accented contemporary decor provides a Zen backdrop to the artfully presented cuisine, with soft woods, exposed brick, and a cedar-wood bar with metal wine racks suspended like hammocks from the ceiling. The food is a sensuous overload of flavors, textures, and aromas. The zingy freshness and purity of flavor of the tuna tartare appetizer is worth a visit alone. Very expensive.

Kinzie Chop House **400 N Wells St, at Kinzie ⓣ312/822-0191; Brown or Purple Line to Merchandise Mart.** Business traffic from nearby Merchandise Mart keeps this steakhouse – hunkered right under the El – hopping, especially at lunch, when it's a cheaper but usually just as good, less-crowded alternative to the pricier steakhouses. There's also plenty of other dishes available, from peppercorn halibut to sesame-encrusted *ahi* to rock shrimp risotto. Steaks ranging from $24–35 will tip the budget, but most other dishes are, on average, $15. At lunchtime, they also serve burgers, sandwiches, and salads (less than $10). Expensive.

Klay Oven **414 N Orleans St, at Kinzie ⓣ312/527-3999; Brown or Purple Line to Merchandise Mart.** More menu items than you'll know what to do with at this popular Indian restaurant. The wide selection of tandoori and vindaloo should satisfy any palate. The restaurant's signature oven cooks up eight tempting varieties of their delicious breads. There's a good-value all-you-can-eat lunch. Moderate.

Le Lan **749 N Clark St ⓣ312/280-9100; Red Line to Chicago**. Acclaimed Chef Arun Sampanthavivat of *Arun*'s (see p.203), fuses French panache and Vietnamese mystique with aplomb at *Le Lan*, which opened with much fanfare in 2005. Discreet and tasteful Asian decor features fresh bamboo, a jade tiled floor, and an eye catching dragon mural designed by Arun's artist brother. The creative flourishes continue on the plate as fresh oysters float in sweetcorn soup and a smoked squab perches beneath an olive chocolate tuile. The intricate flavors reach their zenith with the dessert menu, highlighted by exotically composed chocolate and banana tart with coconut sorbet and lavender sauce. Intriguing drinks include the signature house libation, a sensual lychee Bellini, as well as an excellent selection of world wines. Closed Sunday. Expensive.

MK **868 N Franklin St, at W Chestnut ⓣ312/482-9179, ⓦwww.mkchicago.com; Brown or Purple Line to Chicago.** Trendy, upscale place which has perfected the concept of minimalist chic, offering New American and continental cuisine alongside a great wine list and an imaginative dessert selection (banana brioche bread-pudding with salted-peanut ice cream). If you're in town in the summer, be sure to try the six-course taster's menu, around $68. Reservations are a must. Jackets recommended for men. Very expensive.

Nacional 27 **325 W Huron St, at Orleans ⓣ312/664-2727; Brown or Purple Line to Chicago.** This Nuevo Latino restaurant is named for the twenty-seven nations of Latin America and its menu makes a valiant and exciting effort to include each and every one of them. Flavors range from the piquant to the zingy to sturdy homestyle dishes. Try the hearty Cuban-style stuffed potatoes, citrusy Mexican-style ceviche and a selection of innovative empanadas, the ubiquitous Latin American hunger blaster. The cocktail list specializes in potent Brazilian *caipirinhas* and feisty Cuban *mojitos*. Closed Sunday. Moderate to expensive.

Naha 500 N Clark St, at Illinois ⓣ312/321-6242; Red Line to Grand. Exciting, high-end dining that takes an American-Mediterranean menu and gives it a twist. A veteran on the local restaurant scene, *Naha*'s confidence shows from the minimal, natural beauty of the interior to the always intriguing menu which combines sweet and savory ingredients with panache: sea scallops are infused with vanilla bean; trout glazed with honey; and foie gras set atop a rhubarb and strawberry tatin. If you just want to sample, rather than commit, there is a casual lounge area with a menu of small plates, notably spicy tuna, lamb kebabs, and flatbreads. Closed Sunday. Very expensive.

Osteria Via Stato 620 N State St ⓣ312/642-8450; Red Line to Grand. New on the scene in 2005, this rustically hip Italian with pre dictable decor – stone walls and chunky wooden communal tables offers a novel approach with the menu – a three-course prix fixe ($36): you choose your entree and the antipasti and pasta/risotto courses are prepared according to the chef's whim. Each dish, with a purist's approach to traditional Italian preparation, is sufficient without being overwhelming. Desserts, notably silky *gelato*, and an array of Italian cheeses, are priced separately. The wine bar next door serves small, tapas-style plates ($3–$7) and wine flights, starting from $15. Expensive.

SUSHISAMBA Rio 504 N Wells ⓣ312/595-2300; Brown or Purple Line to Merchandise Mart. This high-energy bar and restaurant attracts Chicago's glamorous and gilded with its ambitious Latin-Japanese fusion dishes, flamboyant decor, and carnival vibe. Small plates of ceviche, tartare, skewered meat and fish, empanadas, and sushi rolls predominate; try the South American beef *maki* or the Brazilian vegetable roll filled with pineapple, *palmito*, and gin. Avoid the overpriced *yamato* roll ($19) with tuna, foie gras, caviar, and, well, gratuitous gold leaf, of course. There is a rooftop terrace, if you want to see and be seen. Very expensive.

Vermillion 10 W Hubbard ⓣ312/527-1060; Red Line to Grand. The scene is as engaging as the concept – Latin-Indian cuisine served in a minimalist dining room while Indian dance music and Latin salsa and meringue alternate in the background. Tapas dishes are great for a light meal; try the spinach empanadas with chorizo and black olives or go with the chef's daily selection. Main dishes feature lobster steamed in coconut and curry-leaf gravy, tamarind babyback-ribs with sweetcorn salsa and yucca fries. For dessert try the *mojito* cheesecake. With a gregarious lounge vibe and a dj spinning on Saturday nights (when the restaurant serves until 2am), the atmosphere can feel rather like a nightclub. Expensive.

Vong's Thai Kitchen 6 W Hubbard St, at State ⓣ312/644-8664; Red Line to Grand. Formerly known as *Vong*, this is the Chicago outpost of chef Jean-Georges Vongerichten's noted Manhattan eatery – this time with a delectable French-Thai menu and lazy, opium-den ambience paired with more reasonable prices – all entrees are less than $20. There are creamy curries to choose from and spicy fish, meat, and seafood dishes, including a fruity tamarind-glazed tilapia. Or, sample a selection of the tantalizing appetizers, ranging from satays to a tuna-wasabi pizza. Moderate.

The Magnificent Mile and Streeterville

Cafés and light meals

Café Spiagga 980 N Michigan Ave, at E Oak St, ⓣ312/280-2755; Red Line to Chicago. Unlike its namesake next door (*Spiagga* restaurant), the café offers flawless Italian-French food without the stuffiness or the high prices – though to be sure, the food here is impeccable. It's a great spot to enjoy a relaxed weekend brunch after shopping on the Magnificent Mile. The decor is inspired by fifteenth-century Italy with marble floors, frescos, and Venetian light fixtures. There are lovely views over Michigan Avenue and the lakefront from the floor-to-ceiling glass window – rather like being in a fish bowl, open to the envied glances of passing shoppers on Michigan Avenue. Moderate.

Zest in the InterContinental hotel, 525 Michigan Ave ⓣ312/321-8766; Red Line to Grand. One of the best places for lunch on the Magnificent Mile, this airy hotel restaurant with floor-to-ceiling glass windows overlooking Michigan Ave, with an ambience that feels more California than Chicago, offers a delightful array of dishes ranging from wholesome Mediterranean salads to satisfying quesadillas and bacon-wrapped scallops. The breakfasts are also wonderfully decadent with slabs of French toast smothered in lemon curd. The cocktails are an alluring tonic after a long morning of shopping on Michigan Avenue. Inexpensive to moderate.

Restaurants

▽ *Billy Goat Tavern*

Billy Goat Tavern 430 N Michigan Ave, at Kinzie ⓣ312/222-1525; Red Line to Merchandise Mart. Dingy and beloved bar/grill lurking in the shadows underneath Michigan Ave, with dangerously greasy burgers. No fries (potato chips only), a minimal beer selection, and wood panelling reminiscent of a 1970s rec room – either great atmosphere or none at all, depending on your view. *Tribune* scribes regularly inhabit the grimy old stools. The staff's legendary "doublecheezburger" rants were immortalized by John Belushi, Bill Murray, and Dan Aykroyd on *Saturday Night Live*.

Lawry's 100 E Ontario St, at Michigan Ave ⓣ312/787-5000; Red Line to Chicago or Grand. Yes, the same *Lawry's* that produces those bottles of seasoned salt available in supermarkets, but the best prime-rib in town, a big, juicy, savory slab served from a rolling cart. The menu is rather limited: ribs, lobster tail, a fish of the day, and a bountiful "spinning salad," but this is one of the rare places where you can enjoy a side of Yorkshire pudding, perfect alongside creamed spinach and fluffy peaks of mashed potato. The restaurant itself is something of an institution, located in a grand old mansion, with intimate alcoves and a regal spiral staircase, built roughly a century ago by the McCormick family. Expensive.

NoMi in the Park Hyatt, 800 N Michigan Ave, at Chicago ⓣ312/239-4030; Red Line to Grand. *NoMi's* 7th-floor views of Streeterville and the lake beyond are reason enough to pay a visit (especially from the small outdoor terrace). The French-inspired menu jumps all over the place with a seasonally influenced selection which could feature anything from sushi appetizers to a succulent monk fish in a coconut broth to creamy risottos and Maine lobster. If dinner is off limits, enjoy an early-evening cocktail in the bar, at the very least. Very expensive.

Tru 676 N St Clair St, at E Huron St ⓣ312/202-0001; Red Line to Chicago. If you've got the patience and the bank account to handle the long, prix-fixe-style experience and skyscraper-high prices, this is consistently one of the top fine-dining options in this part of the country. Select your tasting-menu theme (from vegetarian, $90, to the grandiose "Chef Tramoto Selection," $135). You will be dazzled by gourmet dishes such as the galaxy of intriguing mousses and the caviar staircase (has to be seen to be believed). The impeccably white, minimalist decor is a serene backdrop for each global fusion dish's artful conception. The finale is definitely the seductive desserts; highly recommended are the delectable chocolate-mousse crêpes engulfed by banana bisque and topped with candied mint. Reserve well in advance. Closed Sunday. Very expensive.

Viand Bar and Kitchen 155 E Ontario, at N Michigan ⓣ312/255-8505; Red Line to Grand.A very popular newcomer, *Viand* specializes in small plates of reinvented comfort-food classics. The space is a heady Art Deco palace, all crystal, frosted glass, and a palette of red, white, and black. The food is both heartwarming and curious, with lobster and cheese sandwiches, corn fritters basted with honey, lamb lollipops with mint sauce, and rum-glazed pork with sweet-potato hash. The martinis pack a punch, even more so on a Tuesday when they are half price. Moderate to expensive.

Gold Coast and Old Town

Cafés and light meals

Ashkenaz Delicatessen 12 E Cedar St, at State ⓣ312/944-5006; Red Line to Clark/Division. It's about as barebones as you can get, just a counter and a couple of tables, but the serious kosher food – one of the only good delis in this part of town – is worth going for. Corned-beef sandwiches are lean and huge, the rugelach (small rolled pastries) a sweet finish, and the staff chatty. Inexpensive.

Original Pancake House 22 E Bellevue Place, at N Rush ⓣ312/642-7917. Old-fashioned, ultra-casual breakfast joint, always reliable for just about everything on the menu. Egg dishes are hot and fresh, while the pancakes are fluffy – try the sticky apple-pancake house special – and the coffee surprisingly full-bodied for a diner. Other locations: 2020 N Lincoln Park in Lincoln Park, and 1517 E Hyde Park Blvd close to the University of Chicago. Inexpensive.

Restaurants

Adobo Grill 1610 N Wells St, at North Ave ⓣ312/266-7999; Red Line to North/Clybourn. Next door to the *Second City* comedy club, this upscale Mexican place is known for excellent guacamole – mixed at your table to taste – and strong margaritas (made from your choice of eighty tequilas); try their highly potent signature *Adobo Margarita* made with fresh lime (ask for *reposado* or *añejo* Herradura tequila instead of the standard *blanco*). The reasonably priced food is a worthy rendition of haute Mexican fare. Try such appetizers as goat-cheese empanadas or a fruity tuna ceviche with mango and cilantro. For a main course, there's grilled tilapia served with a herbed potato-cake and mushrooms, and a seared *ahi* tuna with green salsa. Arrive early as service is far from swift. There is another branch with a more laid-back atmosphere, opened in 2005, in Wicker Park at 2005 W Division. Moderate to expensive.

Dinotto Ristorante 215 W North Ave, at Wells ⓣ312/202-0302, ⓦwww.dinotto.com; Red Line to North/Clybourn. The cozy and ever-thriving *Café Dinotto* does a brisk trade in no-frills Italian fare (average entree $15), including pasta tricolor *rotolo* in a cream tomato sauce, steamed mussels, and chicken with gorgonzola, all highly praised. Good dinner spot after a movie or live show at *Piper's Alley* across the street. Service can be erratic. Moderate.

Edwardo's Natural Pizza 1212 N Dearborn St, at E Division St ⓣ312/337-4490; Red Line to Clark/Division. Just a takeout joint with a few booths, but this local chain's monumentally proportioned deep-dish pizza is something to behold. Their fresh ingredients are underscored by the taste, from crispy crust to spicy sausage and crunchy vegetable toppings, drawing a loyal following among discriminating Chicagoans. Good lunch specials. Inexpensive.

Gibson's 1028 N Rush St, at Bellevue Place ⓣ312/266-8999; Red Line to Clark/Division. Just off the Magnificent Mile, in the appropriately nicknamed "Viagra Triangle," the restaurant's bar is something of a scene and popular with a 40s-and-over crowd. The steakhouse, which is always lively with loud banter, offers excellent cuts and impeccable service; the waitstaff even brings your pre-cooked steak to the table for inspection. True enough, it has a real "old boys" club vibe, but that doesn't put off the movie and theater celebrities working in town and Chicagoans who devour faultless filet mignon ($32) and porterhouse ($37) with abandon. Reserve well in advance. Very expensive.

Hugo's Frog Bar and Fish House 1024 N Rush ⓣ312/640-0999; Red Line to Clark/Division. Under the same ownership as *Gibson's* next door, *Hugo's* is its maritime alter-ego but with all the brawn of a steakhouse. Gilded Chicagoans pack into the boisterous, wood-panelled bar-restaurant, complete with marlin fish sculptures, and black-and-white vintage photographs, for seafood dining on an epic scale. The Australian lobster tail – widely considered the best in town – drenched in lemon and butter is mouthwatering, the blackened swordfish and seared tuna with wasabi are perfectly cooked and flavorsome. Gasp in awe at the size of the desserts; all are big enough for four, at least, to share. It's a toss-up between a glorious Key Lime pie with crunch and zest in all the right places, and a decadent muddy bottom pie. With a porterhouse steak nudging $40 and a lobster tail flipping over $60, it certainly isn't skimpy on the wallet or the waistline. Very expensive.

Kamehachi of Tokyo 1400 N Wells St, at Schiller ⓣ312/664-3663, ⓦwww.kamehachi.com; Red Line to Clark/Division. Opened in 1967 and the first Japanese restaurant in Chicago, *Kamehachi* still offers supremely fresh sushi, but its premier status has certainly been usurped by the newer, more inventive arrivals on the scene. The dragon rolls and Chicago crazy rolls (tuna, yellowtail, salmon, and crab), and *gomae* (blanched spinach with peanut sauce) are all worth trying. There are now four other locations, one at 240 E Ontario, 320 N Dearborn, in the suburbs at 1320 Shermer in Northbrook, and at 275 Parkway Drive in Lincolnshire. Moderate.

Le Colonial 937 N Rush St, at Walton ⓣ312/255-0088; Red Line to Clark/Division. The atmosphere merges French chic with Asian exoticism – all airy white space, swirling fans, palm trees, and rattan furniture – while the menu gives gourmet zing to tasty Vietnamese dishes like wok-seared monkfish. There is also a lively bar and terrace upstairs and sidewalk café open in summer. With most dishes well under $20, it's unlikely to induce a wallet hemorrhage. Moderate to expensive.

Morton's of Chicago 1050 N State St, at Maple St ⓣ312/266-4820, ⓦwww.mortons.com; Red Line to Clark/Division. The original location of this upscale steakhouse-chain serving one of the best and probably the largest steak in town. The formally attired waiters describe the menu in such delectable detail that you can't decide between the 20oz New York sirloin or the 24oz porterhouse or the double-cut filet mignon with a *Béarnaise* sauce. Even if you don't think it's the best steak in town, the old-style Chicago atmosphere and faultless service make it an unforgettable, classic dining experience. Don't leave without trying the Godiva cake for dessert. Very expensive.

Old Jerusalem 1411 N Wells St ⓣ312/944-3304; Red Line to North/Clybourn. The hummus, served with piping-hot pita bread, is to die for at this cheap, barebones eatery that thrives on its takeout business, while the rest of the standard Middle Eastern offerings (tabouli, *baba ganoush*) are hard to beat on price. The falafel, especially, has character, served hot and crispy with garlicky tahini. Inexpensive.

Salpicón 1252 N Wells St, at W Scott St ⓣ312/988-7715; Red Line to North/Clybourn. Second only to *Frontera Grill/Topolobampo*, authentic but original Mexican haute cuisine is served in a funky, colorful interior. Smaller and mellower than *Adobo*. The menu ranges from tequila-marinated halibut to chile-infused chicken and cool, sweet desserts like *naranjas en dulce* (boiled orange quarters in a cinnamon-orange syrup). The tequila list is, of course, extensive and the attentive staff only too pleased to impart their knowledge. Expensive.

Topo Gigio Ristorante 1516 N Wells St, at Schiller ⓣ312/266-9355; Red Line to North/Clybourn. Always crowded Italian hotspot in Old Town, with relaxed outdoor seating and reasonably priced dishes like chicken *cacciatore*, veal *saltimbocca*, and *escolar* tuna. The exceptional pasta dishes, from spaghetti with meatballs or seafood, to creamy *allpanna*, or spicy *arra'bbiata*, keep it pure and simple, and taste straight from a Tuscan kitchen. Moderate.

Twin Anchors 1655 N Sedgwick St, at W Concord ⓣ312/266-1616. The long waits and loud, crowded dive-bar surroundings only seem to enhance the reputation of this decades-old institution (a speakeasy once upon a time), where the succulent barbecue meat slides off the bone. There's also steak and fried chicken offered up. Moderate.

Vinci 1732 N Halsted St, between North and Willow ⓣ312/266-1199, ⓦwww.vinci-group.com; Red Line to North/Clybourn. While the convenient location – just up the street from Steppenwolf Theatre – is the major draw (the troupe of actors has their own table here), this warm and inviting place serves up sizeable and tasty portions of rustic Italian fare. The menu runs the gamut of pasta and meat classics from pasta alfredo to chicken parmesan. Moderate.

South Loop and Near South

Cafés and light meals

Manny's Deli 1141 S Jefferson St, at W Roosevelt Rd ☎312/939-2855; Green, Red, or Orange Line to Roosevelt. One of Chicago's only New York–style delis – and definitely one of the best in the city – with everything from matzo-ball soup and giant corned-beef sandwiches to cheese blintzes and tongue sandwiches, served up cafeteria-style. Located next to the University of Illinois at Chicago, it draws a studenty crowd, along with some grizzled locals. Inexpensive.

Restaurants

Chicago Firehouse 1401 S Michigan Ave, at 13th St ☎312/786-1401; Green, Red, or Orange Line to Roosevelt. Inviting restaurant in a historic South Loop building that until 1905 used to be – big surprise – a firehouse. While the four-square food (meatloaf, steaks, variations on the potato) here can be inconsistent, this is one of the few dining options in the area and very convenient to some South Loop bars and nightclubs. Moderate.

Emperor's Choice 2238 S Wentworth Ave, at W 22nd Place ☎312/225-8800; Red Line to Cermak/Chinatown. Chinatown's most acclaimed restaurant, *Emperor's Choice* offers excellent seafood, with some unusual items on the side for adventurous eaters, like the soft-shell crab with red peppers and jalapeño. Service is attentive, but not aggressively so. Moderate.

Gioco 1312 S Wabash Ave, at 13th ☎312/939-3870; Green, Red, or Orange Line to Roosevelt. Stylish, white-tablecloth Italian that has been bringing in a hip South Loop crowd by virtue of its simple but never-dull dishes like hand-rolled penne in cream sauce and rabbit with pureed fava beans. Expensive.

Hackney's 733 S Dearborn St, at W Harrison ☎312/461-1116, ⓦwww.hackneys.net; Red Line to Harrison. Beloved local burger chain – which started in Glenview in 1939 – serving plenty of solid comfort food from its beautiful Printers Row building, known for the lean and wonderful Hackneyburger (get it on dark rye, with blue cheese) and midriff-enlarging French-fried onion loaves. On the downside, the rough-and-ready ambience is not always to everyone's taste. Inexpensive.

Hong Min 221 W Cermak, at S Wentworth Ave ☎312/842-5026; Red Line to Cermak/Chinatown. Hands down one of the least attractive restaurants in the city when it comes to the decor, but the food — whole pike, Mongolian shrimp, and massive, delectable potstickers – makes you forget all about your surroundings. Inexpensive.

Opera 1301 S Wabash St ☎312/461-0161; Green, Red, or Orange Line to Roosevelt. A former film studio, *Opera* maintains its theatrical overtures with embroidered curtains in luxuriant reds and gold, multicolored bricks, illusory mirrors, fantasy art work, and nude sculptures. While the echoing industrial space and carnival ambience preclude intimacy, you can reserve your own private dining booth. The menu is a bewildering take on traditional Chinese food. A golden shrimp appetizer is seared with peppercorn glaze, while entrees (average $24) include a whole red snapper liberally seasoned with soy lotus root and ginger. Also try the Kung Pao beef or the General's chicken, a crispy chicken-breast with cashews, lychee, and a spicy sweet and sour sauce. Moderate to expensive.

Penang 2201 S Wentworth Ave, at W 22nd Place ☎312/326-6888; Red Line to Cermak/Chinatown. More upscale and stylish than your average Chinatown place, *Penang* specializes in Malay cuisine with a hint of Japanese. The menu has over 100 dishes on it – including chargrilled beef satay – and dozens of sushi offerings (though certainly not the best sushi you will ever taste). Inexpensive to moderate.

Three Happiness 209 W Cermak Rd ☎312/842-1964; Red Line to Cermak. Not to be confused with the *Three Happiness* on the main Wentworth strip, the spartan decor of this tiny namesake belies its highly praised Mandarin and Cantonese food. The dim sum dishes are worth a visit alone, filled with chicken or lotus seed or custard. The entrees, including stir-fried crab with a fiery chilli seafood sauce, and Mongolian beef are all inexpensive (average $8). Open until 2am every night. Inexpensive to moderate.

Bucktown and Wicker Park

Cafés and light meals

Bongo Room 1470 N Milwaukee Ave, between Evergreen Ave and Honore St ⓣ773/489-0690; Blue Line to Damen. Hip brunch spot with ambient music and a lounge-bar vibe – stroller yuppies start lining up early – with long waits and a slightly overpriced menu, but the food is worth it, especially the sweeter selections; try the stack of Black Forest pancakes. Moderate.

Café de Lucca 1721 N Damen ⓣ773/342-6000; Blue Line to Damen. Great coffee and light meals are served at this Italian-style café that exudes old-world allure, albeit of the contrived variety. Murals of washing lines, crumbling walls, vintage movie posters, and a laissez-faire vibe provide the perfect backdrop to hang out with Bucktown's denizens. French toast, oversized grilled panini and salads can be munched long into the evening. There is also a full bar and street-side seating in summer. Inexpensive.

Earwax Café 1564 N Milwaukee Ave, at North Ave ⓣ773/772-4019; Blue Line to Damen. Excellent coffeehouse that serves plenty of satisfying vegetarian fare. Has a fun, hip, and quirky atmosphere pitched at the area's hipster residents. There's a few sandwich items for meat eaters. You can rent videos here, too. Inexpensive.

Hilary's Urban Eatery 1500 W Division St, at N Milwaukee Ave ⓣ773/235-4327; Blue Line to Division. It's an unlikely location for this arty breakfast spot where scruffy romantics canoodle over dishes as disparate as pancakes, veggie lasagna, and salmon cakes. Try the well-prepared daily specials, like the *huevos rancheros*. Closed Tuesday. Inexpensive.

Iggy's 1840 W North Ave ⓣ312/829-4449; Blue Line to Damen. A good late-night bar and restaurant where artichoke fritters, burgers, fried calamari, and salads mop up the copiously consumed beer, wine, and cocktails. With its industrial decor, red and black color scheme, and off-beat vibe, it's a great place to people-watch. The breezy rooftop patio with reservation-only areas partitioned by white muslin drapes is a great spot for afternoon lunch, especially when there is a dj or local musicians playing. Moderate.

Letizia's Natural Bakery 2144 W Division St, at Hoyne Ave ⓣ773/342-1011; Blue Line to Damen. Delicious panini made with *focaccia* bread and laden with melted mozzarella, pasta, pizza, coffee, and pastries are on offer at this tiny café, with an outdoor patio – all of them made on site and without bleached flour by Letizia herself, who hails from Rome. Open until 11pm, it's great for late-night snacking. Inexpensive.

▽ *Margie's Candies*

Margie's Candies 1960 N Western Ave, at W Armitage Ave ⓣ773/384-1035; Blue Line to Western. Famous neighborhood ice-cream parlor (it opened in 1921) that serves a cavity-inducing array of home-made candies and deliciously creamy shakes and malts. Try and finish the World's Largest Sundae, a full half-gallon of ice cream – gargantuan even by Chicago standards. There's a second branch at 1813 W Montrose. Inexpensive.

Toast 2046 N Damen Ave, at W Armitage Ave ⓣ773/772-5600; Blue Line to Damen. Delicious omelets, a French Toast Orgy (French-toast slabs stuffed with fruit or mascarpone cheese and filled with granola, fresh fruit, and honey) and other eggy breakfast staples are served in a small dining room with an outdoor patio which is very popular with Bucktown's yuppified, beautiful young things. The huge sandwiches, ranging from retro peanut butter and jelly to steak and Gorgonzola, are worth building up an appetite for – and you will – long waits of up to an hour are common at the weekend. There's another smaller branch at 746 W Webster. Inexpensive.

Vienna Beef Factory Store & Deli 2501 N Damen Ave, between Fullerton and Diversey avenues ⓣ773/235-6652. Sit elbow to elbow with the factory workers having their breakfast or lunch, munching on steaming hot dogs right off the assembly line. Many other fine Vienna meat products are available, including corned beef, pastrami, and Polish sausages. You can buy dogs by the dozen at the company store. Closed Sunday. Inexpensive.

Restaurants

Café Absinthe 1954 W North Ave, at N Milwaukee Ave ⓣ773/278-4488; Blue Line to Damen. You pay for the atmosphere at this trendy North Avenue restaurant – a dark, curtained haunt for beautiful people where you enter through a back alley to the sound of moody jazz. The wine list is extensive, and the food (entrees around $25), a tasty blend of *nouveau* American and French (Pernod-glazed lamb, Baileys chicken *au jus*, and grilled ostrich), has some imaginative touches. Expensive.

Hot Chocolate 1747 N Damen Ave ⓣ773/489-1747; Blue Line to Damen. Mindy Segal, former pastry chef at the venerable *MK* (see p.187,) has launched her own chocolate haven to seduce Bucktown's arbiters of chic. The front drips down the exterior glass windows like melted chocolate and everything from the walls, industrial piping, chairs, bar, and even the gracious staff are clad in tones of chocolate and caramel. The major draw here, not surprisingly, are the worthily praised desserts, which includes a posh take on a Snickers, hot chocolate tasters, vanilla-layered strawberry and rhubarb cake, and caramelized bananas with banana coffee cake and banana ice cream. On the downside, the menu's scant savory selections (brie with brioche, goat-cheese salad, tuna melt, and kobe beef skirt-steak) are mediocre, the vibe borders on gimmicky, and the long waiting times can be frustrating. Moderate to expensive.

La Bonita 2165 N Western Ave ⓣ773/486-7340; Blue Line to Western. With a new, more pronounceable name (the restaurant was formally known as *Ixcapuzalco*), and a new location, *La Bonita* has also slightly toned down the gaudy decor of its previous incarnation. While the walls are still covered in heady Mexican folk art, it does not detract from chef-owner Tomas Behana's six famed *mole* sauces (one for each day: *La Bonita* is closed on Tuesdays) which bring serious gourmands from all over the city. Skip the bland appetizers and dive straight in to the inventive entrees, including tender pork loin, and shrimp in creamy vanilla sauce. Moderate to expensive.

Le Bouchon 1958 N Damen Ave, at W Armitage Ave ⓣ773/862-6600; Blue Line to Damen. Tiny and romantic French bistro, with inexpensive appetizers like *escargot* and steamed mussels (about $7) and entrees like frog legs with pasta ($16), sautéed rabbit and duck in a red-wine sauce (about $18). Later on in the evening, Bucktown's bohemians take over from an older, early-evening crowd. The tables can be too close together for some tastes. Closed Sunday. Moderate.

Meritage Café and Wine Bar 2118 N Damen Ave, at W Dickens Ave ⓣ773/235-6434; bus #50, #73. Bold and innovative Pacific Northwest fusion cuisine – seared foie gras on caramelized French toast, duck with *medjool* and date bread pudding, seared *ahi* with chilled gazpacho – which rotates seasonally, keeps this small, but romantic dining room perennially crowded and the courtyard buzzing with urban sophisticates in summer. Entrees $18–28; brunch is served on Sundays. Expensive.

Spring 2039 W North Ave, at N Damen Ave ⓣ773/395-7100; Blue Line to Damen. New American food with an Asian twist (and even some Middle Eastern accents) in one of Chicago's top restaurants. Decor is clean and peaceful, like a rock-garden-turned-restaurant, and the menu features interesting flavor minglings like cod with oxtail and red grouper with couscous. Expensive.

Thyme Café 1540 N Milwaukee ⓣ773/227-1400; Blue Line to Damen. A 120-year-old building at the Bucktown epicenter (the intersection of Damen, North, and Milwaukee), with exposed bricks, low lighting, watercolors, and simple banquet seating provides the setting for this casual bistro. The deftly conceived menu of French-accented classics, including *steak frites*, salmon with poached fennel, home-made ravioli, and timeless desserts – the *crème brûlée* and chocolate banana crêpes are sublime. With main courses under $20, it's very affordable and a great launch pad for an evening hanging out in Bucktown. Moderate to expensive.

Lincoln Park

Cafés and light meals

Bourgeois Pig 738 W Fullerton Ave, at N Burling St ☎773/883-5282; Brown or Purple Line to Fullerton. Around forty different teas are available at this coffee shop, though some may gripe about the small cups. Still, the atmosphere is appropriately dark and literary, even if Marxists may be hard to find here these days. There's a good selection of panini and sandwiches and a seductive display of pastries, muffins, and cakes. Don't miss the black-and-white photos of Old Chicago upstairs. There's outdoor seating and a balcony in summer. Inexpensive.

Chicago Pizza and Oven Grinder 2121 N Clark St, at W Dickens Ave ☎773/248-2570; Red Line to Clark. No-frills local favorite serving trademark "grinders" (Italian sausage sandwiches), a limited selection of pizzas, and excellent salads; waits can be long – plenty of time for you to check out the site of the St Valentine's Day Massacre across the street (see p.120). Inexpensive.

Potbelly Sandwich Works 2264 N Lincoln Ave, at W Webster Ave ☎773/528-1405. The original location of this popular, no-frills sandwich shop with decor dating from its days as an antique shop (selling *potbelly* stoves, naturally). The lines are always long – *Potbell* has certainly cornered the market in deli-style sandwiches – but the result is certainly worth the wait. Try "The Wreck" (salami, roast beef, turkey, and ham with Swiss cheese) or the turkey with provolone cheese, all served on fresh-tasting crispy Italian rolls, then watch as it's heaped with your choice of deli toppings, to get your $4 worth. Around twenty branches are scattered throughout Chicago, and the number is rising. Inexpensive.

Restaurants

Alinea 1723 N Halsted ☎312/867-0110; Red Line to North/Clybourn. This discreet townhouse close to where virtuoso chef-owner Grant Achatz first launched himself on the restaurant scene at *Charlie Trotter's* (see p.196) was the most anticipated restaurant opening of the last few years. The attention to detail is impeccable, from the service to every morsel of the three different prix-fixe tasting menus: eight courses, $75, twelve courses, $110, and the epic 24 courses, $175. Dining at *Alinea* requires religious commitment; allow plenty of time, an elastic waistband, and a willingness, to abdicate total control to the chef and sommelier – the wine pairings will push the bill even further into orbit. Each menu changes frequently but you could expect one course to be something along the lines of a solitary grape dipped in peanut butter then neatly wrapped in brioche, or hearts of palm perched on a china pedestal, or a bowl of hyacinth blossoms surrounded by a shellfish custard lake. Open Wednesday–Sunday. Very expensive.

Ambria in the Belden Stratford Hotel, 2300 N Lincoln Park W, at Belden Ave ☎773/472-5959. Brown, Purple, or Red Line to Fullerton. Excellent French cuisine served in a quiet, dim, romantic setting exuding old-world grandeur and priced accordingly. Rich pickings include foie gras, oysters, sweetbreads, rack of lamb, and venison. Or, opt for one of the degustation menus – petit, vegetable, shellfish, or the eight-course "grand" menu – priced $65–85, they are a much better deal. Don't peak too soon: the desserts are a fine finale, especially the chef's signature chocolate and Grand Marnier soufflés. Very expensive.

Athenian Room 807 W Webster Ave, at N Halsted St, near Oz Park ☎773/348-5155; Brown or Red Line to Fullerton. Students from nearby DePaul University flock to this Greek diner for the cheap, tasty gyros, Greek fries, and salads. Decent and cheap if you're in the area looking for a quick bite, but not worth going out of your way for. Service hovers between casual and invisible. Inexpensive.

Boka 1729 N Halsted ☎312/337-6070; Red Line to North/Clybourn. A stylish choice close to the Steppenwolf Theatre, *Boka*'s sleek, eye-catching decor includes a soundproof phone booth to ensure cell-phone protocol is strictly observed and striking fabric "sculptures" draped across the ceiling. The inspired global menu, which changes weekly, is divided into hot and cold small plates ($7–12) and larger plates ($19–35). Pan-seared rainbow trout with Peruvian white beans, halibut with port wine syrup, or pork chops served atop lobster risotto are all prepared with aplomb. The wine list is monumental – some 150 bottles, the service sharp and attentive, and the atmosphere poised. In summer, the outdoor patio services the local see-and-be-seen Lincoln Park hipsters. There's a prix-fixe tasting menu from Thursday to Saturday. Reservations are recommended. Expensive.

Bricks 1909 N Lincoln Ave, at Wisconsin ⓣ773/255-0581; bus #11 to Lincoln or #22 to Clark. Snazzy pizzeria, with a cheerful ambience and walls decorated with Pop Art, that eschews the familiar deep-dish route for perfectly executed thin-crust variations, with an innovative choice of meat, seafood, and vegetarian toppings; the prosciuto and fontina cheese are fine choices. There are over two dozen beers available. Inexpensive.

Charlie Trotter's 816 W Armitage Ave, at N Halsted St ⓣ773/248-6228, ⓦwww.charlietrotters.com; Brown Line to Armitage. Superlative American and continental cuisine in elegant surroundings from one of the country's most renowned chefs, with an extensive wine list and attentive service to match. If you can't get a reservation, try *Trotter's To Go*, mostly a takeout business (1337 W Fullerton Ave, at N Lakewood ⓣ773/868-6510), which has two small tables, plus divine spit-roasted chickens (for about $12) and fabulous beef tenderloin for not much more. Restaurant: Very expensive; *To Go*: Moderate.

Dee's Mandarin Restaurant 1114 W Armitage Ave, at N Sheffield Ave ⓣ773/477-1500. Probably the best Chinese food outside Chinatown, this upscale restaurant offers delectable sesame chicken, wonderfully fresh shrimp, and refreshing Mai Tais. To the chagrin of the faithful, sushi has recently been added to the menu with prices that relect the addition. Inexpensive.

Geja's Café 340 W Armitage Ave, at N Orleans St ⓣ773/281-9101; bus #9 or 22 to Armitage. Perfectly romantic and popular restaurant that serves up excellent fondue in a candlelit setting snugly decorated with oodles of dark wood. Try for one of the curtained-off booths. Expensive.

Green Dolphin Street 2200 N Ashland Ave ⓣ773/395-0066, ⓦwww.jazzitup.com. Hip, west Lincoln Park supper club where the menu caters both to meat–and-potato types and those with a taste for foie gras, brioche, and succulent seafood. The quiet reflection-inducing sea-green interior and black-and-white photos of jazz and blues greats make for a comfortable setting, and the adjoining jazz bar puts on a variety of live music. Expensive.

Lou Malnati's 958 W Wrightwood Ave, at N Lincoln Ave ⓣ773/832-4030. Ex-Chicagoans have been known to have a pie or two Fed-Exed to them in times of need – Lou himself claims the reason you can't get good pizza outside of Chicago is because a mouthwatering crust requires Lake Michigan water. The deep-dish here is perhaps not as monstrous as from *Gino's* (see p.186) or *Giordano's* (see p.183), but it's a densely packed, tastebud-delighting extravaganza nonetheless (with extra-crispy, ever-so-buttery crust). They also make a mean, not-so-thin crust pie and a great apple-pie dessert. Twenty-three locations in the Chicago metropolitan area. Inexpensive.

North Pond 2610 N Cannon Drive, in Lincoln Park ⓣ773/477-5845; bus #22. This is one of the loveliest restaurant settings in the city, nestling beside a pond in Lincoln Park, with views of the skyline. The menu deftly combines fresh organic ingredients to conjure an inpired fusion menu. Appetizers (average $12) include a caramelized onion and goat cheese tartlet and a sautéed soft-shell crab in a coconut and cashew sauce. Entrees ranging from classic American to Asian accented, feature a Gorgonzola-encrusted aged strip-steak and Szechuan pepper duck. A great Chicago Sunday ritual is to linger over a brunch of vanilla-bean pancakes, or an arugula frittata with cheddar paninio, then take a walk in the park. Closed Monday. Very expensive.

Rose Angelis 1314 W Wrightwood Ave, at N Lakewood ⓣ773/296-0081; Brown or Purple Line to Fullerton. Homely, unpretentious, off-the-beaten-path spot that serves mostly vegetarian variations on traditional Italian cooking (there are a few meat dishes, as well); the raviolis are especially inviting as are the prices – average entrees are $13. It's best avoided during peak weekend evenings when the noise can preclude the intimate and romantic ambience which makes it so appealing. Closed Mon. Moderate.

Stanley's Kitchen and Tap 1970 N Lincoln Ave, at W Armitage Ave ⓣ312/642-0007; Purple or Brown Line to Sedgwick. Loved and loathed in equal measure, the hook here is the all-you-can-eat weekend comfort-food brunch, served until 4pm, and tasty Bloody

Marys. Not for the calorie shy, greasy fried chicken, macaroni and cheese, pork chops, and biscuits and gravy will keep you full for the day. The fun and nostalgic bar area leads into a cozy eating section that's never too crowded. The free mashed potatoes, left outside after closing time for hungry passers-by, is an odd, but nice, touch. Inexpensive.

Taco and Burrito Palace 2441 N Halsted St, at Fullerton ⓣ773/248-0740; Red, Brown, or Purple Line to Fullerton. This late-night Mexican joint doles out *chimichangas*, tacos, and exceptional burritos (starting at $2.50). The line snakes out the door late Friday and Saturday nights; play the ancient video games while you wait. Open until 3am. Inexpensive.

Twisted Lizard 1964 N Sheffield Ave, at W Armitage Ave ⓣ773/929-1414; Brown or Purple Line to Armitage. Given the small size of this restaurant's bar and the basement location, the usually long wait can seem even longer. Still, this is a good spot for no-frills filling and tasty Mexican standards – try the *queso fundido* (baked cheese) – and pitchers of margaritas, in one of Lincoln Park's trendiest areas. Moderate.

Via Carducci 1419 W Fullerton ⓣ773/665-1981; bus #9 to Ashland and Fullerton then walk three blocks east. On the western fringes of Lincoln Park, this rustic neighborhood trattoria with a devoted local clientele serves monumental portions of hearty Southern Italian food. Consumed with abandon are the well-priced pasta classics – rigatoni primavera and spaghetti carbonara. Highly recommended dishes are the chickens vesuvio and Parmesan and daily fish specials. Service can teeter on the lackadaisical, but is always gracious. Under the same ownership, the *Enoteca* wine bar next door, with a garden patio, is a good place to get into character. Reservations advised. Moderate.

Lakeview and Andersonville

Cafés and light meals

Ann Sather 929 W Belmont Ave, at Sheffield ⓣ773/348-2378; Red or Brown Line to Belmont. Scattered all over the city's North Side, *Ann Sather* is a chain of cozy Swedish diners that's become Chicago's most popular breakfast spot. The cinnamon rolls are legendary, while the Swedish pancakes with lingonberries are a close second. Stick with the Swedish items on the increasingly American menu. Inexpensive.

Henry's 5707 N Clark ⓣ773/561-1600; bus #22. Great breakfast and lunch place located in Andersonville, serving traditional sandwich options: jerk chicken, turkey, and tuna, and more flamboyant brunch options. Dulce Banana Rumba is thick brioche toast stacked with bananas and sprinkled with toasted pecans and raisins. The pancakes are heavenly, drizzled with a pomegranate bisque, while the wedges of Mediterranean quiche are mouthwatering. Worth the wait – there are very long lines on the weekend. Inexpensive.

Intelligentsia 3123 N Broadway, at W Barry ⓣ773/348-4522; Red Line to Addison. While its coffee – though good – may not be the *Starbucks*-killing super-brew that its proponents claim, there's no doubt that this is a choice spot to kill a few hours with a cup of joe, a pastry, and a *Reader*. There is also an excellent tea selection from white to black to green to oolong. The hum of quiet conversation is never loud enough to break your concentration. Inexpensive.

Southport Grocery 3552 N Southport Ave ⓣ773/665-0100; Brown Line to Southport. Chic café dining at this family-oriented deli/café combines quality ingredients to create a discriminating range of sandwiches ($8), salads ($6), and brunch ($7) delicacies. Home-roasted turkey, roasted sweet red peppers, and pesto-mayo are loaded between slices of delicious nutty wheat bread. The buttermilk pancakes are divine, filled with roasted vanilla walnuts and topped with berries. Wine pairing selections add extra finesse to the menu. There's outdoor seating in summer and a special menu for kids. Open until 6pm during the week, 8pm on the weekend. Closed Monday. Inexpensive.

Swedish Bakery 5348 N Clark St, at W Summerdale ⓣ773/561-8919. This old-fashioned 1920s bakery serves delicious marzipan cake and custard-cup sweet rolls, among other sugary offerings, but the long lines and small, easily crowded space can be annoying. Inexpensive.

Victory's Banner 2100 W Roscoe St ⓣ773/665-0227. The Satisfaction Promise scrambled-egg dish here is one of the best egg creations you will taste – spinach, thick slabs of feta, and sun-dried tomatoes, served with toasted hearth bread, and potatoes. All the breakfast and brunch dishes are indulgent – even the French toast is bathed in cream, while the lunchtime sandwiches and wraps are a little too healthily restrained, not surprising, since the café is run by a Buddhist. The mellow yellow decor and warm and fuzzy atmosphere make for a sedate Sunday antidote to a wild Saturday night. Inexpensive.

The Wiener's Circle 2622 N Clark St, at W Wrightwood Ave ⓣ773/477-7444; bus #22. Whether the staff is arguing amongst themselves or verbally assaulting you (in what appears to be good fun), you'll enjoy some of the best hot dogs in town, best eaten loaded up with all the pickles, peppers, onions, and tomatoes you can get. Inexpensive.

Restaurants

Acqualina 4363 N Lincoln ⓣ773/770-4363; Brown Line to Montrose. A recent addition to the Lincoln Square scene, *Acqualina* offers a restrained minimalist space – apart from the orange light fixtures – and a purist dining experience using fresh, top-quality ingredients. The menu has a distinct Mediterranean slant, with appetizers including plump mussels, gnocchi with pancetta, and a spicy Provençale seafood stew. Entrees feature grilled New York strip, simply served with potatoes and butter. More complex dishes include a pistachio-flavored halibut drizzled with a piquant tomato syrup. The service is attentive without being intrusive. Expensive.

Café 28 1800–1806 W Irving Park Rd, ⓣ773/528-2883; Brown Line to Addison. For lovers of all things Latin, this upbeat, Mexican café with a Cuban influence is a great neighborhood joint. It has just enough polish and a sufficient injection of Latin spirit to woo the crowd of regulars who pack in for deliciously piquant dishes like grilled *chipotle* chicken, almond-encrusted halibut, jalapeño pork chops, and Cuban *ropa viejo*. Add the merriment of salsa music – of course – which is performed live on the weekend, the potent *mojitos*, and it's an uplifting evening on every level. Moderate.

Le Crêperie 2845 N Clark St ⓣ773/528-9050; Brown Line to Diversey. French bohéme prevails at this unpretentious family bistro in an unlikely position close to the prosaic Clark and Diversey nexus. Sweet and savory crêpe concoctions range from creamy chicken curry with mango chutney to seafood soaked in white wine or a decadent thickly loaded chocolate pancake topped with cream. Appetizers including tender *escargots* doused in garlic and French onion soup oozing with cheese provide soothing winter comfort-food. In summer, there's an outdoor patio garden and on Thursday nights, an accordion and trumpet duo meandering through the alluring, aged dining rooms with rickety wooden tables adds to the allure. Closed Monday. Moderate.

Magnolia 1224 W Wilson ⓣ773/728-8785; Red Line to Wilson. This smart, modern American bistro, with neutral decor, high ceilings, soft lighting, and shiny wooden floors is one of Uptown's swankier eating places. Classic dishes are deliciously reinvented and, quite refreshingly, vegetables rank highly on each amply proportioned entree (around $18). Braised lamb shanks, pork chops draped over gooey mac-and-cheese, calamari infused with garlicky pesto marinade atop spaghetti squash, and chicken breast with shiitake risotto, are all well executed. Save room for the sublime desserts, which include home-made ice cream and a flourless chocolate banana cake. Very convenient for a post-dinner visit to the *Green Mill* poetry slam on Sundays; see p.221.

On Common Ground 3800 N Clark St ⓣ773/929-3680; Red Line to Sheridan. Close to Wrigley Field, this accessible, artsy café-bar-restaurant with a welcoming vibe serves an excellent-global fusion brunch. The Montana omelet with bacon, potatoes, and sour cream is a perfect pre-Cubs filler. The lunchtime offerings include Thai peanut salad, organic sesame salmon with miso sauce, and a triple-decker Southwestern club sandwich. With art exhibitions, live music, reading material, and outdoor seating in summer, it's worth lingering for a while. Don't miss a thick, soothing, hot chocolate by the fireside in winter. Inexpensive.

Penny's Noodle Shop 3400 N Sheffield Ave, at N Clark ⓣ773/281-8222; Red Line to Belmont. Cheap, quality, and usually packed noodle joint that spans Asian cuisines, with relaxed outdoor dining – especially the numerous curries, satays, stir-fries, and amazing spring rolls – during the warmer months. Average entrees are less than $6. BYOB. Closed Monday. Inexpensive.

Rise 3401 N Southport Ave ☎773/989-4220; Brown Line to Southport. *Rise* is one of Chicago's best Japanese restaurants. The design is stylish and restrained with floor-to-ceiling windows, ambient background music, and simple wooden tables. The tuna tartare served with crispy rice crackers is sublime, the spicy calamari piquant, and the eye-catching *maki* rolls, while fanciful, still cater to the sushi purist. The large proportions of *nigiri* are fresh and varied – try the *unagi* (eel) and *hamachi* (yellowtail). The "chef's roll" with salmon, tuna, and cucumber is excellent, the scallop tempura, sweet and crunchy. For dessert-style sushi, try their signature *umi maki* – an intriguing combination of banana, shrimp, and *tobikko*. Expensive.

Southport Lanes and Billiards 3325 Southport Ave ☎773/472-6600; Brown Line to Southport. This bowling avenue that opened in 1922 still sets the pins by hand – the only one in the city to do so. A welcoming sports bar, with pool tables and steady Cubs contingent, it's especially lively on game nights. The main reason to come is for the simply fantastic burgers, served with curly fries. The mammoth chopped-chicken salad with bacon, Gorgonzola, olives, and palm hearts is also fresh and tasty. Best bar food in town. Inexpensive.

Tango Sur 3763 N Southport Ave, at W Grace ☎773/477-5466. Small, family-run restaurant specializing in charred, Argentinian-style steaks and ribs along with *parrillada* (short ribs, beef, sweet breads, and black sausage); not much in the way of sides. For the brave and the ravenous. Moderate.

Taste of Lebanon 1509 W Foster Ave ☎773/334-1600. In the Swedish enclave of Andersonville, this hole-in-the-wall Lebanese joint may lack polish but it's a local institution, serving ludicrously cheap, but authentic, Middle-Eastern staples. Nutty falafel is stuffed inside fluffy pita, then drizzled with tahini sauce. The chicken shawarma wraps with a spicy cinnamon sauce are arguably the best in the city, and the stuffed grape-leaves are refreshingly minty and vegetarian friendly. Don't leave without trying the baklava. Across the street, stop by at the family-run Middle-Eastern bakery which sells excellent spinach pies, cheese, hummus, and *baba ganoush* at ridiculously low prices – a great place to prepare for a festival picnic. Inexpensive.

The West Side

Cafés and light meals

Al's Number 1 Italian Beef 1079 W Taylor St, at Aberdeen St ☎312/226-4017; bus #37, #60. Takeout joint that was once the king of Italian beef before numerous copies began arriving – and still turns out a tasty sandwich (around $5), especially the "dipped" varieties. There's another one in River North at 169 W Ontario (☎312/943-3222). Inexpensive.

Café Jumping Bean 1439 W 18th St, at S Loomis St ☎312/455-0019; bus #9. Popular Pilsen hangout for local artists with funky decor – the furniture and walls covered in bright, expressionistic swatches of color – that mixes a coffeehouse groove with Latino café fare. Inexpensive.

Restaurants

Blackbird 619 W Randolph St, at S Jefferson St ☎312/715-0708; Green Line to Clinton. Marvelous and innovative New-American fare in a super-trendy setting, though often overcrowded and pricey. Appetizers include crispy confit of suckling pig and chilled *ahi*. Reworked American classic entrees (average $28) are a delight for ardent carnivores with roasted rabbit, veal, elk loin, and sturgeon with oxtail. Save room for the heavenly desserts – raspberries with Graham-cracker ice cream and chocolate *semifreddo* with waffles. Very expensive.

Costa's 340 S Halsted St, at W Van Buren ☎312/263-9700; Blue Line to UIC/Halsted; bus #8, #126. Spacious, south Greektown joint with live music and large portions of traditional Greek food – the Athenian chicken, mussels Salonika, and *saganaki* (fried cheese) are especially good. Moderate.

De Cero 814 W Randolph St ☎312/455-8114; Green Line to Clinton. This modern taqueria serves fresh Mexican specialties in a sparsely decorated urban setting. Taco selections are diverse with seared *ahi*, salmon with pesto, three-cheese, baked duck, or deep-fried catfish. Sample a few appetizers – especially the *chiles poblanos* – or delve into the more substantial entrees which move from no-frills traditional Mexican dishes – grilled chicken burritos, chicken *mole*, to more global fusion–inspired favorites to the tune of spicy, seared *ahi*. The outdoor patio is a cool place to watch the evening unfold with a signature margarita. Moderate to expensive.

Francesca's on Taylor 1400 W Taylor St, at S Loomis St ⓣ312/829-2828, ⓦwww.miafrancesca.com; Blue Line to Polk. Among the best Italian places in Little Italy, and also the city, *Francesca's* serves up authentic food with zing and verve (including a heavenly carpaccio) in a lively and fun atmosphere. Happily, unlike the other *Francesca* restaurants in Chicago, this one takes reservations. Moderate.

Greek Islands 200 S Halsted St, at W Adams St ⓣ312/782-9855; Blue Line to UIC/Halsted; bus #8, #126. Greek and Middle Eastern food, a cut above most other restaurants in the area, serving faultless classics – the seafood dishes are fresh and creatively executed – in a huge, colorful dining room, with an open kitchen. The service is very attentive and it's open until midnight. Crowded all week long and justifiably so. Moderate.

Green Zebra 1460 W Chicago Ave ⓣ312/243-7100; bus #66 to Noble. Vegetarian food reaches its apogee at this new boutique restaurant with industrial-chic decor. Small taster portions of ambitious dishes such as grilled white mushrooms with silky white-corn polenta and herb emulsion, and crimson lentil cake with spiced shallot and bell-pepper jam, are aimed at providing "high touch" cuisine in a "high tech" world. For die-hard carnivores there's usually at least one meat and fish option. Penance food this definitely isn't, with desserts that include chocolate brownie cake and orange crêpes with birch-syrup mascarpone. With moderately sized portions priced at $8–15, it offers flexibility for the wallet rather than the waistline. Closed Mon. Moderate to expensive.

Marche 833 W Randolph St, at Green ⓣ312/226-8399, ⓦwww.marche-chicago.com; bus #131. One of the highlights of the West Randolph restaurant row, this French bistro packs them in every night with its ballyhooed cuisine – including wonderful bacon-wrapped sea scallops and some amazing desserts – and energetic nightclub-style atmosphere, popular with the glittery, fashionable crowd. Expensive.

Nuevo Leon 1515 W 18th St, at Ashland Ave ⓣ312/421-1517; Blue Line to 18th St. Excellent, traditional Mexican food – among the best in Chicago – served since 1962 in a colorful family-style restaurant in the Pilsen neighborhood, especially lively after Sunday-morning mass. Combine a trip out here with a visit to the nearby Mexican Fine Arts Center Museum (see p.135) and bring your own alcohol; they'll supply a bucket and ice. Moderate.

Parthenon 314 S Halsted St, at W Jackson Blvd ⓣ312/726-2407 ⓦwww.theparthenon.com; Blue Line to UIC/Halsted; bus #8, #126. Longstanding Greektown standby that continues to draw the faithful with its consistent and affordable food. The *taramasalata* (fish roe with sour cream) and *tzatziki* (yogurt with cucumber and garlic) are highly recommended. There's nothing modest about the *Parthenon* – you can feast on a whole roasted suckling pig that could feed a dozen people if your hunger demands it. For the less famished, there are tasty gyros and kaebab platters. It claims to have invented flaming *saganaki* (fried cheese doused with Metaxa brandy); it's worth trying as much for the serving spectacle as for the deliciously rich taste. Moderate.

Red Light 820 W Randolph St, at S Green St ⓣ312/733-8880; bus #8, #131. Dark, upscale West Side pan-Asian restaurant, popular with a young, sleek crowd that comes to munch on the Taiwanese catfish and grilled quail. Expensive.

Rodity's 222 S Halsted St, at W Adams St ⓣ312/454-0800; Blue Line to UIC/Halsted; bus #8, 126. Friendly mom-and-pop place serving first-rate Greek chicken, *avgolemono* (egg-lemon) soup, and *saganaki*. The attentive waitstaff won't rush you either. Inexpensive.

Sushi Wabi 842 W Randolph ⓣ312/563-1224; Green Line to Clinton. For its über-fresh taste and hip, but unpretentious, ambience, *Wabi* is the best sushi restaurant in town, successfully embodying its eponymous ethos of "refined simplicity." Kaleidoscopic *maki*, *nigiri*, and sashimi are served on chunky wooden blocks in a spartan setting of exposed rafters and brick walls, simple banquette seating, and low lighting. The dragon roll with tempura shrimp, *unagi* (eel), and avocado, the Ecuador roll with *maguro* (tuna), and *hamachi* (yellowtail), are as appealing to the eye as they are to the taste. For appetizers, try the *hotategai* (sea scallops in an apple and plum sauce) or *gomae* (spinach with sesame peanut sauce). There is a tiny bar area, serving a wide selection of sake and syrupy sweet plum wine. Reservations advised. Moderate to expensive.

Twisted Spoke 501 N Ogden Ave, at W Grand Ave ☎312/666-1500; bus #65. Out-of-the-way restaurant/bar with rooftop dining and somewhat affected biker atmosphere. You can't go wrong with the half-pound Fatboy burger and the margaritas. If you find yourself here around midnight (a dicey proposition at best), you'll experience "Smut and Eggs," porn projected from TV screens. Moderate.

South Side and Hyde Park

Cafés and light meals

Caffè Florian 1450 E 57th St, at S Blackstone Ave ☎773/752-4100; bus #6. Reliable coffee joint – also serving pizza and sandwiches heavy on the vegetarian side of things – where University of Chicago students and locals deconstruct radical issues. Inexpensive.

Medici on 57th 1327 E 57th St, at S Kenwood Ave ☎773/667-7394; bus #6. Typical college hangout, with two levels of graffiti-covered tables, fine pizza, juicy burgers, and lots of smoke; not to mention the stained-glass windows downstairs. "The Med"'s high point is Sunday brunch, particularly the fresh-squeezed orange juice. Inexpensive.

Negro League Café 301 E 43rd St ☎773/536-7000; Metra to 47th St, then taxi. A tribute to athletes who played in the Negro leagues prior to desegregation in the 1940s, the walls are covered in baseball memorabilia including a "Wall of Fame." The food is also worth the trek, with an innovative, less hearty twist on soul-food classic dishes. Try the chicken wingettes with a spicy peach glaze for appetizer, followed by the catfish with lime. There's also uplifting gospel brunch on Sundays. Closed Monday. Inexpensive.

Restaurants

Army and Lou's 422 E 75th St, at S Martin Luther King ☎773/483-3100. This South-Side institution has a wide selection of satisying soul food for the choosing: short ribs, cornbread, chitterlings, and sweet potatoes have been bringing its regular customers in from all over the city for decades. Inexpensive.

Dixie Kitchen & Bait Shop 5225 S Harper Ave, at 53rd St ☎773/363-4943; Metra to 53rd. Delicious Southern cooking at good prices, served in a room with playful 1930s decor. The menu ranges from delicious Southern BBQ to hot Cajun and Creole gumbos and jambalayas. The fried-green-tomato appetizer is a must and the service simply wonderful. Inexpensive.

La Petite Folie 1504 E 55th St, at Lake Park Blvd ☎773/493-1394; bus #6. Hyde Park's only upscale French restaurant – in terms of the menu and decor, not the price – is tucked away in a tiny mall beside Walgreen's. This smart but cosy bistro with pristine white tablecloths and warm baguettes and butter as a preamble, serves classic French cuisine; roulade of sole, veal tenderloin, and a tasty foie gras variation – perhaps the cheapest you will find anywhere. The prix-fixe menu (three courses, around $28, served between 5–6pm) is often the best deal. Closed Monday. Moderate.

Mellow Yellow 1508E 53rd St ☎773/667-2000; Metra to 53rd Street. A 1970s retro classic with a well-honed menu of spit-roasted chicken, burgers, savory crêpes, six different kinds of chilli (a resounding winner at the Taste of Chicago summer food festival; see p.257), and old-school desserts like apple pie, bread pudding, and Oreo milkshakes. The time-warp decor with lava lamps, leafy foliage, and a laid-back vibe has made it a Hyde Park landmark for almost thirty years. Inexpensive.

Pearl's Place **3901 S. Michigan ⓣ773/285-1700; Green Line to Indiana.** Despite the rather soulless facade and unfortunate location, next to a motel, *Pearl's* Southern soul food with a Creole twist is as soulful as it comes. Main dishes (average $8) including juicy fried chicken, collard greens with smoky pork bits, and potato pie with a melt in your mouth crust, are as comforting for the stomach as they are for the wallet. Great for the area's post-church Sunday brunch, although be prepared to wait in line, a long time. Inexpensive.

Piccolo Mondo **1642 E 56th, at S Hyde Park Blvd ⓣ773/643-1106.** One of the few Italian restaurants on the South Side, serving basic fare like rigatoni Gregorio and rotolo Rossini. There's a deli counter up front. Moderate.

Ribs 'n' Bibs **5300 S Dorchester Ave, at E 53rd St ⓣ773/493-0400.** For no-frills takeout ribs, this Hyde Park institution is the place to go. Go for the Lil' Bronco, half a slab of their dripping-with-sauce ribs and fries. Wear an old shirt, as this food splatters. Inexpensive to moderate.

▽ *Ribs 'N' Bibs*

Oak Park

Cafés and light meals

Petersen's **1100 W Chicago Ave ⓣ708/386-6131; Green Line to Oak Park.** This ice-cream über-parlor has been drawing the salivating masses since 1919. *Petersen's* flavor temptations include scoops of black walnut, New York cherry, cookie dough, bubble gum, or not so plain old vanilla, $6.95, petite (rather a misnomer) size $4.95. Sundaes are just devilish. The Tin Roof Sundae is lashings of vanilla and chocolate ice cream drenched in chocolate syrup, then smothered with caramelized Spanish peanuts ($7.95). The brownie and apple pie à la modes, milkshakes, and root-beer floats are retro heaven.

Restaurants

Amarind's **6822 W North Ave ⓣ773/889-9999; Green Line to Oak Park.** A former chef from the superlative *Arun's* (see p.203), Rangsan Sutchatit demonstrates the same culinary wizardry and artistic panache at *Amarind's* to create traditional Thai classics like a salty-sweet beef Panang curry and a fine pad thai with tenderness and crunch in all the right places. If you like it hot, ask for extra spice – like at *Arun's*, this is very much a westernized interpretation of Thai cuisine. With all dishes under $10, it makes for an inviting lunch stop-off. Closed Monday. Inexpensive.

Café le Coq **734 Lake St ⓣ708/848-2233; Green Line to Oak Park.** This is the best restaurant in Oak Park, serving French bistro classics with flair and panache. The decor has more than a whiff of turn-of-the-century France, with a tiled floor, storefront windows, a tin-panelled ceiling, and fleur-de-lis wallpaper. The menu triumphs in restraint and respect for classic French bistro fare, with Lyonnaise salads, onion soup, mussels in parsley, garlic sauce, *steak frites*, *escargot*, onion tart, and braised rabbit. The extensive wine list is predominantly French. Moderate to expensive.

Geppettos Pasta and Pizza **113 N Oak Park Ave ⓣ708/386-9200; Green Line to Oak Park.** This archetypal small-town restaurant serves great thin-crust pizzas, soups, a wholesome salad bar, freshly baked Italian breads, and a medley of satisfying deli sandwiches and pasta dishes. The thin-crust pizza is the star, ranging from traditional margarita to a spicy Mexican and a surprisingly good deli pizza swirled with mustard. An endless list of toppings and friendly staff allow you to customize at will. There is a credible selection of wine and imported and domestic beers. Inexpensive

Rogers Park and the North Shore

Restaurants

Arun's 4156 N Kedzie Ave ☎773/539-1909; bus #80. Hailed as the best Thai restaurant in Chicago and, indeed, the country, chef-owner and all-round Renaissance man, Arun Sampanthavivat, conjures a delectable twelve-course prix-fixe odyssey ($75) through the intricate sensations of Thai cuisine. The sumptuous decor centers on Thai silks and paintings from Arun's private collection. Following a discussion of your spice tolerance and gastro-aversions, six appetizers are served in sequence before the evening's climax, four entrees presented banquet style, before dessert duo finale. Event dining in the extreme, it is well and truly worth splashing out on and venturing north for. Reservations are a must. Very expensive.

Hema's Kitchen 6406 N Oakley, at W Devon Ave ☎773/338-1627; bus #155. If you can live with the tacky decor and erratic service, this unsung gem serves value inexpensive Indian/Pakistani dishes from the traditional recipe collection of Hema Potla. The lamb sautéed with peppers and *sag mug* (chicken with peppers and spices) are two of her scrumptious specials. *Hema's* popularity has extended to her second locale near Lincoln Park at 2411 N Clark. Early close at 9.30pm. Inexpensive to moderate.

Viceroy of India 2520 W Devon Ave, at N Campbell Ave ☎773/743-4100; bus #155. A huge and always dependable eating palace in the heart of Devon Ave's Indian community, serving excellent North Indian cuisine; the chicken tandoori here is hard to beat. It's slightly more expensive than most in the area, but for the improved quality of the food, decor, service, and atmosphere, it's definitely worth it. There is a suburban outpost at 555 Roosevelt Rd, Lombard. Moderate.

15

Drinking

Chicago has been defined by its boisterous **drinking scene** since at least the early 1900s, when Schlitz, a major local brewery, owned more land than anyone else in town, save another pillar of the community, the Catholic Church. Muckraking journalist George Turner estimated in 1907 that in some "wards" (neighborhoods) there was roughly one bar per 150 residents.

The city's hard-drinking reputation was cemented during the Prohibition era of the 1920s and 1930s, when the need for beer and bathtub gin consumed Chicago in the gangland violence that has become one of the city's most notorious historical associations. While the mobsters and speakeasies are a thing of the past, these days, drinking still remains a serious business; you'll find more **sports bars** here than in New York and Los Angeles combined. Only slightly less ubiquitous are the city's popular **beer gardens** – casual outdoor patios that teem in summer with people who've made up ingenious excuses to skip out of work early. Just about every kind of bar imaginable exists, from Irish bars and chic velvet-rope places to movie houses and bowling alleys that double as drinking establishments.

Many of the new lounge bars also function as restaurants – the food certainly transcends the standard greasy bar fodder; see "Eating," Chapter 14, for more potential listings.

Chicago's bar scene tends to be quiet early on in the week, picking up on Wednesday and through the weekend. Long weekend brunches are prime drinking times as there's always some game on the big TVs at most bars. Late-night drinking is also a hallmark of the city's bar scene: the average 2am weekday **closing time** extends to 5am on Saturdays in some places. Bars are packed right up to closing time, and late-night bars often have lines at 2am that are longer than the ones you'll see earlier in the night.

Remember to carry **photo ID** or your passport with you; many bars won't let you in without it. You have to be 21 to drink in Illinois and the law is rigorously adhered to in all bars – if you look under 35 years old you will almost certainly be carded. **Smoking** is allowed in Chicago bars.

AUTHOR PICKS

Duke of Perth p.213
Hopleaf p.213
John Barleycorn Memorial Pub p.212
Matchbox p.215
Moody's Pub p.215
Narcisse p.208
Old Town Ale House p.209
Signature Room p.209
Tiny Lounge p.214

Drink prices are fairly reasonable compared to other major US cities, except in the most upscale bars. **Beer** is usually cheap, between $3.50 and $6 a pint, and many bars have happy hours (roughly 4–8pm) featuring drink specials, usually half-price drafts of domestic beers, or a bucket of six bottles for the price of five. Local favorites include **Old Style**, a mass-produced lager brewed in Milwaukee, and the many varieties of **Goose Island**, a robust Chicago beer from a brewery that runs a few of its own bars in the city (see p.212).

Mixed drinks and **wine** are more expensive, typically from $6.50 to $13, depending on the fanciness of the establishment. A few odd cocktail combinations have persisted here, like the brutal but effective **Car Bombs** – a shot of whiskey dropped into a full pint of Guinness and downed in one swoop.

Drinking by neighborhood

While every neighborhood has its own cluster of bars, with distinct flavors and themes, **Near North** has more per square mile than anywhere else in Chicago, with most of them concentrated around the raucous intersection of **Rush** and **Division** streets.

River North has some fancy places for cocktails, as does the Mag Mile, where luxury hotel chains have poured tons of money into their sumptuous lounges. The *Drake Hotel* exudes turn-of-the-century grandeur, while the *W* hotels draw the urban sophisticates with their self-consciously sleek and sexy vibe. Conservative, collegiate **Lincoln Park** is known for its dozens of sports bars – with a recent leaning towards cultivating a less macho veneer – but also has a number of quality lounges and pubs. Despite the clutch of Cubs bars around Wrigley Field, nearby **Lakeview** has perhaps the best mix of types of bars ranging from the ubiquitous Irish theme pub to alternative scene bars, poised wine bars, and gregarious singles' hunting grounds. The bohemian denizens of **Bucktown**, **Wicker Park**, and the **Ukrainian Village** frequent an eclectic mix of bars ranging from grungy saloons with beer-soaked floors to sleek lounges with exotic fish tanks.

△ Drinks at *The Berghoff*

The **Loop** mostly caters to an after-work office crowd and theatergoers, though there are a couple of excellent taverns in the more isolated, but increasingly gentrified **South Loop**.

There isn't much in the way of destination drinking on the **South Side**, with the exception of **Hyde Park** and the traditionally Irish neighborhood of **Beverly/Morgan Park**, at Western and 103rd Street, which hosts the nation's largest neighborhood St Patrick's Day parade, see "Festivals and events," Chapter 21. If you happen to be around during one of its other street festivals (see pp.254–259), though, there's plenty of drinking to be found, usually accompanied by live music.

The Loop

See map on p.48 for drinking locations.

Atwood Café in the Burnham Hotel, 1 W Washington St, at State ⓣ312/368-1900; Brown Line to Washington. Restored American bar-café, exuding classical grandeur, located in a legendary Chicago Style building designed by Daniel Burnham (see p.168). While the food is decent, the atmosphere and people-watching from the giant windows is the major draw, and is best appreciated accompanied by one of the classic pre-dinner cocktails.

Berghoff 17 W Adams St, at State ⓣ312/427-3170; Brown Line to Jackson. Though known primarily for its food, this German-American institution also serves its own much-vaunted beer and root beer in the atmospheric *Stand Up Bar* upstairs, amid aging woodwork and antique fixtures. Oktoberfest here is something to behold with raucous drinking, eating, and live music.

The Big Downtown in the Palmer House Hilton, 124 S Wabash St ⓣ312/917-7399. A 1940s retro vibe permeates with a blues theme, railway station memorabilia, and colorful "Old Chicago" murals. Spacious, interconnecting rooms with comfortable booths and sidewalk seating endear it as much to local business crowds as to hotel guests. The food, comprising the usual classic American suspects, is also very good. Great spot for a relaxing lunchtime drink.

Cardozo's Pub 170 W Washington ⓣ312/236-1573. This hard-edged subterranean pub close to City Hall is where the political movers and shakers head for an industrial-strength lunchtime drink, sustenance, and TV time out. With a raw ambience, it makes for interesting people-watching and eavesdropping.

Cavanaugh's 53 W Jackson Blvd ⓣ312/939-3125. Located inside the landmark Monadnock Building, this unassuming joint with a historic, pleasingly unpolished, Chicago ambience is easy to miss – look for the green-and-white awning down the side alley. Once inside, the cozy, wood-panelled interior, shiny brass fixtures, and green leather bar and stools is a welcoming retreat from the frenzy of the Loop. A resolutely locals' watering hole where men in suits exchange lively banter with the genial barstaff.

Monk's Pub 205 W Lake St, at Wells St ⓣ312/357-6665; Blue Line to Clark. Noisy, unassuming, wood-panelled neighborhood bar with a good line-up of beers and a wide selection of pub fare; great half-pounder burgers with a multitude of toppings and chilli, the house special. Packed between noon and 1pm with business workers engaged in animated chatter or gripped by the CNBC ticker on the TV screen.

Whiskey Blue in the W Hotel, 172 W Adams St, at Wells St ⓣ312/782-4933; Brown, Orange, or Purple Line to Quincy. One of the few spots in the Loop for upscale drinking ($11 martinis, $12 cosmopolitans). The leggy waitresses are a trademark of *W Hotel* bars, while the lounge decor and low lighting is sleek and sexy.

Near North

See map on p.75 for drinking locations.

The Bar at the Peninsula Chicago 108 E Superior St, at N Michigan Ave ⓣ312/337-2888; Red Line to Chicago. Reminiscent of a men's club, with leather armchairs and a signature "Gentleman's Retreat Tea" – a selection of appetizers, a glass of bourbon, and a cigar – this plush lounge attracts a well-heeled, debonair crowd. There is an extensive array of high-priced cocktails and cigars, not to mention a stunning view of the city.

Bar Louie **226 W Chicago Ave, at N Franklin St ⓣ312/337-3313; Brown or Purple Line to Chicago.** The first in the now-ubiquitous bar chain, this one serves drinks and food late (until 4am on Friday, 5am on Saturday). With a mixed and youthful crowd, it's loud, unromantic, and unpretentious. The walls are covered with evocative murals depicting Chicago in the Roaring twenties, and sparkling mosaic tiles encrusted above the smart wooden bar lined with red leather stools. There are over twenty beers. The bar food is a cut above average, with some tasty sandwiches, burgers, and salads.

Basil's **in the Talbott Hotel, 20 E Delaware ⓣ800/525-2688.** This lordly English country-manor-style bar is a dandy spot to sip a single malt whiskey, a Cognac, or an *añejo* tequila amidst deep mahogany furniture, shiny brass fixtures, and foxhunting paintings.

Blue Frog **676 N LaSalle St, at W Erie St ⓣ312/943-8900; Red Line to Chicago.** An almost-hidden dive bar in River North, this mellow joint is popular for its shelves of near-complete board games, from Operation to Battleship to Kerplunk. There are over 20 kinds of bottled beers and an outdoor deck in summer. A refreshingly fun alternative to all the chains in the area.

Brehon Pub **731 N Wells St, at W Superior St ⓣ312/642-1071; Brown or Purple Line to Chicago.** Family-owned *Brehon* (Gaelic for lawyer), a neighborhood fixture for over twenty years, is a casual Irish-American pub complete with green painted ceiling, Irish flags, an antique bar, and more than a whiff of genuine Irish hospitality. There are 12 beers on tap, an adequate beer garden, plus a pool table, dartboard, and a jukebox. On St Patrick's Day, just about every pub-crawl gang makes a pit stop here.

▽ *Celtic Crossings*

Celtic Crossings **751 N Clark St, at W Chicago Ave ⓣ312/337-1005; Red Line to Chicago.** One of Chicago's more authentic Irish pubs. With no TVs, it's best suited for a pint and good conversation. Choose from a dozen beers on tap, mostly imports, including Murphy's, Newcastle Brown, and Guinness. The Irish owners keep it real, the crowd is mature, the vibe unpretentious. Irish bands often play on Saturday nights and Sunday afternoons.

Charlie's Ale House **700 E Grand Ave, on Navy Pier ⓣ312/595-1440.** A branch of the original Lincoln Park ale house and the best of the Navy Pier restaurant/bars, serving more than forty types of beers, along with liquor. The patio is a great place to sidestep the Navy Pier throngs in summer, while the interior is reminiscent of a snug, old-English pub. The restaurant serves salads, sandwiches, tasty meatloaf, and chicken pot pie.

Clark Street Ale House **742 N Clark St, just south of Chicago Ave ⓣ312/642-9253; Red Line to Chicago.** Relax at the handsome cherry-wood bar with one of the vast selection of domestic beers (almost one hundred including 25 draft beers, a couple of good house brews, and local specialties), dozens of Scotches, and cigars. There's also a pleasant outdoor garden in summer. Lively atmosphere, popular with the after-work crowd and graduate students.

Cru Café **888 N Wabash Ave, at E Chestnut St ⓣ312/337-4078; Red Line to Chicago.** Just south of the Rush drinking corridor, at Rush and Division, there's great people-watching at this corner wine bar replete with chandeliers, fireplace, and poised vibe. Order one of the hundreds of wines or a glass of port, munch on a cheese platter or tuna carpaccio and relax in the muted candlelight to an ambient house soundtrack. On the downside, the service can be erratic.

Harry's Velvet Room **56 W Illinois St, at N Dearborn St ⓣ312/828-5600; Red Line to Grand.** Super-snazzy underground River North lounge with leather booths, dim lighting, swank dj tunes, cigars, decadent desserts, and dozens of Martinis to die for. There is a $10 cover on weekends, and a suitably gilded clientele in their finest attire. Smart dress is recommended, but not required.

Kaz Bar **in the House of Blues Hotel, 329 N Dearborn St, at W Kinzie St ⓣ312/923-2453; Red Line to Grand.** This Moroccan-styled lounge takes pseudo-Arabic ornate to another level, with its tents and draped fabrics everywhere. They serve a broad repertoire of Martinis ranging from spicy to sweet; try the Hot-Tini (dirty martini with Tabasco) or the German Chocolate Cake (Frangelico, French Kiss, Godiva, Malibu, and cream, ($10)). There's occasional live music on weekend nights.

Luxbar 18 E Bellvue Place ⓣ312/642-3400. Opened in summer 2005, this swanky bar successfully, and quite uniquely, combines stylish decor – all marble, onyx, brass, and leather – with a casual neighborhood ambience. The chatty, convivial scene is enhanced by the centerpiece fireplace, classic mahogany bar, and comfort food with a contemporary spin, which is worth pairing with one of the well-executed cocktails or glass of wine. *Luxbar* is under the same management as the venerable *Gibson's* and *Hugo's*; see p.190.

Martini Ranch 311 W Chicago Ave, at N Franklin St ⓣ312/335-9500. At this Gallery District den, it's all about the martinis – more than 40 in all shapes and varieties, and some of the best in the city if you like them strong and sweet. A smoky, snug place usually with standing room only, it has a clubby vibe, courtesy of the djs spinning dance, house, and hip-hop. There is also plenty of greasy bar food on offer.

Motel Bar 600 W Chicago Ave ⓣ312/822-2900. One of the latest and most innovative hot spots in the fashionable River North district, the *Motel Bar* replicates with retro zeal the 1970s motel-lobby experience. Orange booths, brown sofas, and an understated old-school vibe predominates amidst the 30-something cocktail purists who imbibe Tom Collins, Gin Fizz, and Harvey Wallbangers. The motel theme extends to the late-night eats with room-service classics like grilled-cheese sandwiches and buffalo wings.

Narcisse 710 N Clark, at Superior ⓣ312/787-2675; Brown Line to Chicago. Appropriately named, this ultra-swanky lounge, dripping with chandeliers, velvet, marble, and serious attitude draws the A-list celebrities and local wannabees dressed to the nines, with its decadent vibe and suave milieu. If money is no object, the high-class menu including oysters, caviar, lamb carpaccio, and filet mignon, is hard to fault and best enjoyed with one of their fine signature champagne cocktails.

O'Callaghan's 29 W Hubbard St ⓣ312/670-4371. Down-to-earth River North after-work bar, with a vaguely Irish-pub feel, that attracts a mixed crowd. The drinks are nothing special, but the welcoming staff keeps regulars coming back for more.

Pippin's Tavern 806 N Rush St, at E Chicago Ave ⓣ312/787-5435; Red Line to Chicago. An actual, honest-to-God hole-in-the-wall, this friendly down-to-earth bar, predating the yuppie scene along the Rush strip by decades (it opened in 1949), is a tiny oasis of dark wood, holiday lights, and an extensive choice of beer – the drink of choice for the casual, twentysomething, and Loyola student contingents.

The Redhead Piano Bar 16 W Ontario St, at N State St ⓣ312/640-1000; Red Line to Grand. Known for its cabaret acts, this suave bar also serves excellent martinis – thirty types in all, as well as an extensive list of Scotches, tequilas, and port. Usually draws a mature singles crowd, though it's not uncommon for crooners better suited to the karaoke circuit to start belting them out here.

Rockit Bar and Grill 22 W Hubbard ⓣ312/645-6000. It's saloon chic at this Wild West–themed split-level bar-grill with antler chandeliers, brown leather chairs, and distressed wooden tables. The rugged vibe extends to the menu with the specialty Kobe Rockit burger, thick slabs of crab cake, and calamari. On the second level plasma TVs and pool tables draw the tie-shedding, post-work crowds.

Sea of Happiness 640 N Wabash, at E Erie St ⓣ312/787-2721; Red Line to Grand. Adjoining the budget *Cass Hotel*, *Sea of Happiness* is quite the antithesis of the gamut of River North lounge bars and Irish pubs. A pleasingly raw watering hole decked out in all manner of nautical kitsch, it makes for a friendly place to relax with local Chicagoans and enjoy a cheap beer.

Whiskey Sky in the W Hotel, 644 N Lake Shore Drive, at E Erie St ⓣ312/255-4463. The views of Lake Michigan from this 33rd-floor lounge are great, but the place is so popular that you have to put your name on the guest list in advance if you hope to even drink here on a Friday or Saturday night. A haven for models, sports figures, and business types, none of whom blinks at the $11 martinis.

Chicago **food**

Celebrated as the "hog butcher of the world" by the poet Carl Sandburg during the city's early-twentieth-century heyday as the nation's meatpacking powerhouse, Chicago staked its claim early as a place where food is paramount. Large portions were – and still frequently are – the order of the day. This is reflected in several dozen venerable steakhouses for which the city is renowned, from packed yet homey *Chicago Chop House* to the mansion elegance of *Lawry's* to *Morton's of Chicago*, famous for serving the largest steak in town, some 64 ounces.

Chicago steak

Street treats

Simpler cravings are met by an array of local fast-food specialties. King of all is the **hot dog**, introduced at the World's Columbian Exposition of 1893, and more ornate than the variety already being served up on New York's Coney Island. This beef frankfurter-in-a-bun – then called the "hot dog sandwich" – was an instant hit with the fair's millions of visitors as a cheap, filling meal, and quickly caught on in homes as well as at baseball parks around the country. The sausage was served in a fashion that would come to be known as "Chicago style," with toppings that are still standard today. The steamed, poppyseed bun is filled with a boiled or steamed (though not grilled) wiener, but note that ketchup is never used. Indeed, many of Chicago's classic hot-dog houses, such *Portillo's Hot Dogs, The Wiener's Circle*, or *Superdawg* refuse to sully their beloved frankfurter with the red stuff.

The city's historic obsession with red meat is further evident with the **Italian beef sandwich**, which became popular during the Depression. When beef was scarce, cooks in the West Side's Little Italy sliced the meat super-thin and served it on chewy rolls loaded with thin gravy. Today, the sandwich is served at walk-up stands and restaurants in Little Italy and throughout the city, with toppings ranging from sweet and hot peppers to cheddar or mozzarella cheese.

Everything but the ketchup...

Possible toppings for the classic Chicago hot dog

- ✔ mustard
- ✔ green relish
- ✔ pickle spears
- ✔ tomato wedges
- ✔ chopped onion
- ✔ sport peppers (a type of pickled hot pepper)
- ✔ celery salt

Chicago-style pizza

Invented in 1943 at Pizzeria Uno's original location at 29 E Ohio St, **deep dish** or "**Chicago-style**" pizza is the city's most legendary foodstuff. Unlike the crust of a typical Neapolitan-inspired pizza, which is thin and flat, Chicago-style pizza crust is more like the Sicilian variety, thicker and pulled up high on the sides of a deep dish pan, resulting in a substantial, truly pie-like crust that's topped with a thick layer of mozzarella, then sausage or other meat and vegetable toppings and, finally, a layer of tomato chunks (also unlike typical pizza, which starts with a tomato sauce base before adding cheese). Not surprisingly, the final product is massive enough to require a knife and fork.

Uno's may have introduced this deep-dish style (and the chain has indeed grown to 200 locations across the country), but the question that inspires passionate arguments among local pizza aficionados even today is, "Who does it best?" Ask a dozen Chicagoans and you may get a dozen different answers; perennial contenders include *Lou Malnati's*, *Gino's*, and *Giordano's*.

Polish *Kielbasa*

Ethnic cuisines

Greek pastries

Arriving during the late-nineteenth and early twentieth centuries, European immigrants quickly made their impact on Chicago life. As these pockets of **Polish**, **German**, **Swedish**, **Greek**, and **Ukrainian** settlers spread throughout the city, so did their cooking traditions, resulting in a city rich with a variety of ethnic cuisines.

Wander the various neighborhoods and you'll come across shops selling everything from **Polish sausages** to **pierogi** (doughy, half-moon-shaped dumplings stuffed with meat, mushrooms, or sauerkraut). Greektown is the obvious place to head for a hearty **moussaka** or **Greek pastries**, while Andersonville is the home of fine **Swedish cuisine** and baked goods – be sure to try **pickled herring**, and **lutefisk** (cod soaked in lye, a highly unlikely delicacy); if you can't make it out there, try out one of the many branches of *Ann Sather*, a Chicago chain that serves Swedish dishes among other foods.

With one of the fastest-growing Mexican populations in the US, Chicago's **Pilsen** neighborhood boasts some mind-blowing **Mexican fare** – some of the best you'll find outside of Mexico. A trip to the **Maxwell Street Market**, an open-air banquet of affordable and authentic Mexican delicacies, should not be missed.

Food vendors at the Maxwell Street Market

While visitors and Chicagoans alike frequent the dim sum restaurants of **Chinatown**, the more adventurous make the pilgrimage north to Rogers Park's "Little Bombay," where Chicago's sizeable South Asian population is thriving along **Devon Avenue**. Here, you'll find a plethora of exotic Indian, Bangladeshi, and Pakistani restaurants, ranging from cheap curry houses to world-class four-star dining.

Gourmet dining at *Frontera Grill*

Gourmet aspirations

Over the last two decades, Chicago's dining scene has worked hard to transcend its meat-and-potatoes roots; the results have been some of the finest, and most diverse, eateries in the country. The god of Chicago's epicurean innovation was **Charlie Trotter**, whose namesake restaurant, which opened in the late 1980s, pioneered the concept of elegant fusion dining, with an innovative tasting menu served in a formal and serene Lincoln Park townhouse.

A crop of celebrity chefs swiftly followed in Trotter's footsteps. The indefatigable **Rick Bayless**, recognizable from his TV show and numerous cookbooks, singlehandedly subverted the notion that Mexican food is all chips and enchiladas with his superb *Frontera Grill* – which has assumed the mantel of best Mexican restaurant in the US. In the process it changed the common perception in Chicago that haute cuisine begins and ends in the kitchens of France; a taste of one of the restaurant's chile braises or *moles* should let you know why.

In recent years, with its fervent embrace of every global culinary trend, Chicago has become a prominent center of the progressive food movement. In 2005, *Alinea*, with provocative chef/owner **Grant Achatz** at the helm, achieved national acclaim with a futuristic form of fine dining that tantalizes, engages, and sometimes perplexes the senses. The first course of an epic tasting menu of 6, 12, or 28 creations could be anything from flavored gas that you pump into your mouth with an atomizer, to fruit that becomes paper, or a grape wrapped in peanut butter served atop a device that resembles a steel torture implement.

If none of these novelties appeal, you can always head to the next steakhouse.

Gold Coast and Old Town

See map on p.87 for drinking locations.

Bella Lounge 1212 N State Parkway ⓣ312/787-9405. This sultry, suave lounge bar opened at the end of 2004. Decked out in suede and leather, and doused with attitude, it features three bars and four lounges. There is a "limo" room – no explanation required – and a "VIP" area, with smooth library decor. Pretensions aside, the cocktails are worthy of the hype. Try the signature Bellatini – Belvedere vodka, passion fruit puree, and lime, or the Sweet Violet Tini – Effen Black Cherry Vodka and pineapple juice served in a grape-sugar-rimmed glass. Open until 1am during the week and 2am on the weekends with a dj spinning nightly.

Butch McGuire's 20 W Division St, at N Dearborn St ⓣ312/337-9080. An institution on the singles scene since the 1960s, *Butch*'s is the most popular of all the Division Street bars, which means that on Friday and Saturday nights it heaves with prowling singles and has all the sophistication of a frat house. The Christmas tinsel, stuffed animals, and motorized trains add to the suffocation.

Coq d'Or in the Drake Hotel, 140 E Walton St, at N Michigan Ave ⓣ312/787-2200; Red Line to Chicago. Smoky, speakeasy-style environs popular with suits at lunch and an older after-work Martini crowd. Elegant cabaret tunes complete the atmosphere of rare sophistication. Choice burgers and what may be the finest club sandwich in the city.

The Leg Room 7 W Division St, at N State St ⓣ312/337-2583. Sandwiched in between the crowded Division Street drinkeries, this velvety little lounge with ice-cold martinis and perfectly tacky leopard-print decor is one of the coolest bars in the area. It maintains a subdued vibe despite the trendy crowd dancing to dj spun grooves.

Melvin B's Truck Stop 1114 N State St ⓣ312/751-9897. In summer, the huge outdoor patio teems with a mix of joggers, rollerbladers, and business types who come to drink like fish and munch on the above-average bar food. Come winter, the menu slims down to just the staples (pizza, hot dogs, chilli) and a tamer sports-themed indoor scene.

Mother's 26 W Division St ⓣ312/642-7251. Immortalized in the 1980s movie *About Last Night*, *Mother's* provides the quintessential Division Street experience – a frenzied singles scene where the young and the raucous writhe on the dancefloor to a cacophonous medley of tunes.

Old Town Ale House 219 W North Ave, at N Wieland St ⓣ312/944-7020. A favorite with artists, photographers, and literary types since it opened in 1958, this dimly lit, smoky dive, with its antique decor and lending library, has character to spare; check out the mural behind the bar that honors *Second City* alumni including John Belushi and Bill Murray. Some *Second City* members have even tied the knot here, while others hung out, played pinball, and drank copiously. Open until 4am during the week and 5am at the weekend.

P.J. Clarke's 1204 N State Parkway, at E Division St ⓣ312/664-1650. The two-story sibling of the famed New York City burger joint serves great comfort food and legendary burgers but is, in essence, a classic neighborhood drinking den, which draws a crowd of regulars and also serves as a pick-up joint for less sp types. The atmosphere is fun and friendly and there's an impressive selection of imported beer and Scotch.

Signature Room 875 N Michigan Ave, at E Chestnut St ⓣ312/787-7230. An unashamedly touristy, but quintessential Chicago ritual. Take the elevator to the 96th floor of the John Hancock Building, order a cocktail, relax, and take in the breathtaking views of the city. Especially beautiful on a snowy winter's day when the lake is frozen over. The decor is shabby, the service frustratingly slow, but the experience unforgettable.

Tavern on Rush 1031 N Rush St, at Bellevue ⓣ312/664-9600. Airy, spacious restaurant and lounge catering to a young, trendy crowd. The menu is nothing exciting – ideally, stick to drinks – but the modern and stylish surroundings are made for young bright things and the tall windows ideal for people-watching.

Whiskey Bar and Grill 21 E Bellevue Place, at N Rush St ⓣ312/475-0300. The local branch of this chainlet of style bars run by Cindy Crawford's husband should not be confused with *Whiskey Blue*, at the *W*. It's still a scene-maker type of place, with beautiful people elbowing their way toward the more beautiful bartenders, but a little easier to get into.

Zebra Lounge **1220 N State Parkway, just north of W Division St ⓣ312/642-5140.** Kitsch decor and eccentric personalities mix and mingle at this black-and-white, closet-sized piano bar which has been drawing lounge singers, middle-aged swingers, transvestites, and young preppies since the 1930s. Rollicking until the early hours, the keyboardist only enhances its corny appeal.

South Loop and Near South

See map on p.95 for drinking locations.

Alcock's Bar **411 S Wells St, at W Congress Parkway ⓣ312/922-1778, ⓦwww.alcocks.com; Brown, Orange, or Purple Line to LaSalle.** This bar overflows with Bears fans whenever the team plays at home, and financial types from the nearby Board of Trade during the week. Otherwise it's a mellow joint with rock 'n' roll blaring from the jukebox, bottled beers, and pizzas, pasta, sandwiches, and hot dogs at lunch. Closed Sundays.

Tantrum **1023 S State St, at E 11th St ⓣ312/939-9160; Red Line to Roosevelt.** Slick, mellow, little lounge drawing local loft-dwellers, and after work financial movers and shakers from the rapidly revitalizing South Loop zone. Step up to the gorgeous mahogany bar for one of their thirty ingenious Martinis and let time slip away. As the story goes, the bar's name comes from the tantrum the owners were forced to throw in order to get their liquor license.

Bucktown, Wicker Park, and Ukrainian Village

See map on p.107 for drinking locations.

California Clipper **1002 N California Ave, at W Augusta Blvd ⓣ773/384-2547, ⓦwww.californiaclipper.com.** This former speakeasy, near Humboldt Park, has plenty of retro appeal with vintage booths, Art Deco bar, and low lighting. Frequent free live music at the weekends, and Monday is bingo night. Open until 2am during the week, until 3am on Saturday.

Celebrity **1856 W North Ave ⓣ773/365-0091; Blue Line to Damen.** Savvy new Wicker Park bar with a hip, clubby vibe, opened in 2005, with an emphasis on pretty cocktails, elitist bar food (think ceviche rather than wings), and hip-hop, R&B, and dance music spun by notable local djs. A kaleidoscopic entranceway gives way to a tasteful minimalist interior with cube furniture, candles, and exposed brick. Rather pretentious.

Club Lucky **1824 W Wabansia Ave, at N Honore St ⓣ773/227-2300; Blue Line to Damen.** Retro Rat Pack–styled hangout, where the drinks are strong and the moderately priced food is straightforward and satisfying.

Gold Star Bar **1755 W Division St, at N Wood St ⓣ773/227-8700; Blue Line to Division.** All-business, old-fashioned Ukrainian Village bar where the focus is on drinking cheap beer ($2 bottles of Budweiser) in strictly blue-collar surroundings with a great classic and alt-rock jukebox.

Hideout **1354 W Wabansia Ave, at W Willow St ⓣ773/227-4433, ⓦwww.hideoutchicago.com; bus #72.** Tucked away among the warehouses between Old Town and Bucktown, *Hideout* is a sedate bar that just happens to be the center of Chicago's alternative country-music scene. A refreshing change to the crop of rather self-conscious bars, it attracts an eclectic, straight-talking, plain drinking (mostly beer) crowd for the almost nightly shows (which range from readings to film and documentary screenings).

Holiday Club **1471 N Milwaukee Ave, at N Honore St; ⓣ773/486-0686, ⓦwww.swingersmecca.com; Blue Line to Damen.** Recreating a Vegas-style lounge from the 1950s and 1960s, *Holiday* is one of Wicker Park's more popular nocturnal destinations and a self-proclaimed "swingers Mecca" (beyond the novelty theme there is scant evidence, but who knows). There's good bar food, drink specials several nights a week, and pool tables as well.

Leopard Lounge **1645 W Cortland Ave, at N Ashland Ave ⓣ773/862-7877; bus #73.** Clubby lounge bar that sees mainly Lincoln Park and Bucktown residents, who dress up a little to match the cool environs (like the big fish tank behind the bar) and for a chance to hook up. There's an outdoor garden and pool table and a fireplace, perfect for chilled, out winter's evenings.

Map Room **1949 N Hoyne Ave, at W Armitage Ave ⓣ773/252-7636; Blue Line to Western.** One of Bucktown's best bars, the *Map Room* offers a wide selection of beers (over one hundred varieties) in a travel-themed setting – bookshelves lined with *National Geographic*, guidebooks, and such, as well as Internet terminals. Crowded every night (there's usually some drink special on tap), the friendly, family-owned bar has live music on the weekend and a popular "international night" on Tuesday – a buffet focusing on a single country's cuisine; a couple of beers earns you a free plate. In the mornings it functions more as a coffee shop, a laid-back place to read and soak up the local vibe over coffee and bagels.

Marie's Rip-Tide Lounge 1745 W Armitage Ave, at N Hermitage Ave ⓣ773/278-7317; bus #73. A small, late-night tavern, which peaks after midnight, between Lincoln Park and Bucktown, that serves a mixed crowd – everyone from yuppies to blue-collar types to artist-wannabes and determined bar-crawlers who've been tossed out of every other tavern in the neighborhood. The staff – especially the adorably testy and cantankerous Marie herself, who has been part of the local scene since the 1960s – is part of its appeal. Have a beer or a straightforward mixed drink: this is far from trendy cocktail country.

Nick's Beergarden 1516 N Milwaukee Ave, at W North Ave ⓣ773/252-1155; Blue Line to Damen. Right under the El tracks, the rather slovenly *Nick's* succeeds largely because it's one of the few late-night bars in Wicker Park (open till 4am Sun–Fri, 5am on Sat). Still, it's a congenial place with a beer garden (open May–Nov) and live music (usually blues) on weekends. Most people don't start arriving until midnight, when the unusually large space fills up fast.

Northside Café 1635 N Damen Ave, at W Wabansia Ave ⓣ773/384-3555; Blue Line to Damen. While bars come and go in trendy Wicker Park and Bucktown, the gregarious and unbuttoned *Northside* has carved a lasting place for itself with its huge, mouth-watering burgers devoured by the largely beer-drinking crowds of young pretty people who fill the year-round outdoor patio.

Pontiac Café 1531 N Damen Ave ⓣ773/252-7767; Blue Line to Damen. One of the best bars in the city, this gritty former garage is the center of Wicker Park's outdoor drinking scene. Punkish, with an alternative vibe, it's one of the best places to people-watch on a sunny afternoon or get loaded before a show at the nearby *Double Door* (see p.222). Beer is the drink of choice, all bottled – Bud and other basics – the wine list minimal. It's also a good spot for lunch, the wholesome lentil salads, marinated slabs of Portobello sandwiches, and juicy burgers are better than they have any right to be.

Quencher's 2401 N Western Ave, at W Fullerton Ave ⓣ773/276-9730, ⓦwww.quenchers.com; bus #49, #74. This hip microbrewery in the northern reaches of Bucktown has been around since 1979, long before the trend hit the mainstream. There's an astonishing array of more than 200 beers (including everything from New Hampshire's Smutty nose Old Brown Dog Ale to the Brazilian Xingu Black), a good enough reason to brave the bar's semi-obnoxious party-hearty attitude. Live music every night.

Rainbo Club 1150 N Damen Ave, at W Division St ⓣ773/489-5999; bus #50. An old neighborhood standby that's become chic by virtue of its trendy Ukrainian Village location. Graced by artists past and present – including Nelson Algren – there is an authentically retro feel to the place (pinball machine and photo booth), complimented by both the above-average music that spans all genres and the inexpensive beers that satisfy all tastes. Lounging in the comfy booths, the crowd ranges from glam twentysomethings to boho students and hipster moms.

Subterranean 2011 W North Ave, at N Damen Ave ⓣ773/278-6600, ⓦwww.subt.net; Blue Line to Damen. One of the best bars around the six-corner intersection of N Milwaukee, W North, and N Damen aves, this one-time brothel and gambling house (thus the chandelier and ornate woodwork) is now a three-floor cabaret, lounge, and dance club, housed in a nineteenth-century building. The first floor, *The Lounge*, achieves a sexy, red-light-district vibe, while the two-floor *Cabaret* upstairs is a cool live-music venue featuring everything from reggae and hip-hop to house, Motown, and open music mics. There are drinks specials each night.

Lincoln Park

See map on p.116 for drinking locations.

Black Duck 1800 N Halsted ⓣ312/664-1801; Brown or Purple Line to Fullerton. Conveniently located for a pre/post Steppenwolf Theatre drink, the smart-casual, dimly lit *Black Duck* draws a post-work yuppie crowd during the week, while more frat-style groupings predominate on the weekend. The dining area to the rear serves reasonable food if you can bare the thick wafts of smoke and amped-up chatter and tunes.

Charlie's Ale House 1224 W Webster Ave ⓣ773/871-1440; Brown or Purple Line to Fullerton. Homely pub with intimate alcoves and plenty of deep mahogany, which is lightened by expansive mirrors. While the crowd can be a bit J Crew, *Charlie's* is still a great place to kick back with a few pints in the popular, vine-covered, outdoor garden-patio after a walk through Lincoln Park.

Delilah's 2771 N Lincoln Ave, at W Diversey Parkway ⓣ773/472-2771; Brown Line to Diversey. A resounding locals' favorite, *Delilah's* is out of place in sedate Lincoln Park, with all-black decor, punk rock on the jukebox, and cult movies that screen here on weekends. Featuring an extensive selection of over 200 whiskeys and over 150 types of beer, its main draw are the excellent djs spinning everything from classic punk to alt-country and R&B. Upstairs, there's a pool hall that's usually less crowded than the bar.

Glascott's 2158 N Halsted St, at W Dickens Ave ⓣ773/281-1205; Brown or Purple Line to Fullerton. Also known as *Glascott's Groggery*, this friendly neighborhood pub has been around since 1937, run by a family that's been in the business since the 1800s. Popular with baseball-cap-wearing, bar-hopping types.

Goodbar 2512 N Halsted St, at W Fullerton Ave ⓣ773/296-9700; Brown or Purple Line to Ful lerton. This funky tavern has stripped floors, gold and red fabrics, and ottomans drawing a young, attractive clientele. There is also an upstairs lounge and rooftop beer garden (open during the summer only). Alternative pop and rock is spun in the back of the bar during the week and the djs prefer hip-hop and house on the weekend.

Goose Island 1800 N Clybourn Ave, near N Sheffield Ave ⓣ312/915-0071, ⓦwww.gooseisland.com; Red Line to North/Clybourn. The rare case of a successful Chicago microbrewery – a huge, multi-level space that was once a warehouse, serving dozens of fabulous home brews (especially their crisp India pale ale). One of the first brewpubs in the US, and widely considered the best, there are tours of the brewery on Sundays at 3pm, which include a beer tasting. They also have a Wrigleyville location at 3535 N Clark (ⓣ773/832-9040).

▽ *John Barleycorn Memorial Pub*

John Barleycorn Memorial Pub 658 W Belden Ave, at N Lincoln Ave ⓣ773/348-8899, ⓦwww.johnbarleycorn.com; Brown or Purple Line to Fullerton. One of the city's most popular bars and beer gardens, this former speakeasy draws on a nautical theme to attract a mix of students from nearby DePaul University, young couples and families and beer lovers (more than thirty brews to choose from). Though it can get crowded on weekends, it's not uncomfortably so. There's another location near Wrigley at 3454 N Clark (ⓣ773/549-6000).

Liar's Club 1665 W Fullerton Ave, at N Clybourn Ave ⓣ773/665-1110; bus #73. Located in an industrial no-man's-land, the dark and decaying *Liar's Club* is a singles bar verging on a dance club, bathed in red lights, with everyone grooving to the Ramones or drum 'n' bass with a total lack of pretension. For more chilled ambience, there are pool tables and sofas on the second floor. The drinks are cheap and the weekend cover charge is just $5, although be prepared to wait a while to get in.

McGee's 950 W Webster Ave, at N Sheffield Ave ⓣ773/549-8200; Brown or Purple Line to Ful lerton. Beneath the El tracks, this Irish sports bar with dozens of TV screens, has cheap, cheap drinks and serves excellent pub food, but it's an overwhelmingly college/sports kind of place packing in the student crowds and twentysomething urban sophisticates.

Red Lion Pub 2446 N Lincoln Ave, at W Montana St ☎773/348-2695; Brown or Purple Line to Fullerton. A friendly English pub where you'd be comfortable dropping by solo. Claiming to be haunted, it has a host of dedicated regulars (many UK expats) and features a series of weekly readings (usually in the fantasy vein). English pub grub includes sausage rolls, beans on toast, and Welsh rarebit.

Walsh's Schubert Inn 1301 W Schubert Ave, at N Lakewood Ave ☎773/472-7738; bus #11. This fine North Side neighborhood tavern – located in a two-story house – has a facade typical of the homes in this area; it's easy to walk right past without noticing it. *Schubert's* boasts a convivial mix of young locals, business folk, and old-timers, and also has one of the nicer beer gardens in the city (walk through the service entrance, down the metal ramp).

Webster's Wine Bar 1480 W Webster Ave, at N Clybourn Ave ☎773/868-0608. In a surprising location, this candlelit bar with a European ambience is a relaxing spot for a glass of wine – choose from the monumental list (35 wines available by the glass, over 400 served by the bottle), which includes excellent themed two-ounce sample servings if you are struggling to commit. The knowledgeable and friendly staff is always willing and able to help you choose. It's a very popular spot with young couples who pair off in the dim lighting among the book-covered walls. There are some better-than-average appetizers, like the exceptional pear and brie quesadilla, salads, sandwiches, and cheese platters.

Lakeview, Wrigleyville, and Andersonville

See map on p.123 for drinking locations.

Cubby Bear 1059 W Addison St, at N Clark St ☎773/327-1662; Red Line to Addison. Opened in 1953, the spacious, crowded, and loud *Cubby Bear* would be just another sports bar if it weren't for Wrigley Field across the street. When the Cubs are in town, the twelve 32" TVs and two large projectors turn on and the crowds squeeze in to down the beer specials of the day soaked up with greasy wings, dripping Italian beef sandwiches, and succulent burgers. They also have a sporadic line-up of live touring rock and hip-hop groups.

Cullen's Bar & Grill 3741 N Southport Ave, at W Waveland Ave ☎773/975-0600; Brown Line to Southport. One of the favored night spots in the burgeoning Southport Avenue corridor, this boisterous Irish pub draws young groups of Lakeview professionals with its welcoming staff, above-average pub food (try the delectable mashed potatoes), and live Celtic music several nights a week. There's also outdoor seating in warm weather.

Duke of Perth 2913 N Clark St, at W Oakdale Ave ☎773/477-1741; bus #22. The city's only Scottish pub, with more than seventy kinds of single-malt Scotch whiskey, all-you-can-eat fish'n'chips on Wednesday and Friday ($9.20), and a full line-up of Scotch delicacies like leek pie and Scotch eggs. All pints of beer are $3.50 on Thursdays. The staff is enthusiastic and the atmosphere is relaxed and unassuming. During summertime, the beer garden is a perfect retreat.

Ginger Man 3740 N Clark St, at N Racine Ave ☎773/549-2050; Red Line to Addison. One of the only defiantly non-sports-related drinking establishments in Wrigleyville, next to the Metro music theater. This no-frills bar has pool tables in the back room, an absence of screaming Cubs fans, over fifty bottled beers, and a cool, rocker vibe.

Hopleaf Bar 5148 N Clark St ☎773/334-9851. If you are looking for a spot in Uptown or Andersonville, be sure to stop by this stellar North Side bar, sporting one of the most extensive beer selections in Chicago (over 200 to choose from, half of which are Belgian). The decor, with European vintage posters, also takes its inspiration from the country with one of the finest beer cultures and even the food pays homage with wonderful steamed mussels served with fries, duck, and gooey Gruyère cheese and ham sandwiches. With no TV, conversation reigns, and there's even a good selection of magazines for those drinking alone.

Hye Bar 3707 N Southport Ave, at W Waveland Ave ☎773/244-4102; Brown Line to Southport. A wise stop on a Southport bar hop, this dark-mahogany-furnished neighborhood joint is given a slightly Irish flavor by virtue of the beers on tap and hospitable bartenders. Mainly a young professional hangout, the place also draws Cubs fans from nearby Wrigleyville. "Car bombs" (a whiskey shot in a pint of Guinness) are so popular here that the staff may even join you for one.

The Irish Oak 3511 N Clark St ⓣ773/935-6669; Red Line to Addison. This Irish pub – the entire establishment was designed and made in Ireland and shipped over – with less than a decade under its belt has quickly become a local favorite. Located near Wrigley Field, it's a pleasant alternative to the raucous sports bars on game days, and features live music on Thursday, Friday, and Saturday, plus great shepherd's pie, 25¢ wings on Mondays, and all-you-can-eat fish 'n' chips on Friday.

Jacks/404 Wine bar 2856 N Southport Ave ⓣ773/404-4619; Brown Line to Diversey. Doubling as a lively sports bar and smart, low-key wine bar, this is a down-to-earth locals' bar befitting most moods. In the *404* wine bar, cozy leather sofas, wooden tables with tea candles, three fireplaces, and bookcases offer a relaxing place to peruse the extensive wine list and nibble on paired cheese and fruit platters, salads, and thin-crust pizzas. Next door, in the more upbeat sports bar, you can play pool, watch a game on the large-screen TV, and munch on classic burgers, sandwiches, quesadillas, brownies, and ice cream.

Jet Vodka Lounge 1551 N Sheffield Ave ⓣ312/730-4395; Red Line to Belmont. As the name suggests, over 130 different kinds of vodka (try the vodka flights) are served in a crisp, bright white aviation-themed space, where "flight attendants" strut along the aisle to a mega-decibel hip-hop, dance, and house music soundtrack spun by djs ensconced in corner booths. Youthful crowd and expensive covers ($5–20) most evenings after 10pm.

Pops For Champagne 2934 N Sheffield Ave, at W Oakdale Ave ⓣ773/472-1000, ⓦwww.popschampagne.com; Red Line to Belmont. This sophisticated jazz bar – a destination on special occasions – has been pouring more than a hundred kinds of Champagne, and liquor, too, since 1982. Prices range from $11.50 per glass to sky high, and while there's not an official dress code, *Pops* pitches itself at those who like to sprinkle some "class" over their evening forays – leave the jeans and sandals behind.

Redmond's 3358 N Sheffield Ave, at W Roscoe St ⓣ773/404-2151; Red Line to Belmont. A world apart from the traditional sports bar, this upscale, uplifting place with welcoming staff, offers a full menu of comfort food dishes, including ribs, mac and cheese, and Guinness stew, plush booths, and 30-some beers. Sample them in the outdoor patio area.

Resi's Bierstube 2034 W Irving Park, at N Lincoln and N Damen aves ⓣ773/472-1749. Located beyond Lakeview's northern reaches, *Resi's* is worth the trek if you're looking to immerse yourself in some hearty German ambience – this bar is hard to beat. Choose from more than thirty Bavarian beers on tap, 150 bottles of imported beer, and fifteen *Weiss* (wheat beers). There's also a veritable smorgasbord of bratwurst, knackwurst, schnitzel, and wieners while surrounded by Oktoberfest posters and souvenirs. There's also a pleasant beer garden out back.

Sheffield's Wine and Beer Garden 3258 N Sheffield Ave, at W Belmont Ave ⓣ773/281-4989; Red Line to Belmont. When the weather's warm, lines wrap around the entrance of this leafy outdoor beer garden for the fine assortment of wines and beers (20 drafts, plus bottles). The indoor bar is intimate with lots of nooks and crannies in which to hide away.

Simon's Tavern 5210 N Clark St, at W Foster Ave ⓣ773/878-0894; bus #22. This former speakeasy, now an aged Swedish bar (dig the Viking-style decorations and hunting paraphernalia), has a beautiful, long wooden bar and good Andersonville neighborhood cred. The friendly staff, full of historical info, tend to a crowd that's a mix of Swedes, gays and lesbians, and people who come for a slice of chilled-out, Chicago-style conversation and excellent deals on cocktails.

Tiny Lounge 1814 W Addison St ⓣ773/296-9620; Brown Line to Addison. Improbably located under the Addison El stop, this smart and aptly named lounge bar serves killer Martinis – try the heady Bubbleini made with Champagne, triple sec, peach schnapps, and garnished with a cherry. Arrive before 9pm for a leather booth or when it gets snug pitch up on one of the comfy, velvety bar stools. Votive candles, black velvet drapes, a frosted glass unisex bathroom, and a VIP-style back room with scarlet sofas and ottomans all add to the intimate, urban cool. Live music on a Wednesday features the acoustic talents of former Swimmer lead singer, Nicolas Barron.

The West Side

See map on p.131 for drinking locations.

Betty's Blue Star Lounge 1600 W Grand Ave, at N Ashland Ave ☎312/243-8778; Green Line to Ashland. A barebones, late-night bar (until 4am during the week, 5am on Saturdays) and live music venue that brings in a hip but relaxed crowd for the cheap beers and the soulful ambience. Live music tends to focus on hip-hop and house courtesy of local djs and musicians, and weekends bring a carnival dance party vibe with hard-core revellers showing up and picking up the pace around midnight.

Jaks Tap 901 W Jackson Blvd, at S Peoria St ☎312/666-1700; Blue Line to UIC/Halsted. Forty draft beers (Bellhaven to Warsteiner) and an extensive brewpub menu are the highlights of this University of Illinois-Chicago area bar. Exposed brick walls and lots of gleaming wood add to the atmosphere. The bar food is a cut above average drawing local workers at lunchtime. Decent pizzas will satisfy the late-night munchies.

Matchbox 770 N Milwaukee Ave, at N Ogden Ave ☎312/666-9292; Blue Line to Damen. Be prepared to get up close and personal with some of Chicago's most idiosyncratic locals at this slender bar – one of the smallest and most intriguing places in the city. The very tight space, excellent Martinis, and friendly atmosphere make for a fun, communal experience.

Plush 1104 W Madison ☎312/491-9800; Brown or Purple Line to Fullerton. An unpretentious lounge bar with a playfully decadent vibe complete with velvet sofas, and decorated in lavish tones of gold and crimson. Middle Eastern overtures include fragrant hookahs and belly-dancing nights on Tuesdays. Martinis and Champagne are the libations of choice. There is also a dinner menu featuring global-fusion dishes.

Tasting Room 1415 W Randolph St, at N Ogden Ave ☎312/942-1212. A two-story, tastefully decorated wine bar complete with sofas and armchairs that's more about the wine than the ambience, *the Tasting Room* employs several sommeliers to help visitors with their choices which can be paired with tasty appetizers (from cheese selections, including global cheese tasters to pizzas, to meat and seafood plates). Don't miss the great views of the skyline from the second floor. The wine is also available for purchase in the Randolph Wine Cellars, attached to the bar.

South Side and Hyde Park

See map on p.138 for drinking locations.

The Cove Lounge 1750 E 55th St, at S Everett Ave ☎773/684-1013. A Hyde Park hole-in-the-wall that caters mainly to a handful of regulars, except on Thursday nights when crowds of UC students take full advantage of the $4 pitchers. Not the best, but a reliable option in a surprisingly bar-free zone.

Jimbo's 3258 S Princeton Ave, at W 33rd St ☎312/326-3253; Red Line to Sox/35th. A no-frills neighborhood bar that succeeds because of its proximity to Comiskey Park. It's usually packed with Sox fans before and after games as it's one of the only places to drink near the park.

Jimmy's Woodlawn Tap 1172 E 55th St, at S Woodlawn Ave ☎773/643-5516. Referred to strictly as "Jimmy's" after the bar's late owner, this dimly lit bar is an oasis for locals and students alike, who love its bookish airs and cheap drinks and burgers. With just three smoky, unadorned rooms, two bars carrying a modest selection of beer and liquor, and a lone pinball machine, it's the kind of place to "hear and be heard."

Keegan's Pub 10618 S Western Ave, at W 106th St ☎773/233-6829. Wood-panelled walls, flags, portraits of Irish writers, finely poured Guinness, a fireplace, and fervor for the White Sox are the name of the game at this classic neighborhood joint in Beverly, the South-Side Irish enclave. It's a friendly enough drinking den even if the staff is not overly excited to wait on a new face and certainly the best bet for a drink if you are heading to a Sox game.

Rogers Park and North Shore

See map on p.157 for drinking locations.

Moody's Pub 5910 N Broadway, at W Rosedale Ave ☎773/275-2696; Red Line

to Thorndale. Far up north lies this little gem, an intimate dim-lit bar with a medieval aura, hidden behind chunky wooden doors. It oozes charm and serves a prime selection of beer and refreshing summertime cocktails. In winter, punters hang out by the fireplace munching burgers (highly recommended) and slurping hot chocolate, while in summer the languorous beer garden has been known to suck people in for entire afternoons.

16

Live music and clubs

Being the crossroads that it is, Chicago has one of the best **music scenes** in the US, often reflecting the changing musical landscape of the country as a whole. From the early days of jazz and blues to the rise of alternative rock in the mainstream, Chicago has made its mark, albeit in its characteristically down-to-earth way.

Although Louis Armstrong and scores of other top musicians brought jazz from New Orleans in the early 1920s, Chicago's musical identity is rooted in the **blues**; indeed, Chicago is considered the capital of modern electric blues. During the genre's heyday in the mid-twentieth century, blues clubs lined the streets of Chicago's South Side around the influential Chess Records studio (see p.105), where blues legends Muddy Waters, Willie Dixon, Junior Wells, and Koko Taylor all recorded. Economic forces have more or less pushed – or pulled – blues clubs from the South Side to the city's North Side, and on an average weeknight, you'll find five or six different blues acts performing in Near North and Lincoln Park alone. One would think **jazz** would be bigger in Chicago than it is; what it lacks in size, though, it more than makes up for in quality, with serious crooners like six-time Grammy nominee Kurt Elling and Patricia Barber performing locally on a regular basis. Indeed, finding live jazz on any night of the week won't be hard – a visit to premier jazz club *Green Mill* deserves at least a night (see p.221).

Besides blues and jazz, Chicago has a burgeoning **alternative rock** scene that came of age in the 1990s, with breakthroughs early in the decade by the Smashing Pumpkins and Liz Phair, followed more recently by Wilco, champions of the now-established **alternative country** (or "alt country") scene which popped up in the late 1990s. As far as dance music goes, **house** and **techno** basically started in Chicago in the mid-1980s, and that's what you'll hear in many of the dance clubs, which thump till the wee hours, mostly on Thursday through Sunday nights. Indeed, the legacy of Chicago house djs like Frankie Knuckles and Marshall Jefferson is so strong that in 2005, Mayor Richard M. Daley declared August 10 "House Unity Day" to commemorate the birthplace of the genre. In the past few years, the city's **hip-hop** scene has gained serious cred, too, and taken a foothold in the city's dance clubs thanks to smash albums from Grammy-winning producer and performer Kanye West and veteran local rapper Common. The venues in Chicago are another distinction: the city has some of the country's best **rock halls**, many of them former movie palaces and theaters converted into concert spaces. Just about every major American band, it seems, includes the city on their itineraries, and you'll be able to hear them here for not much more than $25 a ticket.

As for a sampling of where to go: **Near North**, **Lincoln Park**, and **Lakeview** have the highest concentration of blues and dance clubs; **Bucktown** and

Getting tickets

The most convenient way to buy **tickets** is through a ticket agency like Ticketmaster (☎312/559-1212, www.ticketmaster.com), though be prepared to pay a fee on top of the ticket price. You can also go to the venue's box office and save yourself the fee.

Expect to pay $5–12 for tickets to shows at small clubs like the *Double Door* and *Schubas*; $15–35 at mid-sized venues like *Metro*, *The Vic*, *The Aragon*, and $30 and up at stadiums like the United Center and the Allstate Arena. Bear in mind that bars and clubs strictly enforce the legal **drinking age** (21), and you won't be admitted without **proper ID** (a driver's license or passport).

Wicker Park cater to alternative and indie rockers, while rock 'n' roll can be heard just about anywhere there's a stage and a tap. Ethnic and world music get their due at venues like *HotHouse* and *Old Town School of Folk Music*, as do gospel, hip-hop, reggae, samba, and country.

For **current music listings**, pick up the excellent free weekly *Chicago Reader* – copies come out Thursday afternoon in street boxes and bookstores all over town and are usually all gone by Saturday. Other good free sources include the weekly *New City* and the gay and lesbian *Windy City Times*. Full listings also appear in the Friday issues of the *Chicago Sun-Times* and the *Chicago Tribune*, and *Chicago* magazine has useful arts and restaurant listings. The Gramaphone Ltd **record store**, at 2843 N Clark St (☎773/472-3683), is the best place for details on one-off **dance** nights.

Major concert venues

Allstate Arena 6920 N Mannheim Rd, Rosemont ☎847/635-6601; Blue Line to River Road, transfer to Regional Transportation Authority (RTA) bus #221 or #222. $15 parking for concerts. Soulless, out-of-the-way stadium northwest of Chicago in Rosemont, pulling in big-name concerts, with seating for 18,000-plus.

Jay Pritzker Pavilion Randolph Street and Michigan Avenue, in Millennium Park ☎312/742-1168; Green, Brown, Orange, or Purple Line to Randolph. Intricate, Frank Gehry–designed outdoor stage and lawn that plays host to free seasonal concerts, including the Grant Park Music Festival and September's World Music Festival. For details, see Chapter 21, "Festivals and events."

Petrillo Music Shell Columbus Drive and Jackson Blvd, in Grant Park; Red Line to Jackson. Multi-purpose outdoor stage and lawn in the Loop, often used for free summer concerts – notably the Chicago Blues Festival (see p.256). If you want to see the performers, get a seat near the stage; otherwise just camp out on the lawn with a blanket.

Ravinia Festival Ravinia Park Road, Highland Park ☎847/266-5100; reachable via Metra train (Union Pacific North Line). A Chicago gem, this performance complex is located on the North Shore about 25 miles north of the Loop. Just a fifteen-minute ride on the Metra commuter train (board at the Ogilvie Transportation Center and get off at the Ravinia Park stop), the pavilion makes for the most intimate outdoor music venue in summer, featuring top acts of nearly every musical genre, with numerous performances by the Chicago Symphony Orchestra. Bring a picnic and sit on the lawn or buy a ticket for a seat in the pavilion (there are also concerts in the two small theaters). Ticket prices vary, though usually not less than $15.

United Center 1901 W Madison St, West Side ☎312/455-4500; public transportation not recommended for safety reasons. Home to the Chicago Bulls and Blackhawks, this stadium on the sketchy side of the neighborhood also draws superstar music acts. With a 20,000-plus capacity, it's not the most intimate place to hear music by any stretch, but if you want to see the top performers, you'll go.

△ Live blues at Lincoln Park's *B.L.U.E.S*

Blues

Some sixty **blues clubs** are scattered throughout the city, most of them small, loud, smoky, and adorned with all manner of blues memorabilia. Chicago blues was born on the South Side (see Contexts, p.289), and for true aficionados, a visit to one of the few remaining clubs there is almost mandatory – though take care, as the area can be sketchy, especially after dark. That said, excellent blues can also be heard in any number of clubs right in the heart of the city, and many bars and clubs include live blues acts in their line-ups. Names to watch out for include Son Seals, Vance Kelly, Melvin Taylor, and Buddy Guy – any one of these bluesmen can put on a powerhouse show.

Cover charges range from next to nothing to about $25, depending, usually, on the club's proximity to the tourist circuit; some require a two-drink minimum. If you happen to be around in the summer, there are plenty of outdoor music concerts to be had, including June's massive Chicago Blues Festival (see p.256). The city also runs neighborhood blues and gospel **tours** from time to time; for details. (For more on blues history, see Contexts, p.289.)

Blue Chicago 536 N Clark St, at W Ohio St ⓣ312/661-0100 and 736 N Clark St, at Superior St ⓣ312/642-6261, ⓦwww.bluechicago.com; Red Line to Grand. Touristy blues joints featuring mostly female vocalists – they won't disappoint if you're looking for a blues scene close to the Near North hotels – there's almost always one loud, audience-involved rendition of *Sweet Home Chicago*. The $8 cover charge gets you into both clubs, the smaller of which (no. 536) is not much bigger than a closet.

B.L.U.E.S. 2519 N Halsted St, Lincoln Park ⓣ773/528-1012; Brown or Red Line to Fullerton. Open since the 1970s, this intimate club has hosted all the greats, and has live blues every night of the week. They sometimes have deals with *Kingston Mines* across the street (see p.220). The cover on weekends is around $10, less on weekdays.

Buddy Guy's Legends 754 S Wabash Ave, South Loop ⓣ312/427-0333; Red Line to Harrison. This large club, owned by the veteran guitarist and vocalist, has great acoustics and atmosphere, and live blues every night (Guy himself has an extended stint each January). The roster features new talent and established greats, and though somewhat touristy it's worth dropping by, if only because it's a classic. Monday nights are jam nights. Covers range from $8 to $12 during the week, $15 to $25 on weekends.

House of Blues 330 N Dearborn St, Near North ⓣ312/527-2583, ⓦwww.hob.com; Red Line to Grand. Despite its name, this swish concert venue puts on all kinds of music, including blues, but with a schedule of mostly touring acts, you won't find much local flavor here. The acoustics are phenomenal and the waitstaff attentive, though, and the popular Sunday Gospel Brunch ($41.50) alone merits a visit. Concert tickets start around $17.

Kingston Mines 2548 N Halsted St, Lincoln Park ⓣ773/472-2031; Brown or Red Line to Fullerton. Opened in 1968, this Chicago blues staple is one of the city's oldest blues clubs, appropriately dark, loud, and smoke-filled. It's packed every night and consistently delivers some of the finest blues around. Bands alternate on two stages, keeping up a constant stream of music throughout the evening; big names perform till 5am on Saturdays. Cover $12–15.

Lee's Unleaded Blues 7401 S Chicago Ave, South Side ⓣ773/493-3477. Small, friendly juke joint in one of the most rough-and-tumble parts of the city. About twenty blocks south of the University of Chicago, *Lee's* does attract a student or two, but mostly it's staple for locals who come for a nightly (except Mondays, when the bar is closed) dose of classic blues, jazz, or R&B. Best to come here by car or taxi.

Rosa's Lounge 3420 W Armitage Ave, West Side ⓣ773/342-0452. Run by an Italian mother-and-son duo, *Rosa's* is a soulful, welcoming, and excellent blues club, with a solid calendar of shows (Tues–Sat). The only drawback is the location: it's about thirty blocks west of downtown, so you'll need a taxi. Tuesdays with Melvin Taylor, one of Chicago's unsung guitar virtuosos, are a highlight. Covers vary ($5–15).

Underground Wonder Bar 10 E Walton St, Near North ⓣ312/266-7761; Red Line to Chicago. Cramped subterranean bar (not for lightweights or wallflowers) with live music 365 days a year, ranging from blues and jazz to reggae, performed well into the wee small hours (until 4am during the week and 5am on Saturdays). A bit dark and louche, in a good way. Impromptu celebrity appearances have been known to happen, but more likely you will catch a performance from owner Lonie Walker and the Big Ass Company Band. If it's your birthday, beware. Cover charges ($5–10) apply.

Jazz

Jazz clubs are, by no means, as abundant in Chicago as they are in New York, and a good portion of the jazz that Chicago hears happens in bars not entirely devoted to the genre. On the other hand, two clubs easily hold their own against the country's best: the historic *Green Mill* in Uptown and *Jazz Showcase*, in Near North, the spot for renowned jazz artists passing through town.

Andy's 11 E Hubbard St, Near North ⓣ312/642-6805; Red Line to Grand. A casual fixture on Chicago's jazz scene, popular for its lunchtime concerts and Monday-night improv jam sessions. While many Chicago bars offer occasional "jazz" trios and such, *Andy's* is devoted entirely to jazz – traditional, mainstream, and bebop. The crowd is a mix of drinkers, jazz lovers, and diners here for the menu of pizza, ribs, steaks, and seafood. Mon–Fri 6.30pm–midnight, Sat till 1am. Cover $5–10.

Chicago Cultural Center 78 E Washington St, the Loop ⓣ312/346-3278; Red Line to Washington. Home to the city's main visitor center (see p.50), this splendid old building also has gallery spaces where classical and jazz groups host weekly free lunchtime and evening concerts. The crowd is a real mix – suits on lunchbreak, travelers, and music lovers in the know.

The Cotton Club 1710 S Michigan Ave, South Loop ⓣ312/341-9787; Green or Red Line to Roosevelt. Venue that attracts two crowds: a mellow, older set for jazz and blues in the Cab Calloway front room, and a younger group for hip-hop and step-dancing in the Gray room in the back. Definitely a people-watching scene, with everyone decked out in their finest duds (think Zoot suits). Modest cover. Mon–Fri till 4am, Sat till 5am.

Green Dolphin Street 2200 N Ashland Ave, Lincoln Park ⓣ773/395-0066, ⓦwww.jazzitup.com. This sophisticated and casually elegant restaurant and jazz bar attracts a mixed crowd. The music, depending on the night, could be anything from Afro-Cuban to big band. Kick back with a cigar from the floor-to-ceiling humidor or tuck into the eclectic menu (see p.196).

Green Mill 4802 N Broadway, Uptown ⓣ773/878-5552, ⓦwww.greenmilljazz.com; Red Line to Lawrence. This former speakeasy and Al Capone haunt is pure Jazz Age Chicago and should not be missed. Though far from downtown, it's the most revered jazz club in the city, both for its acts, which range from bebop to progressive jazz as well as a notable weekly poetry slam, as well as its atmosphere – the beautiful interior still retains its period charm. Open till 4am. Cover varies, usually around $5.

Jazz Showcase 59 W Grand Ave, Near North ⓣ312/670-BIRD, ⓦwww.jazzshowcase.com; Red Line to Grand. If you're looking for top talent and are willing to pay a hefty cover, then the late Chicago music mogul Joe Segal's place might be for you. Since 1947, it's been the venue of choice for mainstream jazz artists, from Gillespie to Hargrove and Brubeck. Shows at 8pm & 10pm Tues–Thurs, 9pm & 11pm on Fri and Sat, and 4pm, 8pm & 10pm on Sun. Students get a discount. $20–25, cash only.

Velvet Lounge 2128 1/2 S Indiana Ave, Near South ⓣ312/791-9050, ⓦwww.velvetlounge.net. This relaxed tavern run by Chicago jazz institution Fred Anderson has live jazz five nights a week, and is a good place to catch the more exploratory side of recent Chi-town jazz. Open-mic nights on Sundays 5–9pm.

Rock

One look at the music listings in *The Reader* will reveal dozens of **rock bands** performing any night of the week, mostly on the city's North Side in Lincoln Park, Lakeview, and Wicker Park. Catching a show in one of the rock halls is a quintessential Chicago experience, especially at venues like *Metro*, *The Riviera*, or *The Vic*. For smaller shows in more down-to-earth surroundings, Wicker Park's *Double Door* and *The Empty Bottle* in the Ukrainian Village offer some of the best in the city.

The bigger venues

The Aragon Ballroom 1106 W Lawrence Ave, at N Broadway, Uptown; ⓣ773/561-9500, ⓦwww.aragon.com; Red Line to Lawrence. The acoustics may be wanting at this 5000-seat behemoth, but the ornate decor and size (room for 4000-plus) keep it on Chicago's short list of top, mid-sized concert venues.

The Congress Theatre 2135 N Milwaukee Ave, Bucktown ⓣ773/252-4000, ⓦwww.congresschicago.com; Blue Line to Western. This former movie palace with Gothic trimmings now attracts mainly indie and punk acts, popular djs, and a smattering of up-and-coming rock acts. Cover charges vary.

Metro 3730 N Clark St, Lakeview ⓣ773/549-0203, ⓦwww.metrochicago.com; Red Line to Addison. This club's excellent acoustics and reputation as a top venue for national and local indie acts pull in Chicago's party crowds. The *Smart Bar*, in the same building, is a dance club (see p.224).

Park West 322 W Armitage Ave, at N Clark St, Lincoln Park; ⓣ773/929-5959, ⓦwww.parkwestchicago.com. Spacious standby that tends to host mellow solo artists and troubadours and the sensitive folks who follow them.

The Riviera Theatre 4746 N Racine Ave, Uptown ⓣ773/275-6800, ⓦwww.rivieratheatre.com; Red Line to Lawrence. Part of this area's music triumvirate (joining *Aragon* and *Green Mill*), the aging but characterful *Riviera* hosts major rock acts. Always nice to catch some jazz at the *Green Mill* after a concert here.

The Vic 3145 N Sheffield Ave, Lakeview ⓣ773/472-0449, ⓦwww.victheatre.com; Brown or Red Line to Belmont. Huge former vaudeville theater that now sees a steady flow of popular rock, folk, and comedy acts. A great place to catch a show – the acoustics are good and there's ample space to stand (on the floor) or sit (in the balcony). The only drawback is its tendency to be louder and sweatier than most other venues. Also hosts "Brew & View," movie screenings accompanied by beer and pizza (see p.232), when there's not a concert on.

The smaller clubs

Cubby Bear 1059 W Addison St, at N Clark St, Wrigleyville ⓣ773/327-1662, ⓦwww.cubbybear.com; Red Line to Addison. Busy by day with crowds from neighboring Wrigley Field, this boisterous sports bar features alternative rock bands after dark (Wed–Sat), though music takes a backseat to the sports scene. Cover $5–7.

The Double Door 1572 N Milwaukee Ave, Wicker Park ⓣ773/489-3160, ⓦwww.doubledoor.com; Blue Line to Damen. This club has been on top of the alternative music scene since it opened in 1994; its stage has been graced by a who's who of rock acts, from Smashing Pumpkins and Veruca Salt to Liz Phair and even the Rolling Stones. There's usually some indie band playing on most nights; the crowd is very Wicker Park (unshaven, consignment-store dress, messy hair), and there are pool tables downstairs if the music gets too loud. Covers vary, though it's usually half what the big North Side music venues charge.

Elbo Room 2871 N Lincoln Ave, Lakeview ⓣ773/549-5549, ⓦwww.elboroomchicago.com; Brown Line to Diversey. Known around Chicago as the place where band Liquid Soul got their start, this easygoing venue has lost a bit of its edge over the years, though it still puts on music most nights of the week, from ska and alternative rock to funk and acid jazz.

The Empty Bottle 1035 N Western Ave, at W Cortez St, Ukrainian Village ⓣ773/276-3600, ⓦwww.emptybottle.com; Blue Line to Division. A hole-in-the-wall club that showcases some top talent, ranging from up-and-coming indie bands to avant-garde jazz and progressive country. Truly loud (earplugs sold at the bar), though rarely overfilled and always enjoyable, with a crowd that's just as all over the map (hip college kids, urban yuppies, slacker twentysomethings) as the music.

The Note 1565 N Milwaukee Ave, Wicker Park ⓣ773/489-0011, ⓦwww.thenotechicago.com; Blue Line to Damen. Music venue that survives more on its location than from the talent performing on its stages, which is a bit of everything, including jazz, reggae, hip-hop, funk, and salsa (Tues–Sat). There's a pool table in the front room if you want to cool down between sets.

Schubas Tavern 3159 N Southport Ave, Lakeview ⓣ773/525-2508, ⓦwww.schubas.com; Brown Line to Belmont. A small mainstay of the neighborhood, booking an impressive roster of rock, alternative country, and roots revival bands. The intimate setting and wide range of up-and-coming acts make this a great place to see a show. The bar in front is very popular between sets and on weekends; the side room, *Harmony Grill*, serves up tasty American fare. Fri till 2am, Sat till 3am. Cover varies.

Folk, country, and world music

Chicago's **world music** scene is surprisingly healthy, with Irish and rootsy folk music leading the list. Almost any of the neighborhood taverns will have Irish or Celtic music on weekends, especially on Sundays, while a smaller number put on some form of **country** or **folk music**. The South Loop's *HotHouse* and the *Old Town School of Folk Music*, northwest of Lakeview (see p.223), are perhaps the city's best venues for world-music lovers – their diverse concert offerings range from Afrobeat and Latin dance to local hip-hop and Caribbean jazz.

While we've listed some excellent venues below, note that many of them are somewhat out of the way.

Abbey Pub 3420 W Grace St at N Elston Ave, Old Irving Park ⓣ773/478-4408, ⓦwww.abbeypub.com; Blue Line to Addison. One of Chicago's unsung supporters of aspiring musicians and new music, with live performances every night (Irish music on Sun). The only drawback is its location in Old Irving Park, northwest of Lakeview. Covers vary.

Equator Club 4715 N Broadway, Uptown ⓣ773/728-2411; Red Line to Lawrence. Former speakeasy owned by Al Capone now features live African and Caribbean music, sometimes by internationally recognized recording artists.

Exodus II 3477 N Clark St, Wrigleyville ⓣ773/348-3998; Red Line to Addison. Across the street from the *Wild Hare* (see below), this smaller, lesser-known reggae venue is less crowded and also a bit seedier, but if reggae's your thing, chances are you'll overlook the drawbacks. Rarely a cover.

FitzGerald's 6615 W Roosevelt Rd, Berwyn ⓣ708/788-2118, ⓦwww.fitzgeraldsnightclub.com; Blue Line to Harlem. Excellent venue for alternative country, Cajun, and zydeco, but it's way out in the western suburb of Berwyn and hard to reach without a car. The club has live music every night, and despite the location, it's right alongside the *Abbey*, *Schubas*, and the *Double Door* – the cream of Chicago's small-scale music venues.

Hideout 1354 W Wabansia Ave ⓣ773/227-4433, ⓦwww.hideoutchicago.com; Red Line to North/Clybourn. This small, eclectic roots and country-music bar is located two blocks north of North Avenue, in a no-man's-land east of Bucktown and Wicker Park; best to call for directions. The music might as well be right in your lap and the crowd relishes the club's low profile. Fri till 2am, Sat till 3am.

HotHouse 31 E Balbo Drive, at S Wabash Ave, South Loop ⓣ312/362-9707, ⓦwww.hothouse.net; Red Line to Harrison. Not your typical live music venue but a not-for-profit performing arts center that usually has a great line-up of world music and some jazz, blues, and folk. Two-drink minimum; Fri till 2am, Sat till 3am.

Kitty O'Shea's 720 S Michigan Ave, South Loop ⓣ312/294-6860; Brown Line to Harrison. Inside the *Hilton Chicago and Towers*, this great Irish pub offers Irish music most nights, starting at 9.30pm. The crowd is a mix of hotel guests and conventioneers, as well as a few discerning locals. Daily 11am–2am.

Martyr's 3855 N Lincoln Ave ⓣ773/404-9494, ⓦwww.martyrslive.com; Brown Line to Irving Park. Restaurant and bar offering an eclectic roster of live entertainment by touring artists, with traditional Irish music on Monday and open-mic rockabilly on the first Thursday of each month.

Old Town School of Folk Music 4544 N Lincoln Ave, Lincoln Square ⓣ773/728-6000, ⓦwww.oldtownschool.org; Brown Line to Western. Fabulous school and concert space in Lincoln Square (east of Uptown) for one of the city's enduring folk music traditions. Folk isn't all you'll hear, though; you might catch a concert of merengue or Western swing, or performances of African dance. Concerts start around 7pm, and tickets range from $5 to $25. Its curriculum of music classes (everything from fiddle to African drums) is the best in the city.

Wild Hare and Singing Armadillo Frog Sanctuary 3530 N Clark St, Wrigleyville ⓣ773/327-4273, ⓦwww.wildharereggae.com; Red Line to Addison. Chicago's premier venue for reggae. There's no cover before 9pm, and the whole place feels like a Jamaican dancehall and gets packed and sweaty. Smoking not allowed.

Dance clubs

Chicago's **club life** is ever-changing, with new venues popping up all the time, especially in the old warehouses west of the Loop. In fact, the city owes its thriving club scene to the birth of house music here during the early 1980s. Many of those warehouses have since evolved into extravagant dance clubs, with velvet couches, VIP rooms, mega-dancefloors, and expensive lighting and sound systems. You don't have to haunt the clubs to hear top djs, though – many of the late-night bars and lounges downtown have resident djs spinning on weekend nights. These days, the "hot" club of the moment seems almost arbitrary – rather confusing given that they all offer, more or less, the same thing. In general, the larger and more ostentatious the club, the younger the crowd; the smaller, lesser known clubs tend to attract a late 20s and early 30s crowd with their more intimate settings.

Cover charges range from $5 to $25, and dress is typically upscale. Do not wear jeans or athletic shoes, or you're likely to be turned away at the door. Also, be prepared for long waits to get in ($10–20 will usually persuade a bouncer to let you in immediately, though).

The clubs listed below have proven their staying power and are also among the best; if in doubt, or looking for the new hot thing, consult any number of the listings sections mentioned at the beginning of the chapter.

Betty's Blue Star Lounge 1600 W Grand Ave, at N Ashland Ave, West Side ⓣ312/243-1699, ⓦwww.bettysbluestarlounge.com. Casual bar/club that transforms into a raging after-hours hot spot for a twenty- and thirtysomething crowd. Up-and-coming and established djs spin funk, dub, classic house and hip-hop every night of the week, and cheap drinks pull in both clubbers and some serious drinkers. Sun–Fri 7am–4am, Sat 11am–5am. Take a cab there and back.

Crobar 1543 N Kingsbury St, west of Old Town ⓣ312/266-1900, ⓦwww.crobar.com; Red Line to North/Clybourn. Hyper-trendy warehouse club near the river, spinning old-school house, techno, and hip-hop from standout resident djs like Felix da Housecat. More exclusive than the other big-name clubs – without ostentatious dress you may be turned away at the door. Thurs, Fri & Sun 10pm–4am, Sat till 5am.

Excalibur 632 N Dearborn St, Near North ⓣ312/266-1944; Red Line to Grand. An institution in the city, and quite touristy because of it – not to mention for its location – blasting rock, techno, and R&B on several floors; Thursdays are dedicated to Latin music.

Funky Buddha Lounge 728 W Grand Ave, West Side ⓣ312/666-1695, ⓦwww.funkybuddha.com; Blue Line to Grand. Small and fashionably plush dance lounge, open every night. A favorite of younger clubgoers for having a thoroughly mixed crowd and the city's top djs.

Le Passage 937 N Rush, Gold Coast ⓣ312/255-0022, ⓦwww.lepassage.tv; Red Line to Chicago. Hidden in an alley off Rush Street is the entrance to this chic French-Moroccan restaurant/lounge, with a touch of South Beach and New York. It's popular with an after-work, thirtysomething crowd, and, oddly, people do come here to eat, but the house music and dance scene is the reason to come here. The location's convenient if you're staying downtown, the crowd is upscale (as is the dress), and covers can be hefty ($20).

Rednofive 440 N Halsted St, near Grand Ave, West Side ⓣ312/733-6699, ⓦwww.rednofive.com; Blue Line to Grand. Dark, underground space that heads up Chicago's A-list clubs with its cutting-edge dj styles.

Reserve 858 W Lake St, West Side ⓣ312/455-1111, ⓦwww.reserve-chicago.com. At this swank, Asian-inspired club (think candles, brushed copper, and dark wood furniture), the city's most fabulous late-night crowd – mostly moneyed thirtysomethings – lounges to European "mash" music and indulges in pricey bottle service. Call ahead to get on the guest list. Weekend cover men $20, women $10. Open Tues–Fri 6pm–2am, Sat 7pm–3am.

Smart Bar underneath Metro, 3730 N Clark St, Wrigleyville ⓣ773/549-0203, ⓦwww.smartbarchicago.com; Red Line to Addison. Great techno and old-school house on the weekend (with occasional appearances by legendary dj Derrick Carter) in the neighborhood's post-industrial surrounds. Weekdays see a mix of punk, Goth, and Eighties nights. Open late – till 5am on Fri and Sat, and especially crowded when shows at the *Metro* (see p.221) let out. Cover after 11pm (around $5).

Sonotheque 444 W Chicago Ave ⓣ312/226-7600, ⓦsonotheque.net. Designed to offer an acoustically perfect listening experience, this minimalist, linear lounge emphasizes sophisticated international djs spinning an eclectic mix of down-tempo fare, and attracts a likewise upscale crowd. Occasional cover $2–10 for guest-dj sets. Open Sun–Fri 7pm–2am, Sat 7pm–3am.

Sound-Bar 226 W Ontario St ⓣ312/787-4480, ⓦwww.sound-bar.com; Brown Line to Chicago. The neighborhood's newest mega-club boasts a sleek decor of stainless steel and smoked glass and a 4000-square-foot dancefloor filled with club kids grooving to sets by acclaimed resident djs Chris Eterno, John Curley, and others. Sunday is gay night. No cover before 11pm with RSVP, $10–$20 after. Open Thurs–Fri 9pm–4am, Sat 9pm–5am.

Performing arts and film

Second only to New York in the US, **Chicago theater** is downright phenomenal, a unique blend of traditional "Broadway" plays and offbeat works by one of its soulful theater companies, the Steppenwolf or the Goodman.

The **classical music** is equally stellar: the Lyric Opera of Chicago is internationally renowned, and the Chicago Symphony Orchestra is one of the best in the country, performing hundreds of shows a year. A few smaller groups also routinely put on free concerts around the city. Two **dance companies**, the classically inclined Joffrey Ballet and the more avant-garde Hubbard Street Dance Chicago, are regarded as US emissaries to the world dance community, yet manage to remain quite visible throughout the city. Second City, with all its lore, has brought the spotlight to Chicago's **improvisational comedy scene**, and should not be missed on even a short stay in town. And if none of this appeals, there is also a strong **film** presence in Chicago, with ample opportunity to catch even the most obscure indie film or documentary.

For **current information** about what's on, there is no better source than the free weekly *Chicago Reader*, available at cafés, bars, and newsstands throughout the city. The *Chicago Tribune* and the *Chicago Sun-Times* are also good places to look for current listings.

Theater

Typical of Chicago, its inhabitants have developed theater in their own style – daring and in-your-face – with two major theater companies leading the charge: the basement-born **Steppenwolf Theatre** in Old Town, and the slightly more refined **Goodman Theatre** in the Loop. In recent decades, Chicago actors and writers, following in the footsteps of noted actors and Steppenwolf alums John Malkovich, Joan Allen, and Gary Sinise, saw the local stage as a springboard to the bigger and better, which is to say New York's Broadway – the pinnacle of American theater. But on the heels of much success and many a Tony Award, the trend is changing, and Chicago has become a stage where actors strive to remain. Garage theaters and local one-room theaters have grown in number and, as such, they've become a wonderful complement to the city's revived **Theatre District**

Information and tickets

For current **information** on plays and **tickets**, check with the **League of Chicago Theaters** (228 S Wabash Ave, Suite #900 ⓣ312/554-9800, ⓦwww.chicagoplays.com), a local alliance of most Chicago theaters formed to promote the scene, with all the current information on what's running where. **Hot Tix**, the service for last-minute, half-priced theater and dance tickets, has **booths** (72 E Randolph St; the Chicago Water Works Visitor Center, 163 E Pearson St; and the Tower Records stores at 2301 N Clark St and 214 S Wabash Ave) and a **website** (ⓦwww.hottix.org), which are invaluable sources for tickets.

The *Chicago Reader* (ⓦwww.chireader.com) is always great for **listings and showtimes**, as are the *Chicago Sun-Times* (ⓦwww.suntimes.com) and the *Chicago Tribune* (ⓦwww.chicagotribune.com). Alternatively, ⓦwww.broadwayinchicago.com is the website for three big-name, downtown theaters – the Cadillac Palace, Oriental Theatre, and the LaSalle Bank Theatre (formerly the Shubert Theatre). Two radio stations, WBEZ 91.5 FM (ⓦwww.wbez.org) and WFMT 98.7 FM (ⓦwww.networkchicago. com/wfmt), are other sources of events happening around the city.

in the Loop along Randolph Street. Here in the Loop, gloriously restored old vaudeville theaters and movie palaces like **the Oriental Theatre**, **the Cadillac Palace**, and **the Chicago Theatre** host touring productions of Broadway shows as well as pre-Broadway launches of productions, making the city one of the finest theater destinations in the country.

Away from the Loop, a number of mid-sized venues like **Victory Gardens** and **The Royal George** put on a mix of dramas, musicals, and comedies – most of them locally produced – and smaller companies like **Black Ensemble Theatre** and **Red Orchid** ply their trade. The lists below represent only select venues and companies as the full list is far too long to include; consider them as a jumping-off point.

Theatre District auditoriums

Cadillac Palace Theatre 151 W Randolph St, at N LaSalle St ⓣ312/977-1700, ⓦwww.broadwayinchicago.com; Brown, Blue, Green, Orange, or Purple Line to Clark. The facade has a boring high-rise look about it, but step inside and you'll see a space a bit reminiscent of a French chateau, dripping with crystal chandeliers, huge mirrors, and gold add-ons. This huge (2300 seats) theater was built in 1926 – it succeeded and suffered over the years, but thanks to recent renovations it's now back on the national circuit for touring Broadway plays and musicals.

The Chicago Theatre 175 N State St, at E Lake St ⓣ312/902-1500, ⓦwww.thechicagotheatre.com; Brown, Green, Orange, Purple, or Red Line to State/Lake. Built in 1921 in the French Baroque style, the Chicago was created with grand intentions, faced economic pressures, and nearly succumbed to the wrecking ball. But in 1986 the theater was restored and reopened with a gala performance by Frank Sinatra, and now welcomes touring Broadway shows and big-name musicians.

LaSalle Bank Theatre 22 W Monroe St, at S State St ⓣ312/977-1700, ⓦwww.broadwayinchicago.com; Blue or Red Line to Monroe. Restored in late 2005, the former Shubert Theatre is one of Chicago's classier, elder Loop venues. Originally a vaudeville show house, the space is a prime destination for big-name, big-budget Broadway shows.

Oriental Theatre, Ford Center for the Performing Arts 24 W Randolph St, at N Dearborn St ⓣ312/977-1700, ⓦwww.broadwayinchicago.com; Brown, Green, Orange, Purple, or Red Line to State/Lake. Opened in 1927, the Oriental, with its ornate and bizarre interior – impressive domed ceiling, swank chandeliers, and an abundance of sculpted seahorses, goddesses, and elephants – was built to resemble an Asian temple. It reopened in 1996 after a massive restoration project and is currently home to a big-budget, open-run production of the Broadway smash *Wicked*.

Mainstream companies

Chicago Shakespeare Theater 800 E Grand Ave, at Navy Pier, Streeterville ⓣ312/595-5600, ⓦwww.chicagoshakes.com. Spanking new Navy Pier stage that hosts the city's only all-Shakespeare company, in an intimate, courtyard-style theater (the actors perform on a catwalk-like stage that juts out into the audience). Constantly sold out, this company puts on consistently professional, if occasionally staid, productions of the Bard's plays.

Goodman Theatre 170 N Dearborn St, at E Randolph St, the Loop ⓣ312/443-3800, ⓦwww.goodman-theatre.org; Brown, Green, Orange, Purple, or Red Line to State/Lake. Even though they're the city's oldest and perhaps most respected company, the Goodman puts on contemporary interpretations of classics, from Shakespeare to O'Neill, in a recently built, state-of-the-art theater complex. The Goodman has two theaters: the 856-seat Albert Ivar Goodman Theatre, and the Owen Bruner Goodman Theatre, a moveable courtyard theater, with roughly 400 seats. Ask about "Tix-At-Six" for half-priced tickets that go on sale at 6pm the day of performance (tickets go fast, so it's best to show up by 5.30pm). For further ticket information, call or stop by the box office.

Lookingglass Theatre Company 821 N Michigan Ave, Near North ⓣ312/337-0665, ⓦwww.lookingglasstheatre.org. This edgy group headquartered in the Chicago Water Works Visitors Center boasts past productions that include the original staging of *Metamorphoses*, Mary Zimmerman's 2002 Tony Award–winning play performed in and around an onstage pool of water.

Steppenwolf Theatre 1650 N Halsted St, at W Willow St, Old Town ⓣ312/335-1650, ⓦwww.steppenwolf.org; Red Line to North/Clybourn. The cornerstone of the Chicago theater scene; for history, see box below.

Off-Loop theaters

Apollo Theater 2540 N Lincoln Ave, at W Wrightwood Ave, Lincoln Park ⓣ773/935-6100, ⓦwww.apollochicago.com; Brown, Purple, or Red Line to Fullerton. Four-hundred-forty-seat space in Lincoln Park that hosts children's productions on the weekends and has been home to wildly popular open runs of female-friendly shows like Eve Ensler's Vagina Monologues and, more recently, Menopause The Musical.

Athenaeum Theatre 2936 N Southport Ave, at W Oakdale Ave, Lakeview ⓣ773/935-6860, ⓦwww.athenaeumtheatre.com; Brown Line to Wellington. This old performance complex (built in 1911) is one of the more widely used theater and performance venues on the North Side – there's always something happening on either the main stage or the smaller studios.

Bailiwick Arts Center 1229 W Belmont Ave, at N Racine Ave, Lakeview ⓣ773/883-1090, ⓦwww.bailiwick.org; Brown, Purple, or Red Line to Belmont. Chicago's leading gay and lesbian theater center, which frequently offers concurrent performances.

Black Ensemble Theater 4520 N Beacon St, at W Sunnyside Ave, Uptown ⓣ773/769-4451, ⓦwww.blackensenbletheater.org; Brown Line to Montrose. A wonderful success story, this small and perennially popular company is basically a front for founder, director, producer and actress Jackie Taylor's long-running theatrical homages to legends like Ella Fitzgerald, Jackie Wilson, and Etta James.

Briar Street Theatre 3133 N Halsted St, at W Fletcher St, Lakeview ⓣ773/348-4000 ⓦwww.blueman.com; Brown, Purple, or Red Line to Belmont. This no-frills Boystown theater is the current home of the long-running Blue Man Group show, a bizarre, multi-sensory production starring three famously bald, blue-headed men. Pop Dadaism for the masses.

Chicago Dramatists 1105 W Chicago Ave, at N Milwaukee Ave, West Town ⓣ312/633-0630, ⓦwww.chicagodramatists.org; bus #66. A small, bare-bones space that presents dramatic works by up-and-coming local playwrights. Always top quality (and affordable).

Court Theatre 5535 S Ellis Ave, at E 55th St, South Side ⓣ773/753-4472, ⓦwww.courttheatre.org. On the South Side's University of Chicago campus, the Court produces historically classic comedies and dramas, each deftly written. It will often host two shows simultaneously, and tickets range from $24 to $34, though half-price tickets are available two hours before the show.

The Steppenwolf Theatre

The **Steppenwolf** is Chicago's most innovative company; it's a brand still seen today in the work of long-time members like **John Malkovich** and **Gary Sinise**, who occasionally return to grace the group's stage. Three actors (Sinise, Jeff Perry, and "Oz" star Terry Kinney) founded the company in a church basement in the far north suburb of Highland Park in 1974. In the decades since, it has grown to three stages in a sleek, modern edifice in Old Town, and a 34-actor company which now includes familiar names like Joan Allen, Kevin Anderson, John Mahoney, Laurie Metcalf, and Martha Plimpton. Their emotionally raw 1982 production of Sam Shepard's *True West*, directed by Sinise and starring Malkovich and Metcalf, was an unparalleled success, running for four months before transferring to New York (the first of many Steppenwolf productions to do so) and is regarded as seminal by many in the theater world. Subsequent high points include 1986's live stage extravaganza of Tom Waits' concept album, *Frank's Wild Years*, at the Briar Street Theatre, and the Tony Award–winning adaptation of *The Grapes of Wrath* in 1990. More recently, the theater has seen the world premiere of ensemble member Tracy Letts' Pulitzer Prize finalist *Man from Nebraska* in 2003, and welcomed Malkovich back in 2005 for the premiere of Stephen Jeffreys' *Lost Land*.

Drury Lane Theatre Water Tower Place 175 E Chestnut St, Near North ⓣ312/642-2000, ⓦwww.shopwatertower.com. This former movie theater was renovated and reopened in the summer of 2005 as a 575-seat theater which will stage Chicago and American premieres of new musicals and plays as well as Broadway crowd-pleasers like *The Full Monty* and classics like *Grand Hotel*. Tickets are $36–$48.

ETA Creative Arts Foundation 7558 S Chicago Ave, at E 75th St, South Side ⓣ773/752–3955, ⓦwww.etacreativeartsfoundation.org. The leading African-American arts organization on the South Side that's been putting on successful, often family-oriented, plays for some thirty years now.

Mercury Theatre 3745 N Southport Ave, at W Grace St, Lakeview ⓣ773/325-1700; Brown Line to Southport. Smallish live-theater venue (300 seats) two doors north of the Music Box Theatre. Open only since 1996, it's quickly become one of the city's small-stage favorites, often hosting plays of the family-friendly variety for months at a time.

Royal George Theatre 1641 N Halsted St, at W Willow St, Old Town ⓣ312/988-9000, ⓦwww.theroyalgeorgetheatre.com; Red Line to North/Clybourn. Right across Halsted from Steppenwolf (see p.228), this is a modest, two-stage theater that hosts both long-running comedy shows and touring dramas.

Theater on the Lake 2400 N Lake Shore Drive, at W Fullerton Parkway ⓣ312/742-7994. Waterside venue where local theater groups like Steppenwolf and Second City put on sampler shows for a couple weeks at a time during the summer.

TimeLine Theatre 615 W Wellington Ave, at N Broadway St, Lakeview ⓣ312/409-8463, ⓦwww.timelinetheatre.com; bus #22. Currently in a small space tucked away on a quiet residential street, this spunky little group will be moving to the renovated Three Arts Club in 2007.

Victory Gardens Theater 2257 N Lincoln Ave, at W Webster Ave, Lincoln Park ⓣ773/871-3000, ⓦwww.victorygardens.org; Brown, Purple, or Red Line to Fullerton. This Tony-winning company has produced a considerable number of premieres (more than any other in Chicago), and is known for helping nurture new and less experienced talent, especially of the local variety. After the 2005–'06 season, the group is set to move to a new home in the historic Biograph Theatre at 2433 N Lincoln Ave; restoration and renovation (including the addition of two 195-seat theaters and a 60-seat studio theater) is scheduled to be completed in the fall of 2006.

Fringe theater and itinerant companies

About Face Theatre 1222 W Wilson Ave ⓣ773/784-8565, ⓦwww.aboutfacetheatre.org. This groundbreaking company addresses issues of gender and sexuality in smart, visually stunning productions. Recent hits include the Chicago premiere of *Take Me Out*, the world premiere of the musical *Winesburg, Ohio*, and the original production of the multiple-Tony-winning *I Am My Own Wife*.

Redmoon Theater 1463 W Hubbard St, West Side ⓣ312/850-8440, ⓦwww.redmoon.org. Experimental company specialiing in "theatrical spectacles" that fall somewhere between *outré* performance art, puppet shows, and surrealist theater.

Stage Left Theatre 3408 N Sheffield Ave ⓣ773/883-8830, ⓦwww.stagelefttheatre.com. Founded in 1982, this collective of actors, directors, writers, and designers produces mostly new plays that raise debate about political and social issues, from 9/11 to apartheid and the death penalty.

Comedy

Comedy on stage in Chicago is almost entirely made up. That is, there's an improvisational comedy troupe – based on a model invented by the legendary **Second City** theater back in the late 1950s – on seemingly every block and in every little theater space (most of them are itinerant) ready to take audience suggestions and spin them into a (possibly) funny routine; check the *Reader* for weekly listings. One of the few exceptions is the venerable **Zanies**, a straight-up standup-comic joint in Old Town.

ComedySportz Theatre 2851 N Halsted St, at W Wolfram St, Lakeview ⓣ773/549-8080, ⓦwww.comedysportzchicago.com; Brown or Purple Line to Diversey. A wholly Chicago creation, this blend of sports and comedy – two teams of comics battle against each other in song and scenes – is a fun, audience-driven experience, that you'll find outright weird or just plain funny. "Competitions" happen Thurs–Sat, beginning at 8pm; $17.

ImprovOlympic 3541 N Clark St, at W Addison St, Wrigleyville ⓣ773/880-0199, ⓦwww.improvolympic.com; Red Line to Addison. A couple of former *Second City* folks founded this improv landmark back in the early 1980s. Their particular style of improv – called "The Harold" – takes one audience suggestion and spins it into a piece of instant comic theater lasting a half-hour or more. Alumni include Mike Myers, Andy Dick, and Tina Fey.

Neo-Futurarium 5153 N Ashland Ave, at W Foster Ave ⓣ773/275-5255, ⓦwww.neofuturists.org; bus #22. Up on the far North Side resides this strange little place, wherein is performed the long-running *Too Much Light Makes the Baby Go Blind*, a blitzkrieg of thirty mini-plays in sixty minutes. The $8–$13 admission is determined at the door by a pair of dice.

The Playground 3209 N Halsted St, at W Henderson Ave, Lakeview ⓣ773/871-3793, ⓦwww.the-playground.com; Brown Line to Addison. Solo, skit, team, and improv comedy shows run every Thursday through Sunday night.

Second City 1616 N Wells St, at W North Ave, Old Town ⓣ312/337-3992, ⓦwww.secondcity.com; bus #22. For over four decades, *Second City* has been a breeding ground for the nation's top comics, launching dozens of fledgling comics to stardom. The troupe performs a nightly series of sketches mixed with improvisation – never less than hilarious. There's also a smaller stage – *Second City e.t.c.* (1608 N Wells St) – producing similar material in the same building. Cover charge and two-drink minimum. See box on p.93 for more.

Zanies 1548 N Wells St, at W North Ave, Old Town ⓣ312/337-4027, ⓦwww.zanies.com; bus #22. Pretty much the only place to see standup comedy in the city, *Zanies* packs them into their somewhat rough-at-the-edges club with two or three shows a night. Often the comics are less than stellar, but you can occasionally catch big names slumming. Cover charge and two-drink minimum.

Classical music and opera

Chicago's classical music scene is a straightforward affair – there's the internationally acclaimed **Chicago Symphony Orchestra** (CSO) and then all other

groups a tier or two lower. The city is also home to several top-notch summer music **festivals** at Ravinia and in Grant Park (see p.256).

The Chicago Symphony Orchestra

The CSO performs at Symphony Center, 220 S Michigan Ave (☎312/294-3000, Ⓦwww.cso.org), about ten times a month Sept–June when they're not touring domestically or internationally, which they do several times per year, generally for 1–2 weeks at a time. After having George Solti at the helm for many years, since 1991 the one hundred-plus members of the CSO have followed the lead of Daniel Barenboim, a gifted, multiple Grammy Award–winning conductor who has brought more contemporary music into the CSO repertoire, with frequent guest artists like Yo-Yo Ma, Wynton Marsalis, Itzhak Perlman, and others. (At the time of writing, Barenboim had announced he will not be returning to the rostrum of the CSO after the 2005–06 season; a replacement has not been announced. Tickets for the CSO can be pricey, between $25 and $200, the cheapest tickets for seats far away in the gallery.

Alternatively, CSO offers "RUSH" seating, general admission for any available seat just before the performance. Seats are not confirmed, so you may be asked to move to a free seat elsewhere if the original ticket-holder should arrive late. Inquire about this last-resort option with the ticket agent in the lobby just before showtime.

Smaller orchestras and chamber groups

The Chicago Chamber Musicians 2 Prudential Plaza, 180 N Stetson St ☎312/819-5800, Ⓦwww.chicagochambermusic.org. This cadre of devout musicians put on some fifty concerts a year, many of which are held at DePaul University's Concert Hall, 800 W Belden Ave (☎773/325-7260), in Lincoln Park. They are best known (and loved) around town for their "First Monday" series – free lunchtime performances underneath the Cultural Center's Tiffany dome on the first Monday of every month.

Chicago Chamber Orchestra ☎312/922-5570, Ⓦwww.chicagochamberorchestra.org) Founded in 1952, the 35-member orchestra also perform at the Cultural Center, with monthly shows encompassing works from the Baroque to the present.

Chicago Sinfonietta ☎312/236-3681, Ⓦwww.chicagosinfonietta.org. This Evanston orchestra under the leadership of Mahler Award–winner and Emmy nominee Paul Freeman, has a multicultural feel to the music they produce, and tends to fuse classical with modern – everything from solos to orchestra-backed marimba performances. They hold a good number of their concerts at Symphony Center.

The Chicago Youth Symphony Orchestras ☎312/939-2207, Ⓦwww.cyso.org. A full (110-piece) orchestra comprising elite high-school musicians from the Chicagoland

Other classical groups

Beyond the CSO, there are a number of classical music groups in Chicago performing nearly every day of the week, at the Symphony Center during the summer and when the CSO is off touring. **Chicago Chamber Musicians** (see above) present intimate monthly concerts of classic works by composers like Haydn and Brahms; **Music of the Baroque** (☎312/551-1414, Ⓦwww.baroque.org) focuses on earlier works for chorus and orchestra. Also, smaller, **free concerts** are frequent at the Chicago Cultural Center, 78 E Washington (☎312/346-3278 for details), Newberry Library, 60 E Walton, The 4th Presbyterian Church of Chicago (across from the John Hancock Center), Old St Pat's Church, 700 W Adams, Holy Name Cathedral, 735 N State St, The Museum of Contemporary Art, 220 E Chicago Ave, and a few other venues. Check the *Reader* or call venues for complete event listings.

area; they perform a fall and a winter show each year, usually held at Symphony Center.

Music of the Baroque ⓣ**312/551-1414,** ⓦ**www.baroque.org.** The Midwest's largest group (60 musicians) playing sixteenth- and seventeenth-century music, perform in Old St Pat's Church, St Paul's Church, Holy Name Cathedral, as well as a bunch of suburban venues, weekdays throughout the year – single event tickets are available.

Opera

Nearly as acclaimed as the CSO, the **Lyric Opera of Chicago** is tops for opera in Chicago and is, indeed, one of the finest opera companies in the world, having welcomed performers ranging from Maria Callas and Pavarotti to dancer Rudolf Nureyev in the magnificent – and recently restored – Art-Deco Civic Opera House, 20 N Wacker Drive (ⓣ312/332-2244, ⓦwww.lyricopera.org). Its season is from mid-September to early February, and most performances are sold out. If you want even a chance at a (pricey, $30–165) ticket, you'll have to put yourself on the Lyric Opera mailing list and they'll send out a "Priority Individual Ticket brochure" in late July – this will have instructions about purchasing tickets and current availability.

If you can't land a ticket to the Lyric, the **Chicago Opera Theater** (ⓣ312/704-8414, ⓦwww.chicagooperatheater.org) is a viable, slightly less costly ($35–$115) alternative, with lower-budget productions of lesser-known classics and contemporary works, often at the Athenaeum Theatre in Lakeview.

Cinema

Chicago is definitely on the shortlist of US cities with a big film culture, which means several things: there are growing lists of decent – and public – **film festivals**, a bunch of cool venues to see classics, indies, foreign flicks, and documentaries, and a respectable number of mainstream theaters citywide, each pumping out the Hollywood hits. Venues range from mega-sized Omnimax theaters to music auditoriums that double as film houses to standard three- or four-theater first-run complexes.

For **information**, the free *Reader* (ⓦwww.chireader.com/movie) always has up-to-date lists of showtimes, as does *New City* (ⓦwww.newcitychicago.com/chicago/film). **Moviefone** (ⓣ312/444-3456) is a great way to find shows and showtimes at any theater in Chicago, though you'll need either the zip code or the theater's approximate area of town.

Generally, the price of admission is about $9, though many of the smaller and second-run houses show films for half as much.

First-run cinemas

600 North Michigan Avenue Near North ⓣ**312/255-9340; Red Line to Grand.** Nothing special, but this nine-screener upstairs from Eddie Bauer shows a decent mix of mainstream and semi-arty films.

Esquire 58 E Oak St, at N Rush St, Gold Coast ⓣ**312/280-0101; Red Line to Chicago.** New releases and art/indie films at this tall, skinny theater slipped in between Oak Street boutiques.

Landmark Century Centre Cinema 2828 N Clark St, at W Diversey Parkway, Lakeview ⓣ**773/248-7744; bus #22.** On the top couple floors of this vertical shopping mall, showing independent and foreign-language films – one of the city's better-run theaters.

Music Box 3733 N Southport Ave, at W Waveland Ave, Lakeview ⓣ**773/871-6604,** ⓦ**www.musicboxtheatre.com; Brown Line to Southport.** The owners of this grand old neighborhood theater bill it as a "year-round film festival," and, while it's not quite that, it is a good place to watch interesting flicks – cult, classic, indie, horror, whatever. Funky interior, and live organ music between films.

Film festivals

Black Harvest International Festival of Video and Film (Aug ⓦwww.artic.edu/webspaces/siskelfilmcenter). A long-running and fascinating annual collection of new African and African-American works rarely (if ever) screened anywhere else in the country. Held at the Gene Siskel Film Center (see below).

Chicago Outdoor Film Festival (mid-July to Aug ⓣ312/744-3315). Free movie festival on Tuesday nights at Butler Field in Grant Park (Monroe St and Lake Shore Drive), where you can sit on a blanket with a picnic and watch classic flicks like *Vertigo* and *West Side Story*.

Chicago Underground Film Festival (late Aug ⓦwww.cuff.org). A little more unbuttoned than most, this fest was born out of frustration with the relative inaccessibility and mainstreaming tendencies of other fests. Two students started it in 1993 and it's been a hit ever since, showing indie, experimental, and documentary films.

Chicago International Film Festival (Oct ⓣ312/683-0121, ⓦwww.chicagofilmfestival.org). Held over a couple of weeks throughout the city, this is now the oldest competitive film festival in North America (1964), and, though it doesn't have the reputation of say, the Sundance Film Festival, it is a highly respected event in the US motion picture world. Categories range from feature films, to first- and second-time directors, documentaries, short films, student, and animated films.

Chicago International Children's Film Festival (Oct–Nov ⓣ773/281-9075, ⓦwww.cicff.org). The oldest and largest of its kind in the country, this showcases hundreds of feature and short films for (and often made by) children all over the world and also includes hands-on film workshops for kids. Held over two weeks in October and/or November at Facets Cinémathèque (see below).

Reeling: the Chicago International Gay and Lesbian Film Festival (late Aug to early Sept). See "Gay and lesbian Chicago," p.239.

Pipers Alley 1608 N Wells St, at W North Ave, Old Town ⓣ312/337-0436; bus #22. Three-theater complex in Old Town, always has a good pick of artsy movies that verge on mainstream.

River East 21 322 E Illinois St, at N Fairbanks Court, Streeterville ⓣ847/765-7262; bus #65. Recently opened Streeterville complex with a whopping 21 screens – good for watching blockbusters, since they're generally playing on three to four screens here.

Second-run and indie flicks

Brew & View at The Vic Theatre 3145 N Sheffield Ave, at W Belmont Ave, Lakeview ⓣ773/929-6713, ⓦwww.brewview.com; Brown, Purple, or Red Line to Belmont. The name says it all: the place to come to watch flicks and drink beer (50¢ per cup, $2 per pitcher). Second-run movies, classics, and audiences that tend to sing and quote along. Admission is only $5; must be 18 to enter, 21 to drink.

Facets Cinémathèque 1517 W Fullerton Ave, at N Greenview Ave, Lincoln Park ⓣ773/281-4114, ⓦwww.facets.org; Brown, Purple, or Red Line to Fullerton. Daily screenings of cutting-edge films and, in their attached rental store, an enormous (and nationally renowned) cache of cult, experimental, and hard-to-find videos. Also hosts several annual film festivals.

Gene Siskel Film Center 164 N State St, at Randolph St, the Loop ⓣ312/846-2600, ⓦwww.artic.edu/webspaces/siskelfilmcenter/; Brown, Green, Orange, Purple, or Red Line to State/Lake. Splashy, sleek, new Loop two-screen complex (named for the beloved, late *Chicago Tribune* film critic), part of the School of the Art Institute of Chicago, with classics, revivals, indie premieres, festivals, etc.

Three Penny Theater 2424 N Lincoln Ave, at W Fullerton Ave, Lincoln Park ⓣ773/525-3449, ⓦwww.3penny cinema.com; Brown, Purple, or Red Line to Fullerton. Aged but cheap little theater with two screens, showing second-run films, right across from the storied Biograph Theatre. See Victory Gardens, p.228.

Univ. of Chicago DOC Films 1212 E 59th St, at S Woodlawn Ave, Hyde Park ⓣ773/702-8575, ⓦwww.docfilms.uchicago.edu. On the University of Chicago campus and an appropriately brainy movie-house with daily screenings of just about any type. The longest continuously running student film-society in the nation, it was founded in the 1930s as an informal film society.

Village Theater 1548 N Clark St, at W North Ave, Lakeview ⓣ312/642-2403; bus #22. Divey movie-house that always shows recently second-run films – with occasionally some stranger, cult, fare and midnight flicks – at discounted prices.

Dance

Two companies, the **Joffrey Ballet** and **Hubbard Street Dance Chicago**, are Chicago's real gift to the world dance community, though there are a number of smaller dance companies that inevitably are a part of the local dance scene.

For current what's-on information, the **Chicago Dance and Music Alliance** (ⓣ312/987-1123, ⓦwww.chicagoperformances.org) is a great source, the 2001 combination of the Chicago Music Alliance and the Chicago Dance Coalition. The Alliance website is loaded with numbers and venue information.

Companies

Ballet Chicago Studio Company ⓣ312/251-8838, ⓦwww.balletchicago.org. Roving like the Joffrey but not nearly as renowned a classical ballet troupe, Ballet Chicago does have a school, and has been performing – and training – since it opened doors in 1997. Geared toward the style of George Balanchine, famed twentieth-century choreographer.

Chicago Moving Company ⓣ773/880-5402, ⓦwww.chicagomovingcompany.org. Modern dance under the guidance of Nana Shineflug, modern-dance leader of great repute in Chicago. Concerts and classes since 1972.

Hubbard Street Dance Chicago 1147 W Jackson Blvd ⓣ312/850-9744, ⓦwww.hubbardstreetdance.com. More contemporary than Joffrey Ballet but equally talented, continually turning out some of the nation's best dance, with its characteristic blend of jazz, modern, ballet, and theater-dance.

Joffrey Ballet 70 E Lake St ⓣ312/739-0120, ⓦwww.joffrey.com. The city's prime classically-oriented dance company, one of the

△ Hubbard Street Dance Chicago

country's best. Transplanted from New York in 1995, the group uses Chicago as a home base, performing at the Auditorium Theatre (see below), with tickets between $35 and $75 per seat.

Mordine and Company Dance Theater **Ⓣ312/654-9540, Ⓦwww.mordine.org.** One of the nation's longer-running contemporary dance companies (1968), right behind the Joffrey Ballet and alongside the River North Dance Company. They were for many years headquartered at the Dance Center of Columbia College.

Muntu Dance Theatre Ⓣ773/602-1135, Ⓦwww.muntu.com. Dance troupe that performs all sorts of African tribal dances, with a contemporary take on everything. They usually perform only a few shows a year, sometimes at the Museum of Contemporary Art, or Hyde Park's DuSable Museum, among others.

River North Dance Company Ⓣ312/944-2888, Ⓦwww.rivernorthchicago.com. Created by four standout Chicago dancers in the late 1980s, River North (performing mostly at the Athenaeum Theatre; see below) comprises a mostly Midwestern cast, and devotes itself to jazz and contemporary dance.

Venues

Athenaeum Theatre **2936 N Southport Ave, at W Oakdale Ave, Lakeview Ⓣ773/935-6860 or 312/902-1500.** See p.227 for details.

Auditorium Theatre **50 E Congress Parkway, at S State St, the Loop Ⓣ312/922-2110 or 902-1500, Ⓦwww.auditoriumtheatre.org; Red Line to Harrison.** Beautiful Sullivan-designed theater with exceptional acoustics, which hosts the Joffrey Ballet as well as touring music acts and Broadway shows.

Chicago Cultural Center **78 E Washington Blvd, at N Michigan Ave, the Loop Ⓣ312/744-6630; Brown, Green, Orange, or Purple Line to Randolph.** The loft-like Sidney R. Yates Gallery on the fourth floor of the Cultural Center has frequent free dance performances, among them the "About Dance" program, which combines discussions about dance with performances by groups like Dance Africa Chicago.

Dance Center of Columbia College **1306 S Michigan Ave, at E 13th St, South Loop Ⓣ312/344-8300, Ⓦwww.dancecenter.org; Red Line to Roosevelt.** Theater in a Columbia College building a few blocks from the main campus, with contemporary dance concerts from troupes like Bebe Miller Company, Merce Cunningham Dance Company, and experimental group The Seldoms, plus classes in the other six studios.

Harold Washington Library **400 S State St, at E Congress Parkway, the Loop Ⓣ312/747-4300; Red Line to Roosevelt.** The Library often hosts dance and music performances from mostly local artists – recent acts have included the Chicago-based Nucleus Dance Collective and The Chicago Jazz Orchestra – in its lower-level auditorium.

Joan W. and Irving B. Harris Theater for Music and Dance **205 E Randolph Drive, the Loop Ⓣ312/334-7777, Ⓦwww.harristheaterchicago.org; Brown, Purple, Orange, or Green Line to Randolph.** Boasting prime acoustics and excellent sightlines, this dazzling, 1525-seat gem in Millennium Park hosts performances of ballet, contemporary dance by Hubbard Street Dance Chicago, and classical, chamber, opera, and folk music.

Museum of Contemporary Art Theatre **220 E Chicago Ave, at N DeWitt Place, Streeterville Ⓣ312/397-4010, Ⓦwww.mcachicago.org; Red Line to Chicago.** The MCA's street-level theater often hosts dance performances by local troupes, like tap troupe Chicago Human Rhythm Project.

Ruth Page Center for Arts **1016 N Dearborn St, at W Oak St, Gold Coast Ⓣ312/337-6543, Ⓦwww.ruthpage.org; Red Line to Clark/Division.** Designed to accommodate dance and theater groups in search of a permanent home, it hosts the performances of the various groups in residence there at any one time; recent groups have included River North Dance Company, Luna Negra Dance Theatre, and Mordine & Company Dance Theater (see above).

18

Galleries

While it may not have the diversity and edge of New York or Los Angeles, Chicago's **art scene** has come a long way since the early 1970s, when any visitor to the city would have had great difficulty in finding an art community of any description. With the gradual metamorphosis of the gritty warehouse district of **River North**, with its epicenter at Huron and Superior streets, into a thriving artistic enclave of loft studios and boutiques, the art scene has been on the rise. However, following a fire that devastated over a quarter of River North's studios in the late 1980s, many galleries packed up and moved to other neighborhoods, a trend which has been compounded over the last few years by escalating property prices.

Today, Chicago's artistic fervor has been pulsating in the **West Loop**, a far less commercial kernel in which more avant-garde and experimental exhibitions are thriving, especially installations, giving an irreverent alter-ego to Chicago's traditionally mainstream art world. **Wicker Park and Bucktown** also have a lively art scene centered around the Flat Iron Building at the intersection of Damen, North, and Milwaukee avenues, which hosts the Around the Coyote Art Festival each September (see "Festivals and events," Chapter 21). Over the last decade, however, gentrification in the Wicker Park area has diluted its traditionally bohemian vibe and subsequent high rents have prevented the establishment of emerging, innovative talent in the area. Many young artists have relocated to the southwest, to the Mexican enclave of **Pilsen**, where you will find an active artistic community. To the north, **Evanston** has a burgeoning art scene, and while it's not worth going out of your way for, the galleries are worth a visit if you happen to be in the area. You'll find that most galleries usually host receptions for new shows on Friday evenings (5–8pm), and there are plenty of Chicago glitterati on hand for great people-watching.

Two **openings** are worth noting: the second or third Friday in September kicks off the **fall gallery season**, while on the second Friday in January, all of the galleries have coinciding openings. For information of current events and occasional **free trolleys** that run between the River North galleries and the Michigan Avenue museums, pick up a copy of the free *Chicago Gallery News*, available from most hotels and galleries.

River North Gallery District

Andrew Bae Gallery 300 W Superior St; Tues–Sat 10am–6pm ⓣ312/335-8601, ⓦwww.andrewbaegallery.com. Predominantly Asian theme with a stirring and serene collection of prints, sculpture, and decorative arts by emerging artists from Japan and South Korea. The imagery, often naturalistic, tends to be simple, but the themes are complex and often metaphysical. There is a focus on bringing together Eastern and Western art techniques and their philosophical ideals.

Anne Nathan 218 W Superior St; Tues–Fri 10am–5.30pm, Sat 11am–5pm ⓣ312/664-6622, ⓦwww.annenathangallery.com. An eclectic assortment of paintings, sculpture, and ornate furniture by famous and up-and-coming regional and national artists.

Bucket Rider 119 N Peoria St #3D; Tues–Sat noon–6pm ⓣ312/421-6993, ⓦwww.bucketridergallery.com. One of the more out-there galleries, whose self-purported mission is to "step beyond the market-induced boundaries and present experimental artworks." Since moving from Pilsen in 2003, it has broadened its focus to feature international as well as local artists. Covering one wall of the white cube-like space, there are fanciful illustrations rendered on canvases and skateboards by Chicagoan Cody Hudson.

Gwenda Jay/Addlington Gallery 704 N Wells St; Tues–Sat 11am–6pm ⓣ312/664-3406, ⓦwww.gwendajay.com. The Gwenda Jay specializes in American and European fine art, featuring a wide range of contemporary styles, subjects, and media.

Jean Albano 215 W Superior St; Mon 11am–4pm, Tues–Fri 10am–5pm, Sat 11am–5pm ⓣ312/440-0770 ⓦwww.jeanalbanogallery.com. Dynamic, innovative, loft space with a maze of galleries that displays conceptual and flamboyant contemporary painting, sculpture, and mixed media. The permanent collection includes the works of abstractionist Valerie Beller, and Argentine native Luciana Abnit whose desolate images and enigmatic landscapes expose themes of human absence. Represented Chicago artists include Margaret Wharton, Valerie Beller, and Gladys Nilsson.

Monique Meloche 118 N Peoria St; Tues–Sat 11am–6pm ⓣ312/455-0299, ⓦwww.moniquemeloche.com. After working at the Museum of Contemporary Art for six years, Monique opened her own gallery with the intent to showcase a left-of-field collection of international and national artworks. Installations incorporating photography, sculpture, painting, and video with a self-deprecating, satirical tone are used by Argentine Alexa Horochowski to explore her Latin roots and how it impacts her Midwestern identity.

Primitive Art Works 706 N Wells St; Mon–Sat 11am–7pm ⓣ312/943-3770, ⓦwww.primitiveartworks.com. With more than one hundred cultures represented here, the four floors of jewelry, textiles, and other artifacts can certainly take up several hours of an afternoon. The knowledgeable staff will explain every piece in the house, from obscure and ancient Himalayan pieces to magical amulets worn by West African warriors. Integral to the stunning building is a restored Chinese house. There is a "Buddha Room" containing sculptures from all over the world, large painting collection on the fourth floor, Indian collection, and an ornately hand-painted room containing a library.

Printworks Gallery 311 W Superior, Suite 105; Tues–Sat 11am–5pm ⓣ312/644-9407, ⓦwww.printworkschicago.com. Established in 1980, this excellent gallery specializes in contemporary fine art and photography. A substantial collection of local and international artists are represented, many of which are globally acclaimed for their contributions to art history. Look for the political and figurative paintings of Leon Golub, whose highly politicized and controversial work has been featured in the collections at MoMA in New York and the Tate in London. There is an "Affordable Art Work" section that shows paintings priced at $300 and under. Usually closed for two weeks in the summer; call ahead.

Zg Gallery 300 W Superior St; Tues–Sat 10am–5.30pm ⓣ312/654-9900, ⓦwww.zggallery.com. Contemporary art from local, national, emerging, and established artists in a variety of media. There are plenty of abstract pieces on view, especially in the temporary exhibitions.

Zygman Voss 222 W Superior St,1E; Tues–Sat 10am–5pm ⓣ312/787-3300. Gallery that specializes in seventeenth–twentieth century art, including Renoir, Picasso, Toulouse-Lautrec, and Miró. There are also impressive temporary exhibitions featuring themed collections of great masters or the gallery's resident artists.

Michigan Ave and Streeterville

Colletti Gallery 67 E Oak St; Mon–Thurs 10am–6pm, Fri 10am–7pm, Sat 10am–6pm, Sun noon–5pm ⓣ312/664-6767. This Oak Street gallery showcases vintage, late nineteenth- and early twentieth-century posters and decorative arts spanning the Belle Epoque, Art Nouveau, Art Deco, and contemporary periods. Among the superlative masterworks are lithographs by Henri de Toulouse-Lautrec and Jules Chéret.

Fine Arts Building 410 S Michigan Ave, Suite 433; Wed–Sat noon–6pm ⓣ312/913-0537, ⓦwww.FABGallery.com. Built in 1885 as the former showroom for Studebaker Company's carriages, and with a legacy of artistic denizens from L. Frank Baum to Frank Lloyd Wright, the Fine Arts Building is now a showcase for up-and-coming and established artists. Roger Bole's realistic urban scenes capture Chicago's soul lurking within the gritty day-to-day banality, while the landscape photography of Bart Harris is also Windy City–inspired. Receptions are often held from 5–8pm.

RH Love Galleries 645 N Michigan Ave; Mon–Fri 9am–5pm, Sat 10am–5pm ⓣ312/640-1300, ⓦwww.rhlovegalleries.com. Mainstream gallery focusing on American artists, spanning the colonial period through the twentieth century. There is a large collection of Impressionist and Post-Impressionist paintings as well as still life, folk art, and academic realism. The most captivating works are from the Ash Can School, notably Everett Shinn, John Barber, and William Glackens, whose works captured the raw details of every-day urban life in turn-of-the-century New York.

Richard Gray Gallery 875 N Michigan, Suite 2503 John Hancock Center; Mon–Fri 10am–5.30pm, Sat by appointment ⓣ312/642-8877, ⓦwww.richardgraygallery.com. One of the forerunners of Chicago's buoyant gallery scene, this compelling gallery space, still at the cusp of the Chicago art scene, specializes in the finest modern art. Impressive exhibitions rotate the gallery's extensive collection, which includes such contemporary masters as Jackson Pollock, Georgia O'Keeffe, Roy Lichtenstein, Mark Rothko, and Willem de Kooning.

Bucktown and Wicker Park

Ancient Echoes 1022A W Armitage St; Mon–Fri 11am–7pm, Sat 10am–6pm, Sun noon–5pm ⓣ773/880-1003, ⓦwww.ancientechoes.com. Always featuring on the lists of top US retail experiences, this glittering emporium, the brainchild of Ivy Hofstadter, specializes in innovative jewelry, accessories, and hand-crafted furnishings from a diverse array of international designers. Highly affordable, necklaces start at around $55. Of special note is the flamboyant costume jewelry of one of the world's leading designers, Israeli Ayala Bar, whose colorful, mosaic creations are encrusted with beads and rhinestones, and the nature-inspired work of American master mold-maker and caster, Michael Michard.

The Contemporary Art Workshop 542 W Grant Ave; Tues–Fri 12.30–5.30pm, Sat noon–5pm ⓣ773/472-4004, ⓦwww.contemporaryart-workshop.org. Since its inception in 1949, the CAW has been a launch pad for young emerging artists, providing them with exhibition exposure and low-cost studios in what was once a former dairy. If you spend time in the Lakeview area of the city you may see sculptures of one of the CAW's resident artists, John Kerney, whose quirky steel animal representations are made from welded car-bumpers.

The Leigh Gallery 3306 N Halsted St; Wed noon–5pm, Thurs & Fri 11am–7pm, Sat & Sun 11–9, Mon & Tues by appointment only ⓣ773/472-1865, ⓦwww.theleighgallery.com. Informal and accessible gallery representing dozens of emerging artists across a variety of media: watercolors, ceramics, jewelry, and photography. Featured artists include Illinois-based Ron Nepereny whose eclectic style ranges from commercial computer-generated graphic images to acrylic fine-art landscapes and still life, and the more classical oil and pastel paintings of Chicago-based Grace Cole, a graduate from the Art Institute of Chicago, whose purported aim is to capture the "essence of beauty and dignity."

West Loop and Pilsen

Chicago Arts District 1945 S Halsted St; opening hours are individual to each studio ⓣ312/923-1010, ⓦwww.chicagoartsdistrict.com. This thriving artist community, just southwest of the Loop, covers twelve blocks – from 16th Street to the north, to Canalport Street to the south. For over forty years this traditionally down-at-heel area, now largely comprised of bright and airy lofts, has provided a center for contemporary artists, photographers, sculptors, and performance artists as well as art teachers. With hundreds of talented young artists from different backgrounds, it's here you are likely to see some of Chicago's most innovative, daring, and thought-provoking artworks.

Frederick Baker Inc 1230 W Jackson Blvd; Mon–Fri 10am–5pm, and by appointment ⓣ312/243-2980, ⓦwww.frederickbakerinc.com. This expansive gallery houses the Midwest's largest collection of European and American fine prints. There is a selection of 1930s–1940s lithographs by the quintessentially regionalist painter Grant Wood ($2500–7500). Their inventory has also included a 1974 artist's-proof lithograph by Marc Chagall, entitled *Autoportrait* ($22,500). You will also find one of the largest and most rewarding collections of Chicago images, including the stellar works of Ken Auster, Nick Bridge, Mark McMahon, and Bascove.

Thomas McCormick Gallery 835 W Washington St; Tues–Sat 10am–5.30pm ⓣ312/226-6800, ⓦwww.thomasmccormick.com. Located in the West Loop gallery district, this expansive loft space focuses on early twentieth-century modern art as well as presenting select works of young emerging artists. Of special note are the abstract expressionist works of New York avant-garde painters Melville Price, Mary Abbott, and Bostonian Perle Fine. In addition to its permanent collections, the gallery also hosts travelling exhibitions.

Evanston

Gillock Gallery 930 Ridge Ave, by appointment only ⓣ847/864-3799, ⓦwww.gillockgallery.org. This alternative space located in the Victorian home of gallery-owner Connie Gillock specializes in figurative paintings and landscapes by Midwestern artists. Call ahead for details of the rotating exhibitions, which change several times each year.

Maple Avenue Gallery 1745 Maple Ave; Tues & Wed 10.30am–6pm, Thurs, Fri & Sat 10.30am–8pm, Sun noon–5pm ⓣ847/869-0680, ⓦwww.mapleavenuegallery.com. In downtown Evanston, this sleek industrial space, whose artworks are aimed more at the consumer rather than the collector, features around thirty local and international artists at any one time, across a variety of different media including paintings, original prints, mixed media, and sculpture. Of particular interest are the works of Jim Martin, Lily Balasanavo, and Carol Sams.

19

Gay and lesbian Chicago

As the metropolis of the Midwest, Chicago has long been a cultural and social magnet for small-town **gays and lesbians**, who make up a sizeable minority here and are fairly visible, not just at the **Pride Festival** or **Northalsted Market Days**, two of the city's most popular summer events. This visibility has had a small political impact: in 2001, Illinois' first openly lesbian mayor, Joanne Trapani, was elected in suburban Oak Park, while the Chicago city council in 2002 passed an ordinance outlawing discrimination against transgendered people. Cultivating a spirit of inclusiveness, Chicago's Mayor Daley, never one to shy away from polemics, said he would have "no problem" issuing gay marriage licenses.

Gay life in Chicago revolves around the North Side area known as **Boystown** (the moniker coined by Mayor Daley), a part of the Lakeview neighborhood that stretches east from Halsted Street to the lake and north from Belmont Avenue to Grace Street. **Halsted** in particular has been the long-standing center of gay life, and most of the action in Boystown focuses on the street's gay bars and gay-friendly restaurants around Roscoe Street.

Increasingly, however, the more affordable and less-congested Swedish enclave of **Andersonville** (see p.127) to the north has been steadily luring gays and lesbians away from Lakeview for several years, with a host of increasingly stylish restaurants, bars, and shops, focused around N Clark and Foster, catering to the gay community and a hip crew of straight denizens. And even further to the north, still-developing **Edgewater** and **Rogers Park** seem destined to be the next pockets in Chicago's already robust gay, lesbian, bisexual, and transgender scene.

You can get a feel for Chicago's gay scene by picking up a copy of the *Chicago Free Press* (Ⓦwww.chicagofreepress.com) or *Windy City Times* (Ⓦwww.outlineschicaco.com), both **weeklies** with extensive gay and lesbian news and local event listings. For nightlife info, try *Gay Chicago* or *Boi Chicago*, weekly rags that detail just where the boys (and, occasionally, girls) will be partying next. All are free and can be picked up at corner boxes or in bars. **Lesbians** should check out the Chicago-specific Ⓦwww.dykediva.com, a fun, helpful site that lists upcoming lesbian parties, readings, concerts, and seminars. For a list of other gay resources and organizations in Chicago, see p.244.

Accommodation

While few properties in the area cater exclusively to gay men and lesbians, you'll feel right at home in just about every hotel in and around Boystown. Prices range from $70–250, based on the cheapest double-room rate available during high season.

The Ardmore House 1248 W Ardmore Ave, Lincoln Park ⓣ & ⓕ773/728-5414 (call before faxing), ⓦwww.ardmorehousebb.com; Red Line to Thorndale. Cozy, exclusively gay, B&B in a comfortably furnished, restored Victorian on a quiet residential street close to the lake and a gay beach (Hollywood Beach). Three rooms share two full baths, plus an outdoor hot tub with secluded sundeck. Other amenities include Internet access, satellite TV, and a nightly social hour, as well as continental breakfast on weekdays and full hot breakfast on weekends. Reservations required; two-night minimum stay on weekends. $70–150

Best Western Hawthorne Terrace 3434 N Broadway, Wrigleyville ⓣ773/244-3434 or 1-888/860-3400, ⓕ773/244-3435, ⓦwww.hawthorneterrace.com; Red Line to Belmont. Close to Wrigley Field, this boutique hotel with vintage charm draws a pretty even mix of gay and straight guests. Most spacious rooms are equipped with Internet and satellite facilities, refrigerators and microwaves. There is a patio terrace and parking. Complimentary breakfast is included. $100–150.

Hotel Burnham 1 W Washington St, the Loop ⓣ312/782-1111 or 1-866/690-1986, ⓕ312/782-0899, ⓦwww.burnhamhotel.com; Red or Blue Line to Washington; Brown, Green, Orange, or Purple Line to State/Lake. This gorgeous boutique hotel oozes turn-of-the-century grandeur and is very gay-friendly – mention the "pride rate" for a significant discount. Marble, mosaics, crystal, and mahogany at every turn complement original features from 1895. A pet-friendly hotel, so even your pooch can bask in the luxury. Check ⓦwww.burnhamhotel.com/html/bur_hotdates.php for fantastic discounts. $150–250.

City Suites Hotel 933 W Belmont Ave ⓣ773/404-3400 or 1-800/248-9108, ⓕ773/404-3405, ⓦwww.cityinns.com; Brown, Purple, or Red Line to Belmont. Within easy reach of Boystown, although the price you'll pay is the grinding noise from passing trains and traffic. A friendly boutique hotel, the rooms, while nothing special, are reasonably well equipped with data ports and refrigerators. The Art Deco lobby has been given a welcome facelift and a decent continental is included in the price. Eclectic mix of gay men, artists, and performers. $100–140

Days Inn Lincoln Park-North 644 W Diversey Parkway, Lincoln Park ⓣ773/525-7010, ⓕ525-6998, ⓦwww.lpdaysinn.com; Brown or Purple Line to Diversey. Gay-friendly hotel of particular appeal for its good location just a ten-minute walk from Boystown. What it lacks in character and charm it makes up for in convenience, service, and value. $70–100

Flemish House of Chicago 68 E Cedar St, Gold Coast ⓣ312/664-9981, ⓕ664-0387, ⓦwww.chicagobandb.com; Red Line to Clark/Division. Gay-owned and friendly, but mostly straight clientele at these B&B apartments in a beautifully renovated 1892 row house. Six guest rooms done in attractive English Arts & Crafts style, each with full kitchen, bath, TV, and phone. Rates include self-serve continental breakfast. No smoking, no children; two-night minimum stay. $100–200

The Gold Coast Guest House 113 W Elm St, Gold Coast ⓣ312/337-0361, ⓕ337-0362 ⓦwww.bbchicago.com; Red Line to Clark/Division. Relaxed, gay-friendly B&B with easy access to Mag Mile shopping and dining. For more details, see p.174. $100–150

Majestic 528 W Brompton Ave, Boystown ⓣ773/404-3499 or 1-800/727-5108, ⓕ773/404-3495, ⓦwww.cityinns.com; Red Line to Addison. Quiet, elegant inn near the lake on a residential Boystown street. For more details, see p.177. $100–150

Villa Toscana 3447 N Halsted St, Boystown ⓣ773/404-2643 or 1-800/404-2643, ⓕ773/404-2416, ⓦwww.thevillatoscana.com; Red Line to Belmont. Six clean, smallish rooms in a gay-owned Victorian B&B, with a mostly gay male clientele. The house, in the heart of Boystown, set back from the street with a private sundeck, has three rooms with private bath; others are shared. No smoking, no pets. Basic amenities include phone, cable TV, and self-serve continental breakfast. Reserve at least a month ahead. $99–$139

Cafés and restaurants

While many Chicago **restaurants** attract a sizeable gay following (*Dinotto Ristorante* in Old Town, Randolph Street's *Blackbird*, and *Marche*, for instance), the places listed below have become fixtures on the city's gay and lesbian scene.

The following reviews use four **price ranges**: inexpensive (below $15), moderate ($15–25), expensive ($25–40), and very expensive (over $40).

Angelina 3561 N Broadway, Boystown ⓣ773/935-5933; Red Line to Addison. Romantic, low-lit atmosphere and reasonable prices (average entrees $20) make this cozy Italian date-spot a neighborhood favorite. Well-balanced menu features goat cheese and beet salad, duck risotto with caramelized onion, lamb shank with chianti broth, and hot chocolate bread pudding topped with vanilla-bean ice cream for dessert. Moderate–expensive.

Ann Sather 929 W Belmont Ave, Lakeview ⓣ773/348-2378; Red Line to Belmont. Local Swedish chain, which has developed into something of a gay institution, bearing the hallmark of its proprietor, gay activist Tom Tunney; see p.197.

Arco de Cuchileros 3445 N Halsted St, at W Cornelia, Boystown ⓣ773/296-6046. Excellent tapas bar on the north end of Boystown, bustling with a predominantly gay clientele, that provides dozens of tasty possibilities in a no-frills but comfortable setting. Stay a while with a pitcher of delectable sangría. Moderate.

Caribou Coffee Company 3300 N Broadway, Boystown ⓣ773/477-3695; Red Line to Belmont. Not your typical chain coffee shop. Affectionately nicknamed "Cariboy," this comfortable, cruisy café is packed most nights and weekend afternoons with gay men reading, lounging in easy chairs, and watching the scenery go by. Inexpensive.

Cornelia 738 W Cornelia, Boystown ⓣ773/248-8333; Red Line to Addison. This rustically elegant restaurant with crisp white tablecloths, black-and-white photographs of gay icons, and a centerpiece piano, serves a broad menu of bistro fare ranging from shiitake pancakes to fried calamari, inventive salads, and predictable classics such as lemon-butter chicken and salmon with spinach. When it's good, it's fantastic, but consistency is not *Cornelia*'s strong point. There is outdoor seating in summer and great service. Closed Monday. Moderate to expensive.

Firefly 3335 N Halsted St, Boystown ⓣ773/525-2505; Red Line to Belmont. This recent arrival, just down the block from the boy bars, is a loungey, late-night space offering creative French bistro fare at reasonable prices. Don't miss the creamy parmesan deviled eggs or the flaky, tender grilled salmon with crunchy veggies. Open till 1.30am (Sun till 12.30am); closed Tuesdays. Moderate to expensive.

Joy's Noodles 3257 N Broadway, Boystown ⓣ773/327-8330; Red Line to Belmont. Good, super-cheap, pan-Asian plates bring the boys out in full force at this very casual neighborhood BYOB joint. Delicious *lard na* (fried rice noodles with chicken and broccoli), chicken satay, baby egg-rolls, and more. The service is friendly, the atmosphere inviting, and there is an outdoor garden in summer. Inexpensive.

Jin Ju 5203 N Clark, at Foster Ave, Andersonville ⓣ773/334-6377; Red Line to Berwyn. A local favorite, this approachable Korean restaurant caters to the western palate and the budget-minded with reworked traditional dishes such as *te gim* (tempura), *bi bim bop* (rice with beef, vegetable, and egg), and spicy ribs. The decor is stylishly understated with soft lighting and a hip clientele. The drinks are one of the major draws, with the signature *sojutini* (Korean grain liquor made from sweet potato). Moderate to expensive.

Kit Kat Lounge and Supper Club 3700 N Halsted St, Boystown ⓣ773/525-1111; Red Line to Addison. At this cool South Beach–inspired lounge club, the decor – exposed brick contrasts with bright white *Miami Vice* booths and leopard-skin prints. The menu features upscale comfort food with a smattering of exotic, coconut-infused delicacies. Mouthwatering. Camp entertainment comes in the form of drag queens who strut through the narrow room, mimicking gay icons from the 1940s and 1950s. Closed Mondays. Expensive.

Tomboy 5402 N Clark St, Andersonville ⓣ773/907-0636; Red Line to Berwyn.

Lesbian-owned standby with a hip gay and lesbian crowd and comfortably chic exposed-brick decor. Each dish is perfectly executed and artfully presented. The signature dish is a seared yellow-fin tuna steak with *wasabi*, while more Mediterranean flavors include a goat-cheese-stuffed chicken breast, gazpacho soup, and filet mignon. Desserts are worth saving room for; try the much-vaunted bread pudding. BYOB (corkage $5) in addition to a fully stocked bar. Expensive.

Tweet 5020 N Sheridan Rd, at W Argyle Ave, Andersonville ⓣ773/728-5576; Red Line to Argyle. The quirky and perky *Tweet* is a relative newcomer with a small but perfectly formed menu of wholesome bistro classics including *escargots*, *caprese* salads, lamb chops, and strip steak, and heavenly desserts, like vanilla *crème brûlée* and chocolate *soufflé*. The prix-fixe is menu is served before 7pm. BYOB. Moderate.

Yoshi's Café 3257 N Halsted St, Boystown ⓣ773/248-6160; Red Line to Belmont. If you can get past the generic, upscale diner decor, you're in for a treat. The French cuisine, infused with Japanese flavors and textures, results in delicious concoctions like chicken and mushroom spring roll with cucumber salad or grilled sea scallops with green-tea pasta in pesto sauce. The desserts, including *crème brûlée* and chocolate mousse layered with berries and crunchy caramelized *mille feuilles* are delicious. Outdoor seating in summer provides great people-watching. Brunch is served on Sundays with doughy *brioche* and fresh carrot juice. The service is sleek and the wine list comprehensive. Closed Mondays. Expensive.

Bars and clubs

Most gay and lesbian **bars** in Chicago do not charge a cover; those that do are noted below. The minimum drinking age is 21 and strictly enforced – always carry a **photo ID**. Many of the places listed are frequented by a mixed crowd, and you'll find that even bars and clubs that tend to be exclusively gay will still be welcoming to a straight clientele.

@mosphere 5355 N Clark St, Andersonville ⓣ773/784-1100; Red Line to Berwyn. This far North Side neighborhood bar, with exposed brick walls and metal decor, attracts a crowd of mostly straight and gay men and some lesbians. There's a small dancefloor if the dj music so moves you – 80s on Wednesdays and pop and house on Saturdays. The requisite lure of drink specials features $2 Bud on Fridays and $12 pitchers of Stoli on Wednesdays.

Baton Show Lounge 436 N Clark St, Near North ⓣ312/644-5269; Red Line to Grand. You won't believe your eyes when you see the drag queens at this famed River North club, which draws more straight men, tourists, and bachelorette parties than gay men. Showtimes Wed–Sun 8.30pm, 10.30pm, and 12.30am. $10–14 cover with two-drink minimum.

Berlin 954 W Belmont Ave, Lakeview ⓣ773/348-4975; Red Line to Belmont. Legendary dance spot where a pumped, mixed crowd grooves to some of Chicago's hottest djs. The boys come out for "Testosterone Tuesdays," while ladies gather for "Women Obsession Wednesdays," every week except the last of the month. The last Sunday of every month is a Prince Night – where the artist's tunes are played and the crowd is decked out in the requisite flamboyant attire. Cover $3–5.

Big Chicks 5024 N Sheridan Rd, Andersonville ⓣ773/728-5511; Red Line to Argyle. A fixture on the scene, this laid-back Far North favorite features a dancefloor, pool table, and despite its name, an eclectic, mostly gay male crowd. With the owner's eclectic artwork covering the walls, erotic outpourings on the TV monitors, and djs on the weekends, this is a night of fun and fetish, guaranteed. Free Sunday-afternoon barbecues in summer pack the place. Free parking in the alley behind the bar.

Charlie's 3726 N Broadway, Lakeview ⓣ773/871-8887; Red Line to Addison. Sporting brassy buckles and lashings of leather fringing, Midwestern cowboys strut their stuff on the large dancefloor which takes up most of the small space at this popular late-night country bar. Free line-dance lessons Mondays and Wednesdays at 7.30pm and

Saturdays at 9pm. There's karaoke on Tuesdays and after 2am on Friday and Saturday nights, the dj spins house music until the wee hours. Small cover on weekends. Open Mon & Tues till 2am, Wed–Fri till 4am, Sat till 5am.

Circuit Nightclub 3641 N Halsted St, Lakeview ⓣ773/325-2233; Red Line to Addison. After a makeover in 2004, this cavernous nightclub is the place to be for circuit boys and club kids on Saturday nights, when the glowsticks come out and the techno starts pumping. The front room or "Rehab Lounge" hosts disco bingo on Mondays and karaoke on Tuesdays, while the amped-up, camped-up, back room is dedicated to unbridled grooving with a spicy Thursday Latin night, plus a wild ladies dance party on Fridays. Cover $5–15. Open Sun–Wed till 2am, Thurs & Fri till 4am, Sat till 5am.

The Closet 3325 N Broadway, Lakeview ⓣ773/477-8533; Red Line to Belmont. Tiny, aptly named late-night lesbian hangout with a small bar and an even smaller dancefloor. It's also very popular with the boys, who flood the place on weekends when the 2am Halsted bars let out. Open Sun–Fri 2pm–4am, Sat noon–5am.

Crobar Nightclub 1543 N Kingsbury St, Lincoln Park ⓣ312/337-5001; Red Line to North/Clybourn. Following massive renovations, *Crobar* returned in 2003 with a disco-industrial look and continues to be the pinnacle of Chicago's adrenaline-fueled, and liquor-infused, hard-core dance club scene. Put on your tightest, most glittery clubwear for Sunday "Anthem" Club (Gay, Lesbian, and Everything Else), a hugely popular night of progressive dance music for muscle boys and glam girls in the enormous *Crobar* dance complex. Cover $10–30.

Gentry of Chicago 440 N State St, Near North ⓣ312/836-0933; Red Line to Grand. This intimate cabaret, popular with showtune lovers and piano barflies, features live entertainment every day of the week and draws a mostly male crowd of suits from the neighborhood. The main room features a Martini bar and lures a more mature crowd, while the lower level has video projections and a more youthful vibe. Sunday nights are open mic. Two-drink minimum cover.

Red Dog 1958 W North Ave, Bucktown ⓣ773/278-1009; Blue Line to Damen. A young crowd hits this dance club on Monday nights to groove at the club's weekly gay night extravanganza, "Boom Boom Room," featuring lively, cutting-edge house music. Cover $5.

▽ A Boystown favorite

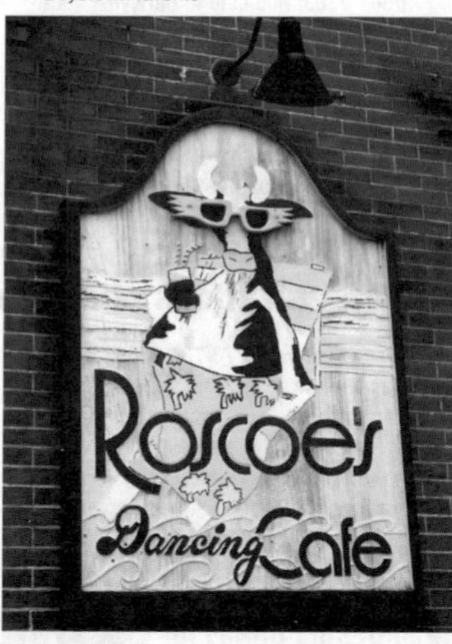

Roscoe's 3356 N Halsted St, Lakeview ⓣ773/281-3355; Red Line to Belmont. Boystown's best hangout for younger guys, this comfortable video bar and club has five rooms befitting different moods, a pool table, fireplace, plus a large dancefloor, which packs in the leather-clad cheek by jowl. The outdoor patio, open in summer, serves light meals, and is prime cruising territory in summer. Theme nights include karaoke Mondays and game show Wednesdays. Small cover on Saturdays.

Sidetrack 3349 N Halsted St, Lakeview ⓣ773/477-9189; Red Line to Belmont. This sleek, friendly video bar draws a thirty something male crowd and sprawls over four connected rooms, including the airy "glass bar," with lofty ceilings, a rooftop deck, and a wall of windows looking out onto Halsted. Great frozen drinks, including a potent, purple Ketel One Crush, which fatally slides down as easy as lemonade. Music is generally pop divas – Madonna, Britney, Kylie, and Cristina. Theme nights are huge, particularly Sunday showtunes and Thursday comedy clips.

Spin 800 W Belmont Ave, Lakeview ⓣ773/327-7711; Red Line to Belmont. A tattooed and pierced, mixed crowd call this bar and dance club home. Dollar drinks draw a big crowd on Wednesdays ($5 cover), as does the Friday shower contest. Small cover on Saturdays.

Star Gaze 5419 N Clark St, Andersonville ⓣ773/561-7363; Red Line to Berwyn. Chicago's main lesbian hangout, this dance club and restaurant draws an all-ages mixed crowd, including some straight men. There's an inviting outdoor beer garden, plus pool tables, darts, and a limited menu of bar food, salads, and pastas. Fridays feature salsa music, with $2 drinks on Thursdays and karaoke on Sundays. Closed Mondays.

T's 5025 N Clark St, Andersonville ⓣ773/784-6000; Red Line to Lawrence. This casual, colorful Andersonville spot hosts a laid-back mixed crowd and offers bar-food staples such as cheesy fries and chicken tenders up front. There are couches and a pool table in the back, where on Wednesday nights there's open mic; popular with the lesbian crowd. Half-price bottles of wine on Tuesdays.

Gay organizations and resources

About Face Theatre ⓣ773/784-8565, ⓦwww.aboutfacetheatre.com. Well-respected and exploratory theater company that analyzes issues of gender and sexuality both on stage and in workshops at area schools. Previous productions have included *Monsieur Proust*, the work of Tony Award–winner Mary Zimmerman, produced in association with the Steppenwolf Theatre; see p.228.

Brown Elephant 3651 N Halsted ⓣ773/549-5943; Red Line to Sheridan. All proceeds from this Wrigleyville resale shop go towards the Howard Brown Health Center which specializes in HIV- and AIDS-related treatments and

Festivals and events

Fireball early Feb (ⓣ773/244-6000, ⓦwww.heartsfoundation.com). Three days of nonstop dancing at clubs around the city. Proceeds benefit the Hearts Foundation, which supports local HIV/AIDS service organizations.

International Mr Leather weekend before Memorial Day (ⓦwww.imrl.com). A fabulous extravaganza – if you are gay or straight – of fetish, fun, and S&M at this quite surreal event – usually hosted in the most unexpected of locations (in 2006, at the *Palmer House Hilton*). Leather-loving men (and women) come from all over the world to mingle, buy the latest leather, props, toys, and reading and video material, and to check out the competition to crown the hottest leather man of all.

Chicago Pride Festival late June (ⓣ773/348-8243, ⓦwww.chicagopride.com). The Gay Pride month-long series of events celebrating Chicago's gay community, culminates with the Gay Pride Parade as 250 colorful floats, pop music, food, and frivolity gather along Halsted St and Broadway on the last Sunday in June. Throughout June, look out for theater, panel discussions, athletic events, and religious services.

Northalsted Market Days early Aug (ⓣ773/883-0500, ⓦwww.northalsted.com). This two-day street fair is one of the largest in the Midwest and offers some great people-watching. Staged in Boystown, it draws more than 250,000 people with live music played on three stages, hundreds of vendors and food from dozens of local restaurants.

Windy City Rodeo third weekend in Aug (ⓣ312/409-3835, ⓦwww.ilgra.com). At this annual gay fundraising event, whip-cracking cowboys and cowgirls from across the US compete in roping, bull riding, and racing, sandwiched between bar crawls, music and dancing, and victory galas.

Reeling: the Chicago International Gay and Lesbian Film Festival late Aug to early Sept (ⓣ773/293-1447, ⓦwww.reelingfilmfestival.org). Established festival, running for two weeks at venues around the city showing a quality mix of shorts, documentaries, and feature-length movies with both entertaining and avant garde themes and production.

counselling. An Aladdin's cave of everything from books and CDs to jewelry and clothes, computer accessories, and knick-knacks. Open daily noon–6pm.

Chicago Area Gay & Lesbian Chamber of Commerce 1210 W Rosedale ⓣ773/303-0167, ⓦwww.glchamber.org; Red Line to Thorndale. Helpful community organization offering info packets for visitors and listings of shopping resources, jobs, and more.

Gerber/Hart Library 1127 W Granville Ave ⓣ773/381-8030, ⓦwww.gerberhart.org; Red Line to Granville. North of the city, in Edgewater, this circulating library holds more than 13,000 books and an extensive archive of periodicals, videos, and artifacts relating to gay, lesbian, bisexual, and transgender individuals. Run by volunteers, the Gerber is very active in the gay community with outreach programs and a strong Gay Pride event presence.

Illinois Gender Advocates 47 W Division St Suite 391 ⓣ312/409-5489, ⓦwww.itstimeil.org; Red Line to Clark/Division. A political advocacy group for the transgender community, organizing demonstrations and vigils, publishing newsletters, and more.

Illinois HIV and STD HELPLine ⓣ773/929-4357. Provides crisis counseling and information on gay-related health issues. Mon–Fri 9am–9pm, Sat and Sun 10am–6pm. National AIDS hotline: ⓣ1-800/342-2437.

Unabridged Books 3251 N Broadway ⓣ773/883-9119; Red Line to Belmont. Longstanding, friendly, independent Boystown bookstore with extensive gay and lesbian sections, from literature to erotica, as well as a great travel section, and a treasure-trove of sale shelves. Mon–Fri 10am–10pm, Sat & Sun 10am–8pm.

Women & Children First 5233 N Clark St ⓣ773/769-9299, ⓦwww.womenandchildrenfirst.com; Red Line to Berwyn. One of the nation's largest feminist bookstores, this Andersonville favorite stocks over 30,000 women's-interest books, children's books, and gay and lesbian titles. Frequent readings and discussion groups, too. Mon & Tues 11am–7pm, Wed–Fri 11am–9pm, Sat 10am–7pm, Sun 11am–6pm.

Sports and activities

In Chicago, professional-sports attachments seems to permeate all levels of society, and you'll find that just about everyone has a handle on Major League Baseball, the NFL, and the NBA, as well as the local outfit's respective standings. Supporting the local pro teams is a huge part of the Chicago mindset; walk the streets and you won't go far without passing some Chicago sports paraphernalia plastered across store windows or inside a crowded sports bar.

Attending a **professional sports event**, be it a baseball, football, basketball or hockey game, should be a priority for any visitor. At the top of the list is a Cubs game at Wrigley Field, where you can experience Chicago at its most prideful while soaking up the atmosphere of one of the great standing shrines to old-school sports stadiums.

Locals are just as enthusiastic about **participatory activities**, from biking to bowling, and the city has been blessed with mile upon mile of lakefront parkland, fantastic for jogging, cycling, in-line skating, swimming, volleyball, fishing, boating, golfing, or simply lazing on a beach. Most of the action happens throughout Lincoln Park, the wide swath of greenery that stretches six miles north of downtown, the largest urban park in the country.

Spectator sports

"Going to the game" in Chicago is a year-round pastime, since there's always a sport in season: football in the fall and winter; hockey and basketball in the fall, winter, and spring; baseball in the spring and summer; and baseball and soccer in the spring, summer, and fall. When it's too cold for most locals to be active

Getting tickets

Buy **tickets** to most professional sporting events in Chicago through Ticketmaster (Ⓣ312/559-1212 or 559-1950, Ⓦwww.ticketmaster.com); it's also possible to buy them at one of several Ticketmaster outlets throughout the city (inside Carson Pirie Scott, Tower Records, and at the Hot Tix booths at 72 E Randolph St. and 163 E Pearson St).

You can also buy directly from the individual team's box office, especially at the last minute. If all else fails, you can try ticket brokers, although they usually charge higher prices. Try either Gold Coast Tickets (Ⓣ1-800/889-9100, Ⓦwww.goldcoasttickets.com) or ticketsnow.com (Ⓣ1-800/927-2770).

themselves – be it playing softball or tennis or jogging by the lake – you'll often find them packed into sports bars in a sort of hibernation until warm weather comes and everyone floods outside again.

Baseball

Chicago boasts one of America's most beloved ballparks, **Wrigley Field** at 1060 W Addison St, at Clark St (see p.124), and one of the country's perennially mediocre baseball teams, the **Chicago Cubs** (ⓣ773/404-2827, ⓦwww.cubs.com). Although the Cubs haven't won a World Series since 1908, the team's fans are famously loyal, and most home games sell out each season. Seeing a game there is a must even for non-baseball devotees. For a true Wrigley experience, sit in the general admission outfield bleachers, home to the rowdiest of fans, known as the "bleacher bums," who follow their own set of rules for each game, such as always throwing back a home-run ball hit by the opposing team.

While the popular Cubs have remained consistent non-achievers, their South Side rivals, the less celebrated **Chicago White Sox** (ⓣ312/674-1000, ⓦwww.chisox.com) have fared far better winning the 2005 world series, their first world series win since 1917. They now play at the more modern but sterile U.S. Cellular Field at 35th Street and Dan Ryan Expressway – the previous stadium, Comiskey Park (see p.139), was demolished not many years ago, and used to be right next to where the new one is.

The baseball season runs between April and September. Ticket prices for Cubs games are $6–250; $7–57 for Sox games.

Basketball

Neither the **Chicago Bulls** (ⓣ312/455-4000, ⓦwww.nba.com/bulls) nor the city of Chicago had any real idea what impact one acquisition – **Michael Jordan** in the 1984 draft – would have on their next fifteen years. Jordan went on to become quite simply the best player in the history of professional basketball, almost single-handedly changing the fortunes of the Bulls and the game as a whole. He led the team to win six NBA titles in the 1990s, and his gravity-defying heroics still inspire the next generation of basketball hopefuls. His retirement from the Bulls in 1999 left the team reeling, and the squad is just starting to recover, thanks to an influx of young players, who helped propel the 2004–05 team to the playoffs for the first time since Jordan's departure.

The basketball season begins in the fall, and playoff games stretch into the summer. Tickets for Bulls games, played at the **United Center** at 1901 W Madison St start at $10 for 300-level seats, with courtside seats costing $600.

Football

Known as the "Monsters of the Midway," football's **Chicago Bears** (ⓣ312/295-6600, ⓦwww.chicagobears.com) have been playing at **Soldier Field** at 425 E McFetridge Drive since the 1930s. The stadium recently underwent a massive $600 million renovation (see p.103), which basically constructed a new, modern stadium within the historic colonnades and exterior walls of the old park, resulting in a hodgepodge of architectural styles that has justly gained it the nickname "the mistake by the lake."

Despite years of down seasons, the Bears still pack the stadiums come fall, and tickets are highly coveted. As with other Chicago professional sports teams, fans are extremely loyal (verging on the obsessive), and routinely fill the seats despite the sub-zero temperatures at the lakefront stadium. Founded in 1920 as the Decatur Staleys by legendary coach George Halas, the team was the nation's first

△ Statue of Michael Jordan outside of the United Center

pro football squad, and became the Chicago Bears in 1922. The 1985 team, under the lead of coach "Iron Mike" Ditka lost one game all season, won the Super Bowl, and ranks as one of the great teams of all time.

The football season opens the first week of September and runs through December. Tickets for Bears games are $50–330.

Ice hockey

In this rough-and-tumble city, professional hockey has a major following – or at least it did until 2005, when a prolonged players' strike ended the 2004–05 season before it started. Though the strike was resolved, only time will tell whether the fans will come back to the troubled league. In the team's heyday in the early '90s, with star players Jeremy Roenick, Chris Chelios and Ed Belfour, Blackhawk games earned a reputation as one of the loudest sporting events in the country, and when the October to April season rolls around, tickets to **Chicago Blackhawks** games (ⓣ312/455-7000, ⓦwww.chiblackhawks.com) are generally hard to get.

If you want to catch a Hawks game while in town, you'll have to see them at the **United Center** because the team's owners refuse to broadcast home games on TV – another reason the Hawks haven't quite gained the popularity of the city's other major sports teams. Tickets for games start at $10, with rinkside seats going for $250. (For details on the United Center, see p.132.)

Alternatively, you can catch a minor league game at **Allstate Arena** at Mannheim Road and Lunt Avenue, in Rosemont, with the **Chicago Wolves** (ⓣ847/724-4625, ⓦwww.chicagowolves.com), and while the play won't be as spectacular as you'd see at a Blackhawks game, it's another entertaining way to get a taste of Chicago's intense sports scene.

Soccer

Ironically, one of Chicago's most successful professional sports teams in recent years is also one of its most underappreciated: the **Chicago Fire** (ⓣ1-888/MLS-FIRE, ⓦwww.chicago-fire.com), of Major League Soccer. Since joining the league in 1998, the squad – with an international roster of players from Mexico, Jamaica, Africa, Eastern Europe, and the US, has advanced to three MLS Cup finals in only seven years of existence.

Big things are afoot for the team in April of 2006, when it will start the new season in its brand-new $70 million, 20,000-seat soccer stadium in southeast suburban Bridgeview at 71st and Harlem. The team will finish out the 2005 season with games through October at **Soldier Field**, before moving to the new stadium. Tickets for Fire games range from $15–75.

Horse racing

One of the country's best tracks for thoroughbred horse racing is located northwest of Chicago in Arlington Heights – a half-hour's ride on Metra commuter rail. **Arlington Park Race Course**, 2200 Euclid Ave (ⓣ847/385-7500), is open May through September (Wed–Sun), with gates opening at 11am and post time (first race) usually at 1pm. The highlight of the season is the running of the high-stakes **Arlington Million**, a 1.25mile turf race that draws top steeds from around the world for a seven-figure purse.

Besides the usual races, the track also hosts "Party in the Park" on Friday afternoons, pulling in the after-work crowds with cheap drinks and live music on the front lawn; the first race doesn't start till 3pm.

To get here, board the Union Pacific Northwest line at Ogilvie Transportation Center and get off at the Arlington Park stop (round-trip $7.40). The train drops you right at the park.

Activities

Chicagoans tend to hibernate during the winter, taking shelter from the cold and the wind and the snow that hits the city between November and March (and sometimes later). But when the weather finally shifts in the spring, locals break outside and take advantage of the warmth with countless outdoor activities, from jogging, biking, or playing volleyball along the lake, to tennis, golf, softball, sailing, and birdwatching. Most of the action centers in Lincoln Park (see p.250), whose bike paths and green space are particularly inviting to the city's young, physically fit crowd.

Bicycling

With hundreds of miles of **bike trails** and a fifteen-mile paved path along the lakefront, Chicago is a bicyclist's dream. This main path alone spans 15 miles, from the far northern neighborhood of Edgewater to the University of Chicago in Hyde Park on the South Side – passing by the heart of downtown – and it makes for one of the best outdoor experiences in the city. The path is easily accessible, too, with entrances at every underpass along Lake Shore Drive. The city's streets are also handy for cycling, with 120 miles of bike lanes on stretches of Halsted Street, Wells Street, Lincoln Avenue, and Damen Avenue, among others. The North Shore area of Chicago is a popular destination for cyclists too; the nine-mile asphalt and crushed-stone **Green Bay Trail** from Wilmette to Highland Park is a particular favorite. The City of Chicago publishes a **free map** with bike lanes and paths and recommended routes through the city and suburbs. Call ⓣ(312) 742-2453 for a free copy.

Bike Chicago Navy Pier ⓣ312/755-0488, North Avenue Beach ⓣ773/327-2706, ⓦwww.bike chicago.com. This outfit has more or less cornered the bike rental market in Chicago, and with two key (and relatively accessible) rental outlets, it should be your first call for bikes and in-line skates. Prices start around $10/hour or $35/day; day rates drop to $10 if you rent for a minimum of four days during the week. All rentals include locks and maps.

Chicagoland Bicycle Federation ⓣ312/42-PEDAL, ⓦwww.chibikefed.org. Organization that promotes cycling in the city, hosts cycling tours and events, and offers services like bike registration and safe bicycling tips.

Chicago Cycling Club ⓣ773/509-8093, ⓦwww.chicagocyclingclub.org. Local social club that organizes rides every Saturday and Sunday between April and October, most leaving at 8.30am from the clock tower in Lincoln Park (at Waveland Avenue and the lakefront path, just south of the golf course). Rides range from 15 to 100 miles and are open to riders of all experience levels.

On the Route Bicycles 3146 N Lincoln Ave ⓣ773/477-5066, ⓦwww.ontheroute.com. Full-service bike shop that also rents road bikes, mountain bikes, and city bikes; the latter rent for around $35/day (24 hours), $20/half-day.

Birdwatching

Chicago's best place for **birdwatching** is the Magic Hedge, an area of trees and shrubs east of Lake Shore Drive at Montrose Point (look out for the sign on Montrose Harbor Drive). Jutting out into Lake Michigan, this grassy area is right in a major migration path and can be visited year-round. Sightings of more than three hundred species of birds have been recorded on this sandy hill.

The best time to visit is during spring and fall migrations, but on any given day you're likely to spot up to fifty-odd species, including warblers, swallows, and falcons; especially eye-catching are the thousands of purple martins that flock here in early August.

Boating

As the city sits right on an enormous lake, the popularity and accessibility of boating is no surprise (see "Fishing," p.252, as well). The **Chicago Sailing Club**, 2712 N Campbell Ave (Ⓣ773/871-7245, Ⓦwww.chicagosailing club.com), organizes sailing lessons, rentals and charters from dock B at the north end of Belmont Harbor, at Belmont and the lake. Rentals are available to the public, with J22 boats from $35 to $55/hour, and J30 boats from $70 to $90/hour. (To get to Belmont Harbor, take Lake Shore Drive north of Belmont to Recreation Drive, then turn right and follow the road back to the harbor.) The club also offers windsurfing lessons and equipment rentals, often from Montrose Beach, just north of the harbor.

Between May and September, there's a paddleboat rental service on Lincoln Park's South Pond, outside *Café Brauer*, 2021 N Stockton Drive ($10/30min or $15/hr). Boat rental is open from 10am to dusk.

The Chicago Area Sea Kayaking Association Ⓦwww.caska.org. Web-based organization offers evening paddles on Lake Michigan and is a good source for current information on kayaking around Chicago.

The Lincoln Park Boat Club Ⓣ773-549-2628, Ⓦwww.lpbc.net/Paddling. This social club offers paddling and rowing classes, just south of W Fullerton Avenue, at the Lincoln Park Lagoon.

Bowling and billiards

Bowling fans will find plenty of alleys in Chicago – including two new spaces that give the pastime a trendy spin. All but two of the following alleys offer both bowling and billiards facilities.

10Pin 330 N State St, in Marina City, River North Ⓣ312/644-0300, Ⓦwww.10pinchicaog .com. Trendy downtown bowling lounge with 24 lanes and a 128-foot HDTV video wall, plus a casual menu of gourmet pizzas and comfort food (before 5pm $4.95 per person per game; after 5pm $6.95 per person). Sun–Thurs 11am–midnight, Fri 11am–2am, Sat 11am–3am.

The Corner Pocket 2610 N Halsted St, just north of W Wrightwood Ave, Lincoln Park Ⓣ773/281-0050. Closer to a neighborhood pool hall (with a bar, and a kitchen in front) than the larger, more sterile places, with nine regulation-size pool tables ($10/hr, Fri & Sat $12/hr after 8pm). Mon–Fri 4pm–2am, Sat & Sun noon–3am.

Diversey River Bowl 2211 W Diversey Parkway Ⓣ773/227-5800, Ⓦwww.drbowl.com. A cheesy yet fun place to bowl amid flashing strobe lights, smoke machines, and loud Eighties music. Lane prices vary by the day: Mon–Thurs $19/hr, Fri & Sat $32/hr, and Sun $26/hr. Shoes $3. Open daily noon–2am, Sat till 3am.

Lucky Strike 322 E Illinois St, Streeterville Ⓣ312/245-8331, Ⓦwww.bowlluckystrike.com. Hollywood-based nightspot draws a club-ready crowd with 18 lanes, 11 pool tables, three separate bar areas, and American fare like burgers and buffalo wings. (bowling $4.95–$6.95 per person per game; pool $10–$14 per hour). Daily 11am–2am.

Seven Ten Lounge 2747 N Lincoln Ave in Lincoln Park Ⓣ773/549-2695. This Art Deco alley, with eight lanes and six pool tables, has two bars as well as decent finger food. The lanes may not be the best in the city, but the ambience makes up for it. Lanes cost $15/hr and shoes $2, while pool tables are $10/hr Sun–Thurs, $12/hr Fri & Sat. Mon–Fri 4pm–2am, Sat noon–3am, Sun noon–1am.

Southport Lanes & Billiards 3325 N Southport Ave, Lakeview Ⓣ773/472-6600. Really a bar with four bowling lanes and a few pool tables, but the vintage setting – complete with human pinsetters – makes this a fun place to bowl. You'll need to call ahead to reserve a lane, as the place is extremely popular. Rates are a little cheaper than usual ($16/hr, $2 for shoes). During the week, lanes are less busy, opening at 6pm and closing when demand falls off or when the bar closes, usually around 1am. On weekends lanes open in the early afternoon and stay open later (but are often occupied by private parties and groups). As for pool, there are six regulation-size tables ($10/hr during the week, going up to $12/hr on peak nights).

Waveland Bowl 3700 N Western Ave, one block north of W Addison St, Roscoe Village; Ⓣ773/472-5902, Ⓦwww.wavelandbowl.com; Red Line to Addison. The rare bowling alley that's open 24hr, 7 days a week – it's often full with leagues until around 9.30pm. Open since 1959, the recently refurbished alley

Chicago's beaches

In summer, the city's beaches are swamped with locals trying to escape the intense heat and humidity. While none are secluded or private in any way – Lake Shore Drive is buzzing nearby – they are a pleasant place to take a break and catch some rays.

The city's main beaches are listed below; several other popular beaches are located further north in Rogers Park and on the North Shore (see p.159 for more information).

All of the beaches listed below are free and usually open 9am–9.30pm between May and September, and you'll find public restrooms in the vicinity.

The main beaches

Foster Avenue Beach Sedate, clean beach near the northern tip of Lincoln Park. The beach house has concessions and outdoor showers.

Fullerton Avenue Beach Just east of Lake Shore Drive, this concrete stretch is popular thanks to the adjacent Theater on the Lake, which occasionally hosts evening shows on weekends during the summer (see p.228).

Montrose Beach Wide, sandy beach with volleyball courts; less crowded than the North Avenue and Oak Street beaches. You'll find Lincoln Park's bait shop here, as well a fishing pier (see "Fishing," p.252).

North Avenue Beach Just east of Lake Shore Drive, the city's most popular beach has volleyball nets, a Bike Chicago outlet (see p.250), and a boat-shaped beach house with concessions, and volleyball equipment rental, along with *Castaway's Bar & Grill*.

Oak Street Beach A place to see and be seen, this busy, fashion-conscious patch of sand just east of Michigan Avenue is decked out with volleyball courts and a bistro, with skyscrapers as a backdrop.

has three regulation-size pool tables, an arcade, and a little theater showing Disney flicks for kids. Prices depend on when you play, but expect to pay between $1 and $6 per game, with games being more expensive after 5pm and on weekends. Prices for pool table rental also vary, though you'll generally pay between $8 and $12/hr.

Fishing

Few people come to Chicago with **fishing** in mind, but the city has several places where anyone can put a line in the water. Chicago is, after all, on a lake well-endowed with fish (especially coho and king salmon), and though angling trips and charter service are by no means plentiful, they do exist.

Most charter boats launch from north or south of the city, though a few service downtown fishermen (see below). Check the **Chicago Sportfishing Association**'s website (Ⓦwww.great-lakes.org/il/fish-chicago/) for a list of charter boat operators. Prices usually start from $400 per six people per four hours.

If fishing from a boat doesn't appeal, there are a number of places where you can fish from shore. Popular fishing spots include Lincoln Park's **South Lagoon**, the pier at **Montrose Harbor**, and just about anywhere there's a cement embankment along the lake. Fly fishermen often head to the pier at the south end of the North Pond to practice their casting – it's surrounded by floating rings that serve as targets.

The Park Bait Shop, at Montrose Avenue and Harbor Drive (Ⓣ773/271-2838), can set you up with bait (minnows and worms).

Captain Al's Charter Service 400 E Randolph Drive Ⓣ312/565-0104, Ⓦwww.captainalscharters.com

Captain Bob's Lake Michigan Charters Ⓣ1-888/929-3474, Ⓦwww.confusioncharters.com

Spendthrift Charters Ⓣ1-800/726-7309, Ⓦwww.spendthriftcharters.com

Golf

There are dozens of excellent **golf courses** within the greater Chicago area, as well as a few courses close to downtown.

Diversey Driving Range & Mini-Golf 141 W Diversey Parkway ⓣ312/742-7929, ⓦwww.diverseydrivingrange.com; Brown/Purple Line to Diversey. A terrific alternative to Waveland (see below), this driving range is open daily 7am–10pm, year-round (they have 25 heated mats), and rents clubs; a bucket of sixty balls costs $7, with the last bucket sold around 9.30pm.

Harborside International Golf Center 111th St and Bishop Ford Expressway ⓣ312/782-7837. One of the best courses in the area – a links-style eighteen-hole course far down on the South Side. The only drawback is that you'll need your own transport to reach the course. Tee-time must be booked in advance, and greens fees start around $75 for eighteen holes.

Jackson Park Golf Course 63rd Street and Lake Shore Drive ⓣ773/667-0524. An eighteen-hole course on the South Side that's open year-round, from dawn to dusk. Greens fees start around $20.

Sydney R. Marovitz Golf Course 3600 Recreation Drive ⓣ773/667-0524. Also known as "Waveland," this popular nine-hole course is right on the lakefront near downtown and best suited for casual players who want to squeeze a few holes into their day (you'll need to book in advance, though). Rounds start around $15.

Jogging

Jogging remains one of the city's favorite athletic pastimes, thanks in large part to the extensive park system and the lakefront trail, where the majority of the city's runners tend to congregate; jog either on the paved bike path or the dirt path – scenic routes either way. You can join the trail at most avenues and gauge your run using the mile markers along the way. Aside from the lakeshore path, the city's parks offer miles of gravel-lined and paved jogging and walking trails; call the Chicago Park District at ⓣ312/742-PLAY for more information.

The **Chicago Area Runners Association** (ⓣ312/666-9836, ⓦwww.cararuns.org) organizes runs that meet at the north end of Diversey Harbor (membership not necessary). They can also provide information on upcoming races, as well as training for the **Chicago Marathon**, the city's biggest running event (ⓣ312/904-9800, ⓦwww.chicagomarathon.com), which occurs on the first or second Sunday in October.

21

Festivals and events

During the freezing winter, Chicagoans tend to hibernate, with just a handful of citywide events able to lure locals out into the cold. But after St Patrick's Day, the Windy City comes alive with a host of **festivals and events**, with just about every neighborhood hosting its own weekend party. For a complete list of festivals, contact the Chicago Convention and Tourism Bureau (ⓣ1-877/CHICAGO) or check out their website at ⓦwww.chicago.il.org. Dates tend to change from year to year; call the numbers listed and check the local press for exact dates and times.

For a list of national public holidays, see Basics, p.40. Select festivals are listed in "Gay and lesbian Chicago," pp.239–245, and "Performing arts and film," pp.225–234.

January

Chicago Boat, RV, & Outdoors Show early Jan ⓣ312/946-6200, ⓦwww.chicagoboatshow.com. Boat-lovers' extravaganza at McCormick Place, where you can check out more than 600 boats, 300 RVs, and hundreds of booths catering to outdoor enthusiasts from all over the Midwest.

Chicago Cubs Convention mid-Jan ⓣ773/404-CUBS. Cubs fans pay upwards of $40 to attend this popular weekend at the *Hilton Chicago and Towers* to meet and get autographs and photos taken with their favorite players. Proceeds benefit Cubs Care, the team's charity organization.

Chicago Winter Delights Jan–March ⓣ877/244-2246, ⓦwww.877chicago.com. Family-friendly weekends of gourmet tastings, free blues and jazz shows, and discounts at city museums, hotels, restaurants, and shops all over the city.

Information lines

Chicago Convention and Tourism Bureau ⓣ1-877/CHICAGO (244-2246) or 1-866/710-0294 (TTY)

Chicago Cultural Center ⓣ312/346-3278

Mayor's Office of Special Events ⓣ312/744-3315

February

African American Heritage Month all month ⓣ312/747-2536. Exhibits, special events, and programs celebrating black history and culture all over the city, with many held at the South Shore Cultural Center.

Chicago White Sox "Soxfest" early Feb ⓣ312/565-0769. Fans of the South Side sluggers get their fix of player autographs and photos at this weekend event at the *Hyatt Regency Chicago*.

Chicago Auto Show mid-Feb ⓣ630/495-2282, ⓦwww.chicagoautoshow.com. The nation's largest auto show, a 10-day event at McCormick Place where the world's top automakers show off nearly 1000 different vehicles, from tame trucks to futuristic concept cars.

Chinese New Year Parade date varies ⓣ312/225-6198 or 689-0338, ⓦwww.chicagochinatown.org. Painted horses, traditional lion dancers, and a 100-foot-long dragon snake along Wentworth from Cermak to 24th St. The parade also features Miss Chinatown and her court, and a flurry of fireworks at the neighborhood's biggest celebration of the year.

March

St Patrick's Day Parade Sat before St Patrick's Day ⓣ312/942-9188, ⓦwww.chicagostpatsparade.com. One of the city's most raucous celebrations, with the Chicago River dyed an emerald green for the occasion. Parade starts at Balbo and goes north on Columbus past Buckingham Fountain.

South Side Irish St Patrick's Day Parade St Patrick's Day ⓦwww.southsideirishparade.org. Less touristy and more authentic than the city event, this is the nation's largest neighborhood parade, drawing up to 300,000 revelers as it meanders through Irish communities Beverly and Morgan Park on Western from 103rd to 115th streets.

Flower & Garden Show second week ⓣ312/222-5086, ⓦwww.chicagoflower.com. Lush gardens, hands-on demonstrations, and hundreds of product and educational booths highlight this weeklong event for green thumbs at Navy Pier.

Smelt Fishing varies ⓦwww.chicagolandfishing.com. For a couple of weeks each spring between March and May, thousands of finger-sized smelt (salmon-like fish, tasty when pan-fried) swarm along the lakeshore to spawn around 2–3am. When the call goes up ("The smelt are running!"), grab a net and head to the water; just south of Navy Pier's a good spot.

April

Hellenic Heritage Parade early April ⓣ773/775-4949. A Chicago tradition for more than 40 years, with one hundred-plus Greek-American religious and civic organizations marching through Greektown along Halsted St between Randolph and Van Buren streets.

Earth Day Festival all month ⓣ312/742-PLAY. Month-long, city-wide festival of activities including park clean-ups, nature studies, and celebrations with live music and puppet shows.

Kids & Kites Festival last Sat ⓣ312/744-3315. Kids make and fly their own kites and watch professional flyers strut their stuff at this family-friendly event celebrating National Kite Flying Month at Montrose Harbor.

May

Cinco de Mayo Festival first week ⓣ312/399-9644. Five-day party celebrating Mexico's 1861 victory over the French, with live music, food vendors, soccer tournament, and a parade that winds through Pilsen along Marshall Blvd, between Cermak Rd and 26th St.

Polish Constitution Day Parade first Saturday ⓦwww.chicagosocietypna.org. Polish folk dancers, marching bands, and local Polish organizations march up Columbus Drive downtown in this, the nation's largest parade commemorating Poland's constitution of May 3, 1791.

Art Chicago at Navy Pier early May ⓣ312/587-3300, ⓦwww.artchicago.com. Works by more than 3000 international artists are on display and for sale at this Navy Pier contemporary art show, which also features lectures, panel discussions, and special exhibitions like "The Stray Show," which gives exposure to ten emerging galleries and projects from around the US.

△ The Chicago Blues Festival in Grant Park

Bike Chicago mid-May to mid-June ⓣ312/744-3315, ⓦwww.cityofchicago.org/specialevents. Month-long festival promoting Chicago's bike-friendly streets, with a full slate of neighborhood rides, bike safety clinics, the Bike to Work Rally, and more.

Asian-American Festival late May ⓣ312/744-3315. From Thai food to Indian stand-up comedy, this five-day event at Daley Center Plaza celebrates Asian culture with food vendors, activities, and live entertainment.

Memorial Day Parade Sat before Memorial Day ⓣ312/744-0565. One of the nation's largest Memorial Day parades, with more than 10,000 participants and close to 300 marching units, veterans' groups, and bands making their way from Balbo to Monroe along Columbus Drive.

Chicago Blues Festival late May to early June ⓣ312/744-3315. ⓦwww.cityofchicago.org/specialevents. Without a doubt the best blues festival in the world, it's also Chicago's largest music festival, with four days of free performances in Grant Park by more than seventy performers, usually a roster of all-time legends.

June

Printers Row Book Fair first weekend ⓣ312/987-9896, ⓦwww.printersrowbookfair.org. Booksellers from around the country peddle their wares – new, used, and antiquarian - under five tented blocks in the historic district on Dearborn St between Congress Parkway and Polk St.

57th Street Art Fair first full weekend ⓣ773/493-3247, ⓦwww.57thstreetartfair.org. Hyde Park fair with more than 300 artists displaying and selling their work in painting, photography, jewelry, sculpture, and other media.

Chicago Gospel Music Festival first full weekend ⓣ312/744-3315. Free concerts on three stages in Grant Park draw enthusiastic crowds of gospel music fans, some of whom sing a few bars themselves at the open-mic sessions in the Youth Tent.

Ravinia Festival early June to early Sept ⓣ847/266-5100, ⓦwww.ravinia.org. Pack a picnic basket and head north to suburban Highland Park, where for $10 you can get lawn seats to concerts ranging from the Chicago Symphony Orchestra to Tony Bennett.

Wells Street Art Festival second weekend ⓣ773/868-3010, ⓦwww.chicagoevents.com. Fine-art fair/street party for North Side yuppies, with 250 exhibitors competing for attention. There's a live music stage, food vendors, and children's theater, all on Wells St between North Ave and Division St.

Andersonville Midsommarfest second weekend ⓣ773/665-4682, ⓦwww.andersonville.org. Everybody's a little Swedish on this weekend, as the city's Scandinavian enclave puts on a fun two-day party with live music, street vendors, and a pet parade, all along Clark St from Foster to Balmoral avenues.

Old Town Art Fair second weekend ⓣ**312/337-1938,** ⓦ**www.oldtowntriangle.com.** Crowded but fun weekend in one of the city's prettiest neighborhoods, with hundreds of booths hawking art, plus food and drink. Several lovely residential gardens are opened to the public.

Juneteenth Celebration mid-month ⓣ**773/684-6070 or 247-6200.** Celebrating the end of slavery, with events at venues like the Old Town School of Folk Music (see p.223) and the Chicago Children's Museum, with live music, storytelling, song and dance, food, and a spirited parade along 79th St from Stony Island Ave to South Shore Drive.

Northcenter's Ribfest mid-month ⓣ**773/525-3609,** ⓦ**www.northcenterchamber.com.** Weekend-long neighborhood street party on Lincoln Ave between Irving Park Rd and Warner Ave, with a car show, two live music stages, an amateur cook-off, and ribs aplenty.

Chicago Country Music Festival last weekend ⓣ**312/744-3315.** Big names often turn out for this free, foot-stomping two-day festival in Grant Park, which coincides with the opening weekend of Taste of Chicago (see below). With line dancing, dance lessons, and music on two stages.

Taste of Chicago late June to early July ⓣ**312/744-3315,** ⓦ**www.cityofchicago.org/specialevents.** More than three million people packed like sardines in Grant Park enjoy free concerts and scarf down deep-dish pizza, cheesecake, and hot dogs at this massive ten-day festival in the heat of summer.

July

Rock Around the Block first weekend ⓣ**773/665-4682,** ⓦ**www.starevents.com.** Lakeview traffic comes to a standstill as this local music festival takes over the intersection of Lincoln, Belmont, and Ashland avenues, with thirty local bands jamming continuously on three stages.

Independence Eve Fireworks Spectacular 3rd ⓣ**312/744-3315.** Cool, free, pyrotechnic display in Grant Park accompanied by the Grant Park Symphony Orchestra, which opens the evening with a concert of patriotic favorites like *God Bless America* and *Stars and Stripes Forever*.

Chicago Yacht Club Race to Mackinac mid-July ⓣ**312/861-7777.** Prestigious, invitation-only race from Chicago's Monroe Harbor, 333 miles to Mackinac Island, Michigan. Watch the boats parade past Navy Pier with their ceremonial flags raised before the race.

Old St Pat's World's Largest Block Party 3rd weekend ⓦ**www.worldslargestblockparty.com.** Touted as one of the city's best places to meet your mate, this church fundraiser draws 20,000 randy singles for food, drink, and live music in the West Loop to raise money for its namesake church.

Sheffield Garden Walk 3rd weekend ⓣ**773/929-9255,** ⓦ**www.sheffieldfestivals.org.** Lincoln Park neighbors open their posh private gardens to the public (more than 100 on view), while attendees stroll through the neighborhood, guzzle beer, and check out the decent live music.

Venetian Night late July/early Aug ⓣ**312/744-3315.** Half a million onlookers lounge along the lake at dusk as more than 35 elaborately decorated and illuminated boats promenade from the Shedd Aquarium to the Chicago Yacht Club, with further entertainment provided by the Grant Park Symphony Orchestra and a post-parade fireworks display.

Tall Ships Chicago late July/early Aug ⓣ**312/744-3315.** Majestic racing yachts, clipper ships, and replica trading schooners drop anchor along the lakefront; you can actually climb aboard and explore the impressive vessels during their five-day stay.

August

Retro on Roscoe first weekend ⓣ**773/665-4682,** ⓦ**www.starevents.com.** Yet another neighborhood street party, this one in fun, funky Roscoe Village (Roscoe St and Damen Ave), featuring an antique car and motorcycle show, food and craft vendors, and a full line-up of bands playing tunes from the 1970s, 80s, and 90s.

Chicago 16" Softball Championship second weekend ⓣ**312/744-3315.** More than one hundred men's, women's, and co-ed teams compete in six classes at this Grant Park softball tournament, played with a 16-inch ball and no mitts.

Bud Billiken Parade second Sat ⓣ**312/225-2400.** The largest African-American parade in the US, named for a mythical guardian of children. Drill teams, dancers, and local school kids march along King Drive from 39th to 51st streets, then live it up at a music festival and barbecue in Washington Park.

Chicago Air & Water Show mid-month ⓣ**312/744-3315.** Sleek military aircraft zoom over the lake performing aerobatic stunts for onlookers; prime views can be had along the lakefront between Oak St and Fullerton Ave. Skip the water show, unless you don't mind fighting the crowds for a glimpse of the lackluster "Ski Show Team."

¡VIVA! Chicago Latin Music Festival late Aug ⓣ**312/744-3315.** Tropical, merengue, salsa, and mariachi bands jam in Grant Park at this two-day event, alongside local merchants selling traditional food, clothing, and jewelry.

Mrs T's Chicago Triathlon weekend before Labor Day ⓣ**773/404-2281,** ⓦ**www.caprievents.com.** Iron men and women swim, bike, and run for glory along Lake Michigan in one of the world's largest triathlons.

Chicago Jazz Festival Labor Day weekend ⓣ**312/744-3315.** A mellow holiday-weekend crowd enjoys free jazz on three stages in Grant Park; there's an arts and crafts fair and wine garden, too.

September

German-American Festival early Sept ⓣ**773/728-3890,** ⓦ**www.lincolnsquare.org.** The old German neighborhood of Lincoln Square throws a party with live oompah music and dancing, and more beer and schnitzel than you can shake a stick at.

Mexican Independence Day early Sept ⓣ**312/654-5314 or 773/579-1200.** The official holiday is Sept 16, but most of the festivities – including three separate parades at 26th St, 47th St, and on Columbus Drive – happen in the two weeks before.

Berghoff Oktoberfest mid-Sept ⓣ**312/427-3170,** ⓦ**www.berghoff.com.** This beer bash on Adams St in front of the legendary German restaurant packs the streets with after-work revelers enjoying the live music and gorging on knackwurst and potato salad.

Around the Coyote Arts Festival mid-Sept ⓣ**773/342-6777,** ⓦ**www.aroundthecoyote.org.** No beer tent and no bad live music, just local artists displaying and selling their works for a weekend in studios, galleries, and even bars and restaurants, in the Wicker Park neighborhood.

Chicago Celtic Festival mid–Sept ⓣ**312/744-3315.** Free art fair and music festival in Grant Park, with several stages of live music, dance, and storytelling, plus vendors hawking handmade clothing and jewelry, and plenty of Guinness.

World Music Festival late Sept ⓣ**312/744-3315.** Musicians from as far as Niger, Turkey, and Brazil take the stage at venues all over the city.

Italian Market Days late Sept to early Oct. Lively lunchtime event at Block 37 (the empty lot at State and Washington streets), where Italian singers and dancers entertain and vendors sell pastas, breads, and cheese along with handmade dolls and masks.

October

Chicaglo Oct–Dec ⓣ**1-877/244-2246,** ⓦ**www.877chicago.com.** Three months of city-sponsored holiday events, from special markets and ethnic celebrations to ice-skating and parades.

Chicagoween all month ⓣ**312/744-3315.** Family-friendly Halloween events, from pumpkin-carving and spooky storytelling to haunted houses and even the Haunted "L" – a spooky tour of the Loop with costumed storytellers.

LaSalle Bank Chicago Marathon second Sun ⓣ**312/904-9800 or 1-888/243-3344,** ⓦ**www.chicagomarathon.com.** The fastest marathon in the world (thanks to the flat terrain), this event draws some of the world's best runners and creates a party atmosphere with thousands of spectators along the race route – especially around mile seven at Broadway and Belmont Ave, where a cheering station of drag queens makes even the most tired runner smile.

Northalsted Halloween Parade 31st ⓣ773/868-3010, ⓦwww.chicagoevents.com. The ghouls come out in full force for this parade and costume contest on Halsted St from Belmont Ave to Roscoe St.

November

Day of the Dead 1st ⓣ312/738-1503, ⓦwww.mfacmchicago.org. Traditional Mexican celebration of life and death; the Mexican Fine Arts Center Museum on 19th St (see p.135) boasts the nation's largest Day of the Dead exhibit, with colorful paintings, photography, and sculpture from Mexico and the US.

Dance Chicago all month ⓣ773/935-6860, ⓦwww.dancechicago.com. Dance festival showcasing the Joffrey Ballet, Hubbard Street Dance, and more than 200 other local jazz, ballet, tap, and modern dance troupes.

Lincoln Park ZooLights late Nov to early Jan ⓣ312/742-2165, ⓦwww.lpzoo.com. Light displays, ice carving, train rides, and a nightly laser show at the sea lion pool keep things hopping at this free zoo – though you will pay admission for this event (adults $8, kids 4–12 $6, free to kids 3 and under).

Magnificent Mile Lights Festival Sat before Thanksgiving ⓣ312/409-5560, ⓦwww.themagnificentmile.com. Mag Mile shops kick off the holiday season with an all-day celebration leading up to the lighting of more than one million lights strung from Oak St to Wacker Drive, followed by a fireworks show at the river.

Thanksgiving Parade last Thurs ⓣ312/781-5678, ⓦwww.chicagofestivals.org. More than a million spectators brave the cold to watch Kermit the Frog and the other balloons go by with marching bands on State St from Congress Parkway to Randolph St.

Holiday Tree Lighting Ceremony day after Thanksgiving. At Daley Plaza at 4pm, the mayor flips a switch and *voila* – the city's holiday tree (actually made of many smaller fir trees) lights up.

Christkindlmarket late Nov to mid–Dec ⓣ312/644-2662, ⓦwww.christkindlmarket.com. Dozens of festively decorated timber booths at Block 37 (State and Washington sts) sell handcrafted ornaments, nutcrackers, and other holiday trinkets, along with German fare like bratwurst, sauerkraut, and hot, spiced red wine.

December

Carol to the Animals first Sun ⓣ312/742-2000, ⓦwww.lpzoo.com. Carolers sing traditional holiday songs to the animals in the Lincoln Park Zoo; whether the animals like it or not is anyone's guess.

Winter WonderFest mid-Dec to early Jan ⓣ312/595-7437, ⓦwww.navypier.com. Family festival at Navy Pier with hundreds of decorated trees and plenty of entertainment, including puppet shows, storytellers, a skating rink, and Santa himself.

Kwanzaa Dec 26 to Jan 1 ⓣ773/947-0600, ⓦwww.dusablemuseum.org. The DuSable Museum of African American History (see p.147) celebrates Kwanzaa (an African-American holiday based on various African harvest festivals), with an exhibit of colorful textiles, paintings, and artifacts that explores the holiday's history and meaning.

Ethnic Market Chicago late Dec ⓣ312/744-3315. Last-minute Christmas shoppers escape the cold and sift through arts and crafts items from around the world inside a timber house set up at Daley Plaza (Clark and Washington sts).

Holiday Sports Festival last weekend ⓣ312/744-3315. All-ages event at McCormick Place where casual players try their hand at golf, martial arts, bowling, badminton, boxing, and more hard-core types compete in volleyball, soccer, table tennis, and basketball tournaments.

New Year's Eve Fireworks 31st ⓣ312/744-3315. Countdown to the New Year with Buckingham Fountain's own fireworks display, followed by the main pyrotechnic event above the lakefront at Montrose Harbor.

22

Shopping

Shopping is one of Chicago's strong suits, right up there with blues music and modern architecture. Long on classy department stores nestled in historic buildings, especially within the confines of the Loop and Near North, Chicago ranks right up there near New York among US cities in terms of variety and experience; in addition, the spacious stores and down-to-earth service make shopping here relatively hassle-free. You'll be able to shop even in the dead of winter, thanks to the abundance of huge indoor malls, though eventually you'll come in contact with the freezing temperatures outdoors, not the most delightful proposition.

As for shopping **categories**, the city is especially strong in **malls** you'd actually be interested in visiting, esoteric **music** shops, and **vintage and thrift stores**. This doesn't mean that trendy **boutiques** and the most modern fashions aren't accounted for as well; in truth, whatever you're looking for should be relatively easy to find.

Shopping by neighborhood

Shopping is concentrated in a few key areas of the city, all of them reachable by the El – we've indicated stops with each neighborhood overview below.

The Loop

As you might expect in the business district, some major department stores, like Marshall Field's and Carson Pirie Scott, line **State Street**, while **Wabash Avenue** has the pick of most everything else – camera shops, T-shirt stores, and other smaller service shops that are in no way specific to Chicago.

You'll have no trouble getting here as all El trains stop in the Loop.

The Magnificent Mile and Near North

The **Magnificent Mile**, or North Michigan Ave, Chicago's most famous shopping destination, draws throngs of shoppers for its malls and stores of all breeds, from big-name designers (Gucci, Armani) to commercial shopping (Niketown, The Gap, Bloomingdale's, Saks Fifth Avenue) to small Chicago-only establishments like Garrett Popcorn. Pick one of the malls or an end of the street, and work your way in the opposite direction.

To reach N Michigan Avenue on the El, take the Red Line to Chicago or Grand.

The Gold Coast and Old Town

Boutique shopping at its priciest happens along **Oak Street**, adjacent to the north end of Mag Mile. It's never very crowded, and for those with some extra coin to throw around, it's the best place to do so – home to lots of ultra-fashionable designers. As for Old Town, the little strip of **Wells Street** between Division and North Avenue has a fair number of lesser-known boutiques.

The Gold Coast is reachable on the Red Line (get off at Clark/Division and head east toward State Street), while the Brown Line stops at Sedgwick in Old Town.

Bucktown and Wicker Park

The shopping in these parts happens on two main strips, **Milwaukee and Damen avenues**. South of the "six corners" intersection of North, Milwaukee, and Damen avenues, Milwaukee Avenue more or less defines Wicker Park retro chic, with all sorts of oddball stores. Prices jump up as you head over to Damen Avenue, and then north of the six corners: boutiques are geared more toward the yuppie than the starving artist, as the area grows a bit more in tune with its Lincoln Park neighbor.

To get to Bucktown and Wicker Park on the El, take the Blue Line to Damen. You can also hop to Lincoln Park from here on the efficient crosstown #73 bus, which runs along Armitage Avenue.

Lincoln Park

The center of the Lincoln Park shopping scene is the intersection of **Armitage Avenue and Halsted Street**, and for most Chicagoans, it's the best place to shop: away from the throngs on Michigan Avenue, reachable by the El or by car (with easy parking on the side streets), and with plenty of restaurants, cafés, and bars to take a break from it all. The shops on Armitage tend to be of the local variety, many of which have been here for ages. Halsted Street receives plenty of spillover.

You can reach Lincoln Park on the El by taking the Brown Line to Armitage. The #73 Armitage bus runs to Bucktown and Wicker Park from here.

Lakeview

One thing to remember with Lakeview shopping: take the El, or hop a cab; if you're driving, most shops do not have their own parking and you're likely to search for a spot on the street for quite some time. **Belmont Avenue**, loaded with alternative and retro shops, is your best bet. **Clark Street**, which crosses through many neighborhoods, in fact hits its most interesting stride at its intersection with Belmont, though that's not to say that the rest of Clark isn't worth exploring.

Take the Red Line to Belmont to reach Lakeview.

Arts, crafts, and antiques

Alaska Shop 104 E Oak St, Gold Coast ☎312/943-3393. This small shop and gallery, hidden behind a jewelry store (Silver on Oak), has a fine selection of Inuit carvings, sculpture, and scrimshaw.

Ancient Echoes 1022A W Armitage Ave, Lincoln Park ☎773/880-1003. Beaded lampshades, stamped copper photo albums, fancy pewter sculptures and switchplates, handmade jewelry, pins, and artful furniture are a few of the handcrafted items at this eclectic boutique.

Broadway Antique Market 6130 N Broadway, Edgewater (north of Uptown) ☎773/743-5444. In this 20,000-square-foot, two-story space, more than 75 antique dealers peddle everything from vintage advertising signage to metalware, fine art, pottery, art glass, furniture, and lighting.

Faded Rose 1017 W Armitage Ave, Lincoln Park ☎773/281-8161. Cozy store with a nice selection of delicate linens and small housewares (bath products, picture frames, candlesticks), as well as custom-made

living room furniture. Adjoins Tabula Tua (see below).

Findables 907 W Armitage Ave, Lincoln Park ☎773/348-0674. This aptly named all-in-one gift boutique stocks a wide array of jewelry, china, candles, ornaments, picture frames, and the like.

Fourth World Artisans 3727 N Southport Ave, Lakeview ☎773/404-5200. Handcrafted folk art, clothing, textiles, musical instruments, and jewelry from Africa, India, Australia, and North and South America are featured in this gift shop on the Southport strip.

Gallery 37 Store 66 E Randolph St (inside Gallery 37 Center for the Arts), the Loop ☎312/744-7274. Works by emerging and apprentice artists on view at the Loop's Gallery 37 – part of the School of the Art Institute of Chicago (see p.66) – can be bought in the gallery's store, be it lawn ornaments, mosaics, jewelry, or furniture. Closed Sundays.

Pagoda Red 1714 N Damen Ave, Bucktown ☎773/235-1188. Huge showrooms on two floors carrying high-quality eighteenth- and nineteenth-century Chinese art (pottery, rugs, furniture, etc) – a nice change from the funky, casual secondhand stores in the neighborhood.

Poster Plus 200 S Michigan Ave, the Loop ☎312/461-9277. Three stories of fine art and vintage posters, as well as art-themed trinkets and custom framing.

Primitive Art Works 706 N Wells St, River North ☎312/943-3770. Intriguing River North gallery featuring four floors of ethnic artifacts – jewelry, furniture, textiles, etc, – that makes for a fascinating hour's worth of browsing. The staff's enthusiasm for the place is infectious.

Tabula Tua 1015 W Armitage Ave, Lincoln Park ☎773/525-3500. Linked to Faded Rose (see above), this small kitchenware store has unusual platters and place settings, engraved cheese spreaders, and other gift-worthy items.

Books

General bookstores

Barnes & Noble 1441 W Webster Ave, Lincoln Park ☎773/871-3610; 659 W Diversey Parkway, Lakeview ☎773/871-9004. Either of these huge outlets will have any recent or note-worthy title you'd ever want, except perhaps for academic textbooks or highly specialized works. Occasional author readings and children's storytelling; call for complete schedule.

Borders 150 N State St, the Loop ☎312/606-0750; 830 N Michigan Ave, Near North ☎312/573-0564; 2817 N Clark St, Lakeview ☎773/935-3909. Massive, well-stocked book and music store. The N Michigan Avenue branch is the biggest and best of the city's chain bookstores, centrally located right on Mag Mile, with a café, frequent readings and signings, and loads of room to sit and browse.

Europa Books 832 N State St, Near North ☎312/335-9677. This quaint neighborhood bookstore packs a lot into little space, including an excellent selection of foreign-language books, newspapers, and magazines.

Rare, used, and specialty books

Abraham Lincoln Book Shop 357 W Chicago Ave, River North ☎312/944-3085. You'll find more than eight thousand new, used, and antiquarian books on the shelves, covering the Civil War and other US military history, plus a host of collectibles and, of course, tomes on Lincoln himself.

Afrocentric Bookstore 4655 S King Drive, the Loop (inside Chicago Music Mart at DePaul Center) ☎773/924-3966. The city's best selection of African-American–related books, along with plenty of magazines, calendars, and greeting cards. The store also hosts occasional readings.

Chicago Rare Book Center 703 Washington St, Evanston ☎847/328-2132. Specializes in hard-to-find children's literature, jazz and blues, modern literature, art, Chicago, and the Midwest.

Myopic Books 1564 N Milwaukee Ave, Wicker Park ☎773/862-4882. Artsy and academic Wicker Park book haven selling both new and used rare titles.

O'Gara & Wilson 1448 E 57th St, Hyde Park ☎773/363-0993. Great little bookstore that has sold new and used books (both popular and obscure) since the late 1930s.

Prairie Avenue Book Shop 418 S Wabash Ave, the Loop ☎312/922-8311. Serene and spacious place where you can browse the phenomenal architecture selection (12,000+ titles) to your heart's content. The store also hosts frequent readings and signings.

Rain Dog Books and Café 408 S Michigan Ave, the Loop ⓣ312/922-1200. Smallish bookstore carrying new and used books, known for its antiquarian collection (upstairs). Usually a sedate place to sit, read, have a coffee, and listen to the ambient live jazz played by some of the city's finest musicians.

Savvy Traveller 310 S Michigan Ave, between W Jackson Blvd and W Van Buren St, the Loop ⓣ312/913-9800. Travel guides, electronic translators, maps, and anything else you might need on your trip, from travel insurance and wine carriers to games and luggage tags.

Seminary Co-op Books 5757 S University Plaza, Hyde Park ⓣ773/752-4381. Cavernous basement bookstore with a devout following, where row upon row of shelves is crammed with academic titles.

Unabridged Books 3251 N Broadway, Lakeview ⓣ773/883-9119. This Boystown favorite carries much gay and lesbian literature and a good all-around selection of fiction and non-fiction titles, children's literature, and travel guides. Great sale section in back.

Clothes and fashion

Chain stores

Anthropologie 1120 N State St, Gold Coast ⓣ312/255-1848; 1780 Green Bay Rd, Highland Park ⓣ847/681-0200. Major fashion chain that blends in well with the neighborhood. Expensive women's clothing and home furnishings with a romantic/bohemian slant.

Banana Republic 744 N Michigan Ave, Near North ⓣ312/642-0020; 2104 N Halsted St, Lincoln Park ⓣ773/832-1172. The ubiquitous chain's flagship store is on Michigan Avenue, whose casual men's and women's clothes are snapped up by huge swaths of the country's 20–40 age group.

Burberry 633 N Michigan Ave, Near North ⓣ312/787-2500. Michigan Avenue branch of the British stalwart clothier, known for its distinctive plaid; once conservative, the label is now popular with trendy urban types.

The Gap 555 N Michigan Ave, Near North ⓣ312/494-8580. Affordable men's and women's basics (jeans, T-shirts) that coordinate with just about anything.

Designer stores

Boss Hugo Boss 520 N Michigan Ave, Near North ⓣ312/660-0056. Tailored men's and women's clothing, sportswear, and accessories in an elegant Westfield North Bridge shop.

Cynthia Rowley 808 W Armitage Ave, Lincoln Park ⓣ773/528-6160. This Chicagoan's designs cater to pretty young things, with a good selection of flirty dresses and dainty separates.

Giorgio Armani 800 N Michigan Ave, Near North ⓣ312/751-2244. The last word in classically styled luxury Italian fashion.

Gucci 900 N Michigan Ave, Near North ⓣ312/664-5504. Designer Tom Ford's empire of style; it doesn't get more expensive than this.

Ralph Lauren 750 N Michigan Ave, Near North ⓣ312/280-1655. All-American high-end fashion label.

Boutiques

apartment number 9 1804 N Damen Ave, Bucktown ⓣ773/395-2999. Expensive men's boutique with an eye for of-the-moment labels and hot new designers.

Betsey Johnson 2120 N Halsted St, Lincoln Park ⓣ773/871-3961. Very distinctive, brightly colored, and funky clothing from this New York designer; somewhat over the top for conservative Chicago.

Celeste Turner 857 W Armitage Ave, Lincoln Park ⓣ773/549-3390. Armitage Avenue staple, with cool dresses and tops, but a bit pricey – T-shirts might set you back $80, a sweater $180.

Jade 1557 N Milwaukee Ave, Wicker Park ⓣ773/342-5233. Hip women's store with jewel-encrusted bags and belts and trendy clothing lines like London-based Frost-French and Madeleine Press.

Jake 939 Rush St, Gold Coast ⓣ312/664-5533; 3740 Southport Ave, Lakeview ⓣ773/929-JAKE. High-end denim, tees, and casual wear for men and women from exclusive lines like Nudie, Trovata, and Yanuk, plus local designers Kent Nielsen and Cecilie Broch.

Jane Hamill 1117 W Armitage Ave, Lincoln Park ⓣ773/665-1102. Stylish dresses, shoes, and jewelry from local designer Hamill. A good shop to find a sun dress.

Krista K 3458 N Southport Ave, Lakeview ⓣ773/248-1967. Upscale women's apparel – including stylish maternity wear – with a mix of local designers and trendy labels like Seven for All Mankind and True Religion.

Out of the West 1000 W Armitage Ave, Lincoln Park ⓣ773/404-9378. Cowboy-themed clothing and accessories, including boots, Lucky Jeans, Aztec-inspired turquoise jewelry, buckles, picture frames, lamps, and much more.

p.45 1643 N Damen Ave, Bucktown ⓣ773/862-4523. Hip boutique that doubles as an art gallery for designers. Spacious, with an attentive staff, and a chic selection of casual and dressy styles.

Shopgirl 1206 W Webster Ave, Lincoln Park ⓣ773/935-SHOP. Tiny, expensive boutique away from the Armitage strip that does well nonetheless by carrying some trendy labels including Three Dots, Trina Turk, and Shoshanna.

Sugar Magnolia 34 E Oak St, Gold Coast ⓣ312/944-0885. Distinctive upscale Chicago boutique that's managed to hold its own against Oak Street's ultra high-end competition. Stocks new and established designers.

Trousseau 3543 N Southport Ave, Lakeview ⓣ773/472-2727. Tops in women's lingerie, from brightly colored pajamas to lacey French bras.

Vive la femme 2115 N Damen Ave, Bucktown ⓣ773/772-7429. One of the city's only boutiques for stylish, full-figured women (sizes 12–28).

Vintage, secondhand, and thrift

Brown Elephant Resale Store 3651 N Halsted St, Lakeview ⓣ773/549-5943. Secondhand clothing – and actually much more, including records, books, and furniture – with proceeds going to the Howard Brown Memorial Clinic.

Daisy Shop 67 E Oak St, 6th Floor, Gold Coast ⓣ312/943-8880. Those willing to settle for gently worn couture will find a good selection from top designers at reduced – but still steep – prices.

Hollywood Mirror 812 W Belmont Ave, Lakeview ⓣ773/404-4510. Sells more junky trinkets than you'd ever wish upon anyone, but it's a stimulating place nonetheless. While they do sell an assortment of vintage clothing, just as much of a draw here is the kitschy ambience, helped along by the disco ball and lights, and loud punk music.

Lenny & Me 1463 N Milwaukee Ave, Bucktown ⓣ773/489-5576. Friendly consignment store that has a great assortment of women's clothing, though mostly for petite frames.

McShane's Exchange 1141 W Webster Ave, Lincoln Park ⓣ773/525-0211. High-end women's consignment store can be a treasure-trove of bargains, with everything from fur coats to Chanel suits at a fraction of retail price.

Recycle 1474 N Milwaukee Ave, Wicker Park ⓣ773/645-1900. Designer-conscious consignment store, with men's and women's jeans, shirts, and more.

Strange Cargo 3448 N Clark St, Wrigleyville ⓣ773/327-8090. Vintage clothing, jokey T-shirts, used Levis, wigs, costumes, wacky postcards, and all sorts of random kitsch adorn the shelves at this local favorite.

Una Mae's Freak Boutique 1422 N Milwaukee Ave, Wicker Park ⓣ773/276-7002. Affordable vintage clothes, perfumed candles, and an odd array of knick-knacks make this a quintessential Wicker Park locale.

Discount clothing

Filene's Basement 1 N State St, the Loop ⓣ312/553-1055. One of those stores where you can find everything, from soap trays to brand-name clothes, all at discounted prices. Competitor TJ Maxx, in the same building, has a decent selection of housewares.

Marshall's 600 N Michigan Ave, Near North ⓣ312/280-7506. Though you'll have to plow through racks and racks of clothing – from discount to designer labels – you'll usually find a bargain or two.

Nordstrom Rack 24 N State St, the Loop ⓣ312/377-5500. Great deals on high-end men's and women's clothing, home accessories, and particularly shoes.

Shoes

City Soles/Niche 2001 W North Ave, Bucktown ⓣ773/489-2001. Shoes with attitude – imports from Spain, Italy, and elsewhere. Also carries bags and other accessories.

DSW Shoe Warehouse 3131 N Clark St, Lakeview ⓣ773/975-7182. Thirty-five thousand pairs of name-brand and designer men's and women's shoes, from sandals and slippers to athletic and dress footwear. Socks and handbags, too.

Hanig's Footwear 660 N Michigan Ave, Near North ⓣ312/642-5330; also Hanig's Birkenstock Shop, 847 W Armitage Ave, Lincoln Park ⓣ773/929-5568. Carries major brands of walking shoes like Ecco, Mephisto, and Dansko. The Lincoln Park branch has one of the largest selections of sandals in the city.

John Fluevog Shoes 1539 N Milwaukee Ave, Wicker Park ⓣ773/772-1983. Flamboyantly trendy shoes from this Canadian label.

Johnston & Murphy 625 N Michigan Ave, Near North ⓣ312/751-1630. Staple for quality, conservative dress shoes.

Lori's Designer Shoes 824 W Armitage Ave, Lincoln Park ⓣ773/281-5655. The quintessential women's shoe store and one of the best in Chicago; styles run the gamut and there's also a good selection of one-of-a-kind bags and purses.

New Balance Chicago 2369 N Clark St, Lincoln Park ⓣ773/348-1787. Small neighborhood store selling one of the top brands in running shoes.

Niketown 669 N Michigan Ave, Near North ⓣ312/642-6363. This giant Nike retail outlet is a tourist attraction in itself, thanks in part to the video theater and miniature basketball court.

Cosmetics and fragrances

Aroma Workshop 2050 N Halsted St, Lincoln Park ⓣ773/871-1985. A great place for candles, though you'll find scented oils, incense, and the like here as well; there's also a mixing bar where you can create your own scents.

Fresh 2040 N Halsted St, Lincoln Park ⓣ773/404-9776. One of the hottest stores in Chicago, with knowledgeable staff and an extensive – though slightly expensive – selection of candles, soaps, lotions, and other beauty products.

MAC 40 E Oak St, Gold Coast ⓣ312/951-7310. Trendy make-up brand that caters to a youngish crowd, known for its glamour-heavy look.

Merz Apothecary 4716 N Lincoln Ave (at the intersection of Lincoln, Western and Lawrence), Lincoln Square ⓣ773/989-0900. Opened in 1875, this pharmacy is loaded with bath, body, and natural-health products, including some rare European items.

Powder Room 705 W Armitage Ave, Lincoln Park ⓣ773/640-1194. Recently arrived boutique cosmetics shop carries hard-to-find lines like Little Shop of Beauty, Jelly Pong Pong, SugarBaby, and a couple dozen others, all in a cute Lincoln Park storefront.

Stinkerbelle 1951 W Division St, Wicker Park ⓣ312/252-4120. Great selection of natural bath and beauty products from all over the world, including soaps, body washes, and moisturizers from uskincare, Les Basiques, and Pharmacopia. Tees, jewelry, and handmade bags, too, plus occasional workshops and classes.

Department stores and malls

Department stores

Barney's New York 25 E Oak St, Gold Coast ⓣ312/587-1700. Boutique department store carrying a highly edited selection of all the major designers. A more congenial and less-crowded version of its New York counterpart.

Bloomingdale's 900 N Michigan Ave, Near North ⓣ312/440-4460. Flagship Midwest store of the famous New York retailer. You could easily spend half a day in here and skip the rest of the Mile; part of the 900 N Michigan Avenue mall, it's near a movie theater, restaurant, and plenty of other shops.

Carson Pirie Scott & Co 1 S State St, the Loop ⓣ312/641-7000. Long-time competitor of Marshall Field's and always a step below, though it's still a great place to shop. The building itself is a tourist destination, considered a Louis Sullivan masterpiece (see p.54). Like Field's, they put on beautiful holiday-themed window decorations in December.

H&M 840 N Michigan Ave, Near North ⓣ312/640-0060; 22 N State St, the Loop ⓣ312/263-4436. Swedish department store concept offers trendy but affordable European fashions for men, women, and children.

Lord & Taylor 835 N Michigan Ave, Near North ⓣ312/787-7400. Whether this conservative department store succeeds in revamping its slightly dated image remains to be seen, though its sales are usually worth a look. Located in the same mall as the larger Marshall Field's.

Marshall Field's 111 N State St, the Loop ⓣ312/781-1000; 835 N Michigan Ave, Near North ⓣ312/335-7700. The original State Street location is Chicago's most famous store – a must if you intend to see what's behind the city's shopping appeal, especially around Christmas when the windows are decked in elaborate displays. Check out the blue Tiffany dome (see p.55) and the *Walnut Room* restaurant, a Field's institution. The smaller N Michigan branch still carries most designers. Note: All Marshall Field's branches will convert to the Macy's nameplate by Fall 2006.

▽ Marshall Field's famous clock

Neiman Marcus 737 N Michigan Ave, Near North ⓣ312/642-5900. This high-end, designer-oriented store comes with more attitude than the others, but at least there's usually plenty of room to shop.

Nordstrom 55 E Grand Ave ⓣ312/464-1515. Huge high-end retail chain with an excellent shoe department. Known for top customer service.

Saks Fifth Avenue 700 N Michigan Ave, Near North ⓣ312/944-6500. Similar to Neiman Marcus in its clothing lines and high price point, but known for its customer service and sales, and tends to be among the most crowded of the city's department stores. The first-floor make-up department is especially popular.

Sears 2 N State St, the Loop ⓣ312/373-6000. After several years' absence, the department store giant has returned to downtown with its affordable, but rather staid, merchandise.

Malls

900 North Michigan 900 N Michigan Ave, Near North ⓣ312/915-3900. Northernmost of the Michigan Avenue malls and its most upscale, with six levels that are home to Bloomingdale's, Gucci, J. Crew, and some seventy other stores. *The Oak Tree* restaurant (level 5) is a pleasant breakfast and lunch spot with great Mag Mile views.

Chicago Place 700 N Michigan Ave, Near North ⓣ312/642-4811. Eight-story space that includes Saks Fifth Avenue, Joy of Ireland, and fifty other stores, plus the largest food court on the Mag Mile.

The Shops at North Bridge 520 N Michigan Ave, Near North ⓣ312/327-2300. Airy, four-story Mag Mile complex dominated by Nordstrom's, with a clutch of children's stores, shoe stores, and an upscale food court.

Water Tower Place 835 N Michigan Ave, Near North ⓣ312/440-3166. Chicago's first and most famous vertical mall – seven stories and over one hundred big-name stores, including Marshall Field's and Lord & Taylor, plus a massive mezzanine-level gourmet food court.

Food and drink

Breadsmith (Wells Street Bread Co) 1710 N Wells St, Old Town ⓣ312/642-5858. This small, fabulous bread shop is a better alternative to the numerous chain coffee and breakfast joints in the area.

Fox & Obel Food Market 401 E Illinois St, Near North ⓣ312/410-7301. You don't need to be a gourmand to appreciate the superb selection of cheeses, fresh fish, meats, deli items, and baked goods on offer at this gourmet food emporium; there's a café here, too.

Garrett Popcorn Shop 670 N Michigan Ave, Near North ⓣ312/280-0162. Lines routinely stretch out the door at this venerated

▽ Garrett's storefront

Chicago institution, whose caramel-and-cheese flavored popcorns are out of this world. Other popular varieties include cashew, pecan, or macadamia caramel crisp.

House of Glunz 1206 N Wells St, Old Town ⓣ312/642-3000. Small family-run wine shop, purported to be the oldest wine shop in the nation. Great place to pick up some unique, inexpensive wines.

Lutz Continental Café & Pastry Shop 2458 W Montrose Ave, Lincoln Square ⓣ773/478-7785. Half-century-old German-style bakery where you can soak up the old-world ambience in the café at the back or take home delectable strudels, cakes, pastries, and marzipan from the glass cases up front.

Vosges Haut-Chocolat 520 N Michigan Ave (in the Westfield North Bridge Center), Near North ⓣ312/644-9450. Gourmet chocolate boutique renowned for truffles made with unique flavors and spices like ancho chile powder, absinthe, and balsamic vinegar.

Wikstrom's Gourmet 5247 N Clark St, Andersonville ⓣ773/275-6100. Assorted food from all over Scandinavia: Gothenburg sausage, Kavli flatbread, Danish pumpernickel bread, Swedish lingonberries, and the like.

Museum and gallery stores

ArchiCenter Shop 224 S Michigan Ave ⓣ312/922-3432; 875 N Michigan Ave (ground floor of the John Hancock Center), Near North ⓣ312/751-1380. The Chicago Architecture Foundation's retail arm, with a good selection of architecture-related books and knick-knacks.

The Art Institute of Chicago Museum Shop 111 S Michigan Ave, at W Adams St, the Loop ⓣ312/443-3534. Art books, reproductions, and a host of museum-related gift items.

Bariff Shop for Judaica Spertus Museum, 618 S Michigan Ave, South Loop ⓣ312/322-1740. A small shop devoted entirely to Judaica, with art, ceremonial pieces, books, and more.

MCA Store 220 E Chicago Ave, Streeterville ⓣ312/280-2660. Within the Museum of Contemporary Art, this small store carries art-related posters, gift cards, books, and home accessories.

Music stores

Blue Chicago Store 534 N Clark St, Near North ⓣ312/661-1003. The blues club's own store, packed with CDs, shirts, posters, and assorted paraphernalia, including the club's signature art by John Carroll Doyle. For club review, see p.219.

Dave's Records 2604 N Clark St, Lincoln Park ⓣ773/929-6325. Vinyl-only store with largish selection: some 50,000 new and used LPs, 45s, and 12-inch dance music and hip-hop.

Dr Wax 5225 S Harper Ave, Hyde Park ⓣ773/493-8696. This outfit carries new and used CDs, LPs, and tapes, but its strongest suit is its extensive secondhand CD bins.

Gramaphone 2843 N Clark St, Lincoln Park ⓣ773/472-3683. Packed to the gills with an outstanding selection of house, dance, and techno discs, from mainstream to underground, from Chicago and everywhere else. Djs spin in the back, and you can listen to any CD before you buy.

Hi-Fi Records 2568 N Clark St, Lincoln Park ⓣ773/880-1002. One of Chicago's better outlets for used vinyl, not so much for the usual rock and pop stuff as for the 12-inch dance music. You'll also find overflowing bins of super-cheap used LPs, and a used music-book section that turns up some good deals.

Jazz Record Mart 25 E Illinois St, the Loop ⓣ312/222-1467; ⓦwww.jazzrecordmart.com. Billing itself as "The World's Largest Jazz and Blues Shop," with the floor space and stock to back up the claim. In addition to aisles of new jazz and blues CDs, they also carry plenty of used vinyl, plus books and videos. There is also the occasional in-store performance (check website for schedule). A must-stop for blues and jazz lovers.

Reckless Records 1532 N Milwaukee Ave, Wicker Park ⓣ773/235-3727; 3161 N Broadway, Lakeview ⓣ773/404-5080. Chicago branch of the London-based used-music chain, with an extensive selection of CDs, DVDs, and vinyl (especially indie, punk, and imported electronica vinyl) at fair prices.

Rock Records 175 W Washington St, the Loop ⓣ312/346-3489. More than 20,000 music titles fill the bins at this superstore, with everything from classical to rap and hard rock. Posters, concert tees, and thousands of DVDs too.

Symphony Store 220 S Michigan Ave, the Loop ⓣ312/294-3345. One of the city's top spots to visit if you're looking for a classical music title. A wide array of recordings in stock.

Tower Records 2301 N Clark St ⓣ773/477-5994; 214 S Wabash Ave, the Loop ⓣ312/663-0660. A couple of entries in the massive chain, with wide selections and in-store appearances.

Virgin Records 540 N Michigan Ave, Near North ⓣ312/645-9300. The biggest mainstream music store in the city, right in the heart of Mag Mile.

Sporting goods stores

Active Endeavors 853 W Armitage Ave, Lincoln Park ⓣ773/281-8100. A Lincoln Park mainstay and part of the Armitage Avenue shopping route, this small, popular retailer sells outdoor gear and clothes.

Erehwon Mountain Outfitter 1000 W North Ave ⓣ312/337-6400. Probably Chicago's best selection of outdoor adventure clothes and gear.

Londo Mondo 1100 N Dearborn St, Gold Coast ⓣ312/751-2794; 2148 N Halsted St, Lincoln Park ⓣ773/327-2218; 444 W Jackson Blvd, the Loop ⓣ312/648-9188. Excellent selection of designer swimwear, workout clothing, and inline skates for active folks.

The North Face 875 N Michigan Ave, Near North ⓣ312/337-7200. Functional and stylish outdoor clothing and equipment, geared toward affluent adventure enthusiasts.

Orvis 142 E Ontario St, at N Michigan Ave, Near North ⓣ312/440-0662. Mag Mile version of this dependable New England retailer, with fly-fishing gear and ruggedly fashionable outdoor wear.

Running Away 1753 N Damen Ave, Bucktown ⓣ773/395-AWAY. Very cool boutique runner's shop, with a yoga studio downstairs.

Specialty shops

All She Wrote 825 W Armitage Ave, Lincoln Park ⓣ773/529-0100. Warm, family-run stationery store with unique and cool gifts and decorations.

The Alley 854 W Belmont Ave, Lakeview ⓣ773/348-5000. A temple to all things Goth, this landmark of alternative and fetish Chicago is worth a look if you're in the area. Entrance is in the alley.

Central Camera 230 S Wabash Ave, the Loop ⓣ312/427-5580. Century-old camera shop with knowledgeable staff.

Chicago Tribune Gift Store 435 N Michigan Ave, Near North ⓣ312/222-3080. Hats, shirts, and other souvenirs plastered with the *Tribune* logo.

City of Chicago Store 163 E Pearson St (across from the Water Tower), Near North ⓣ312/742-8811. As the name might suggest, Chicago souvenirs of all kinds.

Iwan Ries & Co 19 S Wabash Ave ⓣ312/372-1306. This second-floor cigar shop has been a Chicago family business for nearly 150 years. Over one hundred different cigar brands, and at least 13,000 pipes on hand.

Paper Source 232 W Chicago Ave, Near North ⓣ312/337-0798; 919 W Armitage Ave, Lincoln Park ⓣ773/525-7300. Wonderful paper boutique with a world of stationery, journals, cards, photo albums, and wrapping paper.

Scrapbook Source 557 W North Ave, Old Town ⓣ312/440-9720. From stickers and glitter to albums, paper, cutting tools, and stamps, this store offers a complete selection of scrapbooking supplies, plus table work-space for use by customers.

Spacetime Tanks 2526 N Lincoln Ave, Lincoln Park ☎773/472-2700. If your idea of relaxation means floating in vats of water in complete darkness, this "float center" is for you. Four isolation tanks, each renting at $40/hr. Closes at 9pm every night except Sundays.

Uncle Fun 1338 W Belmont Ave, Lakeview ☎773/477-8223. Wall-to-wall jokes and novelty toys – whoopee cushions, fake body parts, and more.

Waxman Candles 3044 N Lincoln Ave, Lakeview ☎773/929-3000. Scented and unscented columns, tapers, globes, and drip and non-drip candles are handmade at this funky, eclectic storefront, which also stocks cool candlesticks and candleholders large and small.

23

Directory

Airlines Aero Mexico ⓣ1-800/237-6639; Air Canada ⓣ1-888/247-2262; Alaska Airlines ⓣ1-800/426-0333; America West Airlines ⓣ1-800/235-9292; American Airlines ⓣ1-800/433-7300; American Trans Air ⓣ1-800/225-2995; British Airways ⓣ1-800/247-9297; British Midland ⓣ1-800/788-0555; Continental Airlines ⓣ1-800/525-0280; Delta Air Lines ⓣ1-800/221-1212; Frontier Airlines ⓣ1-800/432-1359; Independence Air ⓣ1-800/359-3594; JetBlue ⓣ1-800/538-2583; KLM ⓣ1-800/374-7747; Mexicana ⓣ1-800/531-7921; Northwest ⓣ1-800/225-2525; Southwest Airlines ⓣ1-800/435-9792; Spirit ⓣ1-800/772-7117; United Airlines ⓣ1-800/241-6522; US Airways ⓣ1-800/428-4322.

Area code Chicago has two main area codes – ⓣ312 (downtown as far as 1600) and ⓣ773 (the rest of the metropolitan area) – but you may come across the following too: ⓣ630 (west Chicago), ⓣ708 (south and west suburbs), and ⓣ847 (northern suburbs).

Banks Bank One ⓣ312/732-1164, ⓦwww.bankone.com; branches at 875 N Michigan ⓣ312/664-4600; 1122 N Clark ⓣ312/407-2626; 3730 N Southport Ave ⓣ773/281-7563. Citibank ⓣ1-800/926-1067, ⓦwww.citibank.com; branches at 100 S Michigan Ave ⓣ312/419-9002; 233 N Michigan Ave ⓣ312/977-5881; 11 S LaSalle St ⓣ312/853-5780; 69 W Washington Blvd ⓣ312/977-5131; Northern Trust Bank ⓦwww.ntrs.com; branches at 50 S LaSalle St ⓣ312/630-6000; 120 E Oak St ⓣ312/630-6666; 201 E Huron St ⓣ312/557-6200; 2814 W Fullerton ⓣ773/395-2255.

Bike rental See p.250.

Bus departures Call Greyhound ⓣ1-800/231-2222, in Chicago ⓣ312/408-5800, ⓦwww.greyhound.com; Lakefront Lines ⓣ1-800/638-6338, ⓦwww.lakefrontlines.com; or Indian Trails ⓣ1-800/292-3831 or 1-800/231-2222 (schedules), ⓦwww.indiantrails.com. Departures to Cleveland, Indianapolis, Milwaukee, Minneapolis, New York, and elsewhere are from the Greyhound terminal at 630 W Harrison St, at S Desplaines Street.

Currency exchange American Express: ⓣ1-800/528-4800, ⓦwww.americanexpress.com; offices at 605 N Michigan Ave, Suite 105 ⓣ312/943-7840; 55 W Monroe St ⓣ312/541-5440. Foreign Currency Exchange at terminals three and five, O'Hare International Airport. World's Money Exchange, Mezzanine Level, Suite M1, 203 N LaSalle St ⓣ312/641-2151.

Doctors The Chicago Medical Society (ⓣ312/670-2550) has a physician referral service that can point you to a doctor should you need one.

Electricity 110 volts AC. Plugs are standard two-pins – foreign visitors will need an adapter for any electrical appliances they bring, with the exception of dual-voltage shavers.

Embassies and consulates Australia: 123 N Wacker Drive, Suite 1330, 60606 ⓣ312/419-1480; Canada: Two Prudential Plaza, 180 N Stetson Ave, Suite 2400, 60601 ⓣ312/616-1860; Ireland: 400 N Michigan, Suite 911, 60611 ⓣ312/337-1868; New Zealand: 8600 W Bryn Mawr Ave, Suite 500N, 60631 ⓣ773/714-9461; UK: Wrigley Building, 13th floor, 400 N Michigan Ave, Suite 1300, 60611 ⓣ312/970-3800.

Emergencies Dial ⓣ911 and ask for relevant emergency service.

Film times/tickets For current movie listings or to buy tickets in advance, call *moviefone* (ⓣ312/444-FILM).

Hospitals There is no public health-care system and if you require emergency treatment you will need to show your insurance details or pay the entire amount. Many insurance companies will specify which hospitals you may use, and most companies require immediate notification should you need treatment. Each of the following has a 24-hour emergency center: Cook County Hospital, 1835 W Harrison St ⓣ312/633-6000; Northwestern Memorial Hospital, 251 E Huron St ⓣ312/926-2000, ⓦwww.nmh.org; Rush-Presbyterian 1650 W Harrison St ⓣ312/942-5000 or 888/352-RUSH, or ⓦwww.rush.edu; University of Chicago Hospital, 901 E 58th St, Hyde Park ⓣ773/702-6250.

Internet cafés Available at *BEAN.net* (inside Merchandise Mart), 350 N Orleans St ⓣ312/601-4430; *Bytes & Coffee*, 606 W Barry Ave ⓣ773/281-1600, *Broadband Café*, 58 E Randolph St; *Off the Wall Wireless Café*, 1904 W North Ave, Wicker Park ⓣ773/782-0000; *Hostelling International–Chicago*, 24 E Congress Parkway, the Loop ⓣ312/360-0300; the Harold Washington Library, 400 S State St ⓣ312/747-4999; *Screenz*, 2717 N Clark ⓣ773/348-9300; *Windy City Cyber Café*, 2246 W North Ave ⓣ773/384-6470.

Libraries The main public library is Harold Washington Memorial Library, 400 S State St, in the Loop ⓣ312/747-4999. Alternatively, there's a Lincoln Park branch at 1150 W Fullerton ⓣ312/744-1926 and in Bucktown at 2056 Damen Ave ⓣ312/744-6022.

Tax Chicago sales tax is 9 percent; hotel tax 14.9 percent; restaurant tax 10.25 percent.

Taxis American-United ⓣ773/248-7600; Checker Taxi ⓣ312/243-2537; Chicago Carriage Cab Company ⓣ312/326-2221; Wolley Cab ⓣ312/888-8294; Yellow Cab ⓣ312/TAX-ICAB.

Time Chicago is in the central time zone, which starts at Chicago (on the east end) and continues as far as the west border of Texas. This is six hours behind Greenwich Mean Time (-6 GMT). Daylight saving begins the first Sunday in April and ends the last Sunday in October. If flying from Australia or New Zealand, bear in mind that you will cross the International Date Line, and will, in effect, arrive in Chicago before you have left home.

Tipping Tipping, in a restaurant, bar, taxi cab, or hotel lobby, on a guided tour, and even in some posh washrooms, is a part of life. In restaurants in particular, it's unthinkable not to leave the minimum (15 percent of the bill or roughly double the tax) – unless you actively hated the service.

Train departures Amtrak (ⓣ1-800/872-7245 or 312/655-2101) operates out of Union Station, offering service to both coasts and beyond. You can buy (or reserve) your tickets by phone, or on the Web (ⓦwww.Amtrak.com), but in either case you'll need to pick them up at Union Station before you board. Trains serving the greater metropolitan Chicago area and suburbs are run by Metra (ⓣ312/322-6777, ⓦwww.metrarail.com) and run out of Ogilvie Transportation Center; you can buy tickets at the station ticket office before boarding or pay slightly more on the train.

Travel agencies American Express: 605 N Michigan Ave, Suite 105 ⓣ312/943-7840; 55 W Monroe St ⓣ312/435-2598 (business travel); STA Travel: 1160 N State St ⓣ312/951-0585; 429 S Dearborn St ⓣ312/786-9050.

Weather Both the *Chicago Tribune* and the *Chicago Sun-Times* print five-day weather forecasts. You can also visit weather.com and type in "Chicago."

Contexts

Contexts

A history of Chicago

From fur-trapping backwater through its emergence as a provincial industrial town to becoming one of the world's great cities, Chicago's growth can be seen as a microcosm of the US. And while the nation's self-styled "Second City" is inherently American, the history of the major metropolis of the Midwest is truly unique.

1673–1833: the early years

The first Europeans to arrive officially in Chicago were explorers from New France (now Quebec). **Louis Joliet**, a cartographer, and **Jacques Marquette**, a missionary, had been sent on an empire-building expedition by Louis XIV, the so-called Sun King: Louis' plan was to shore up his country's holdings in the New World by connecting New France and New Orleans with fresh territory. Marquette and Joliet, guided by friendly local **Powatomi Indians**, arrived in what's now Chicago in the fall of 1673.

At this time, the shores of Lake Michigan were a fur-trapping hub, having been settled by **Native Americans** for almost seven hundred years. It's also likely that other European settlers had passed through earlier, and a year after Marquette's and Joliet's arrival, the explorers encountered a fellow French-Canadian, Pierre Moreau – nicknamed "The Mole" – a trapper who'd already also established a thriving, illicit trade in alcohol to the Indians. The word *checagou* derives from Joliet's attempts to phonetically transcribe the local Native American name: it's been variously glossed as "great and powerful," "striped skunk," and "wild onion" (after the plants that grew in abundance locally), although its true meaning has never been confirmed.

Claiming the area for France, Joliet and his party soon moved on, leaving a small settlement of three hundred or so. France hoped this town might become a gleaming metropolis, its answer to the powerful and thriving British settlements of New York and Boston. Sadly, it was a case of bad luck and bad timing: the royal coffers were running on empty, and there was little money left to spend on a town few in France would ever see. Soon, the settlement was abandoned and *Checagou* slipped into obscurity: for the next few years, the territory flip-flopped between colonial powers, eventually landing in American hands after the War of Independence.

Given Chicago's history of often contentious race relations, the fact that the city's acknowledged founder, **Jean-Baptiste Point du Sable**, was black is wryly ironic. A Haitian-born fur trapper, who after arriving in 1779 amassed a sizeable fortune, he married a Powatomi Indian girl and built an estate where the *Chicago Sun-Times* building now stands. Du Sable's settlement was strategically important, and by 1803 – recognizing the continuing colonial threat from a disgruntled Britain – the American government had established a garrison here, known as **Fort Dearborn**. Indeed, open war with Britain broke out nine years later, and Fort Dearborn was the site of a major atrocity when British-backed Indians torched the building, and ambushed the evacuees from the fort, slaughtering two-thirds of them.

After America won the war, Fort Dearborn was soon rebuilt. By the time of Chicago's incorporation as a town in 1833, there were 350 residents living in the area now bounded by Kinzie, Desplaines, Madison, and State streets; that year, the town's first newspaper, *The Chicago Democrat*, went to press. The stop-and-start phase of Chicago's settlement was over: for the next seventy years it would grow at breakneck speed to become one of the largest, most prosperous cities in America and a symbol of nineteenth-century economic success.

1837–70: emerging as a city

In fact, the first sign of Chicago's healthy future had come when the **Erie Canal** opened in 1825: by linking New York City's Hudson River with the hamlet of Buffalo, which sat on the eastern reaches of Lake Erie, the canal opened up the entire state of Illinois to commerce. Some savvy Chicagoans spotted how Buffalo exploded, virtually overnight, into a thriving transport hub, and were soon snapping up swaths of local land for next to nothing.

In the industrialized nineteenth century, Chicago had an advantage that no man could manufacture: its location. Those Buffalo-watchers recognized this, and so invested heavily in infrastructure like waterways and railroads; unusually, they also spent money on better sewers and drains. Indeed, Chicago city planners have always thought big and by treating their nascent town like a city, locals were well prepared to seize economic opportunities when they appeared.

The first of those was the construction of the **Illinois and Michigan Canal**, begun in 1836. This waterway would connect the Illinois River to the Mississippi, and so to the thriving shipping hub of New Orleans; a year later, swelled by the influx of thousands of construction workers, Chicago was large enough to incorporate as a city. Then it hit a snag: a nationwide depression that lasted for three years and was precipitated by President Andrew Jackson's ham-fisted meddling in the rickety national banking system.

After this, construction of the canal slowly resumed, while simultaneously local leaders turned their attention to Chicago's own water system. Since the city was built on marshy, swampy land, no cellars or drains had been possible at first, so now the streets were clogged with sewage. In 1849, an ingenious engineer, who'd recently arrived from New York State, devised a strange but simple solution – **raise the buildings**. Each structure was ratcheted off the ground to a height of four to seven feet, and drainage systems were then installed in the newly created first floor.

The engineer responsible was **George Pullman**, who'd later make his name as a railroad magnate; like Pullman, it's to the railroads that Chicago owes almost everything.

The arrival of the railways

As the railroads laid down tracks to and from the city, Chicago became the **terminus for cross-country travel**: few rail companies operated networks both east and west of the Mississippi River, and so all cargo, both freight and human, had to be unloaded there. This was the first key impact of the railroad: travelers would often stay (and spend) for several days before continuing their journey, while cargo hauling created hundreds of new jobs. In fact, during this time, the population of Chicago more than tripled – from 30,000 in 1850 to 110,000 ten years later.

If this first effect funneled America through Chicago, the second scattered Chicago across America. The rest of the US became a **market for goods** from merchants based in the city: soon, Chicago was the hub of America's grain and lumber trades. Businessmen here were best placed to reach any corner of the country and many became phenomenally wealthy: they then pumped money back into the city, building fabulous mansions and endowing institutions.

Third came the definitive **defeat of St Louis**, Chicago's snazzy southern rival three hundred miles away in Missouri. St Louis was already a thriving city in the early 1830s when Chicago was little more than a hamlet, linked by the Mississippi River to New Orleans and warm enough that its waterways wouldn't ice up in winter. But St Louis relied on the steamboat, which was easily eclipsed by Chicago's cheaper, more efficient railroad network. St Louis struggled on until the Civil War, which was the final, lethal blow: its Confederate economy depended on trade with the South, while Union Chicago was quick to provide the massive northern army with provisions, especially meat.

Chicago's **meatpacking plants** were perhaps the most visible by-product of its pole position in the railroad race – at one point it was even nicknamed "Porkopolis" (though Illinois poet Carl Sandburg's "Hog Butcher to the World" would be the nickname that stuck). Since meat could be quickly transported cross-country from Chicago, it was a natural base during the Civil War, and by 1862, had become the largest meatpacking city in the world. The legendary **Union Stockyards** opened on the South Side in 1865: indeed, the stockyards were so large – ten miles of feed trough on one hundred acres of land – that they became a tourist attraction. Chicago's pragmatic leaders turned butchery into business. There was a disassembly line, where hog slaughter was so efficient that, unlike individual butchers who threw away almost half a carcass (like cartilage and bones), almost nothing was wasted: aside from meat, the plants turned out bouillon, brushes, and even instrument strings. One local bigwig butcher used to boast that he made use of every part of a pig but the squeal.

The railroads didn't just move food and goods, they also moved people: the train made travel speedy and convenient as never before. In essence they created a **commuter class**. Soon, the city's middle class was moving out of downtown and into larger houses and bigger yards further afield – in fact, Naperville, to the west of the city, was the world's first "railroad suburb."

Finally, the spaghetti junction of railroad lines meeting in Chicago spurred reform in one offbeat area: **time**. As late as 1883, there was no standard time in America – it could be 2.30pm in New York City, while a few hundred miles away it was 2.46pm in Washington, DC. Until the industrial age, variable timekeeping like this had caused few problems, but with the railroads came timetables, and so confusion. Often, companies synchronized the clocks along their own lines but this might bear little resemblance to local time; it also meant that many stations had several clocks, featuring the time according to each railroad company *plus* the local time. It's not surprising that Chicago, where fifteen railroad lines met, was one of the key drivers behind New York–based Charles Dowd's reforms of 1869, where he suggested four time–zones, much like those we use today, be created.

Destruction and rebirth: 1871–1895

Chicago's transformation into a modern city was spurred on by a terrible citywide fire, which would turn Chicago from a city of wood to a city of steel,

The men who built Chicago

Remarkably, many of the breathtaking buildings in the Loop were the work of just a handful of gifted architects. While Frank Lloyd Wright (see p.152) and Mies van der Rohe (see p.59) are the most famous and influential among the Chicago architects, several other architectural luminaries designed major works in the Loop.

A forward-thinking architectural giant with an evangelical zeal for city planning, **Daniel H. Burnham** (1846–1912) was one of the driving forces behind the City Beautiful Movement (see box, p.281). He designed and oversaw the 1893 World's Columbian Exposition on Chicago's South Side and later exported his vision to other places, including Washington, DC, and San Francisco. With his partner, John Wellborn Root, he designed the show-stopping **Rookery**, 209 S LaSalle St (p.62), known for its gorgeous light court. Burnham was also the mastermind behind the **Reliance Building**, at 32 N LaSalle (p.54), the world's first steel-framed building and a forerunner of today's giddying skyscrapers.

While **Bertrand Goldberg** (1913–97) was trained at the Bauhaus in Germany and thus influenced by van der Rohe, he soon found his own highly individual style. Technically eccentric, Goldberg saw rectilinear shapes as unnatural and so designed overwhelmingly circular buildings to encourage community and interaction. He also believed round structures had better wind resistance and provided more usable interior space. **Marina City** at 300 N State St is Goldberg's best-known work (p.84) – a controversial, mixed-use complex aptly nicknamed the "Corncobs."

William Holabird (1854–1923) **And Martin Roche** (1855–1927) met while working together in the offices of William Le Baron Jenney (see below). Together, they were pioneers of architecture's "Chicago School" and credited with popularizing the "Chicago window" – a fixed central pane flanked by moveable sash windows. The pair are remembered for the **Marquette Building**, 140 S Dearborn St (p.58); with its open facade and steel frame, it was the prototype for many modern office buildings. After the architects' deaths, the firm was taken over by Holabird's son **John** (1886–1945); together with **John Wellborn Root Jr** (1887–1963), son of Burnham's partner, the

and give the world the skyscraper. Subsequent progress was speedy, culminating with a high point of the World's Fairs in 1893.

The Great Fire of 1871

As Chicago's economic prosperity reached its peak, the most defining event in city history occurred – one which, at first, would seem to have doomed its progress but instead spurred the town to greatness: **the Great Fire of 1871**.

City fires weren't unusual in those days – most major American metropolises, Chicago included, had already suffered at least one. In fact, there was a blaze there on October 7, 1871 (the day before the Great Fire), that had destroyed twenty acres west of downtown.

The subsequent fire started at around 9pm on October 8, in a barn owned by Patrick and Catherine O'Leary; it was situated at what's now the intersection of Jefferson and Taylor streets. The classic story tells how a kicking cow knocked over a nightlight and so started the blaze, but the truth is probably more prosaic. Local cow-championing researchers have uncovered the existence of Daniel "Pegleg" Sullivan, whose mother's cow was also billeted in the same barn. Most historians now agree it's more likely that Sullivan, having stopped by to feed the animal – perhaps in a drunken state - accidentally started the blaze and blamed the cow to save his skin.

younger Holabird designed the one major Art Deco masterpiece downtown, the **Board of Trade**, at 141 W Jackson Blvd (p.61).

Though both **Helmut Jahn** (1940–) and van der Rohe were German expatriates drawn to Chicago by the Illinois Institute of Technology (the former to study there, the latter to help found it), their work could not be more different. Jahn's buildings are a playful counterpoint to Mies's minimalism, combining color, humor, and reflective glass to convey energy and fun. His local masterpiece is the **James R. Thompson Center**, 100 W Randolph St (p.62), with its brightly colored atrium and curving facade.

Known as the "father of the skyscraper," **William Le Baron Jenney** (1832–1907) came to Chicago from Massachusetts in the 1860s to work on urban planning projects, including the railroad suburb of Riverside; after the Great Fire, though, he became heavily involved in the rebuilding of downtown. Despite many technical achievements, his greatest impact was as mentor to many great architects of the late 1800s and early 1900s – Burnham, Holabird, Roche, and Sullivan were all at one time employed by his firm. Don't miss the **Manhattan Building**, 431 S Dearborn St (see "Architecture" color insert) – one of his earliest works that prefigures many later advances in structural engineering. Sadly, his 1883 Home Insurance Building at LaSalle and Adams streets – widely regarded as the "first skyscraper" because it used a metal skeleton to help support the exterior wall – no longer stands.

The rule-breaking genius of **Louis Sullivan** (1856–1924) spawned the revolutionary tenets that were the foundation of the "Chicago School" of architecture. Born in Boston, and trained at MIT and in Paris, Sullivan came to Chicago after the Great Fire to put into practice his maxim, "Form Follows Function" – which soon had many adherents among architects. Often working with brilliant engineer **Dankmar Adler** (1844–1900), he built masterpieces like the **Carson Pirie Scott** department store at 1 S State St (p.54). Note its practical, modular design and nature-inspired cast-iron decorations, among them a touch of the architect's ego – Sullivan's own initials (LHS), woven into the design.

Two factors hindered firefighters' immediate response: firstly, they were all exhausted after spending the previous night dousing the massive West Side blaze; secondly, an inept watchman misjudged the fire's location and sent the alert to the wrong crew. By the time they arrived, the flames were too strong to put out. For two days, until rain came in the early hours of October 10, Chicago burned at the rate of 65 acres each hour. Losses were staggering: exact statistics vary, but around 18,000 buildings were destroyed, damage was estimated at $200 million, and 90,000 people were left homeless. Only 250 people died, thanks in part to the lake, into which many waded for safety away from the flames.

Only the Water Tower and the Pumping Station, gaudy neo-Gothic hulks of stone lurking at the upper end of Pine Street (now N Michigan Avenue) didn't burn (see p.79). An architectural shame, perhaps, but at least the city's drinking-water supply wasn't affected.

The city at its apogee

But Chicago's survival, despite the devastation across downtown, was due to more than clean(ish) drinking water. The only reason the city could bounce back as quickly as it did was that the fire had left Chicago's three major industries – the lumberyards, the stockyards, and the railroads – untouched. Since

Chicago was then at the heart of the country's economy, as well as its geography, businessmen across America turned their attention to rebuilding the city.

Hence, only two years later, downtown had been completely rebuilt. The creative opportunities afforded by Chicago's blank canvas also attracted men like Louis Sullivan and Frank Lloyd Wright (see "Architecture" color insert), whose architectural impact lingers even today. In the years following the fire, Chicago's buildings grew larger and more impressive until, in 1885, the **world's first skyscraper** was constructed downtown. Chicago seemed unstoppable, but the city was starting to show symptoms of urban blight.

The most famous – and telling – incident was the **Haymarket Riots** of 1886. Union leaders, always powerful in Chicago's massive factories and yards, had begun a movement for shorter working hours; a citywide strike was announced for May 1. Three days later, at a protest meeting over worker treatment, a bomb was detonated as police tried to clear the demonstrators. Officer Mathias J. Degan died instantly, while seven other policemen lingered for several days before also expiring. The citywide witch-hunt resulted in the trial of eight so-called "Haymarket Martyrs": seven were condemned to death and the eighth sentenced to fifteen years in prison. In the end, though, only four were executed; one committed suicide while two more saw their sentence commuted to life in prison. Although seven years later in 1893, Governor Altgeld would pardon and release the three remaining men, the Haymarket riots highlighted for the first time worker–owner friction that would reach paralyzing levels in the twentieth century.

If 1893 was the year when Chicago made a headline-grabbing debut on the world's stage, it was also a difficult time for local industry: the country was in a depression and job losses in Chicago were significant. It was the year the paternalistic millionaire **George Pullman** – who'd masterminded the elevation of the city forty years earlier – also went from hero to villain in the eyes of the local working class. Pullman was a railroad millionaire, although he didn't own an inch of track: instead, inspired by the grueling trip he'd made from New York to Chicago, he turned his ingenuity to sleeping cars. Pullman's prototypes were well enough received but it was his flair for publicity, rather than his engineering know-how, that saw him through: after Lincoln's assassination, he offered his namesake car to bring Lincoln's body home to Illinois, and travel through towns across America on its way.

Soon, Pullman cars were a common sight in every station and Pullman himself was a multimillionaire, employing thousands of people at his factory in Chicago. The railroads weren't immune to industrial unrest like the Haymarket Riots; in fact, an 1877 national strike had driven home to Pullman the problems of keeping his workforce happy, or rather, docile. His answer was to build a town for them to live in, and so control every aspect of his employees' lives: buying up chunks of land far on the South Side, he started construction in 1879 and had quickly built a model community (albeit one where rents were 20 percent higher than elsewhere). The town prospered until 1893 when Pullman, his profits slashed by the depression, fired thousands of workers, cut wages by 25 percent, but wouldn't lower rents. In response, union leaders called for a boycott of the sleeping cars across the network; although Pullman's strong-arming saw him eventually emerge victorious, it was at a high price – from then until his death four years later, he was vilified by his employees.

1893: The World's Columbian Exposition

Despite such economic unrest, 1890s Chicago considered itself a grand city, with a righteous claim to be a thriving rival to New York itself. But while

Daniel Burnham and the City Beautiful Movement

By 1910, almost one in two people in the United States lived in a city with more than 2500 inhabitants – and with such mass urbanization, problems like crime and disease were rife. Chicago was no exception, and local architect **Daniel Burnham** began investigating ways of imposing the moral order of a village onto growing cities. The far-reaching ideology he helped develop became known as the **City Beautiful Movement**.

Inspired by the harmony of Europe's new Beaux Arts style, key features of the City Beautiful Movement included wide, tree-lined avenues, monumental buildings, ample greenspace, and frequent plazas or fountains. There were even proscriptions on lampposts, which had to be attractive as well as functional, and straight roads, which had to be broken up by winding streets whenever possible.

Burnham outlined his blueprint for the perfect city at the **World's Columbian Exposition** in 1893, whose construction he oversaw: the fair's structures were uniform, and its parks enormous; a city built on these principles, he argued, would be crimeless due to a combination of civic duty and plenty of police. Burnham's plans weren't popular with everyone, but he began hawking his ideas to cities around the country. Returning to his hometown of Chicago, he self-published plans for the town in 1909 – the first regional urban plans ever published in America, stretching out sixty miles from the lakefront past Chicago's current suburbs. Ultimately, the Chicago Plan Commission only approved two of his ideas: the straightening of the river and, more importantly, the concept of a **public lakefront park**, which, more than any of his buildings, is perhaps Burnham's greatest legacy to the city.

New York had the prestigious Columbia University, the original **University of Chicago** had gone bust several years earlier. William Rainey Harper then masterminded the creation of a new university, located in the newly annexed area of Hyde Park on the South Side. The university would symbolize Chicago's egalitarian, pragmatic attitude: admitting both women and men from the outset, working on a quarters system to allow flexibility for its staff and overseeing an active university press to disseminate its ideals. Harper turned to John D. Rockefeller, nineteenth-century America's answer to Midas and a staunch Baptist to boot (the university was initially conceived as a Baptist bastion), for funds; Rockefeller pledged $600,000, contingent on the city raising $400,000. Since local Baptists couldn't cough up enough cash, the religious mission of the university was revised, and Marshall Field – who until then had never been known as a philanthropist – stepped in with additional funding. The university, designed in a neo-Gothic style, opened in 1892. Sadly, the genial Harper would only live to see his dream realized for another fourteen years before dying at a young age in 1906.

But establishing the university was only a national coup; city bigwigs wanted to hog the world spotlight and turned to the idea of a Great Exhibition. The last fair had been in Paris in 1889, the centenary of the French Revolution; it was decided to hold a fair in America to acknowledge the 400th anniversary of Columbus's arrival. The catfight between New York and Chicago was fierce – in fact, it's where the nickname "Windy City" came from, when a Manhattan journalist derided the braggadocio of Chicago's committee. But the wind blew Chicago's way, and Congress finally voted in its favor: the city would host the **World's Columbian Exposition**, albeit a year late in 1893.

Daniel Burnham and Louis Sullivan, both beloved local architects, were appointed to oversee the fair, alongside legendary planner Frederick Law Olmstead (responsible for New York's Central Park). The site they chose,

The birth of the department store

Chicago may be lauded for launching the skyscraper, but it's rarely credited for its other contribution to modern life: the **department store**. Admittedly, the first such shop, Bon Marché, was actually in Paris (it's still there) but even if the French conceived the department store, it was immediately adopted and raised to adulthood by Chicago's shopkeepers along the "Ladies' Half Mile" of State Street.

The first retail genius was Potter Palmer, who invented the idea of the refund – in fact, for several years, the jaw-dropping practice of accepting returns, no questions asked, was known as the **"Palmer System**." He focused on female customers, greeting them at the door by name and escorting them round his store, and his refund system encouraged women to make impulse purchases for the first time. But it was Palmer's protégé Marshall Field who turned shopping into an art form. Field and his partner, Levi Leiter, bought a controlling stake in Palmer's store in 1865; sixteen years later, he renamed it and ran it solo. Trim, elegant, and highly private, Field held fast to his rigid maxims: "The customer is always right" and "Give the lady what she wants." At its peak in 1900, **Marshall Field's** was serving 250,000 customers a day and employed 8000 people. Among the store's various innovations were bringing goods down from high shelves and putting them on counters so customers could touch and feel them; placing a perfume hall by the doors so that passers-by would be drawn in by the heady smells; opening a bargain basement; offering annual sales and gift certificates; and on down the line.

At the same time as Field was wowing downtown, local entrepreneur Aaron Montgomery Ward was servicing rural shoppers. Having worked at Field's store for two years before becoming a traveling salesman, Ward took what he learned from both jobs and produced a revolutionary new product in 1872: **the mail-order catalog**. Mail-order shopping made merchandise, from basic to luxe, accessible to everyone; Ward opened up an entirely new market for consumer goods, much of it in rural, hard-to-reach places. Ward's business was a nineteenth-century hybrid of Wal-Mart and Amazon.com, buying goods in such vast quantities that he was able to undercut rural merchants by up to 75 percent. Soon, he had a rival in Richard Sears and Alvah Roebuck, who modeled their business after his – and eventually bested him thanks to Sears' instinct for snappy advertising. Both eventually opened brick-and-mortar stores and though Sears is now a household name, sadly Montgomery Ward's went into Chapter 11 bankruptcy in 2000 and has closed its final few doors.

These shopping pashas have left their mark across the city: Marshall Field has his namesake museum (see p.84), the Merchandise Mart (see p.84), and even the University of Chicago (see p.99). Palmer's wife Bertha donated her extraordinary Impressionist collection to the Art Institute (see p.66); while Palmer has the greatest memorial of all – an entire neighborhood. By putting up his first magnificent mansion in what's now the Gold Coast, he encouraged his cronies to follow suit and almost single-handedly created the wealthy enclave (for more on the Gold Coast, see p.86).

Jackson Park, was a swampy marshland close to the new university in the Hyde Park district. What's more, the 1892–93 winter was severe, even by Chicago standards, and hampered progress; so it wasn't until the fair actually opened on May 1, 1893, that anyone knew whether all construction would be completed in time.

The fair was an unqualified triumph and capped Chicago's century: known as the "White City" thanks to its burnished, floodlit white buildings, the fair covered six hundred acres, attracted more than 27.5 million visitors (almost half of the number of people then living in America), and featured 250,000 exhibits from 46 nations. Some of the most popular included the Electricity Building, which showcased the various uses of the new electricity including Elisha Gray's telautograph, a prototype fax machine that was designed to send writing or drawings by telegraph. The Streets of Cairo display was also popular, featuring raunchy belly dancers – although the legendary minx known as Little Egypt didn't, as is popularly supposed, make her debut at the fair: she surfaced for the first time two years later in Coney Island, New York. But it was **George Ferris's wheel** that grabbed the most headlines.

Burnham had challenged engineers across America to come up with a worthy retort to the Eiffel Tower of 1889: he received submissions including a replica of Dante's Hell (probably not a crowd-pleaser) and man-made mountains. But it was Ferris's idea to take the observatory from the Eiffel Tower and pivot it that won Burnham over. Ferris put up his 250-foot wheel in less than five months, using his own money: it was a smart investment, as 1.4 million riders paid 50¢ apiece to ride for two revolutions in one of its 36 cabins.

The fair's only surviving building is now the Museum of Science and Industry (see p.141): Burnham's Palace of Fine Arts, constructed in temporary materials, was painstakingly disassembled to its stone skeleton and then rebuilt in stone. The Midway Plaisance greenspace that Burnham & Co planned as a Venetian canal but had to abandon after flooding problems also emerged out of the fair.

1895–1920: race and reforms

The years up to World War I would transform Chicago yet again, but it would never reach the level of fame and prosperity it enjoyed during the World's Fair. Chicago's always depended on **immigration**, like the laborers who came to work on the first canal and turned it from a town into a city. But the new arrivals from Europe and the Deep South both enriched and complicated city life in new ways.

Some 2.5 million Europeans arrived in Chicago in the forty years from 1880. The largest communities were **Polish**, **Italian**, and **Russian Jewish**, and each contributed in a different way to the new cosmopolitan make-up of Chicago. The Poles – stirred by Polish-language newspapers exhorting them *Swój do Swego* (Support Your Own) – created a self-sufficient, self-contained community that floated on the surface of existing society rather than integrating. The Italians also resisted integration, partly because many men had come alone and planned to return to Italy having earned extra money for their families. Many of the Italians were from rural areas and so avoided working in factories, instead preferring lower-paid, outdoor jobs like construction and railroad maintenance. The Russians established Maxwell Street Market (see p.134) and many worked as peddlers or shopkeepers, so coming into contact with many other immigrant and established groups, and therefore integrating most quickly of all.

African-American immigration during the nineteenth century to Chicago was also significant – and unsurprising: Chicago was one of the main stops on the Underground Railroad, and had always had a liberal attitude to race relations (for example, D.W. Griffith's hit film *Birth of a Nation* [1915], which glorified the KKK, was banned from the city's cinemas). More than such social concerns, though, there were pressing economic reasons: during World War I, European immigration all but ceased, and local white laborers saw their chance to agitate for higher wages; in response, business leaders turned to cheaper, black labor. Again, the railroad was also partly responsible: many Pullman porters on the trains were African American, and they would take copies of *The Chicago Defender*, the city's black newspaper, along with them to distribute during their travels. The net result was that Chicago's African-American population more than doubled from 44,000 in 1910 to 109,000 ten years later.

There was little integration, though: most blacks were confined to a small strip along S State Street, part of which was an entertainment district known as **The Stroll**. Despite the segregation, racial violence wasn't commonplace: the one major exception was the 1919 Race Riots, sparked by the death of a black teenager, Eugene Williams. On July 27, Williams had been out swimming with friends in the lake when they drifted past a "whites only" beach: struck on the forehead by a rock thrown by a white sunbather, he fell unconscious and drowned. When his friends called in the local police and pointed out the man responsible, the officer refused to arrest him. Six days of riots ensued, only calmed when the state governor sent 5000 troops to the city. It's worth noting that there are varying accounts of the Williams story with unreliable, contradictory facts, and that the recession of 1919 and the resultant unemployment, was as much a reason for the violence as his death.

Around this time of massive immigration, the **Progressive Movement** was sweeping the country: this new political sense focused on social justice and the harms of industrialization. Predictably, gritty Chicago was a prime focus – see Upton Sinclair's groundbreaking fictionalized account of the stockyards, *The Jungle*, for an example. Groundbreaking social worker Jane Addams established Hull-House (see p.134) after a trip to London's Toynbee Hall, which was designed to provide social services to the working-class poor. From its founding in 1889, Hull-House mushroomed into a massive complex that even included a library and a gym (for her efforts, Addams was awarded the Nobel Peace Prize in 1931). It was also in the early part of the century that Daniel Burnham conceived of and began to implement his City Beautiful plan, which was as much about civic pride as it was architecture (see box on p.281 for more on this).

Chicago's Roaring Twenties

Despite the city's best efforts to paper over its associations with organized crime, Chicago will always be known as the home of **Al Capone**. It's ironic that the era of molls, mobsters, and murderous ambushes was brought about by zealous reformism like the Progressive Movement. National temperance advocates had jostled for a ban on alcohol for several years and many prominent women's groups focused on its harmful effects on the modern family (in other words, the number of abusive alcoholic husbands it produced). Although Chicago's voters came out 6:1 against **Prohibition**, it was introduced nationwide in January 1920.

Predictably, banning alcohol only glamorized it further, especially among the upper classes for whom serving a cocktail before dinner became a subversive sign of power and wealth. Chicago's illicit alcohol industry was controlled by individual gangs, each of whom supplied different districts of the city: the so-called Beer War, much like many gang murders today, broke out when one man decided to take over the whole city.

That man, born Alphonse Caponi in New York, better known as Al Capone, arrived in Chicago in 1919: running speakeasies before widening his ambitions and to take control of the booze supply on the city's South Side. He was never

△ Al Capone

averse to offing troublesome competitors and ten years after his arrival, Capone made his final, decisive move. On the morning of February 14, his henchmen (dressed as local cops) gathered seven members of the rival Bugs Moran gang, lined the men up against a wall in a garage, and shot them at point-blank range. The so-called **St Valentine's Day Massacre** cemented Capone's legend, as well as scaring off Bugs (who'd overslept and therefore escaped execution); Moran ceded his North Side territory to Capone, who finally controlled the whole city. He wouldn't enjoy his spoils for long: in 1931, Capone was sent to Alcatraz by his nemesis, Eliot Ness, whose band of determined and bribe-resistant investigators earned the nickname "The Untouchables." The gangster was actually convicted of tax evasion, and served a short sentence before retreating to his mansion in Miami where he expired in 1947 of an advanced case of syphilis.

1930–55: The World's Fair, the war, and waning fortunes

By 1933, when it was clear that Prohibition was all but useless, the laws were repealed. Chicago, now known more for robberies than railroads, decided to up its image by launching a new **World's Fair**, this time in celebration of the city's own centenary and called "A Century of Progress." But despite the massive attending numbers (39 million visitors over two years) and the fact that it even operated at a slight profit, the 1933 fair had none of the cultural impact its predecessor had enjoyed. Tellingly, there's little evidence left that it ever took place and its architectural impact was minimal.

There is plenty of evidence of the other major event in Chicago from this era – although the only local reminder is a small plaque on the campus of the University of Chicago. Underneath the squash courts there, on a cold December afternoon in 1942, visiting Italian professor **Enrico Fermi** and his team achieved the first controlled release of nuclear energy. Fermi had been brought to Chicago to undertake such secret experiments only ten months before; at 3.25pm on December 2, he achieved his goal of a controlled nuclear chain reaction. His work paved the way both for fossil fuel–free power stations and the wrenching devastation of the atom bomb, which when dropped on Japan three years later finally ended World War II.

The years after the war were difficult for Chicago, as race relations grew contentious as elsewhere in America: many white locals fled to the new suburbs, leaving downtown an underinvested ghetto. Less than sixty years since its first, world-busting fair, Chicago was on a downward slide until the arrival in 1955 of one legendary man: Richard M. Daley.

The Boss and his wake

Richard J. Daley (aka The Boss) served five consecutive terms as mayor of Chicago, establishing a political dynasty and ruling the city as *de facto* king in a way that few other mayors anywhere in America have ever managed. He secured such governmental *carte blanche* through Chicago's unique local political structure: as a staunchly Democratic city, the local party (Cook County Democratic Party, or CCDP) effectively selects then elects the mayor uncontested. Daley had worked to fill the CCDP (nicknamed, somewhat ominously, The Machine) with his supporters over several years and by rewarding them handsomely – as was expected – after his election, his path to power remained clear.

Born in 1902, Daley was a hardworking but otherwise unremarkable young man; his eventual ascension was never prefigured in his early years. Pragmatic and no-nonsense, Daley's politics were a comfortable fit for this blue-collar, industralized town: he was socially conservative, but financially liberal. He's most infamous for his gross mishandling of the protests around the **1968 Democratic Convention** (see box, below).

Despite this debacle, Daley made many valuable contributions to the city: he was a great builder, if not a sensitive handler of his staff or opponents. He poured money into the Loop, and managed to keep Chicago solvent in the 1970s when cities like New York, Detroit, Cleveland, and Philadelphia were hobbled by their

The riots of the 1968 Democratic Convention

In August of 1968, when the leaders of the National Democratic Party gathered in Chicago to formally select their candidate for the upcoming presidential election, the country was in the throes of the Vietnam War, and America was reeling from the assassination of Martin Luther King Jr, as well as resulting outbreaks of violence across the country.

Several months ahead of the convention, young antiwar activists formulated plans and applied for permits to hold an antiwar protest march during the convention, but all permit requests were denied except one that enabled the group to rally at the Grant Park bandshell. Here, the countercultural **Youth International Party** (called "Yippies"), led by social activist **Abbie Hoffman**, held a "Festival of Life" concert and rally that drew about 5000 protestors. Afterward, when a group of antiwar demonstrators started to protest outside the convention, local police steamed into the crowd and brutalized them in an incident that came to be known as the **Battle of Chicago**. Over the next five days, protestors clashed with thousands of police, Army troops, and National Guardsmen in Lincoln Park and in Grant Park along Michigan Avenue. Television cameras were there to record much of the bloody action; it's not surprising, then, that the media were seen by the police as the enemy – several reporters and photographers were among the victims of violence, which sent more than 100 each of protestors and police to the hospital. When eight demonstrators – including Hoffman – were arraigned in federal court the following year, the circus-like trial mesmerized the media and demonized Daley; it took nearly four years, but the **Chicago Eight** were each found not guilty of conspiracy to induce a riot.

financial troubles. Daley's most visionary act was the attention he lavished on hitherto forgotten Douglas Aircraft field; the city had purchased it in 1946, but left it languishing until Daley realized that a great city like Chicago needed a world-class airport. He thus became the driving force behind the development of **O'Hare Airport**, as the field had been renamed, the largest airport in the United States when it opened and decades later still one of the busiest in the world. Incidentally, its call letters – ORD – derive from its original name, Orchard Airport, when it was under ownership by Douglas.

Both supporters and opponents of Daley were shocked when he died in office in 1976: this political hiccup was compounded when his spunky protégée **Jane Byrne** ran for mayor against an incompetent incumbent in 1979; she in turn was desperately ill-suited to the job. A great headline-grabber (Byrne moved into the deprived Cabrini Green projects for a short but highly publicized period), who'd pledged to fight the grinding wheels of the Machine, she was instead crushed by it and booted out of office by another Democrat, **Harold Washington**, in 1983.

The city's first black mayor was an unwilling victor – he'd never really wanted to run and had already incurred the wrath of the CCDP during his campaign. He won largely because the two other candidates – Byrne and **Richard M. Daley**, Daley Senior's son – split the white vote. Nearly three-quarters of African Americans in Chicago voted during his election, and one precinct on the South Side even called the Board of Elections in mid-afternoon and asked if they should close, since everyone registered in that ward had already voted. Sadly, Washington was a lame-duck mayor during his first term (the CCDP opposed everything he supported and vice versa); when he won for a second time, Washington was slowly achieving a constructive political consensus when, like Daley, he unexpectedly died in office of a heart attack in 1987.

Chicago today

Ever since Washington, it's been Richard M. Daley all the way. Unlike his father, he's a CEO-style mayor, delegating duties and running the city like a corporation. It's a smart move in a place that has always been driven by commerce and, as a city, has always been run by big business. City Hall seems as corrupt as ever, with the past five years seeing countless scandals ranging from ghost payrolling and bribery to corruption in the city's contractor hiring processes; but nothing has come close to toppling the younger Daley. In part, this is because, scandals aside, the city has thrived under his rule: Daley has done much to improve Chicago, from implementing countless civic and educational programs to improve residents' quality of life, from the addition of miles of bike paths and parks to the creation of **Millennium Park**. Indeed, in 2005, Daley was named "the nation's best big-city mayor" by *Time Magazine*.

In the 1990 census, locals were dismayed that Los Angeles's population finally eclipsed Chicago's and seized second place to New York; in fact, with its second-city moniker stolen, in some ways the city is still searching for a new identity. As part of that new identity, Chicago must embrace its role as a truly multicultural city: recent census figures indicate that since 2000, 80 percent of the Chicago area's population growth can be accounted for by the **growing Hispanic population**.

Ironically, the one factor that originally proved such a boon to the burgeoning Chicago – its location in the center of the North American continent – is an albatross for any city that has international ambitions. Recent decisions by corporate giants like **Boeing** and **OfficeMax** to move to or retain their headquarters in the city thus have to be considered a coup, as the city tries to chart its course in twenty-first-century America.

In any case, the city's continued evolution under "Da Mayor" has equaled strong economic growth, and has made the Windy City more attractive to tourists than ever. In 2004, Chicago drew a record 32 million visitors and was also the nation's number-one destination for business travelers. And with McCormick Place set to open its new West Building in 2008, the city would seem to be cementing its status as a premier destination for conventioneers and tourists alike.

Chicago blues

Chicago has been nearly as central to the evolution of modern **blues** as New York was to the evolution of modern jazz. While far from the only area where country blues musicians started to plug in, it was where more decided to do so than anywhere else. Throughout the first half of the 1900s, blacks poured into Chicago from the South, bringing with them the music of their birthplaces, yet also needing to adapt to the ways of the big city. It took a while before loud, stinging electric guitar leads, harmonicas, and a hard-hitting rhythm section became the law of the land. Once this format had established supremacy in the 1950s, though, it pretty much stuck, characterizing not just Chicago blues but most electric blues worldwide.

Early Chicago blues

Between 1900 and 1960, the black population of Chicago increased from about 30,000 to over 800,000. Many of them came from the South, especially Mississippi; by 1930, Chicago had more Mississippi-born residents than any other town outside of Mississippi. Displaced Southerners wanted to hear the kind of blues music they had grown up with, and gravitated toward performers from the lands they had left. At the same time, relocated Southern musicians were adapting their styles to the Northern way of life, playing louder and at a more energetic pace. Chicago blues became more urban throughout the 1930s and early 1940s via fuller ensembles, a more pronounced beat, and some early ventures into amplification.

The most important figure of early Chicago blues was not a performer, but producer/A&R director **Lester Melrose**. Melrose built a stable of Chicago's leading talent under one umbrella, arranging for two major labels, Columbia and Victor, to record **Big Bill Broonzy**, **Memphis Minnie**, **Tampa Red**, **Washboard Sam**, **Big Joe Williams**, **Arthur "Big Boy" Crudup**, **John Lee "Sonny Boy" Williamson**, and **Bukka White** (much of the music was released on the Bluebird label, a subsidiary ofVictor, and thus referred to as "the Bluebird beat"). By using this pool of musicians to back up each other in the studio, Melrose created a "house sound" of sorts, a concept that in the decades to come would be widely applied both within and outside of the blues field. He aimed for a band sound, using not just guitar but also piano, and often a bass and washboard or drums for a rhythm section.

Modern listeners may find the Melrose/Bluebird beat stuff tame even in comparison with the early Chess sides of a few years later, yet they were directly influential upon the performers that would up the wattage. Big Bill Broonzy, who linked folk and blues styles, was a key inspiration on Muddy Waters, who would record a tribute album to Broonzy in the 1960s. John Lee "Sonny Boy" Williamson was crucial in making the harmonica a viable lead instrument in blues. A Southern musician, Rice Miller, would call himself Sonny Boy Williamson after John Lee was murdered in 1948; causing never-ending confusion among record-buyers, Miller recorded his own influential body of work for Chess in the 1950s and 1960s as "Sonny Boy Williamson," and blues reference books have to resort to calling John Lee Williamson "Sonny Boy Williamson I," and Rice Miller "Sonny Boy Williamson II." **Big Maceo** was the king of the early Chicago blues piano players with his forcefully direct style, often accompanied by guitarist Tampa Red; his trademark tune was *Worried Life Blues*, a core nugget of the fatalistic blues repertoire.

Muddy Waters and Chess Records

Lester Melrose seemed to have locked up the Chicago blues market, but after World War II changes in the music business and society made the Bluebird beat sound passé. Independent companies were spurting up to challenge the Columbia/Victor dominance, and a more amplified, rhythm-and-blues-oriented sound was ascendant. One of these labels was **Chess Records**, and after some false starts it would become a major power in the R&B market with the electric Chicago sound, particularly with transplanted Mississippian **Muddy Waters**.

Waters was well known as a young blues player in Mississippi, where he was recorded for the Library of Congress by folklorist Alan Lomax in the early 1940s. His decision to move to Chicago in 1943 was typical of the circumstances that led many to pack up their bags: a dispute with the boss over his sharecropping wages led him to try his luck up north, where discrimination was not so rife and economic opportunity better. Muddy at first found work as a truck driver, but his heart was in playing the blues, as he moonlighted at rent parties and clubs. Like musicians all over the country, he was finding that amplification and a band were needed to make himself heard in urban crowds. Waters didn't dilute his Mississippi Delta blues slide and moaning vocals; he just fleshed them out and made them louder. In a way this was a throwback to a sound that predated the Lester Melrose stable, but it had a clear bite and power that was modern and more forceful.

Waters made his first recordings (unissued at the time) for Melrose, but found a more sympathetic outlet when he began recording for Aristocrat, a label run by brothers **Phil and Leonard Chess**, which was making some tentative forays into the blues market. His 1948 single *I Can't Be Satisfied/I Feel Like Going Home* wasn't much different from what he had sung in the Delta; in fact he had cut both songs under different titles for his Library of Congress sessions. Now he had the urban market, however, and the single became an R&B hit, to be followed by other classics like *Long Distance Call* and *Rollin' Stone*. Despite his success, his studio sound lagged behind the advances he had made as a live performer, heading a full band; still, reluctant to tinker with the winning format of *I Can't Be Satisfied*, the Chess brothers – who had changed the name of their label to Chess by 1950 – recorded Muddy almost as a solo artist, with only a string bass to accompany him. Waters was on the verge of leaving Chess when Leonard Chess relented and starting using a full band, with guitars, harmonica, piano, bass, and drums in the early 1950s.

If for nothing more than his records, Muddy Waters would be a blues giant – *Hoochie Coochie Man*, *I Just Want to Make Love to You*, *Mannish Boy*, *Got My Mojo Working*, and *Trouble No More* are classic staples of rock and blues set-lists, and his B-sides and outtakes were scarcely less accomplished. In addition to being an excellent guitarist, he was more importantly a singer whose confidence suffered no fools, putting over both boasting and sorrowful lyrics with a last-word bearing, absent of any meekness or resignation. Waters also had an eye for assembling the best Chicago blues talent, and several of his sidemen would become star or respected solo artists, including guitarist **Jimmy Rogers**, pianist **Otis Spann**, and a slew of **harmonica players**: Little Walter, Junior Wells, James Cotton, and Walter Horton.

More classic Chess blues

Chess is most associated with the sound of what in-the-know blues hounds call the **four big Ws**: Muddy Waters, Little Walter, Howlin' Wolf, and Sonny Boy Williamson. It had a harsh (in the good sense of the word) sheen with upfront electric guitar leads and searing harmonica, propelled by a granite-hard, propulsive rhythm section. Like Sam Phillips at Sun Records, Chess added an otherworldly echo (with primitive tape delay) that, along with their skill at recording the instruments at slightly over-amplified levels, added to the room-filling depth of the recordings.

Little Walter made his initial impression as harmonica player in Muddy Waters' band in the early 1950s, and started a solo career after his instrumental, *Juke*, tore up the R&B charts in 1952. What Jimi Hendrix was to rock guitar, Little Walter was to blues harmonica, redefining the parameters of the instrument in a way that permanently changed how it was played, and has not been matched to this day. Walter used his harp like a horn, swooping and improvising jazzy phrases, amplifying it so that it could compete on equal terms with electric guitars, and boldly using the more complex chromatic harp to get tones and shadings that were impossible to coax out of standard models. On top of this he was a good singer with an arsenal of great material: the instantly memorable *My Babe* was his biggest hit, while *Mean Old World*, *Mellow Down Easy*, and *Off the Wall* weren't far behind. Although he was still a young man, he went into a dreadful artistic and health tailspin in the 1960s, culminating in death resulting from a street fight in 1968, aged only 37.

Howlin' Wolf was engaged in an ongoing battle with Muddy Waters for supremacy in the Windy City blues scene, and while he never dislodged Waters' unofficial crown, his raspy, haunted voice projected more charisma than any other classic Chicago blues stars did. Wolf was already well on his way to prominence with his recordings at Sun Studios in Memphis in the early 1950s, but after his move north his music grew in frightening intensity and hard-rocking drama. *Smokestack Lightning*, *The Red Rooster* (aka *Little Red Rooster*), *Spoonful*, *Wang Dang Doodle*, and *I Ain't Superstitious* are delightfully bone-rattling performances removed from the reckless thrust of rock 'n' roll by only a thin margin, accounting for the entry of many of his songs into the sets of famous 1960s rock groups like the Rolling Stones and Cream.

Sonny Boy Williamson, aka Rice Miller, had already recorded and performed in Arkansas and Mississippi for a while before hooking up with Chess. In a brazen act of nerve he appropriated the name of the first, late John Lee "Sonny Boy" Williamson; unlike just about everybody else who tried similar tricks throughout the music biz, he got away with it, not least because his talent was equal to or greater than that of the original Sonny Boy. Less experimental and more country in his harmonica playing than Little Walter, Williamson was still a wizard at making wordless witty comments with his riffs. Already in his middle age when he began his stint at Chess, he was also a humorous yet wizened songwriter and vocalist, contributing his own stack of blues standards with tunes like *One Way Out*, *Don't Start Me to Talkin'*, *Eyesight to the Blind*, and *Nine Below Zero*.

The four Ws only represented a fraction of the company's blues output. Chess had some less-adventurous piano-based blues hits with **Eddie Boyd** and **Willie Mabon**, and odd records with **J.B. Lenoir**, whose voice was so high-pitched that many mistook him for a woman, and who exhibited unusual sociopolitical consciousness on numbers like *Eisenhower Blues* and *Korea Blues*. Part of the company's success was based on the presence of session musicians and songwriters that never became widely known to the public as recording artists. Even when signed to Chess as solo artists, some musicians would back up other performers; Little Walter, for instance, was appearing on Muddy Waters songs throughout the 1950s, long after he had made it on his own and stopped performing with Waters live. Drummer **Fred Below**, who appeared on many Chess sessions, was an unsung architect of rock 'n' roll, his jazzy, swinging backbeat laying part of the foundation for the steady, insistent rhythm that would take over popular music. No one was more important to Chicago blues' classic era than **Willie Dixon**, the songwriter who devised stone-cold greats for many of the Chess artists and other performers in the Chicago area: *Hoochie Coochie Man*, *I Just Want to Make Love to You*, *Back Door Man*, *Wang Dang Doodle*, *My Babe*, *Spoonful*, *Little Red Rooster*, and *Pretty Thing* were all from his pen – and Dixon also found time to play bass on many sessions.

1950s blues

Chess was at the vanguard of a mini-explosion of Chicago independent labels that recorded blues in the 1950s. J.O.B., Chance, United/States, Parrot – none achieved anything like the success of Chess, and reissues of their material are far more sporadic, but they recorded fine blues records by solid Chicago bluesmen who weren't quite on the front line of the city's best, such as J.B. Lenoir, Johnny Shines, Sunnyland Slim, Walter Horton, Snooky Pryor, and J.B. Hutto.

Aside from Chess, the most significant of the local labels recording blues was **Vee-Jay** (often abbreviated as **VJ**). Like Chess it wasn't limited to blues, also doing R&B and rock 'n' roll, but it did land two of the most prolific and popular blues singers of the era, **John Lee Hooker** (more appropriately part of the Detroit blues scene) and **Jimmy Reed**. Reed's success was based on his simplicity – he sang with an easygoing, unruffled charm over a steady, rockish beat decorated by simple but effective guitar figures and harmonica riffs. Another fine VJ performer was harmonica player and vocalist **Billy Boy Arnold**, a Bo Diddley sideman whose frugal but stellar VJ output had thumping beats and charged guitar–harp interplay that could stray close to rock.

Most of the early Chicago blues was played in the city's **South Side**, but black neighborhoods were also spreading to the West Side. In the 1950s a style of blues began to be identified with the West Side that was funkier and more modern in nature, in the mold of B.B. King, than the entrenched South Side approach, and sometimes using saxophones. **Cobra** was a notable short-lived West Side blues label, employing Willie Dixon as its musical director when the great songwriter and arranger left Chess for a while in the late 1950s. Cobra's jewel was guitarist **Otis Rush**, the most skilled blues artist bar none when it came to working in minor keys, whose anguished vocals were complemented

△ Chuck Berry

by devilish twisting riffs that both thrill the ears and give you the hives. *Double Trouble, I Can't Quit You, Baby,* and *All Your Love* were instant standards, yet Rush, only in his early twenties when he made his Cobra singles, has never been able to fully capitalize upon his genius. Throughout the 1960s and the first half of the 1970s, he was dogged by lousy record deals that curtailed his studio opportunities. Still active today, he never seems to marshal resources for recording sessions that represent him to the best of his abilities.

Elmore James flitted from label to label often, and did not confine his base of operations to Chicago, also recording in Mississippi, New York, and New Orleans over the course of his nomadic discography. He nevertheless rates as an all-time Chicago blues great, as he was the most influential electric slide blues guitarist of all time. *Dust My Broom*, with its classic opening descending riff, had been around in the blues repertoire since Robert Johnson had cut it back in the 1930s. James was the guy who made it an instantly recognizable standard, though, giving the slide riff a gripping super-amped chill. Though he was to rely on this riff often, he did vary his slide style in interesting ways, creating a crying effect on slow burners like *The Sun is Shining* and its close cousin *The Sky is Crying*. He died in 1963, too soon to see his immense impact upon 1960s rock: Brian Jones of the Rolling Stones was so besotted with James that he called himself "Elmo Lewis" in the pre-Stones days, and Jeremy Spencer of the original Fleetwood Mac based almost his entire style around James's licks.

Chuck Berry and Bo Diddley

In 1955, two Chess guitarists recorded a new brand of blues-rooted music that had the ironic effect of mostly driving hardcore blues off the charts for good. **Chuck Berry**, although from St Louis, recorded at Chess in Chicago, often with stalwart Chess musicians such as Willie Dixon and Fred Below. Berry was not as grounded in country-blues as most of the city's leading players; he was born in St Louis, not a plantation, and had absorbed the innovations of jump-blues stars like Louis Jordan and country and western singers. Slow down the tempo of his first single, *Maybellene*, and you can imagine a hillbilly singer having a hit with it. In fact, it had started out as a demo called *Ida May* that bore some resemblance to a country tune called *Ida Red*, recorded by Bob Wills. But *Maybellene* was rock 'n' roll pure and simple, with its sped-up backbeat and furiously riffing guitar.

Berry has defined much of the basic vocabulary of rock 'n' roll, not only in guitar riffs but in lyrical content, venturing into almost journalistic observations on the nuances and frustrations of teenage and young adult life, and celebrating the joys of rock 'n' roll itself. For the rest of the 1950s, he knocked off one classic after another: *Roll Over Beethoven, Sweet Little Sixteen, Rock & Roll Music, School Day, Johnny B. Goode, Brown Eyed Handsome Man, Too Much Monkey Business*, and *Carol* were some of the best. They were also inspirations for the best rockers of the 1960s – not just the Beatles and the Stones, but also Bob Dylan (whose *Subterranean Homesick Blues* is much like *Too Much Monkey Business*) – to write and sing their own material.

Lagging far behind Berry in sales, **Bo Diddley** over time, proved to be almost as influential. A wild and wacky guitar innovator, he produced oceanic layers of reverb from his ax that sounded like outer-space shock waves by 1950s standards. Like Berry he was a witty songwriter with acute powers of observation, but while Berry kept a detached ironic eye on things Diddley yukked it up like life was just one big put-on. Diddley too was a great performer: Elvis Presley was said to have studied Bo's act closely, and Diddley featured oddly shaped guitars (most famously a square model) and acrobatic antics that anticipated Jimi Hendrix's even bolder moves along those lines in the late 1960s.

Yet above and beyond his deeper skills, Bo Diddley's trademark is his beat. Described sometimes as a "hambone" or "shave-and-a-haircut," its bomp, ba-bomp-bomp, bomp-bomp pattern is one of the most irresistible rhythms known to humankind, and although Diddley used it over and over it didn't get tiresome. Others adapted it for their own ends: Buddy Holly used it for *Not Fade Away*, which when covered by the Rolling Stones gave them their first big British hit. It was that beat, and that wild guitar playing, that made it impossible to call Diddley a bluesman, even though his music was soaked right through with R&B feeling. He built a catalog of wonderful songs – *I'm A Man*, *Bo Diddley*, *You Can't Judge a book by Its Cover*, *Road Runner*, and *Who Do You Love?* – that were ready-to-order for cover by bands all over the US and Britain.

Blues in transition: the 1960s

In the early 1960s blues had became a less significant part of the R&B singles market; rock 'n' roll had eaten into its audience since the mid-1950s, and soul music was beginning to gather steam. Both Chess and Vee-Jay were directing their resources toward their soul stars, and while there was still work for blues musicians in local clubs, there was less opportunity to record and innovate in the studio. However, a blues and folk revival was generating an interest among young, white Americans in blues music that had hitherto been confined to an almost exclusively black listenership; British rock bands were covering blues and R&B tunes, and bringing the original artists to the attention of young white listeners in the US and UK who had never heard the sources. The Rolling Stones were the biggest of such acts; to their credit they didn't limit themselves to covering tunes in their effort to bring their heroes into the spotlight, recording in Chess Studio on their first visit to the US in 1964 (and naming an instrumental, *2120 South Michigan Avenue*, after the address of the Chess building), and having Howlin' Wolf guest on one of their television spots.

Other progress came in the form of how the music was recorded and packaged. **Junior Wells**' *Hoodoo Man Blues* (1965) was a departure in that it was hardcore modern Chicago blues recorded for the local Delmark label as an *album*, not a more or less random array of sessions. It was doubly significant for being the greatest Chicago blues recording of its time. Harmonica player Wells had been on the scene since the early 1950s, doing time in the Muddy Waters band and recording some fine sides as a leader on several labels. Like several of the younger veterans of the 1950s scene, he was not averse to adding some irreverent rock and soul flourishes to his sound. The result took the Chicago blues in new, exciting directions, Wells sometimes coming on like a blues James Brown on cuts like *Snatch It Back and Hold It*, bluesing up rock tunes like *Hound Dog*, even putting in a Latin influence on *Chitlin Con Carne*. The band on the album was tops, too, especially guitarist **Buddy Guy**, who would eventually make a stunning comeback in the 1990s, chalking up a bunch of Grammies with new recordings and establishing one of the city's best blues clubs, *Buddy Guy's Legends*.

Harmonica player **James Cotton**, yet another alumnus of the Waters band, made some fine assertive soul-rock-blues in the late 1960s and was one of the most dependable fixtures of the live blues circuit through the 1990s, although he was always more impressive as an instrumentalist than as a singer. **Magic Sam** was the most mature exponent of the West Side sound, his finger-picked tremolo guitar and R&B-ish material marking him as one of the more versatile performers in the city. He had short hitches with several labels before finding a home on Delmark, where he made a couple of assured albums that found a satisfying midpoint between the soul-flavored direction the blues was being pulled towards, and the loose-limbed spontaneity more characteristic of the 1950s. Unfortunately, he died unexpectedly of heart trouble in 1969, only 32 years of age.

At the same time as young whites were beginning to listen to the blues, they were also beginning to play the blues, not just in Britain but in Chicago too. The local white blues acts tended to be well-meaning but stiff interpretations of the form, the exception being the **Paul Butterfield Blues Band** (which was actually integrated, though its front line was white). Butterfield was only an adequate singer, but a fine harmonica player; his group was more noteworthy for two exceptional guitarists, **Mike Bloomfield** and **Elvin Bishop**. The Butterfield band played lean and mean, and were more open to rock and soul influences than most African-American bluesmen, as was especially evident in Bloomfield's and Bishop's fiery solos.

Although Chess's glory days as a blues powerhouse had passed, the label did record some quality blues in the 1960s. Howlin' Wolf and Muddy Waters made some good sides through 1965 or so, Buddy Guy spent his early career there, and Chicago's best female blues singer, **Koko Taylor**, got her start at Chess. A tough and swaggering belter in the mold of the most aggressive blueswomen, such as Big Mama Thornton, Taylor's anthem was Willie Dixon's *Wang Dang Doodle*. Originally recorded by Howlin' Wolf in 1960, Taylor made the hard-partying song her own and even got to #4 in the R&B charts with it in 1966, when top-selling blues singles had become a rarity. That didn't guarantee an easy ride for Taylor, who in the early 1970s was working as a maid to make ends meet. A long-running association with Alligator Records from the mid-1970s onwards, though, solidified her reign as the queen of the Chicago blues.

Modern Chicago blues

In the last generation, Chicago blues has adopted a brassier polish than its previous incarnations, both figuratively (in its good-time strutting) and literally (in the frequent deployment of horns in addition to guitars and a rhythm section). Soul, rock, and funk shadings have become more prominent than they were in the 1960s; the tempo has generally become slower and funkier, and the vocals more cocksure.

The label mostly responsible for giving both old-timers and newbloods a chance to record is **Alligator**, founded in the early 1970s. In addition to giving steady exposure to artists like Son Seals who had somehow missed out on studio opportunities, it also revitalized the careers of veterans like Koko Taylor, James Cotton, and Billy Boy Arnold. Over the years it expanded its roster to include blues artists from all over the country, but Chicago performers remain central to its release schedule. Alligator's best records (aside from those by Koko Taylor) have been by guitarists. Its first release, by **Hound Dog Taylor**, was a throwback to the spontaneous, just-short-of-sloppy club and juke-joint blues of the 1950s, albeit with fuzzier tones, in a no-nonsense trio featuring Taylor's slide guitar. **Son Seals** was more a man for the times, speaking both through lengthy, feverish solos and gruff, unruffled vocals, using a funky bottom and beefy horn section. **Fenton Robinson**, whose *Somebody Loan Me a Dime* had already been exposed to rock listeners through Boz Scaggs' cover version, was a notable example of Alligator giving a proper chance to an artist who had only been able to record here and there. Other notable Chicago guitarists who took time-honored yet updated styles to a fairly wide audience have been slide guitarist **Lil' Ed Williams** (of **Lil' Ed & the Blues Imperials**), **Jimmy Johnson**, and **Eddy "The Chief" Clearwater**, who still does an uncanny approximation of vintage Chuck Berry.

Since the 1970s, Chicago blues has been in the best of times and the worst of times. On the positive side, general public awareness of the blues is higher than ever, particularly among whites, with clubs featuring blues mostly or occasionally springing up in Chicago and all over the US. The spring of 2005 even saw the opening of the **Chicago Blues Museum** (see p.105), founded by guitarist and bluesman Gregg Parker. On the negative side, the form has grown stale as fewer and fewer young African Americans dedicate themselves to the style, as either listeners or musicians. Its original audience has changed too: blues is still played in some South Side joints, but the very popular clubs are on the affluent North Side, drawing white patrons almost exclusively. Rock, soul, and then rap music siphoned off a lot of talent as trends changed, and musicians in the blues field are now well aware that, with rare exceptions, they will be playing and selling to a specialist market that's a small slice of the industry pie. Chicago blues, like New Orleans jazz and R&B, is in something of a preservationist mode. There's lots of competent, energetic electric blues in classic styles for locals and tourists to enjoy, on stage and on record, but the time of greatest artistic innovation seems gone. Changing public tastes are only part of the reason: the blues is a more rigidly defined style than most American popular styles, and it's difficult to make an original statement when its boundaries and signature riffs have been so firmly laid down.

Discography

The following is a select list of essential blues recordings, which should all be available on CD.

Billy Boy Arnold *I Wish You Would* (Charly). Both sides of Arnold's six Vee-Jay singles from the mid-1950s, plus a couple of rare bonus items. An underrated source point for blues-rock with its propulsive beat and riffs, especially on *I Wish You Would* and *I Ain't Got You*.

Chuck Berry *His Best Vol. 1 & 2* (Chess). Almost every song on this pair of twenty-track anthologies is immediately familiar; if you haven't heard the original version, you've heard it covered by someone. Besides the big hits like *Sweet Little Sixteen*, *Maybellene*, *Johnny B. Goode* et al, there are relatively undiscovered secondary goodies like *Little Queenie*, *Oh Baby Doll*, and *I Want to Be Your Driver*.

Big Maceo *The King of the Chicago Blues Piano* (Arhoolie). Twenty-five sides from 1941 to 1945, sometimes with bass and drums, and even some electric guitar.

Bo Diddley *The Chess Box* (Chess). Two CDs that don't even get to all of his first-rate waxings, but it does have most of 'em: *Bo Diddley, I'm Man, Pretty Thing, Diddy Wah Diddy, Who Do You Love?, Road Runner, You Can't Judge a Book by Its Cover, Mona*, and hidden treasures like *Down Home Special* and *You Don't Love Me*. For less dough there's the single-disc *His Best*, which sticks to the most celebrated tunes.

Buddy Guy *The Very Best of* (Rhino). Serviceable eighteen-song best-of doesn't reach into his 1990s comeback phase, but covers highlights from the late 1950s to the early 1980s, including some Chess sides and supersession-ish tracks with guest spots by Junior Wells, Dr John, Bill Wyman, and Eric Clapton.

Hound Dog Taylor *Hound Dog Taylor & The Houserockers* (Alligator). From the first dirty-amped run of notes, this is Chicago blues at its rawest, in a boogieing trio style that never gets too fussy or shambling. It's much more together and enjoyable, by the way, than the somewhat similar minimal Mississippi juke-joint blues that has gotten so much attention in the 1990s.

Howlin' Wolf *His Best* (Chess). Twenty tracks from the 1950s and 1960s, with a line-up including *Spoonful, Smokestack Lightning', Wang Dang Doodle, Back Door Man, The Red Rooster, Killing Floor*, and *I Ain't Superstitious*. Great stuff that's simultaneously scarifying and exhilarating, and even if you're familiar with the above tunes you'll also be blown away by more obscure items like *Shake for Me*, which has some of the snakiest blues guitar playing ever.

Elmore James *The Sky Is Crying: The History of Elmore James* (Rhino). Collecting James can be frustrating, as he recorded for numerous labels and did multiple versions of some of his best tunes. This smart 21-song compilation of 1951–61 material has the essentials, including the first *Dust My Broom, The Sun is Shining, The Sky is Crying, Shake Your Moneymaker*, and *It Hurts Me Too*.

J.B. Lenoir *Vietnam Blues: The Complete L&R Recordings* (Evidence). Lenoir was a solid journeyman Chicago bluesman in the 1950s, and grew remarkably as a songwriter in the 1960s, exploring Vietnam and racial discrimination with a directness rare in the blues; he also went to an acoustic format with minimal, almost African percussion. These mid-1960s recordings, still largely unknown even in blues circles (they were only available in Europe for a long time), are an intriguing glimpse into a road seldom taken.

Little Walter *The Essential Little Walter* (Chess). Two CDs of Little Walter is not too much, even if you're not a blues specialist. Besides ace standards like *Boom, Boom Out Goes The Light, My Babe*, and *Mellow Down Easy*, there's a bounty of hidden gems like the virtuosic bop-jazzy instrumental *Fast Large One*, the classic minor-key downer blues *Blue and Lonesome* and just plain-hot party blues like *Too Late*, and *It Ain't Right*.

Jimmy Reed *Speak the Lyrics to Me, Mama Reed* (Vee-Jay). There have been, and will always be, a bunch of Jimmy Reed best-of compilations on the market that largely duplicate each other in track selection. This 25-song one is about the best, with the familiar hits and some less overexposed songs.

Otis Rush *His Cobra Recordings, 1956–1958* (Paula). All sixteen of the tracks Rush officially released on Cobra, plus four alternate takes. Most of this is also on the two-CD box *The Cobra Records Story* (Capricorn), which adds some interesting material from the same vintage by Magic Sam, Buddy Guy, Walter Horton, Sunnyland Slim, and others.

Koko Taylor *What It Takes: The Chess Years* (Chess). Eighteen cuts from 1964 to 1971, including *Wang Dang Doodle* and other cuts reinforcing her persona as a woman not to be messed with.

Muddy Waters *His Best, 1947 to 1955* (Chess). Great twenty-song compilation is mostly killer – *I Can't Be Satisfied, I Feel Like Going Home, Rollin' Stone, Hoochie Coochie Man, I'm Ready, Trouble No More,* – and also charts his progress from the spare near-Delta blues of his first recordings to the full-bore electric sound of the mid-1950s. Also worthwhile is the next installment, *His Best, 1956 to 1964* (Chess), which has material not quite as well known, including *You Need Love* (the riff of which was nicked by Led Zeppelin for *Whole Lotta Love*).

Junior Wells *Hoodoo Man Blues* (Delmark). From the opening crash of *Snatch It Back and Hold It*, this varied set grabs your gut and doesn't let go, Wells blowing his harp feverishly and working the vocals like a soul showman while Guy drives things along with sharp and snazzy blues licks. Blues albums don't come any better than this.

Sonny Boy [John Lee] Williamson *Sugar Mama* (Indigo). Twenty-four songs from 1937 to 1942, including one, *Good Morning School Girl*, that became one of the all-time blues standards, covered by everyone from Junior Wells to the Grateful Dead.

Sonny Boy Williamson [aka Rice Miller] *His Best* (Chess). To-the-point twenty-song anthology that zeroes in on his most essential output: *Born Blind, Your Funeral and My Trial, Down Child, Help Me, One Way Out*, and *Bye Bye Bird* just for starters.

Various Artists *The Alligator Records 20th Anniversary Collection* and *The Alligator Records 25th Anniversary Collection* (Alligator). Two double-CD retrospectives of Alligator's output. This doesn't stick solely to Chicago artists, but a lot are on these compilations, including Son Seals, Koko Taylor, James Cotton, Fenton Robinson, Hound Dog Taylor, Billy Boy Arnold, Carey Bell, Big Walter Horton, and Jimmy Johnson.

Various Artists *Blues Masters, Vol. 2: Postwar Chicago* (Rhino). Decent introductory sampler of tracks from 1950 to 1961 within and without Chess, by legends like Howlin' Wolf, Muddy Waters, Little Walter, Jimmy Reed, Buddy Guy, and Junior Wells, as well as significant artists such as J.B. Lenoir, Robert Jr Lockwood, Earl Hooker, and Jody Williams.

Various Artists *The Chess Blues-Rock Songbook* (Chess). This is what you want to have handy if you're dead set on putting someone straight about all the Chess artists who cut original versions of songs that sold a lot more units after getting covered by white guys. Classics like *Spoonful, I Just Want to Make Love to You, Johnny B. Goode*, and less obvious choices like John Brim's *Ice Cream Man* and Willie Mabon's *The Seventh Son*, let the music do the talking.

Various Artists *Chicago: The Blues Today!, Vols. 1–3* (Vanguard). Important series of compilations that documented the mid-1960s Chi-town blues scene with cuts by enjoyable second-line artists such as J.B. Hutto, Otis Spann, Homesick James, Big Walter Horton and Johnny Young, as well as tracks by Junior Wells and Otis Rush.

Adapted from *The Rough Guide to Music USA* (1999), by Richie Unterberger

Books

Where the books we recommend below are in print, the publisher's name is given in parentheses after the title: the US publisher's first, separated, where applicable, from the UK publisher by an oblique slash. Where books are published in only one of these countries, we have specified which one; when the same company publishes the book in both, it appears just once. Books available in only one country are usually easily ordered online at Amazon or similar sites. Books tagged with the ★ symbol are particularly recommended.

History and society

Jane Addams *Twenty Years at Hull-House* (US Signet). Reformer Addams tells the story of her upbringing and remarkable life working at the innovative settlement house she helped start in Chicago's industrial and impoverished West Side. A perceptive, extremely detailed account of the settlement's day-to-day struggles to improve the social conditions in the city's slums in the late nineteenth century.

★ **Nelson Algren** *Chicago: City on the Make* (US U of Chicago Press). Grittily lyrical time capsule highlighting the state of mid-twentieth-century Chicago. Algren has deep affection for the city, but he also has an unsentimental determination to point out its social carbuncles. A must-read for anyone keen to understand the history of blue-collar Chicago.

Eliot Asinof *Eight Men Out: The Black Sox and the 1919 World Series* (Henry Holt). This 1919 scandal – when the heavily favored White Sox threw the final game in the World Series in return for high bribes – rocked America after World War I. This brilliant book astutely examines the cause and effect of what the White Sox did, and frames the story with lashings of anecdotes. A terrific, revealing read, even for non–sports fans.

Adam Cohen and Elizabeth Taylor *American Pharaoh: Mayor Richard J. Daley, His Battle for Chicago & the Nation* (US Little, Brown & Co). Cohen and Taylor take Daley as touchstone for the city, cannily fusing his life story with the story of Chicago itself through the twentieth century. Readable enough, and strong on Daley's poor handling of race relations in the city, but Royko's book (see p.302) is better known and better.

Nadine Cohodas *Spinning Blues into Gold* (US St Martins Press). A lively look at Chess Records, the blues label that began on the South Side of Chicago. Cohodas is strongest when examining the savvy marketing and business flair of the Chess brothers, but much weaker when analyzing the music they packaged in its cultural or musical context.

Robert Cromie *The Great Chicago Fire* (US Rutledge Hill). Picture-packed recap of the Great Fire that's evocative with its imagery, but skimpy on substance – stick with Donald Miller's (see below) detailed, more serious approach if you're looking for hard facts about the fire.

David Farber *Chicago '68* (US U of Chicago Press). Rip-roaring examination of the seminal event in Daley Sr's tenure as mayor – the (mis)handling of hippie protests at the Democratic Convention of 1968. Farber evokes the energy and excitement of the time, though he trips slightly when trying to draw wider conclusions from the highly localized events.

Peter Golenbock *Wrigleyville: A Magical History Tour of the Chicago Cubs* (US St Martin's Press). Riveting account of the lame-duck team in sports-mad Chicago: the Cubs have hobbled from season to season for almost fifty years while headline-grabbers like the Bears and the Bulls have basked in glory. This affectionate, anecdote-packed account of the team provides terrific insight into why and how it kept stumbling.

William J. Helmer and Arthur J. Bilek *The St. Valentine's Day Massacre: The Untold Story of the Gangland Bloodbath that Brought Down Al Capone* (US Cumberland House Publishing). From the author of *The Gun that Made the Twenties Roar* and a former chief of the Cook County Police, this account of the events leading up to the infamous February 14, 1929, shooting on the Near North side reads like a Mickey Spillane potboiler, and makes the argument that the incident was due more to bad timing than to Capone's desire for revenge. A very entertaining read.

Libby Hill *The Chicago River: A Natural and Unnatural History* (US Lake Claremont Press). This eclectic, unusual study follows the Chicago River from its origins through the interference in its flow by man to the present day. It's offbeat and highly readable, taking a refreshingly quirky approach to historical events.

Blair Kamin *Tribune Tower* (US Tribune Co). The *Chicago Tribune*'s Pulitzer Prize–winning architecture critic has written a lovingly detailed, piercingly astute account of his paper's HQ. It's packed with sprightly stories and offers not only a glimpse at the story behind one of Chicago's best-loved buildings, but also an understanding of what happened to the city in the years between World Wars I and II.

Erik Larson *The Devil in the White City: Murder, Magic, and Madness at the Fair that Changed America* (Vintage). It's hard to believe that this gruesome, outlandish tale of a serial murderer on the loose during Chicago's 1893 Columbia Exposition is actually a true story, so vivid and compelling is this work. Larson follows architect Daniel Burnham as he strives to pull off the fair, as well as the sinister doings of H.H. Holmes, who killed between 27 and 200 people (mostly young women) around the time of the fair.

Richard Lindberg *To Serve & Collect* (US Southern Illinois U Press). White Sox historian Lindberg has produced a heavily researched, controversial account of the corrupt cops who populated Chicago's police system for more than a hundred years. His prose can tangle at times, and the text would have been shaped better by a sharper editor, but it's a worthwhile, if depressing, read.

Harold Mayer and Richard Wade *Chicago: Growth of a Metropolis* (US U of Chicago Press). Coffee-table classic, filled with glossy pictures and a correspondingly airbrushed account of the city's evolution. Not the pithiest of histories perhaps, but fun to flick through.

Donald Miller *City of the Century: The Epic of Chicago and the Making of America* (Simon & Schuster). Chicago's apogee was the nineteenth century, and this account of the city from its founding through 1899 takes in every major historical figure from Marquette to Marshall Field. Miller's obsession with detail is admirable, but it also rather clogs his rollicking story; he's on surest footing when writing about later events, notably the World's Columbian Exposition of 1893 and the Great Fire.

Dick W. Simpson *Rogues, Rebels, and Rubberstamps: The Story of Chicago City Council from the Civil War to the Third Millennium* (US Westview). Himself a former local alderman, Simpson brings an insider's relish to the story of America's most battle-scarred, corruption-blighted local government. Simpson's use of Chicago's infamous city council as a touchstone for larger political themes is sometimes questionable, and his prose can be clunky, but it's a fascinating story nonetheless.

Biography

John Kobler *Capone: The Life and World of Al Capone* (US DaCapo Press). Punchy, ambivalent account of the world's greatest gangster, pepped up by a vivid eye for period detail and a refusal to make simple judgements. Capone's the part of its past that Chicago is most determined to forget, but Kobler's juicy biography fills in many of the blanks that the city leaves undiscussed.

Mike Royko *Boss: Richard J. Daley of Chicago* (US New American Library). Local journalist Royko turns his take-no-prisoners sights on Chicago's mythical mayor. Given Royko's well-known antipathy towards his subject, he turns in a readable, surprisingly balanced account that documents the inner workings of the local Democratic party's Machine.

Robert Schoenberg *Mr. Capone* (Quill/Robson Books). A more scholarly, sober-minded take of Capone's myth than Kobler's thrill-ride, this biography adds much on Capone's pre- and post-Chicago lives – from his birth in Brooklyn to his syphilis-riddled final years in Miami. Schoenberg's prose is sprightly enough to keep his story well-paced despite wads of detail. Arguably the definitive account of Capone and his times.

Robert Spinney *City of Big Shoulders* (US Northern Illinois U Press). A brisk survey of city history from its founding to today and one of the best introductions to the city. It's an easier read than Miller's much-lauded tome (see p.301), and makes quicker, punchier points about the city's urban evolution. Highly recommended.

Travel, journalism, and impressions

Mike Royko *One More Time: The Best of Mike Royko* (US U of Chicago Press). The Pulitzer Prize–winning columnist chronicled the foibles and follies of the powerful for more than thirty years; this book brings together some of his pithiest, most enjoyable rants, and shows anyone unfamiliar with his work why his name is legend in Chicago. There is another collection of his columns called *For the Love of Mike: More of the Best of Mike Royko.*

Studs Terkel *Division Street: America* (US New Press). Terkel's the undisputed chronicler of the voice of working-class Chicago – and his reputation was founded on this absorbing, extraordinary book. His first-person interviews with men and women, black and white, as they tell the story of their lives in the city are impossible to put down. For a similarly absorbing collection of personal testimonies from working Chicagoans, read Terkel's *Working: People Talk About What They Do All Day and How They Feel About What They Do* (Random House).

Architecture, music, and photography

Willie Dixon with Don Snowden *I Am the Blues* (Da Capo). The autobiography of the greatest behind-the-scenes architect of modern blues doesn't have as many absorbing stories as hoped. Still, producer, arranger, bassist, and songwriter Dixon offers some fascinating insights into the gestation of numerous classic recordings.

David Lowe *Lost Chicago* (US Watson-Gupthill). Splendid pictorial record – with more than 250 illustrations – of the city's vanished architecture. Spanning the early nineteenth century through the twentieth century, historian Lowe engagingly, and in great detail, dwells on the grand mansions, stockyards, skyscrapers, movie houses, and magnificent train stations that helped shape Chicago's architectural legacy.

Mike Rowe *Chicago Blues* (Da Capo). Originally titled *Chicago Breakdown*, this can get too detailed for the uncommitted blues fanatic, but has a wealth of information on Chicago blues from the 1930s to the 1960s. It includes background on all the big and small Chicago blues labels and all of the city's major classic blues artists, as well as lots of minor ones. Cool vintage photos, too.

Pauline A. Saliga (ed) *The Sky's the Limit – A Century of Chicago Skyscrapers* (US Rizzoli). Lushly illustrated, exhaustive survey of Chicago's significant buildings, emphasizing those that still stand over demolished masterpieces. Useful, detailed background for sightseeing, especially on modernist structures from the 1970s and 1980s.

Franz Schulze and Kevin Harrington (eds), *Chicago's Famous Buildings: A Photography Guide to the City's Architectural Landmarks and Other Notable Buildings* (US U of Chicago Press). Regularly updated pocket guide to Chicago. Though the descriptions are a bit brief, each entry is accompanied by a black-and-white photo. Buildings have been organized by geographical location, including a number in the suburbs.

Alice Sinkevitch (ed) *AIA Guide to Chicago* (Harvest/Harcourt). Pocket-sized encyclopaedia on local buildings, useful mostly for its detailed maps and brief but detailed essays on the city's most important structures. It's let down somewhat by the fact that every entry isn't accompanied by a corresponding photograph.

Susan Sirefman *Chicago: A Guide to Recent Architecture* (Artemis/Ellipsis). This palm-sized guide manages to squeeze in a diverse crop of notable buildings (one hundred in all), built in Chicago within the last decade – from major office-towers to houses and restaurants, and even *McDonald's* hamburger university. Crisp black-and-white photographs accompany architect Sirefman's concise text.

Sandra B. Tooze *Muddy Waters: The Mojo Man* (ECW Press). Competent and lengthy bio of the pre-eminent Chicago blues musician, covering his life thoroughly from his Delta days to his ascendancy to stardom on Chess Records and his final years as a revered elder statesman, but it doesn't catch fire as often as you'd expect.

Fiction and poetry

Nelson Algren *The Neon Wilderness* (Seven Stories Press). Think of Algren's short stories as what Hemingway might have written about Chicago had he not fled the city as soon as he was able. Not the most uplifting collection, but the muscular, no-nonsense style and punchy stories are still a knockout. Of Algren's other titles, the best is probably *The Man with the Golden Arm*.

Saul Bellow *The Adventures of Augie March* (Knopf/Penguin). Given what a grumpy curmudgeon Bellow himself became before his death in 2005, it's refreshing to read this early novel with its relentlessly optimistic hero. Other Chicago-based novels by the Nobel Prize–winner include *Herzog* and *Ravelstein*.

Theodore Dreiser *Sister Carrie* (Penguin). Iconoclastic turn-of-the-nineteenth-century novel, with a resourceful, amoral heroine who sins but still succeeds in this ambiguous fable. Her story also spotlights the power department stores (and their seductive goods) had on working-class women – it's a quiet determination to acquire such finery that drives Carrie's every action.

Stuart Dybek *The Coast of Chicago* (US Picador). Reminiscent of Sherwood Anderson's Midwestern masterpiece *Winesburg, Ohio*, Chicago native Dybek's collection of 14 short stories offers quiet snapshots of life in the city's neighborhoods.

James T. Farrell *Studs Lonigan* trilogy (Penguin). Farrell's legendary novel follows an idealistic Irish-American boy as he's gradually ground down by the drudgery of life. Famed for its realism and unblinking depiction of early twentieth-century urban life, the novel hasn't aged well: its awkward prose can be wearing, especially given how little actually happens to Studs during this door-stopper of a book.

Andrew Greeley The Blackie Ryan mysteries. Outspoken Catholic priest and *Sun-Times* columnist Greeley moonlights as a writer of intriguing thrillers, whose hero, Bishop Blackie Ryan, is a Catholic priest on Chicago's North Side. Try *Happy Are the Peacemakers* (o/p) or *The Bishop and the Missing L Train* (Forge), which centers on a logic-defying kidnapping.

Eugene Izzi *The Criminalist* (US Avon). Izzi's last novel (he hanged himself soon after the book was completed) is one of his best, filled with believably imperfect characters trawling through the grubbiest corners of Chicago. This time, homicide detective Dominick di Grazia investigates the brutal murder of a young, pregnant prostitute with the help of a feisty, fiftysomething female colleague.

Frank Norris *The Pit: A Story of Chicago* (Penguin). A strong companion novel to *Sister Carrie* (see above), Norris's story revolves around a greedy speculator and his complicit, compliant wife. Though less brutally amoral than Dreiser's take, it offers similar lessons about the lure of Chicago's wealth and power, and is a good snapshot of the caffeinated early days of the Chicago Stock Exchange.

Sara Paretsky The V.I. Warshawski mysteries. Paretsky's ballsy, bittersweet female private eye V.I. Warshawski prowls the streets of Chicago solving crime. Try *Bitter Medicine* (Dell/Penguin) where Warshawki's investigating malpractice in an emergency room, or the first book, *Indemnity Only* (Dell/Penguin), centering on the serpentine search for a missing co-ed.

Carl Sandburg *Chicago Poems* (US Dover). The celebrated poet and Illinois native made his literary breakthrough with this earthy, evocative collection of free-verse poetry, a tribute to the beauty and violence of industrial Chicago. Highlights include such well-known poems as *Chicago* and *Fog*.

Upton Sinclair *The Jungle* (Bantam/ Penguin). A hundred years before Eric Schlosser's recent megaseller, *Fast Food Nation*, Sinclair issued his disturbing portrait of the squalid meatpacking industry in Chicago. The muscular prose tells the story of a stockyard worker who eventually finds salvation in socialism. The book is derailed by Sinclair's ideological rants toward the end, yet it's still a vivid story.

Richard Wright *Native Son* (Harper Perennial/Vintage). Bleak but powerful, Wright's potent novel tells the story of an African American in 1930s Chicago who tries to cover up his accidental murder of a white woman with catastrophic results. A searing indictment of ghetto life whose message about racial inequality still resonates seventy years on.

Small print and Index

A Rough Guide to Rough Guides

Published in 1982, the first Rough Guide – to Greece – was a student scheme that became a publishing phenomenon. Mark Ellingham, a recent graduate of English from Bristol University, had been traveling in Greece the previous summer and couldn't find the right guidebook. With a small group of friends he wrote his own guide, combining a highly contemporary, journalistic style with a thoroughly practical approach to travelers' needs.

The immediate success of the book spawned a series that rapidly covered dozens of destinations. And, in addition to impecunious backpackers, Rough Guides soon acquired a much broader and older readership that relished the guides' wit and inquisitiveness as much as their enthusiastic, critical approach and value-for-money ethos.

These days, Rough Guides include recommendations from shoestring to luxury and cover more than 200 destinations around the globe, including almost every country in the Americas and Europe, more than half of Africa and most of Asia and Australasia. Our ever-growing team of authors and photographers is spread all over the world, particularly in Europe, the USA, and Australia.

In the early 1990s, Rough Guides branched out of travel, with the publication of Rough Guides to World Music, Classical Music, and the Internet. All three have become benchmark titles in their fields, spearheading the publication of a wide range of books under the Rough Guide name.

Including the travel series, Rough Guides now number more than 350 titles, covering: phrasebooks, waterproof maps, music guides from Opera to Heavy Metal, reference works as diverse as Conspiracy Theories and Shakespeare, and popular culture books from iPods to Poker. Rough Guides also produce a series of more than 120 World Music CDs in partnership with World Music Network.

Visit www.roughguides.com to see our latest publications.

Many Rough Guide travel images are available for commercial licensing at www.roughguidespictures.com

Rough Guide credits

Text editor: April Isaacs
Layout: Ankur Guha, Diana Jarvis
Cartography: Katie Lloyd-Jones, Maxine Repath
Picture editor: Jj Luck
Production: Julia Bovis
Proofreader: Diane Margolis
Cover design: Chloë Roberts
Photographer: Enrique Uranga
Editorial: **London** Kate Berens, Claire Saunders, Geoff Howard, Ruth Blackmore, Polly Thomas, Richard Lim, Clifton Wilkinson, Alison Murchie, Karoline Densley, Andy Turner, Ella O'Donnell, Keith Drew, Edward Aves, Nikki Birrell, Helen Marsden, Alice Park, Sarah Eno, Joe Staines, Duncan Clark, Peter Buckley, Matthew Milton, Tracy Hopkins; **New York** Andrew Rosenberg, Richard Koss, Steven Horak, AnneLise Sorensen, Amy Hegarty, Hunter Slaton
Design & Pictures: **London** Simon Bracken, Dan May, Mark Thomas, Harriet Mills; **Delhi** Madhulita Mohapatra, Umesh Aggarwal, Ajay Verma, Jessica Subramanian, Amit Verma
Production: Sophie Hewat, Katherine Owers
Cartography: **London** Ed Wright; **Delhi** Manish Chandra, Rajesh Chhibber, Jai Prakash Mishra, Ashutosh Bharti, Rajesh Mishra, Animesh Pathak, Jasbir Sandhu, Karobi Gogoi
Online: **New York** Jennifer Gold, Kristin Mingrone; **Delhi** Manik Chauhan, Narender Kumar, Shekhar Jha, Rakesh Kumar, Chhandita Chakravarty
Marketing & Publicity: **London** Richard Trillo, Niki Hanmer, David Wearn, Demelza Dallow, Louise Maher; **New York** Geoff Colquitt, Megan Kennedy, Katy Ball; **Delhi** Reem Khokhar
Custom publishing and foreign rights: Philippa Hopkins
Manager India: Punita Singh
Series editor: Mark Ellingham
Reference Director: Andrew Lockett
PA to Managing and Publishing Directors: Megan McIntyre
Publishing Director: Martin Dunford
Managing Director: Kevin Fitzgerald

Publishing information

This second edition published April 2006 by
Rough Guides Ltd,
80 Strand, London WC2R 0RL
345 Hudson St, 4th Floor,
New York, NY 10014, USA
14 Local Shopping Centre, Panchsheel Park,
New Delhi 110017, India
Distributed by the Penguin Group
Penguin Books Ltd,
80 Strand, London WC2R 0RL
Penguin Putnam, Inc.
375 Hudson Street, NY 10014, USA
Penguin Group (Australia)
250 Camberwell Road, Camberwell
Victoria 3124, Australia
Penguin Books Canada Ltd,
10 Alcorn Avenue, Toronto, Ontario,
Canada M4V 1E4
Penguin Group (New Zealand)
Cnr Rosedale and Airborne Roads
Albany, Auckland, New Zealand

Typeset in Bembo and Helvetica to an original design by Henry Iles.

Printed and bound in China

320pp includes index

A catalogue record for this book is available from the British Library

ISBN-13: 978-1-84358-615-4

ISBN-10: 1-84353-615-3

1 3 5 7 9 8 6 4 2

Help us update

We've gone to a lot of effort to ensure that the second edition of **The Rough Guide to Chicago** is accurate and up to date. However, things change – places get "discovered," opening hours are notoriously fickle, restaurants and rooms raise prices or lower standards. If you feel we've got it wrong or left something out, we'd like to know, and if you can remember the address, the price, the time, the phone number, so much the better.

We'll credit all contributions, and send a copy of the next edition (or any other Rough Guide if you prefer) for the best letters. Everyone who writes to us and isn't already a subscriber will receive a copy of our full-color thrice-yearly newsletter. Please mark letters: "**Rough Guide Chicago Update**" and send to: Rough Guides, 80 Strand, London WC2R 0RL, or Rough Guides, 4th Floor, 345 Hudson St, New York, NY 10014. Or send an email to **mail@roughguides.com**

Have your questions answered and tell others about your trip at **www.roughguides.atinfopop.com**

Acknowledgments

J.P. Anderson: would like to thank the editors at Rough Guides: Andrew Rosenberg, Richard Koss, and particularly April Isaacs for her eagle eye and insightful feedback; to the always helpful folks at the Chicago Historical Society, the Mayor's Office of Special Events, and the Chicago Architecture Foundation; and especially to Dennis Walsh, who offered endless support during many a late-night editing session, as well as an encyclopedic knowledge of and passion for Chicago architecture.
Caroline Lascom: would like to thank the many staff and volunteers at the Chicago Office of Tourism, Harold Washington Library, University of Chicago, and Chicago Architectural Foundation, who provided their time, expertise and enthusiasm. Thanks also to the Rough Guide team, especially April Isaacs, and special thanks to John Gallucci for his invaluable input, endless support and saintly patience.
The editor would like to thank Caroline Lascom and J.P. Anderson for their hard work and dedication, Jj Luck for her diligent photo research, Diana Jarvis for her clever design work, Ankur Guha for his deft and speedy typesetting, Katie Lloyd-Jones and Maxine Repath for their cartographic wizardry, Diane Margolis for her careful proofreading, Andrew Rosenberg for overall guidance and thanks especially to Richard Koss for sharing his editorial insights, support, time, patience, interior design notions, and most of all, his coffee. Special thanks to Evan Derkacz for sending me songs about Chicago for inspiration.

Readers' letters

Thanks to all the readers who have taken the time to write in with comments and suggestions (and apologies if we've inadvertently omitted anyone's name):
David Houston, Sian Jones, L Tim Kane, Ruth King, Katie Riedinger, Sonja Roidner, and David W Naylor.

Photo credits

All photos © Rough Guides except the following:

Cover

Front picture: Elevated View of Financial District, Chicago, Illinois, USA © Getty
Back Image: Lighted Chicago Sign © Randy Faris/CORBIS

Title page

Chicago skyline © Brian Baker/Alamy

Introduction

Chicago theatre district © Kevin Foy/Alamy
The EL Elevated Train © Mark Segal/Robert Harding
Chicago © Andre Jenny/Alamy
Nightlife on Rush Street © Heeb/Prisma

Things not to miss

01 River Boat Cruises © Bart Harris/Alamy
02 Maxwell Street Market © DK Images
04 Frank Lloyd Wright Home & Studio Photo Don Kalec © FLW Preservation Trust
05 Gospel Brunch © House of Blues
07 Museum of Science and Industry © DK Images
09 Oak Street Beach © Alan Klehr
10 Marquee © Second City
11 Fireplace in Glessner House by Henry Hobson Richardson © Thomas A. Heinz/Corbis
12 Lakefront, Chicago © Andre Jenny/Alamy
17 Khorsabad courtyard © Oriental Institute Museum
18 Concert © Chicago Symphony Orchestra
20 Entranceway © Ravinia Festival
21 Art Institute of Chicago © Directphoto.org/Alamy
22 Bahai Temple © Index Stock Imagery/Photolibrary

Black and whites

p.51 View over Chicago River © Arcaid/Alamy
p.82 Water Tower © DK Images
p.100 Tyrannosaurus Rex skeleton named Sue in the Field Museum of Chicago © David R. Frazier Photolibrary, Inc. /Alamy
p.127 Theater interior © Music Box Theatre
p.136 Dia de los Muertos exhibition © Tim Boyle/Getty Images
p.174 Palm Court © The Drake
p.184 Mr. Beef © Alan Klehr
p.193 Margies Candies © Alan Klehr
p.186 Frontera interior © Frontera Grill/Topolobampo
p.205 Berghoff Restaurant © Alan Klehr
p.219 Chicago Blues Festival © Chuck Eckert/Alamy
p.233 Tabula © Todd Rosenberg
p.248 Michael Jordan Statue at United Center © Bill Bachmann/Alamy
p.267 Garrett Popcorn © Kim Karpeles/Alamy
p.285 Al Capone © Popperfoto/Alamy
p.293 Chuck Berry © Lynn Goldsmith/Corbis

Color Insert: Food

Polish sausage © Eric Rank/Getty Images
Chicago Hot Dogs © Daniel Templeton/Alamy
Grilled steak © Rob Bartee/Alamy
Chicago Chop House © Alan Klehr
Italian beef sandwich © Rick Souders/Foodpix/Photolibrary
Tomatillo-Braised Pork Loin with herby white beans and bacon. Photograph by Gentl & Hyers © Frontera
Deep dish pizza © Lou Malnatis

Color Insert: Architecture

Reliance Building © Angelo Hornak/Corbis
IBM Building © Kevin Foy/Alamy
Monadnock Building © Alan Klehr

Index

Map entries are in color.

N

O

P

R

S

T

U

V

W

INDEX

I

Map symbols

maps are listed in the full index using colored text

80	Interstate	i	Information center
30	U.S. Highway		Post office
1	Highway		Golf course
	Main road		Museum
	Minor road		Church (regional maps)
	Railway		Building
	Airport		Church
	Hospital		Stadium
M	Subway station		Cemetery
METRA	Commuter rail station		Park
	General point of interest